THE BRITISH DREAM

THE BRITISH DREAM

Successes and Failures of Post-war Immigration

David Goodhart

Atlantic Books

LONDON

Published in Great Britain in 2013 by Atlantic Books,
an imprint of Atlantic Books Ltd.

The author and publisher wish to thank the following for permission to reproduce
copyright material:

The Path to Power by Margaret Thatcher. Reprinted by permission of HarperCollins
Publishers Ltd. © 1995 by Margaret Thatcher.

A Postcolonial People: South Asians in Britain edited by N. Ali, V.S. Kalra and S. Sayyid.
Reprinted by permission of C. Hurst & Co. (Publishers) Ltd. © N. Ali, V.S. Kalra,
S. Sayyid and the Contributors, 2006.

Small Island by Andrea Levy. Reproduced by permission of Headline Publishers Limited.
© 2004 Andrea Levy.

Every effort has been made to trace or contact all copyright holders. The publishers
will be pleased to make good any omissions or rectify any mistakes brought to their
attention at the earliest opportunity.

10 9 8 7 6 5 4 3 2 1

A CIP catalogue record for this book is available from the British Library.

Hardback ISBN: 9781843548058
Ebook ISBN: 9780857899750
Paperback ISBN: 9781843548065

Atlantic Books
An imprint of Atlantic Books Ltd
Ormond House
26–27 Boswell Street
London
WC1N 3JZ

www.atlantic-books.co.uk

Text design by Richard Marston
Printed in Great Britain by the MPG Printgroup, UK

To my parents, Philip and Valerie, and to my laptop –
thank you all for not conking out before I finished the book

Contents

Acknowledgements

Thanks to my family – my wife Lucy and children Rosie, Maud, Arty and Stan – and the team at Demos. Thanks also to Toby Mundy and James Nightingale at Atlantic and to Annie Lee for her meticulous copy-editing.

This book has been in gestation since I first started thinking about an essay for *Prospect* magazine about the tension between solidarity and diversity in rich, liberal societies almost ten years ago. In the course of working out my ideas on that and the many related subjects in this book, and in researching the book itself, I have been particularly influenced by and/or helped by a group of around thirty people. I give them special thanks below. There is also a wider group who have given me their time and thoughts on my travels around Britain in the past two years who I would like to thank, and a special thanks to those who were generous with their time despite knowing we had different views. Apologies to those I have left out, and to those who particularly care about titles; I thought it was simpler to have unadorned names.

Special thanks to:

Andrew Adonis; Mohammed Amin; Ralph Berry; Paul Boateng; Liam Byrne; Ted Cantle; Matt Cavanagh; Rob Colls; Geoff Dench; Bobby Duffy; David Edmonds; Ismail Einashe; Kishwer Falkner; Robert Ford; Maurice Glasman; Kat Hanna; Randall Hansen; Michael Ignatieff; Ted Jeory; Sunder Katwala; Eric Kaufmann; Phil Lewis; Michael Lind; Alex Linklater; John Lloyd; Jamiesha Majevadia; Kenan Malik; David Metcalf; David Miller;

Munira Mirza; Maxine Moar; Tariq Modood; Herman Ouseley; Bhikhu Parekh; Trevor Phillips; Robert Rowthorn; Shamit Saggar; Paul Scheffer; Jean Seaton; Siôn Simon; Madeleine Sumption; David Willetts; Max Wind-Cowie.

And thanks also to:

Ishtiaq Ahmed; Mahmood Ahmed; Maqsood Ahmed; Omer Ahmed; Riaz Ahmed; Mohammed Ajeeb; Navid Akhtar; Parveen Akhtar; Stephen Alambritis; Paul Allen; Nuzhat Ali; Ruhana Ali; Rushanara Ali; Sundas Ali; Usman Ali; Rob Anderson; Andrew Anthony; Anjum Anwar; Sher Azam; Willy Bach; Gavin Bailey; Jeff Bailey; Shaun Bailey; Jas Bains; Toby Bakare; Muhammed Abdul Bari; Mike Barraclough; Ann Barratt; John Battye; Halima Begum; Harris Beider; John Benyon; Ashish Bhatt; Philip Blond; Gautam Bodiwala; Henry Bonsu; John Bonsu; Tony Breslin; Paul Broks; Simon Burgess; Phil Burton-Cartledge; Bill Bush; Vicki Butler; David Cannadine; Mark Carroll; John Carruthers; Raj Chada; Jayant Chavda; Jack Citrin; David Coleman; Linda Colley; Michael Collins; Christopher Cook; Graeme Cooke; Zaki Cooper; John Cornwell; Alan Craig; Paul Crosby; Jon Cruddas; René Cuperus; Martha Dalton; John Darwin; Rowenna Davis; Howard Dawber; Neli Demireva; John Denham; Meghnad Desai; Sukhjit Dhaliwal; Gabriella Elgenius; Geoffrey Evans; Frank Field; Catherine Fieschi; Daniel Finkelstein; Alun Francis; Mike Gapes; Len Gibbs; Ameetpal Gill; Neena Gill; David Goldblatt; Rosie Goodhart; Paul Goodman; Matthew Goodwin; Bana Gora; Roger Graef; Andrew Green; David Green; Damian Green; Montserrat Guibernau; Jeff Hanna; Zubaida Haque; Toby Harris; Michael Harvey; Miles Hewstone; Susan Higgins; Ellie Hill; Margaret Hodge; Geoff Holden; Kelvin Hopkins; Tristram Hunt; Shehla Husain; Dilwar Hussain; Naweed Hussain; Tanveer Hussain; Will Hutton; Helen Hylton; Khizar Iqbal; Stephen Jivraj; Lindsay Johns; Nick Johnson; Michael Keating; Michael Keith; Ozlan Keles; Peter Kellner; Madiha Khan; Omar Khan; Sadiq Khan; Wajid Khan; Shiria Khatun; Jytte Klausen; Jurgen Kronig; David Kynaston; David Lammy; James Laurence; Charles Leddy-Owen; Liz Legum; James Lewis; Patricia Lewis; Warwick Lightfoot; Joy Lo Dico; Logie Lohendran; Patrick Macfarlane; Nick Macpherson; Fiona Mactaggart; Khalid Mahmood; Sharaf Mahmood; Mohsin Malik; Zaiba Malik; Gautam Malkani; Sarfraz Manzoor; Sukhdev

Marway; Ehsan Masood; Ed Mayne; Jean McCrindle; Elizabeth McCullough; Siobhain McDonagh; Pat McFadden; Lauren McLaren; Jasper McMahon; Emran Mian; Jaspal Singh Minas; Anshuman Mondal; Margaret Moore; David Muir; Douglas Murray; Maajid Nawaz; Stephen Nickell; Catrin Nye; Duncan O'Leary; Fran O'Leary; Paul Ormerod; Juliana Owusu; Anthony Painter; Charlie Parker; Hyacinth Parsons; Ceri Peach; Jonathan Portes; Bevan Powell; Anne Power; Jonathan Power; Lucinda Platt; James Purnell; Ayesha Qureshi; Yasmin Qureshi; Tariq Rafique; James Ramsey; Phil Riley; Matthew Rhodes; Ahmad Riaz; Chris Roberts; Ben Rogers; Steve Rumbelow; Mark Rusling; Jonathan Rutherford; Nick Ryan; Johnathan Sacks; John Salt; Neena Samota; Ziauddin Sardar; Stafford Scott; Tony Sewell; Shafique Shah; Ghayasuddin Siddiqui; Ramindar Singh; Swaran Singh; Zadie Smith; Will Somerville; John Spellar; Thees Spreckelsen; David Starkey; Marc Stears; Philippa Stockley; Gisela Stuart; Jack Straw; Phil Sumner; Yusuf Tai; David Taylor; Gowri Thamotharampillai; Paul Thomas; Stephen Timms; Adair Turner; Varun Uberoi; Mike Waite; Robin Wales; Mohammed Aslam Wassan; Albert Weale; Martin Whelton; David Wild; Alan Wolfe; Phil Woolas; Simon Woolley; Waseem Zaffar.

A Note on Language

This book is, in part, about describing the patterns of life of large groups of people who are not part of the white British majority. Words and tone matter. As I am a fifty-six-year-old white, British man, I cannot, obviously, describe these patterns from personal experience. Instead, I have tried to write objectively but also directly, aiming to avoid the caveats and obfuscations that disfigure so much of the literature in this field.

It is inevitable that some people will take offence at my words or tone in certain places, but I have not set out to be provocative and I hope that critics will focus on the ideas and arguments behind the words and phrases. Many words in this field carry within them long-standing intellectual disputes – for example, integration and segregation. The word segregation implies, to some people, a process actively managed and promoted by the majority. I mean it in a more neutral sense to signify separateness – sometimes chosen, sometimes not.

For British ethnic minority categories I mainly use the standard Office for National Statistics groups – black African, Indian (as well as Hindu Indian, Sikh Indian and Muslim Indian), Bangladeshi and so on. Sometimes I use the prefix British, as in British Caribbean background, but to avoid clutter I will often just say Caribbeans, Pakistanis or Somalis; it should be clear from the context when I mean settled British groups. When writing about ethnic or racial minorities I often just refer to minorities. I am not including other groups – like gay people or disabled people – who are also categorised as minorities. Sometimes I am just referring to 'visible' minorities and sometimes to all minorities, including white groups like Poles; it should, again, be clear from the context.

Most of the statistics about immigration refer to the UK, though in some cases I use figures that refer just to England or England and Wales. I generally use the word Britain when I really mean the United Kingdom.

Also, although the statistics are often about the UK this is mainly a book written about and from the perspective of England (the immigration stories in Scotland, Wales and Northern Ireland overlap but are somewhat distinct).

Introduction

This book is about post-war immigration to Britain and all the arguments that swirl around it: what the country has got right, and what it has got wrong. It is about the immigrants and their descendants, about how they are progressing in schools and workplaces and how well they are integrated into British life. It is also about the country they have come to and what kind of connection people, of all backgrounds, feel towards it and each other and what place national feeling has in an open, liberal, rich society like ours.

Immigration, race and national identity, and the links between them, are emotional subjects which touch on how people feel about themselves. The conversation has become a more open one in recent years but it is still dogged by many taboos and silences; I want to try to look at matters as they are.

The racial exclusion which marked the first few decades of post-colonial immigration after the Second World War has cast a long shadow. But Britain is now a different place. As Munira Mirza, one of the deputy mayors of London, has put it: 'Racism still exists, but things have improved to a point where many ethnic minority Britons do not experience it as a regular feature in their lives.'

The evidence, as I will demonstrate in Chapter 2, indicates that it is time for liberals to reverse the 'discrimination presumption' and instead to assume that this is an open society struggling, not always successfully, to make good its promise of a decent chance in life to people of all backgrounds. That is not only closer to the truth it is also a more useful story to tell young minority Britons than the alternative of a relentlessly racist country thwarting their lives.

The extensive data – about exam results, pay, social mobility and so on – should also make it possible to generalise in a clear-eyed way about how different minorities are making their way, just as we do about social class. Social class is not destiny and neither is ethnic culture. I do not want to stigmatise particular groups nor to imply that generalisations about ethnic groups apply to everyone from that group; there is great internal variety within groups and in any case we are all individuals and many of us float free of our origins.

But neither do I want to sentimentalise. Political speeches about immigration or minority politics often praise minority groups for their contribution. This may have made sense in the 1970s or 1980s when there was widespread hostility to the minority presence but today it sounds increasingly odd. Political leaders do not thank the people of Cheshire for their contribution. It is also too indiscriminate. Not all minority groups *do* make a great contribution. In thirty years' time British Somalis may be considered as successful and entrepreneurial as the East African Asians are today, but currently only about 30 per cent of them work.

Like most white British people of my age I am happy living in a multiracial society. But unlike most members of my political tribe of north London liberals I have come to believe that public opinion is broadly right about the immigration story. Britain has had too much of it, too quickly, especially in recent years, and much of it, especially for the least well off, has not produced self-evident economic benefit.

What is clearer still is that it has not been well managed. Britain has never had a culture of integrating newcomers, though most have done it for themselves: in the early post-war decades this laissez-faire approach was overlaid first with racial prejudice and then later by a liberalism that was reluctant to intervene in individual choices. Moreover multiculturalism, particularly in the more separatist form that emerged in the 1980s, has allowed 'parallel lives' to grow up in some places and made it harder for ordinary Britons to think of some minorities, and especially Muslims, as part of the same 'imagined community' with common experiences and interests.

Race and identity politics has too often turned minority Britons into a sectional interest with their own 'demands', rather like the trade unions in the 1970s. And too often the demands of minority leaders have been for a separate slice of power and resources rather than for the means to create a common life.

It is a mixed picture. In many places immigration is working as the textbooks say it should: minorities are upwardly mobile and creating interesting new hybrid identities in mixed suburbs. And there are more than 1 million British people of mixed race who are living examples of the most fundamental form of inter-ethnic integration of all. Even if the Somalis do not become the new East African Asians, then others, perhaps the Poles, will. And we have come a long way in a short time. A country that less than 100 years ago believed it was its right to control the destiny of many 'lesser breeds' has now invited them across its threshold and learnt to treat them more or less as equals. One of the great achievements of the past thirty years has been the banishment of overt racism: consider the national furore over a racial expletive uttered by the former England football captain John Terry.

There are places in Britain, however, where the immigration story has been far from successful, notably in the northern 'mill towns' and other declining industrial regions which in the 1960s and 1970s attracted one of the most clannish minorities of modern times, rural Kashmiri Pakistanis. There are some post-colonial groups from developing countries that have quickly caught up with and then passed the white average in education and employment – Hindu Indians, Sikhs, some black Africans, Chinese – and some who generally continue to do worse – Pakistanis, Bangladeshis, Turks, Somalis and African-Caribbeans.

The levels of education and the attitudes that people bring with them have a decisive impact on those outcomes – Britain itself sometimes seems an irrelevant bystander. And we should not be afraid to reflect on how minority lives can be blighted by self-inflicted wounds such as the macho street culture of young, male Caribbeans, or the first cousin marriages of Kashmiri Pakistanis. Muslims have tended to integrate less well not so much because of Islam itself but because most of the British Muslim minority was originally from rural, traditional parts of Pakistan and Bangladesh, and has reproduced many aspects of that life in the streets of northern England, the Midlands and east London. The British Muslims of Indian, East African Asian and urban Pakistani backgrounds are generally far more successful.

The British political class has never done a good job at explaining what the point of large-scale immigration was and whose interests it was meant to serve. That is partly because those questions are hard to answer. The idea that immigration should be unambiguously in the interests of existing citizens was blurred from the start by imperial obligations to the new arrivals, and the difficulty of deciding what the 'interests of existing citizens' are. The result is that compared with many other countries (notably Canada), British immigration has been, at least in the early post-war decades, relatively unselective and those who settled have generally been low-skilled people from poor countries.

The economics of immigration is a big, complex subject. But the economic gains are not as significant as is often assumed. It is true that skill gaps and undesirable jobs have been filled, but poorer British citizens have paid some price in downward pressure on wages and greater competition for public services. There is a psychological as well as a material dimension to this: groups, like individuals, want to feel valued and useful; parts of white working-class Britain have come to feel neither in recent decades and believe that they have been displaced by newcomers not only in parts of the job market but also in the national story itself.

Large-scale immigration has made Britain livelier and more dynamic than it would otherwise have been, but it has not clearly made it much richer or more content. Indeed, it has exacerbated many of the undesirable aspects of British economic life: poverty, inequality, low productivity, lack of training and employer short-termism.

The country would still have functioned perfectly well with half the levels of poor-country immigration we have experienced – it would have been more monochrome, a bit more equal and a lot more Irish. Britain did need more workers in the 1950s and 1960s but they could have come from across the Irish Sea in larger numbers rather than from distant cultures on the other side of the globe – especially as the imperial connection that brought them to Britain was soon to become a source of guilt to the coloniser and resentment to the colonised.

They arrived in two big phases. In the first post-colonial wave, from 1948 to the early 1990s, people came mainly from the Caribbean, India, Pakistan and Africa: by the end of the period the number of ethnic minority Britons (including about half born here) was about 4 million. In the second phase, starting with Labour coming to power in 1997 and continuing to this day, net immigration of non-British citizens has added another 4 million to the population in just fifteen years. Of those 4 million a majority are likely to become permanent residents, and, contrary to popular belief, less than a quarter are from the European Union.

Much of this happened by accident. When the 1948 Nationality Act was passed, giving the right to live and work in Britain to all citizens of the empire and Commonwealth, it was not expected that the ordinary people of poor former colonies would arrive in their hundreds of thousands. Nor was it expected after 1997 that a combination of quite small decisions would lead to such a huge inflow. The 1.5 million East Europeans who arrived after 2004, about half to settle, were as unexpected as those pioneer immigrants after 1948. The second time round Britain was less unwelcoming but no better prepared.

This is a demographic revolution. According to the Office for National Statistics (ONS) census of 2011 the population of England and Wales that was not 'White British' was a fraction under 20 per cent – that included 3 million whites who are not White British, including East Europeans, Australians, Irish, Germans and so on, and around 8 million members of 'visible minority' groups. By the time of the next census in 2021 the visible minority population will have risen from 14 per cent today to around 20 per cent for England and Wales and a few years later for the whole of the United Kingdom. That means the visible minority proportion of the population (including people of mixed backgrounds) will have trebled in just twenty-five years.

Already in some towns and cities, including London, Leicester, Slough and Luton, the White British are in a minority, with Birmingham expected to follow in the near future. The decline in the proportion of the White British population in London to just 44.9 per cent was the biggest surprise of the 2011 census, most experts had not expected it for another twenty years. And what seems to have caught them by surprise is not so much the inflows of various minorities but the huge outflow of 600,000 White British Londoners between 2001 and 2011. London remains around 57 per cent white (including non-British whites) and 43 per cent visible minority but it will almost certainly be majority visible minority by the time of the next census. If Britain had a clear and confident sense of its national culture and was good at integrating people into it, then perhaps this speed of change would be of little concern. But neither has been the case for most of the post-war period.

Immigration prompts not just economic and demographic questions but cultural, political and psychological ones too. What is a modern national community and how quickly can it absorb large numbers of people from very different cultures? Is there a 'core' culture that large-scale immigration diminishes? How much should a host society adapt itself to accommodate newcomers or is the movement all on the other side? Is a more inclusive sense of national identity unavoidably a weaker one?

I had not given immigration much thought until well into my forties – though as a journalist of leftish sympathies I was reflexively in favour of it and aware of having two immigrant grandfathers (both American). But when I saw it through these big political and national identity questions I came to appreciate that it was not only one of the most important stories about modern Britain but also, in the way that it cuts across old left/right distinctions and throws up new political dilemmas, the most interesting.

Then, in February 2004, I became briefly part of the story. I wrote a 6,000-word essay entitled 'Too Diverse?' in the political magazine that I then edited called *Prospect* (subsequently reprinted in the *Guardian*) about what I called the 'progressive dilemma' – the conflict between diversity and social solidarity – and unwittingly raised a storm of often angry argument. I was accused of being a 'liberal racist' and paid my penance on the race and immigration conference circuit for part of the next few years, where I tried to articulate – often with difficulty – why it is possible to worry about the effects of 'difference' without being a racist.

It was David Willetts, the leading Conservative politician known for his intellectual curiosity, who first drew my attention to the 'progressive dilemma'. Speaking at a *Prospect* debate on the welfare state in 1998, he noted that if values and lifestyles become more diverse it becomes more difficult to sustain the legitimacy of a risk-pooling welfare state. 'This is America versus Sweden.

You can have a Swedish welfare state provided you are a homogeneous society with intensely shared values. In the US you have a very diverse, individualistic society where people feel fewer obligations to fellow citizens. Progressives want diversity but they thereby undermine part of the moral consensus on which a large welfare state rests.'

That is to say, people are readier to share and co-operate with people whom they trust or with whom they believe they have significant attributes, and interests, in common. That 'in-group' can be, and is, extended to include people of very different racial, ethnic or class background. But it does not happen automatically or immediately. Modern science confirms our anti-racist intuitions that human beings are all broadly the same. But it is also on the side of a more awkward truth: that humans are group-based primates who favour their own and extend trust to outsiders with caution.

Liberals and multiculturalists have been slow to recognise that strong collective identities are legitimate for majorities as well as minorities. The liberal story about migration too often assumes a society without any pre-existing attachments or sense of community. And this reflects the modern liberal left's ambivalence about community, which is something to be celebrated but also derided and escaped from. People are not blank sheets, societies are not random collections of individuals, and objection to the arrival of a large number of outsiders in a community is not necessarily racist.

And amid the daily entanglement of competition and co-operation that characterises a modern urban society, welfare democracies make big demands on their citizens. Behind every citizen lies a graveyard, as the American political writer Alan Wolfe has put it. Most of us are no longer asked to risk death for our country but we are asked to pay around one third of our income into a common national pool every year and in return the state manages large bits of infrastructure for us – defence, transport, energy, public services and welfare – and attempts to regulate the national economy. For this to work, the modern citizen is expected to conform to a thicket of rules and regulations. And in order to sustain this level of sharing and co-operation we need more than passive tolerance, we need at least some sense of 'emotional citizenship', the belief that despite many different interests we're also part of the same team.

The solidarity versus diversity debate is often a sensitive one. It was made more so back in 2004 by the fact that while I am a privileged white man, arguing from abstract first principles, many of my non-white opponents felt the personal pain of persecution for their 'diversity'.

I often tried in these debates about 'Too Diverse?' to stress that I was not just talking about ethnic diversity, but value diversity in general: the conservative home counties grandmother versus the goth. Even if not a single immigrant had arrived in recent decades, the expansion of individual rights and freedoms since the 1960s would have created an unprecedented range of lifestyles and beliefs in Britain's towns and cities. This new diversity has created a society that is much freer, less violent and in many ways happier, but also more morally confused and with a weaker sense of itself.

Technology and free markets – as well as diversity of many kinds – have loosened the bonds we feel with fellow citizens. Our networks are wider and more international but also shallower. Through this we have both lost and gained. The philosopher Michael Sandel expresses it well: 'In our public life, we are more entangled, but less attached, than ever before.'

There is a lot at stake here, if we don't get the balance right. The miracle of co-operation and institutionalised sharing that is a modern welfare democracy has been hard won over centuries of nation-building and class conflict, yet it could unravel over a generation or two. It is possible to imagine Britain little by little becoming a less civil, ever more unequal and ethnically divided country – as harsh and violent as the United States.

And it is all too easy to imagine a gradual erosion of the willingness to pay for the welfare state as we become richer and more socially distant – indeed, it is already happening. When I wrote 'Too Diverse?' there was little evidence for this; Britain in the mid-2000s was in the middle of a big expansion of public spending and redistribution. Today it is different, with big (and popular) cuts to social security budgets and a big, long-term, fall in support for many aspects of welfare which are seen to be only for the benefit of poorer others. A long period of low growth is bound to exacerbate this.

There is a danger that, as in the US, social security benefits like housing benefit and income support will become increasingly associated with a white underclass and minorities – about 40 per cent of minority Britons are classified as poor compared with about 20 per cent of white Britain, largely the result of the starting point of many uneducated post-colonial immigrants.

The most useful responses to my essay were from people who wanted to avoid that outcome and think about how to mitigate the progressive dilemma. To combine diversity with solidarity, to improve integration and racial justice, it is no good just preaching tolerance, you need *a politics that promotes a common in-group identity*. As the moral psychologist Jonathan Haidt has written, talking about racial division in the US: 'You can make people care less about race by drowning race differences in a sea of similarities, shared goals and mutual interdependencies.'

So the second step in my thinking, and in this book too, came to focus on integration and national identity and to question a form of multiculturalism that was too often indifferent to both. I argued in a pamphlet for the think tank Demos in 2006 (*Progressive Nationalism: Citizenship and the Left*) that moderate national feeling can be a positively progressive force. And as the British national story has weakened somewhat – thanks, inter alia, to globalisation, EU integration, immigration, devolution, the decline of external threats and a big increase in incomes which has allowed us to live less collectivist lives – it has become more important to find new ways of talking about national citizenship that suit a more fluid and multiracial era. Gordon Brown had an interesting failure with his Britishness debate (see my own attempt in Chapter 7, 'The National Question').

One of the creative things about immigration is that it allows us to catch a glimpse of ourselves as outsiders see us; and it is not always very flattering. It has also forced us to think about what it is to be British and to acknowledge that we cannot rely on instinctive understandings any longer, that it is not 'un-British' to talk about Britishness. We may disagree about where the balance lies between the 'civic' and the 'ethnic' – between political principles and institutions on the one hand and ancestry and history on the other – but there is a wider acceptance that the conversation matters, especially since 7/7.

A new British conversation was crystallised for many people by Danny Boyle's opening ceremony for the 2012 Olympics. He captured, in a way that politicians had been unable to do, a sense of a post-racial national story; of a country with an extraordinary past and a promising present. The British national idea still rests on a special relationship between fellow national citizens but it no longer implies *superiority* to other nations or peoples. Nor must it be uncritical or tribal; modern national feeling is comfortably compatible with the idea of the moral equality of all humans – the basic notion behind global human rights.

Anti-nationalists on the left underestimate just how much the nation state has liberalised in recent decades. One might say that the great achievement of post-1945 politics, in Europe at least, has been to 'feminise' the nation state. The nation was once about defending or taking territory and about organised violence. But since collective security has made Britain's participation in a major conventional war highly improbable, the focus has switched to the internal sharing of resources within the nation – and the traditionally feminine 'hearth and home' issues of protecting the young, the old, the disabled and the poor.

The national story has been complicated in Britain, at the political if not popular level, by virtue of the existence of four nations in one state, and also by the inability of the English elite to think in ordinary national terms. This ambivalence has its roots in the supra-national British empire but was later echoed by the left, partly in reaction against the anti-immigration nationalism of Enoch Powell in the 1960s.

This is one reason why in the 1970s and 1980s a multicultural idea of group rights and a 'community of communities' rather than a more integrationist idea of national citizenship seemed the best way of managing majority/minority relations. It is also why US-style patriotic symbols were not offered to newcomers – there was no map of how to become British. That is beginning to change. Britain may never have done 'flags on the lawn' but with the citizenship tests and ceremonies introduced in 2004 we do now have flags and pictures of the Queen in town halls for new citizens.

England itself has remained part-submerged, until recently, because an egalitarian age has been discomfited by its past national dominance – it cannot draw on the small nation solidarity of, say, the Irish or the Danes or the anti-colonial spirit of many newer countries. But two generations after empire, as England has shrunk and the United Kingdom has loosened, the opportunity for a benign, confident English identity to emerge is here: a national story which sees England as special but no longer superior; a blurring of the rigid lines between civic and ethnic forms of identification, and an acceptance that there are many ways to be English.

A confident national identity is an aid, not an obstacle, to integrating newcomers, and only a small number of white Britons believe you have to be white to be British or English. An unembarrassed and unchauvinistic attachment to this country – its language, its history, a sense of a common home – has long been the common-sense, low-key national feeling of ordinary Britain. It was captured and played back to the country by Danny Boyle's opening ceremony and then echoed around the land in celebration of Team GB's remarkable success in 2012.

Most of elite Britain cheered along too, but in the senior common room, the boardroom, and even in Whitehall this liberal nationalism has had to compete with an increasingly global, post-national ethos. I was struck by this dining at an Oxford college in Spring 2011. When I said to my neighbour, one of the country's most senior civil servants, that I wanted to write a book about why liberals should be less sceptical about the nation state and more sceptical about large-scale immigration, he frowned and said, 'I disagree. When I was at the Treasury I argued for the most open door possible to immigration ... I think it's my job to maximise global welfare not national welfare.'

I was surprised to hear this from such a senior figure in a very national institution and asked the man sitting next to the civil servant, one of the most powerful television executives in the country, whether he believed global welfare should be put before national welfare, if the two should conflict. He said he believed global welfare was paramount and that therefore he had a greater obligation to someone in Burundi than to someone in Birmingham.

This encounter re-inspired me to write this book; it had been languishing as a long-term project. But I also realised that I could not write about immigration and multiculturalism and minority Britain without going out to observe it and to talk to as many people as possible about their lives, which is what I have done over the past eighteen months.

Those two men in Oxford reflect a powerful strand in the thinking of Britain's educated liberal baby-boomers. They take for granted the blessings of a national welfare democracy yet are also marked by the anti-national ideology of the 1960s and 1970s, a lingering reaction against the nationalist extremes of the first half of the twentieth century.

Most people are moral particularists, believing that we have a hierarchy of obligations starting with our family and rippling out via the nation state to the rest of humanity. Charity, like our affections, begins at home. But many of the brightest and the best now reject this old homily. Their idealism is more focused on raising up the global poor or worrying about global warming than on helping out the lonely pensioner up the road. The most idealistic fast-stream civil servants usually want to work in DFID, the international development department.

It is true that the world has become a smaller, more interdependent place and many of its biggest problems can only be solved with international co-operation, but it does not follow that the nation state is therefore powerless and irrelevant. Nations remain the building blocks of international co-operation and only they can bring democratic legitimacy to global governance.

Many of the children of the 1960s and today's idealistic, educated youth want to save the world by supporting the freest possible flow of people across what they regard as increasingly anachronistic national borders. The late philosopher Michael Dummett argued that open borders ought to be accepted as the norm and, by extension, that existing citizens in western countries do not have any special rights to 'their' rich and peaceful countries as compared to newcomers. But this offends against democratic common sense and perhaps a deeper intuition that a society is, at least in part, a contract between generations. Moreover, allowing the best educated and most ambitious people from poor countries easy access to rich ones, whether as doctors or office cleaners, may seem generous but it makes it much harder for poor countries to catch up.

The post-national globalists do not agree. Consider the debate over 'British jobs for British workers', the phrase used by Gordon Brown in his speech to the Labour conference in 2007. I was at a birthday party for a Labour MP just after the speech. The people around me entered a bidding war to express their outrage at Brown's slogan which was finally triumphantly closed by one who declared, to general approval, that it was 'racism, pure and simple'.

Gordon Brown, it should be recalled, didn't say British jobs for white British workers. In most places in the world today, and indeed probably in Britain itself until about twenty years ago, his slogan about a bias in favour of national citizens would have seemed so banal as to be hardly worth uttering. Now the language of liberal universalism has ruled it beyond the pale.

The slogan was, of course, cynical because Gordon Brown knew that under EU free movement laws it is illegal for British employers to discriminate in favour of British workers. That law was drawn up in the 1950s when nobody expected a block of countries to join the EU with less than one quarter the income per head of existing members, so giving individuals a strong incentive to seek work in the higher-income countries. Yet that is what has happened. And it has alerted ordinary citizens to the fact that 'fellow citizen favouritism' is increasingly overridden in today's world by liberal economic principles and human rights laws that say it is wrong to discriminate between citizens and non-citizens.

To many commentators this is welcome. Ian Birrell, writing in the *Evening Standard* on 11 October 2011 ('Immigrants saved my family and are crucial to Britain'), attacked the Coalition government's immigration reduction plan on the grounds that it was making it harder to recruit people to care for his seriously disabled child.

Recruiting people for care jobs is a serious issue. Outside London most such jobs are filled by British citizens, but in London and the South-East foreign-born care assistants generally predominate. But such people are not, as Birrell implied, on a higher moral plane to British citizens. They have not come here because they love elderly or disabled British people and want to help them. They have come here for a better life and higher pay than is possible in Colombia, Barbados or Slovakia. Indeed, given that their own poorer countries probably have proportionately higher numbers of suffering and elderly people, one might ask why they have not stayed to look after them.

Their absence from British care homes would not have led to their closure, rather governments and local authorities and private providers would have had to pay more and make the jobs more attractive to lure British citizens to work in them who have more options than Colombians.

The same day, in the *Independent*, Dominic Lawson wrote about the other end of the labour market ('More migrants please, especially the clever ones') and complained that the immigration cap was preventing Britain from recruiting the brightest scientific and entrepreneurial talent. Immigration is here being pressed into service to support a dubious theory of the 'Steve Jobs' economy – the idea that a few heroic CEOs or inventors drive growth. In any case the immigration cap is designed to continue to attract such exceptional people.

The bigger point here is that these arguments in favour of beneficial immigration could apply to inflows at a fraction of current levels. Birrell and Lawson argue from a narrow particular – carers or scientists – and fail to see the bigger picture. The image of the angelic nurse from a developing country or a hard-working Polish plumber must be balanced against the fact that working-age immigrants in general are less likely to work than natives. Unprejudiced local people in places like Bradford and Birmingham saw the point when hard-working immigrants arrived to do useful factory jobs in the period of post-war construction. They now look on bemused at some of the inward-looking communities with low employment levels and high welfare dependency that have emerged in recent decades.

Too much of this debate, in liberal Britain at least, is dominated by what I call an 'immigrationist' story. This semi-mythical account of immigration, in the past and present, starts with the idea of a 'mongrel nation' that has always experienced high inflows of outsiders. But actually from 1066 until 1950 immigration was almost non-existent – about 50,000 Huguenots in the sixteenth and seventeenth centuries, about 200,000 Jews in two waves, and perhaps 1 million or more Irish over 200 years, during most of which time they were internal migrants within one state. Britain is a historic nation (or four separate nations) with an ethnic majority which has recently experienced very high levels of immigration – we are not, or not yet, an immigration nation like the US, Canada or Australia.

Immigrationists, like globalists, typically claim that the nation state is in terminal decline and that large-scale immigration is now inevitable thanks to cheap travel and open economies. Britain is more globally interconnected than fifty years ago, but people are no less dependent on the nation state for physical and economic protection. And after the dust settles from the recent decades of globalisation, and its overblown rhetoric, the national dimension seems to be in reasonable shape still – when banks are collapsing it matters which set of taxpayers are standing behind your savings account.

And mass immigration is not inevitable. It is true that migration flows into rich countries have doubled over the past thirty years, but worldwide only a tiny proportion of the global population live outside the country of their birth. Moreover, as recently as the mid-1990s, when the British economy was only a bit less open than it is today, net immigration was only about 20,000 a year.

Finally, the immigrationist world-view occludes the ways in which post-war immigration is so different from nineteenth-century or early twentieth-century immigration. First, there is simple scale. Since 2004 nearly 500,000 non-British people have arrived in Britain each year to stay for more than a year (with about 200,000 non-British people leaving) – that means more people arrive on these shores as immigrants *in a single year* than in the entire period 1066 to 1950 (excluding the Irish and wartime flows).

Second, Britain is a welfare democracy. Existing citizens have rights of national ownership and a far louder voice than in the nineteenth or early twentieth century. They also inherit valuable social rights with their citizenship. While globalisation has blurred economic boundaries, the welfare state has, if anything, sharpened the boundary between national insiders and outsiders. Extending the idea of equal citizenship to millions of outsiders raises the problem of how to reconcile the special rights of existing citizens with those of new ones.

Third, multiculturalism – meaning for these purposes allowing immigrants not to have to adapt beyond a bare minimum – has changed what we expect of newcomers. As the incoming groups after 1948 became more different, *less* effort was made to integrate them. And the country's messy post-imperial sense of itself made it harder to offer newcomers a clear national narrative to become a part of.

Immigrationists point to the Jews of Whitechapel in the early twentieth century: how alien they seemed then, but how soon they dispersed into the suburbs to become one of Britain's most successful minorities. Surely the

Pakistanis of Bradford and Bangladeshis of Tower Hamlets will soon do the same? Perhaps. But there is, today, a huge difference in scale and in the culturally laissez-faire spirit of our times which slows down the natural integrationist conveyor belt.

At its best multiculturalism allows minority Britons to come to their own hybrid identities without feeling pushed. But by placing ethnic identity before citizenship the multiculturalism that emerged in the 1980s reinforced a separateness that was already developing in some minority neighbourhoods through simple weight of numbers.

This book is not an appeal to stop the tide of history and return to a warm, community-minded Britain of the 1950s. David Kynaston's social history of the 1950s shows that such a place never existed. It is rather an attempt to persuade liberals that large-scale, poorly managed immigration can damage the social contract and that national attachments are a necessary condition of any realistic centre-left project – a 'citizenship state' not a 'market state'.

Yet, squeezed between a 'leave me alone' individualism and a growing number of networks – from immigrant diasporas to computer gamers – which transcend and even disdain national borders, the nation state often appears to be drawing on dwindling intellectual and emotional support.

Sceptics ask, what is there to integrate into? In a complex liberal society it is a hard question to give a simple answer to. New citizens become British not through expressions of national loyalty but by working, going to the shops, sending their children to school, speaking English well enough to have native friends and being able to join the national conversation. The state cannot mandate integration but it has a role in removing obstacles to the creation of a common life and making it easier to join in.

Britain is not just a few political institutions, the NHS and 'shared values' – it is the texture of everyday life from the sprawling conurbations to small villages. Here can be found characteristic forms of behaviour, a certain kind of humour, a richly idiomatic language. Outsiders can often see this more clearly than insiders. The country does still have a 'core' culture – a way of life, a theme, with many sub-cultural variations on that theme – both establishment BBC 1 and anti-establishment Channel 4. This core culture is shifting, hard to pin down. It has a great capacity to absorb newcomers, but not a limitless one.

Immigration is not just a problem. It benefits many people: the immigrants themselves by definition (otherwise they would not have uprooted themselves to come here), and many people in the host society too. When it is regarded as a problem or particular immigrant groups are seen to be underperforming, the debate tends to focus on the failure of the host society to be sufficiently accommodating. But the real failure in Britain in the post-war period was not to control the inflow more overtly in the interests of existing citizens, not to prepare those existing citizens for something as existential as large-scale immigration and not to make a clear, confident offer to newcomers to secure their loyalty and integration. The result is a society that is now more open than most liberals imagine but more separate too.

Well-intentioned attempts to transcend the nation state in the name of 'global welfare' are not in the interests of the majority of citizens in either rich countries or poor. Sustained mass immigration, without appropriate integration, damages the internal solidarity of rich countries while also stripping poor countries of their most dynamic and best-educated people. This is not a sensible way to run the world.

The post-war immigration story is one of the most enormous and perplexing in the whole of British history – and it is still here all around us, perhaps inside us if we are of recent immigrant descent. In the space of less than sixty years a rather homogeneous country at the heart of a multiracial empire became a multiracial country, now without an empire. The empire truly came home and, initially, occupied large parts of the old working-class districts of English cities – London, the west Midlands and the northern industrial towns in particular. And for almost everything you can think of to say about this transformation, something close to its opposite will also be true. It has changed everything, yet perhaps for more than two-thirds of the white population it has changed little at least directly. It is a symptom of Britain's relative decline, but also of its rebirth and reinvention. It has been a triumph of the human spirit which has enriched this island; it has also been a mess of division and conflict.

It might seem odd to call a book that is in places about what a mess we have made of post-war immigration, *The British Dream*. But when a country is changing very fast, as Britain currently is, it needs stories to reassure and guide it. Unlike the American dream, the British dream is a phrase that does not trip off the tongue, the British tradition is more pragmatic than visionary. But it is time we started getting our tongue round the phrase. Telling inspiring stories about the absorption of so many different kinds of people into this country in a very short space of time is one part of the British dream. But we are also an old country with a remarkable past. The historic British people – with all their imagination, creativity and bloody-mindedness – invented much of the modern world, from capitalism and the rule of law to football. The dream is about them too, about connecting majority to minority and old to new. Let me now describe what I have glimpsed of it.

Part One

Setting the Scene

CHAPTER 1

The Bigger Picture: Globalisation and the Economics of Immigration

Nations and People

Our British story is, of course, set in a bigger global one. There are two commonplace assumptions that inform the debate about globalisation and mass immigration. Humanity is on the move on an unprecedented scale and the nation state is inexorably losing power. Neither is true.

Human beings have not given up the largely settled life we have lived since hunter-gathering gave way to the agricultural revolution 10,000 years ago. There is, it is true, a vast movement within poor countries from the rural to the urban, but people have not suddenly become country-hoppers. The number of people living in countries other than the one they were born in is very small. Even within the European Union in 2000, prior to the opening up towards Central and Eastern Europe, less than 0.1 per cent of the EU's population moved to live in another EU country each year. Rootedness remains a strong human impulse.

And nor is the nation state dying out. As the Soviet empire collapsed at the end of the cold war, there was another burst of nation creation, just as there had been earlier in the century with the disappearance of the Ottoman and Habsburg empires and later the French and British empires.

It is true that the world is more economically interdependent than fifty years ago, and more national sovereignty is vested in international institutions such as Nato, the World Trade Organisation and the United Nations.

Moreover, the technology of travel and media reinforces the metaphor of a 'borderless world'. But it is mainly a metaphor. More of us than ever before are rich enough to frequently travel long distances, and sometimes work abroad for a few years, but most of us in the developed world come back to places we call home in solid nation states – we cross national borders into countries with national armies, national economies, national languages (in a few cases more than one).

Indeed, to a remarkable extent ours remains the age of the liberal democratic nation state and of liberal (or in some cases illiberal) democratic nationalism. Not all states are nation states but much conflict in the world – from Palestine to Tibet and Chechnya – involves stateless people seeking nation states of their own. And more of the world's problems arise because nation states are too weak rather than too strong: why was rapid economic development possible in the East Asian tigers but not in Africa? Partly because national solidarity has been too weak in parts of post-colonial Africa to prevent the state being hijacked by sectional or tribal interests.

Why is this remarkable? Only because the ideology of globalisation has told us that it isn't so. Open one of the serious newspapers any day of the week and you will read paragraphs like this one from Philip Stephens in the *Financial Times*.

'Governments have ceded power to mobile financial capital, to cross-border supply chains and to rapid shifts in comparative advantage. Control of information now belongs to 24-hour satellite television and the cacophony that is the web ... Citizens expect national politicians to protect them against the insecurities – economic, social and physical – that come with global integration. Yet governments have lost much of the capacity to meet the demands.'[1] This is not completely wrong. Officials at the UK Borders Agency will tell you that the internet, for example, has internationalised the job, student and even marriage markets. But by focusing on those forces – trade, finance, transport and communications technology, immigrant diasporas – which do flow constantly across national borders, it ends up painting a partial picture. Most of those things are, in any case, still regulated by national laws

1. 28 October 2011.

4

or international agreements drawn up by national governments. It also leaves out of the picture the areas – like welfare – where the nation state is more, not less, enmeshed in people's lives than fifty years ago.

And in some versions of the ideology it is not just describing, it is advocating – it is saying that by transcending the nation state these forces are promoting the cause of peace, economic growth and human well-being.

But nation states still underpin the institutions that manage the greater interdependence of the modern world, and only they can mobilise their publics for global collective action. Global institutions are mainly forums where the great powers try to find common interest. Those that operate a nominally democratic system of 'one country, one vote' like the UN or WTO do not express a global 'demos' and seldom try to impose their will on dissenting states.[1]

Meaningful international agreements are still notoriously difficult to reach, but as global governance grows in importance *so too* must the nation state. As the centre of power close to where people live and have their attachments, it is only the nation state that can confer legitimacy and accountability on global bodies and thus prevent the emergence of global Leviathans like those imagined by George Orwell in 1984.

One group of rich nation states has, of course, gone a bit further and created in the European Union an institution that is partly designed to transcend national interests and identities. But most of the EU's work is just a conventional pooling of national sovereignty to achieve together what cannot be achieved by individual nation states acting alone, in global trade negotiations for example.

Despite the best attempts of the European Commission and Parliament over many decades there is no significant 'European' interest or identity over and above the pooled, and sometimes conflicting, interests of its member states. There is a kind of European democracy in the European Parliament but elections to this body are mainly national affairs. And there is a degree of redistribution between richer countries (and regions) and poorer ones but the sums involved remain small. The recent Euro bail-out funds have so far

---

1. One institution that has rather slipped free of national oversight is the European Convention on Human Rights, which is run by committees of lawyers.

amounted to only about 50 billion euros divided proportionately between Eurozone members, and they are at least in theory loans.

Although the EU mimics the nation state in some trivial ways, it is not a nation state and to the extent that it commands loyalty it is at a far lower level than national loyalty. Very few people would die for the EU and very few would make big economic sacrifices for another EU state. We have seen this clearly in the case of Germany, one of the least overtly nationalistic of the big European states, which was happy to spend about one trillion dollars on unification with East Germany but is very reluctant to spend far smaller sums helping to support the Greek economy and what they call a European 'transfer union'.

The modern law-bound, liberal nation state is not a menacing political institution. You join automatically by birth (or by invitation) and an allegiance to the liberal nation state is compatible with internationalism, with the rapid advancement of developing countries and with support for bodies like Nato and the EU. It is also compatible with a high degree of localism and devolution to sub-national authorities.

Indeed, after a long and often bloody prehistory the modern nation state is the only institution that can currently offer what liberals, of both right and left, want: democratic legitimacy for the exercise of power and upholding of the rule of law; cross-class and generational solidarity and even, in Europe's post-religious age, a sense of collective identification that is bigger than families and neighbourhoods but more tangible than the whole world.

At this stage in human history the liberal nation state is simply the political form that democracy and welfare states take. It is possible in the future that more global or regional institutions might be able to deliver these things; the EU is one prototype but its current difficulties underline what a slow and stuttering process this is likely to be.

This is ultimately a pragmatic argument. The nation state is not about mystical attachments, it is not a good in itself, it is rather the institutional arrangement that can consistently deliver the democratic, welfare, and psychological outcomes that most people, when given a choice, seem to want.

It is true that the mainstream political and media debate can often be stridently chauvinistic in tone, but in left-wing and liberal circles in universities, business, the law, the media and politics the debate is too often the mirror image of this – positively hostile to even moderate national feeling and the idea that one might favour the interests of one's fellow citizens before others (see my Oxford encounter in the introduction).

The progressive assumption seems to be that it is fine to have an attachment to friends and family and perhaps a neighbourhood or a city – 'I'm proud to be a Londoner' – and, of course, to humanity as a whole. But the nation state – especially a once-dominant one like Britain – is considered something old-fashioned and illiberal, an irrational group attachment that smart people transcend or ignore.

One reason why modern liberals are tempted by the globalisation narrative, even those who are critics of global capitalism, is because many of the 1960s generation cut their political teeth battling against the prejudices and conformism of their respective nations in the decades after the Second World War. It was a time when nationalism was tarnished by war and fascism and often resisted the idea of human equality for non-natives.

As I argued in the introduction, the nation state has changed radically since then, especially in rich countries, yet many people on the left are still transfixed by its historic sins. If people are squeamish about the associations of the word 'nation' they should use something else: citizenship or just society.

Raymond Aron, the French political writer, once said that in the second half of the twentieth century 'with humanity on the way to unification, inequality between peoples takes on the significance that inequality between classes once had'.[1] The idea has had a particular resonance in once-imperial Britain.

And there is a bigger story here about western values. In the mid-twentieth century, elites in the liberal democratic west began to embrace what the sociologist Geoff Dench has called the 'universalist shift' – the belief in the moral equality of all people. This meant that differences of sex, ethnicity and, above all, race were no longer deemed obstacles to someone's full membership in a society. Although the idea did not extend to economic inequality

1. From 'The Dawn of Universal History', a lecture given in London in 1961.

it was profoundly anti-hierarchical and socially egalitarian, and demanded that power and rewards in society be justified by performance rather than inherited characteristics (whiteness or maleness).

This political and legal egalitarianism was not new but in earlier eras it was a largely utopian idea associated with religion (we are all equal in the eyes of God) or radical political movements or abstract philosophising – the Enlightenment, the French and American revolutions (not including slaves in the latter case). What brought this idea of moral equality into mainstream politics? Two world wars, the Holocaust, anti-colonial movements and the stirrings of the civil rights movement in the US all combined to change human consciousness, at least in the developed world, in the mid-twentieth century. Moreover democracy itself, which implies an equality of status within the community of citizens – one person, one vote – was only newly establishing itself in most rich countries in the first part of the twentieth century.

After the publication of the 1948 UN Declaration of Human Rights the principle of moral and political equality came to be written into the constitutions and legal systems of all liberal democracies. Along with the American civil rights movement it prompted, for example, Britain's pioneering anti-race-discrimination legislation of the mid-1960s. The moral and legal equality implied in the universalist shift – completing and making real the idea of equality before the law for all groups – was not always fully embraced in practice but it became a standard to judge the behaviour of states and organisations against; and it was so used by the 1968-ers against authority in general and by the leaders of the first, post-colonial, immigrant wave into Britain against racism.

It now seems so banal to believe in the moral equality of all people that we have forgotten what a novel and revolutionary notion it is, and how many people around the world still have traces of more racial and 'groupist' world-views. (The political theorist John Dunn has explained the triumph of liberal democracy as the victory of individualism over collectivism.) And in the lifetimes of many older people still alive today very different official views prevailed. As recently as the 1940s and 1950s respectable strands of British political opinion were arguing that many colonised people were not yet mature enough to govern themselves; they were like children or teenagers not yet able to join the adult community of self-governing states.

Indeed, at the time of the establishment of the League of Nations in 1919, Japan asked for a protocol to be included proclaiming racial equality between all nations. But this idea was scuppered when US President Woodrow Wilson insisted that the vote in favour must be unanimous while knowing that Britain and Australia would vote against, mainly to defend the latter's 'white Australia' immigration policy. Just twenty-nine years later the UN Declaration of Human Rights was drawn up.

All people in mainstream politics in the developed world now believe in human equality. But among some groups, especially on the liberal left, the universalist shift turned into something else – a rejection of all national borders and loyalties. If all people are worthy of equal respect (at least until they have proved themselves unworthy of it) then how can we any longer favour our fellow national citizens over the impoverished masses of the global south?

This 'post-nationalism' is not a dominant view but it is certainly an influential minority view, and it nags away at the conscience of many liberal-minded people. Here are some people who do embrace post-nationalism.

According to George Monbiot, a leading figure of the liberal left, 'Internationalism ... tells us that someone living in Kinshasa is of no less worth than someone living in Kensington ... Patriotism, if it means anything, tells us we should favour the interests of British people. How do you reconcile this choice with liberalism? How, for that matter, do you distinguish it from racism?'[1]

And here is the respected academic Danny Dorling, in the course of an argument for an open-door immigration policy, questioning the moral legitimacy of the rich west: 'At present the proportion of the world's population that enjoys developed economic and social rights and can afford to travel the world on a legitimate passport is, to my mind, rather like the white population of apartheid South Africa in relation to the majority black population.'[2]

1. *Guardian*, 9 August 2005.
2. Open Democracy website, 18 October 2011.

They are not alone in believing that national preferences are wrong or even racist. Shami Chakrabarti, of the human rights group Liberty, argued recently: 'In the modern world of transnational and multinational power we must decide if we are all people or all foreigners now.'

Such views are not exclusive to the liberal left. On a *Moral Maze* programme in 2011 about development aid, the former Tory cabinet minister Michael Portillo said: 'It is quite old-fashioned to think about national borders, and rather nationalistic to say we must help people who are only moderately poor because they happen to be in the UK rather than helping people who are desperately poor because they happen to be a long way away.'

The centrist commentator Oliver Kamm said to me recently that it was morally wrong to discriminate on grounds of nationality, effectively ruling out the 'fellow citizen favouritism' that most people think the modern nation state is based on. This argument seems to confuse national citizenship with race, as did many of the liberal critics of Gordon Brown's infamous 'British jobs for British workers' speech.

Much of this seems to be a kind of category error. It does not follow from a belief in the moral equality of all people that we owe the same obligations or commitments to them all. We feel special obligations to family members but not because they are morally superior to other people. Monbiot and the others seem to elide the necessary political and legal specialness of national citizenship with superiority and even racism.

So ideas about globalisation and the inevitability of mass migration along with this morally appealing ideology of liberal universalism have combined to reinforce a carelessness about national boundaries among intellectual, and business, elites in many rich countries. Britain is especially vulnerable to this carelessness, partly because of its own multinational and imperial history. For the liberal wing of Britain's baby-boom generation guilt about empire has played a similar, albeit less wrenching, role to the post-war German generations' repudiation of the Nazi period.

These attitudes have created a sympathetic audience for the 'immigrationist' ideology I described in the introduction which supports as open as possible a door to newcomers, partly on cultural grounds – Britain is dull and grey and needs leavening from outside – and partly on global economic justice grounds.[1] Thanks to immigrationism many people on the left abandon their normal suspicion of big business and embrace free market assumptions – echoed in the pro-mass-immigration *Economist* and *Wall Street Journal* – about internationally competitive labour markets and the assumption that America, a country built on mass immigration with few collectivist checks, is the global model that the historic nations of Europe are destined to follow.[2]

A key part of the immigrationist story is that mass immigration is an unstoppable aspect of modern life. It is said that 200 million people, and rising, are living permanently outside the country of their birth. This seems an impressively large figure but is in fact just 3 per cent of the world's population.[3]

In several European countries, including Britain, there is a greater sense of population flow because the number of immigrants in rich countries has indeed more than doubled in the past thirty years. Most forced migrants continue to live in adjacent countries in the global south but about three-quarters of all international migrants now live in twelve countries, half of them rich countries (20 per cent live in the US alone).

The idea of an inexorable rise in global migration flows is one possible future but not an inevitable one. The number of global refugees rose sharply in the late 1980s and early 1990s – partly prompted by the conflicts following the break-up of the Soviet Union – reaching a peak of more than 18 million in 1993 but has since fallen back.

Peering into the future, global human flows will depend to a large extent on what happens to population increases, economic growth and environmental change. As big developing countries like China and India become richer and as the world gradually becomes more equal – at least between, if not within, states – the incentive to leave may become less pressing even as the ability to do so rises.

1. Most people on the left believe in a relative, culturally determined, measure of poverty within rich countries but an absolute measure when looking at the world as a whole.
2. As Sunder Katwala, of British Future, has pointed out the two sides in the immigration debate tend to wear each other's clothes: the left borrows free market arguments to defend high levels of migration, and the right worries about the wage and employment squeeze suffered by the urban poor.
3. The number has increased quite sharply in recent decades, but so has the world's population and as a proportion of the latter the percentage has risen only slightly.

And population in most parts of the world is now stable or falling: Europe, China, Russia, South America, Iran. In a few places it is still rising sharply: Pakistan, parts of the greater Middle East and above all Africa. The population of Africa is now just over 1 billion: current projections are that it will stabilise somewhere between 2 billion and 3 billion. If it is closer to the latter there will clearly be greater pressure to migrate. (A semi-arid country like Niger had a population of just 2 million in 1950 and is expected to hit 50 million by 2050. If it fails to cope, millions of people are likely to face a choice between death and emigration.)

Not all developed countries have embraced mass immigration in the manner that Britain has since 1997. Two very successful countries – Japan and Finland – have kept the door quite tightly closed. Moreover, Denmark, having accepted a moderately high level of immigration in the 1980s and 1990s, changed its mind and decided, successfully, to reduce levels. Neither the Japanese nor the Danish model is necessarily desirable, especially for an internationalised 'hub' economy like Britain's, but it shows that if the political will is there the flows can be controlled. And, as I pointed out in the introduction, those in the British debate who argue that huge immigration flows are a fact of life have short memories. As recently as the mid-1990s net immigration was close to zero. Mass immigration is not a force of nature.

Open Borders

There are two broad strands to the case for large-scale immigration to rich countries. The first, more radical one, takes as its perspective humanity as a whole and argues that it is a human right to emigrate and immigrate in an 'open border' world. The second, more conventional case looks out from a rich country like Britain and says that mass immigration benefits both the immigrants and the citizens of the receiving country. It accepts that an open door is politically unrealistic but wants as much openness as reasonably possible.

As the Dutch writer Paul Scheffer has pointed out, the idea behind the 'open border' proposition is that native populations do not have any special rights as compared to outsiders. Why, in other words, should a country belong to its inhabitants? This is not as absurd as it sounds. The idea that the accident of being born in Britain should not automatically entitle you to your country's collective heritage is not so different to questioning the right of children to inherit most of the wealth that their parents have accumulated, and the latter is a commonplace view on the left.

The late philosopher Michael Dummett argued that having a particular birthplace cannot have any moral significance and therefore should not bring with it unearned rewards. Why should a London bus driver get paid ten times more than a Karachi one for performing an easier version of the same task? Part of the answer is that the London bus driver is benefiting from hundreds of years of economic and technological development which has made Britain a much richer country than Pakistan – it is part of his or her national inheritance.

This goes to the heart of one of the main arguments of this book – that modern liberalism has a thin and unhistorical understanding of people and societies; it too often regards society as a more or less arbitrary collection of individuals without any particular ties or allegiances to each other. One might call it the 'cruise liner' theory of the nation, in which people come together for a voyage but have no ongoing relationship. Liberalism's stress on choice and autonomy makes it uncomfortable with forms of identity and experience which are unchosen. It likes the idea of community in theory but does not see that a meaningful one excludes as well as includes. To this kind of liberalism people are rational, self-interested individualists existing apart from group attachments or loyalties. Much of modern economics and law are based on this model of human behaviour, which is why both disciplines (with the notable exception of trade theory in economics) often fail to properly account for national borders and preferences. And if you accept the liberal premises then any defence of tradition or community is likely to appear irrational or, in the case of immigration, racist.[1]

1. Liberal commentators find it very hard to accept that hostility to large scale immigration is not necessarily the same thing as dislike of foreigners. Here is Matthew d'Ancona writing in the *Evening Standard* on the row in November 2012 about East European children being removed from Rotherham foster carers because they were members of UKIP: 'Given UKIP's

But this conflicts with the more historical idea of a society as a cross-generational contract between generations. There is a genuine dilemma here, especially for the left, between the obligations of governments to prioritise the well-being of their own citizens and a more universal ethic that values the well-being of all humanity. As David Miliband has written: 'The left is torn between a commitment to individual human rights for all people, whatever their nationality, and a recognition that communities depend on deep roots.'

It is also a dilemma that is relatively easily resolved, partly by considerations of human nature and organisation but also by considering the likely economic and social outcomes of an open-border world.

All human associations and communities have boundaries of some kind. They can be easier or harder to join but all have some means of demarcating between insiders and outsiders. The modern nation state has become far more internally inclusive in recent generations – the idea of the equal status of all national citizens is underpinned by historically unprecedented social provision, free to all insiders – but towards the outside world it has become, if anything, more exclusionary. There is nothing perverse or mean-spirited about this. As the value of national citizenship in prosperous countries has risen, and the cost of physically reaching those countries has fallen, so the bureaucracy of border control has had to grow.

If that bureaucracy were to be abolished or even relaxed it would lead to more random and pernicious exclusions at a lower level. The American philosopher Michael Walzer talks about 'a thousand petty fortresses'. It is already possible to see signs of this in the growing levels of both ethnic and social class segregation in many of Britain's major towns and cities.

No one knows for sure how many people would come to live in a rich country like Britain if border controls were abolished. But in many poor parts of the world, in Africa in particular, there has been rapid urbanisation without corresponding industrialisation or economic growth or job creation. That has created a large surplus of urban labour well connected enough to know about the possibilities of life in the west and with a miserable enough life to want to

strong position on immigration generally and EU migration particularly – was it wise to place the three EU migrant children with two of its members?'

get there. Who could say confidently that 5 million or 10 million people would not turn up in the space of a couple of years, especially to a country with the global connections that Britain already has?

This claim may appear to conflict with my earlier assumption about human rootedness. But the point is that many of the urban poor in developing countries are already recently uprooted and the promise of security and relative wealth in a diaspora community in the west can override the relatively shallow attachments of life in the slums of Lagos or Nairobi.

The American academic Dani Rodrik plays a game with his economics students, asking them whether they would rather be poor in a rich country or rich in a poor country (where rich and poor refer to the top and bottom 10 per cent of a country's income distribution). Most of them opt for being rich in a poor country. But they are wrong. The poor in a rich country are in fact three times richer than the rich in a poor country, defined as that top 10 per cent and not just the tiny number of the super rich. That means our economic fortunes are primarily determined by what country we are born in and not by our position on the income scale. Being born in a country like Britain, or being able to get here from a poor country, means winning the lottery of life.[1]

There is an argument that says it is the very barriers to immigration that force people to stay in rich countries. Abolish the barriers, runs the argument, and most of what is now permanent migration would become temporary. This is based partly on what actually happened in places like Britain in the 1960s, as immigration controls forced immigrants from former colonial countries to choose this country as their permanent residence. But it does not follow that today's potential arrivals would circulate back and forth as perhaps Asians or Africans might have done in the 1960s. And the experience of internal migration within large countries, such as southern Italians to the north after 1945 or the migration of southern blacks to the northern cities of the US, suggests that temporary movements become permanent, even where it is very easy to move back and forth, if there are big differences in living standards.

1. Dani Rodrik, *Who Needs the Nation State?*, Harvard University and Centre for Economic Policy Research discussion paper.

Is an immigration open door, or even the somewhat open door that we had for some years after 1997 in Britain, in the interests of poor countries? A few of them think so. The Philippines, for example, actively encourages emigration and exports 85 per cent of the nurses it trains. Other countries like Mexico, Turkey and India also actively encourage certain aspects of emigration.

But they are the exception; most poor countries are actively hostile to emigration. And it is hardly surprising. Desperately poor countries cannot afford to lose their brightest and most ambitious and expensively educated people. Phil Woolas, Labour's former immigration minister, recalls a meeting with the Sierra Leone foreign minister in 2008 in which she said: 'Your country has just given me £150 million to invest in infrastructure, and I am very grateful for that, but the trouble is that 90 per cent of our graduates are in the US or Europe. Can you do anything about that for me?'

It is understandable that an individual Ugandan, for example, might not to want to wait the 100 years it might take for his or her country to establish western levels of wealth and security. But when hundreds of thousands of the best-educated Ugandans make that same calculation it helps to push the country's breakthrough ever further into the future.

There are clearly powerful arguments on the other side of this debate. Writers like Philippe Legrain (in *Immigrants: Your Country Needs Them*) and Ian Goldin (together with Geoffrey Cameron and Meera Balarajan in *Exceptional People*) argue that allowing freer movement from poor to rich countries could do more for the economic prospects of developing countries than overseas aid and foreign investment combined.

Goldin claims that a complete opening of borders would produce gains for the world economy of $39 trillion over twenty-five years – far greater than the $70 billion a year now spent on aid or even the $104 billion a year estimated gain from fully liberalising international trade. The gain sounds big, but $1.3 trillion a year is a small fraction of global GDP of $80 trillion and might seem quite a small return for the enormous social disruption in rich and poor countries that would result from open borders. Nor does Goldin explain how the figure is arrived at. If a worker moves from a poor country to a rich country they almost always become far more productive. But there is no attempt to calculate the enormous cost to the economies of sending countries from losing even more of their best-educated people.

The benefits to rich countries from attracting the skilled and hard-working are obvious enough, at least in the short term. They plug skill gaps, fill 'dirty' jobs and promote entrepreneurialism. According to Goldin, in 2000 migrants accounted for 47 per cent of the US workforce with a science or engineering doctorate (though many would be from other rich countries). Further, in 2005 a migrant was at the helm of 52 per cent of Silicon Valley start-ups. Rich countries, or at least some people in rich countries, are also said to benefit almost as much from unskilled immigrants – about 80 per cent of US farm workers are immigrants, mainly from Mexico.

Emigration from poor to rich countries is obviously an economic benefit to the *individuals* – a doctor from Ivory Coast will earn six times more in France and a Chinese junior lecturer can earn five times more in Australia. The benefits to poor sending countries from an emigration 'brain drain' are less obvious, but the remittances sent home is one. Official figures put annual global remittances at $160 billion – $53 billion to South America, $48 billion to East Asia, $40 billion to South Asia but only about $20 billion to Sub-Saharan Africa, which still receives more in foreign aid.[1] In some countries these flows account for a big chunk of GDP, as much as 20 per cent in the case of the Philippines (some put it as high as 40 per cent), 8 per cent in the case of Mexico and even 3 per cent in the case of India.

But just as rich countries can become over-dependent on importing certain kinds of labour, which then reduces the incentive to improve training or the work ethic for the hard-to-employ native citizens, so poorer countries can become over-dependent on exporting labour, which provides a flow of remittance money but prevents the 'take-off' to a more productive economy.

From what is known of the emigrants from poor countries they are usually their better-educated citizens, even if they often end up doing low- or semi-skilled jobs in rich countries. According to Goldin more than 70 per cent of

---

1. Legrain claims that the annual remittance figure is as high as $480 billion, or roughly six times the official aid figure.

graduates from Guyana and Jamaica move to developed countries.[1] And just as there are hidden multiplier benefits from successful immigration, so there are hidden economic and *political* costs of losing precisely the people who should be leading the economic development of poor countries and pressing for political reform as the middle class did in nineteenth-century Europe.

There is a particular concern over the importing of skilled health staff by rich countries. The picture of NHS hospitals full of front-line staff from African and Asian backgrounds is often used as a powerful image to underline the benefits to Britain of immigration. Many of those NHS workers will be the children or grandchildren of immigrants but some will also be recent arrivals, and their employment here is very hard to justify given that many of the poor countries they have recently left have severe shortages of skilled medical staff.

Malawi, for example, lost more than half of its nursing staff to emigration over recent years, leaving just 336 nurses to serve a population of 12 million. Rates of perinatal mortality doubled from 1992 to 2000, a rise that is in part attributed to falling standards of medical care. Excluding Nigeria and South Africa, the average country in Sub-Saharan Africa had 6.2 doctors per 100,000 of population in 2004. This compares with 166 in the UK, 249 in Australia and 549 in the US. Yet despite this some rich countries, including Britain, have been importing doctors and nurses from poor countries on a morally questionable scale.[2]

About 31 per cent of doctors practising in the UK now come from overseas, compared to just 5 per cent in France and Germany. And it is estimated that about 12 per cent of doctors trained in India now live in the UK. There was a spike in overseas recruitment when Labour started investing heavily in the NHS in the early 2000s and before the expansion of medical schools was able to produce a spurt in home-grown staff. In 2004 the NHS agreed not

1. Other places that have high levels of graduate brain drain include Morocco (65 per cent), Tunisia (64 per cent), Gambia (60 per cent), Ghana (26 per cent). For Sub-Saharan Africa the loss is particularly damaging because only on average 4 per cent of the population has a degree.

2. Robert Rowthorn, 'Cherry Picking: A Dubious Practice', *Around the Globe*, vol. 3, no. 2, Spring 2006.

to recruit from developing countries, unless expressly allowed to do so, and there are currently about 150 countries on the 'no go' list. But it is very easy to circumvent, not least by hiring foreign staff from the private sector, and recruitment from poor countries continues on a worryingly large scale.

There are better ways of helping people in poor countries than a mass-immigration system that sucks out their best-educated people while increasing competition for poorer people in rich countries. There is nothing morally objectionable about a country like Britain refusing entry to skilled people from poor countries or insisting that students or temporary workers from such countries return home after their time is up.[1] Indeed, if people return to their country of origin after a few years in a rich country it may produce the best outcome of all, a remittance flow followed by the return of a more skilled and worldly citizen eager for change.

Rich countries can also help to improve conditions in poor countries in such a way that skilled workers are more likely to commit themselves to their homeland. Indeed, rich countries should enter a new contract with poor ones based explicitly around the idea of *bigger financial flows and smaller human flows*. Rich countries should be saying: we will help you to grow faster and thus hold on to your best people through appropriate trade and aid policies; we will also agree not to lure away your most skilled people so long as you agree to take back your illegal immigrants (which many countries don't). The domestic reflection of this idea in British politics is the explicit connection between the Coalition government's reduced immigration goal and its exemption from cuts of the development aid programme.

Another way in which a mutually beneficial 'stay at home' policy might operate is by professional and academic bodies in rich countries encouraging more ongoing contact with counterparts in poor ones. Academic and professional exchanges and other forms of networking can help to reduce the isolation which many professionals in poor countries feel.

1. The argument that Britain must open its doors to the world because about 5.5 million British citizens currently live abroad is not a convincing one. Most of those people are living and working in rich Anglophone countries like Australia, the US, Canada and Ireland; many of them will return to Britain after a few years. There are about 500,000 often rather segregated Britons living in retirement colonies in Spain, but they are not representative.

There is a political as well as an economic dimension to this. Widely drawn definitions of persecution in the UN Refugee Convention can have the effect of driving away the most reform-minded groups in authoritarian societies even when their lives or personal security are not at serious risk, and this acts as a convenient safety valve for the status quo. Easy access to the west encourages too many people to choose 'exit' over 'voice'.

There is a strong case for tightening the legal framework for asylum. When the UN Refugee Convention was established in 1951 the Soviet gulags were a reality and the Nazi genocide a recent memory. It was drawn up on the assumption that a small trickle of refugees might escape such totalitarian states and make their way to the west. Initially it applied only to Europe but was extended to the whole world in 1967.

The convention currently states that anyone is entitled to asylum if they are being persecuted on grounds of 'race, religion, nationality, membership of a particular social group or political opinion'. As Charles Clarke, the former Labour home secretary, has observed: 'These are wide ranging categories which, depending on your definition of persecution, probably cover hundreds of millions, if not billions, of people living in a world where international communications means that more and more people are aware of their "rights" and seek to take them up.'[1] And human rights case law is gradually widening the definitions beyond the rather extreme circumstances imagined in 1951. One recent Appeal Court ruling in London established that homosexuals need not be discreet about their sexuality in a country where it is illegal, which greatly widens the scope for claims from about eighty countries.

But many of the largest groups, such as Somalis, applying to enter Britain and other rich countries as refugees are not facing individual persecution but rather are caught up in regional conflicts or civil wars or even natural disasters. These are not the people for whom the Convention was designed, but in Britain in recent years they have often been granted 'Exceptional Leave to Remain' or what is now called 'Humanitarian Protection'.

There is no reason why the leave to remain should be permanent (in theory in Britain it is reviewed after five years). Civil wars and natural disasters

1. Charles Clarke, *The EU and migration: A call for action*, Centre for European Reform, December 2011.

come to an end and countries need rebuilding. Rich countries should try to provide shelter from the storm for people badly affected but then ensure they return to help that rebuilding. Indeed, in circumstances such as these it would often be better if western states provided neighbouring countries with sufficient aid to build decent but temporary towns in safe areas as close as possible to their former homes. That way people can live securely but not lose touch with their countries (and also be in a good position to judge when it is safe to return) rather than being dumped in the poor parts of rich western cities where they often live segregated and unhappy lives and can become a long-term welfare burden. Of the 4 million refugees who have fled Afghanistan in the latest conflict the majority have gone to live in neighbouring countries and more than 2 million are said to have returned to their old homes.

Some of the brightest and most idealistic people in rich countries, working in NGOs, immigration law firms and so on, are battling to bring as many people as possible from poor to rich countries in the face of overwhelming opposition from their fellow citizens and against the interests of the poor countries themselves. A new 'stay at home' contract can still appeal to altruistic and charitable instincts in the west but would work with, and not against, the majority interest in both rich and poor countries.

There will always be global centres of excellence where the world's leading scientists or financiers or technologists can come together to sharpen their wits. But gathering so many of the world's brightest and best into a few global centres of excellence like Silicon Valley, or even London, seems an oddly lopsided way of arranging global affairs. Surely it would be in the longer-term interests of rich countries and poor to spread development more evenly.

The bigger point here, applied to health or any other sector, is the most basic insight of welfare economics. Just as the marginal extra pound is worth more to a poor person than to a rich person, so the educated and ambitious person is worth more to a poor country that has few of them than to a rich country that already has many.

Indeed, mass emigration from poor countries creates a kind of development distortion, the human equivalent of the global trade and fiscal imbalances: the best-educated people leave countries that badly need them for rich countries that can certainly benefit from their arrival (or at least some people can) but do not need them in any proper sense. Some lucky people end up speeding up the development process for themselves and their families while helping to slow it down for everyone else back home.

Does Large-scale Immigration Benefit Existing Citizens?

No sensible person is opposed to immigration *tout court*. It is a matter of how many people, how quickly, how the process is managed and how it affects the national political community. For the nation state to have any meaning it must in the democratic era – contrary to Michael Dummett – 'belong' to existing citizens; on important matters citizens must have special rights over non-citizens. That means immigration must be managed with the interests of existing citizens in mind. The question is, what are those interests? And what kind, and what level, of immigration should it translate into?

Looked at year on year the numbers arriving in Britain seem tiny. According to the OECD, net immigration to Britain in 2010 was just forty-two people per 10,000 residents. That may not seem many people, but according to the Office for National Statistics persistent immigration at around that rate sees the UK population rising from 62.3 million in 2010 to 81.5 million in 2060 – an increase of 21.8 million. In the absence of migration, the ONS projects that the population would only rise to 64 million by 2060.

In several European countries the immigrant and ethnic minority population is rising to 15 or 20 per cent in the next few years (one leading demographer, David Coleman of Oxford University, has said that on current trends Britain will be 'majority-minority' by 2066).[1] Many large towns are already around 40 per cent minority – Birmingham, Malmö, Marseilles. In London half of those aged thirty were born abroad.

Few people question the economic and cultural benefit of moderate levels of immigration. The arrival of the rich and the skilled and the inventive has long brought blessings to this land. Unskilled immigration brings its benefits

1. 'When Britain becomes "majority minority"', *Prospect*, December 2010.

too. As Philippe Legrain puts it: 'Such immigration allows rich countries to import low cost, low skill, labour intensive services from poor countries. By doing so, we reduce the cost of such services, which allows more people to benefit from them, while freeing up Americans and Europeans to pursue better paid and more productive careers.'

But the justification for such a large and unpopular change would have to be that the economic benefits are significant and measurable. And they are not. There is a widespread assumption in the national debate – at least on the left – that large-scale immigration brings large economic benefits and any problems associated with immigration must be endured or dealt with in order to go on enjoying those benefits. But almost all the economic analyses of immigration in recent years have found the effect on employment, wages, fiscal contribution and per capita growth for the resident population to be marginal.

Moreover, existing British citizens have very different experiences of immigration, depending on where they live and what kinds of job they do. Generally speaking, employers, big and small, and better-off people benefit from imported labour, which is often cheaper, relative to its quality, than the domestic equivalent. In recent years, many millions of people have enjoyed lower prices for cleaners or building work.

Immigrants themselves benefit, of course. But as a consequence of their arrival, low-skilled locals (often recent migrants themselves) face greater competition both in the labour market and in public services. The pressure on public services is offset partly by the extra taxes paid by immigrants. But when inflows are on the scale of recent years short-term problems are often acute – especially in favourite 'landing' destinations such as Slough, Newham or Hounslow.

The last Labour government did establish the Migration Impacts Forum in 2009, which collected evidence of extra costs arising from migration. Extra funds were paid out mainly for schools and the NHS, but the sums were usually regarded as insufficient (and it was abolished by the new government in 2010). Some local authorities also complained about the underestimation of their populations, and therefore of their income from central government, on the basis of the 2001 (and 2011) census – and the complaint was usually based on the under-counting of recent immigration. In some cases they produced their own alternative calculations based on evidence of extra use of local services or even, in the case of Slough, on the extra flow of sewage!

Pressure on housing is another factor. In the first wave of post-colonial immigration, immigrants were generally denied access to public housing by policies that effectively excluded all outsiders (from other boroughs as well as countries). In the 1970s and 1980s legislation shifted to prioritise need, which propelled poorer immigrant families to the front of the housing queue.

Now there is a more general problem of the low supply of all types of housing, especially social housing. This is not caused by immigration but it is certainly exacerbated by it. Recently new household formation in England has been running at about 200,000 a year, of which about 40 per cent is the result of migration – but since 2000 actual housebuilding has lagged behind that rise in households by 50,000 a year.

This pressure on resources begs the question of whether there is an optimal population size for Britain and, if so, whether immigration policy should be subordinated to it. To address that question would require another book. Suffice it to say, there is often a 'more is better' bias on the part of mass immigration advocates. This may be a hangover from the mercantilist view common in the eighteenth and nineteenth centuries that a large population was essential for military and economic power. It is certainly at odds with contemporary environmentalist ideas of sufficiency and sustainability. In any case, small countries today are likely to be as rich, if not richer, than big ones, and within a liberal international order countries like Sweden, Switzerland and Ireland often have influence out of all proportion to their size.

The US is the one western country where, across the political spectrum, an expanding population is regarded as a good thing in itself. And perhaps for the world's dominant power, with its huge armed forces keen to recruit new immigrants, it does make some sense. There is no need for the rest of the world to follow. England is already one of the most densely populated countries in Europe.[1]

---

1. As the Oxford economist Stephen Nickell has put it: 'More people means more houses, more roads, more power stations, more waste incinerators, more airport runways, and so on. And the revealed preference of the existing population is that they dislike most of these

The idea that power and prosperity are driven by immigration-fuelled population growth is the wrong way round. Successful economies and open, liberal societies are magnetically attractive to immigrants – immigrants do not create that success, though they may help to sustain it.

And here I want to drill down deeper into the economic arguments made in defence of large-scale immigration. There are three main claims. First, young immigrants help prevent our societies from ageing and generally pay in more than they take out. Second, immigrants are complementary to natives, not competitive, so bring many benefits for employers but do not take jobs or depress wages for workers. Third, immigrants are a source of growth and innovation.

The first argument about ageing seems a common-sense assumption: our society is ageing, so import lots of young people and encourage them to have large families and, hey presto! we are youthful again. But the truth is that immigrants grow old too, and usually converge quickly on native fertility rates, so for this to work it requires climbing on to a treadmill of high and continuing immigration.

The current age structure of the UK is a result of the rapid growth of the population over the past 100 years, which has risen in that time from about 30 million to a bit over 60 million. To keep the age structure as it is now (with roughly the same ratio of older to younger people) would require a similar surge of population growth. But that is not a popular policy, especially in our more environmentally minded, congestion-conscious times.

The key formula here is the 'potential support ratio' (PSR), which indicates how many people there are of official working age potentially able to support each person of pension age. The ratio falls in Britain around 2020, as the baby-boomer generation born in the 1950s and early 1960s retires. But

---

things ... anywhere near where they live. There is, in fact, plenty of room, but this is not a view shared by many ... So like it or not the relatively high population density in England means that there will be serious problems generated by the rising housing and infrastructure requirements associated with the high rate of population growth generated by high rates of immigration.' See 'Too Many People in Britain? Immigration and the Housing Problem', LSE lecture, 21 June 2011.

the curious thing is how little difference a lot of immigration makes to this ratio. Assuming zero net immigration the PSR is 1.94 in 2074, but add an extra 20 million people to the population by that date and the ratio rises to just 2.11.[1]

As Adair Turner pointed out in a lecture at the LSE in 2007, *Do We Need More Immigrants and Babies?*, arguments for high immigration to keep the support ratio high are usually made on the basis of assumptions that leave the retirement age untouched. He argues that if the retirement age is raised to reflect greater longevity, then half of the change to the support ratio disappears and the problem becomes more manageable. There are other things that can be done: increasing automation and productivity can play a small role, as can bringing more women into the workforce (something that is happening anyway in most rich countries) and, indeed, allowing moderate levels of immigration.[2]

Britain, which has a younger population than many comparable European countries, does not face a big ageing problem – average age for a male is currently thirty-nine and it is projected to rise to forty-two by 2035. The country is ageing slowly enough to adjust to it without relying on enormous levels of immigration. And it can, in the end, gracefully grow a little bit older.

Some scepticism is also required towards the claim that immigrants pay more in than they take out. Highly educated, skilled or talented immigrants, provided they get decent jobs and do not displace native workers, normally make a positive fiscal contribution – they pay more in taxes than they absorb in government spending. Such people come disproportionately from other developed countries. Unskilled immigrants can also make a positive contribution provided that they and their dependants do not make large demands on the welfare state.

There are two influential studies in this discussion. The first was a Home Office study (Gott and Johnston, 2002) which assessed the numbers for 1999–2000 and concluded that immigrants made a net fiscal contribution

1. Goldin in the book *Exceptional People* quotes even more dramatic figures from the UN, suggesting that to maintain the dependency ratio of 2000 to the year 2050 would require an extra 59 million people in the country!
2. Adair Turner, 'Do We Need More Immigrants and Babies?', LSE lecture, 28 November 2007.

of £2.5 billion per annum. The second was a study by the IPPR think tank (Sriskandarajah et al., 2005) which updated the Home Office work and concluded that in 2003–4 migrants paid in £41.2 billion and consumed £41.6 billion. There are many ways in which the numbers can be drawn up but the mainstream conclusion (shared by the Treasury and the government's Migration Advisory Committee) is that overall fiscal contribution is broadly neutral.[1]

This broadly neutral outcome does, of course, hide huge variations between groups. Another IPPR report found that only 1 per cent of Poles and Filipinos claim income support, compared with 39 per cent of Somalis.

Looking beyond the most recent immigration the picture is less positive. Because of the historic legacy of unskilled labour from New Commonwealth countries in the early post-war period, and then the arrival of other large groups with low education levels such as Bangladeshis and Somalis, twice as many minority Britons are classified as poor compared with white Britons.[2] That means minority Britain is, on average, likely to be somewhat more welfare dependent than white Britain, though as we have seen with large variations within both groups.

What about the immigration effect on jobs and wages? There is a broad consensus among economists that when properly managed and at moderate levels, immigration has no overall negative effect on the employment prospects or wages of native workers but greases the wheels of the labour market by filling vacancies that local workers either don't want to do or can't do because they don't have the right skills. This is especially true in countries with relatively flexible labour markets like Britain.

But it is not 'economically illiterate' to suggest that immigrants can

---

1. In *Oxford Review of Economic Policy*, vol. 24, no. 3, 2008, 'The fiscal impact of immigration on the advanced economies', Robert Rowthorn calculated the impact on the British economy being in the range minus 0.47 per cent to plus 0.23 per cent (though if all the indirect public spending costs of immigration are added, for example teaching English to primary school children, the minus figure could be larger). It is also true that migrants are more likely to leave as they age than natives, which has a positive fiscal impact (see the Office for Budgetary Responsibility report, July 2012).
2. About 25 per cent of people living in the most deprived areas of England are non-white. 'Understanding Society', Economic and Social Research Council.

substitute for locals, as well as complement them, as Legrain claims. When the recession struck in 2008, the number of UK-born workers fell sharply by almost 800,000 over an eighteen-month period and has fluctuated around that lower level ever since. Meanwhile, in the four years to the end of 2011 employment of those born outside Britain rose by about 400,000 (with half accounted for by East Europeans). More strikingly, between the second quarter of 1997 and the last quarter of 2011, there were almost 2.7 million extra people employed in Britain, of whom 2.1 million were born outside the country.

The issue of job displacement is a complex and controversial one. What seems to be happening is this. There is a daily 'churn' in the labour market, with about 2,000 jobs disappearing and another 2,000 being created; of those 2,000 new jobs most are taken by British-born workers swapping around or moving up (or down) the employment ladder. But a disproportionate number of *new* jobs (on top of the 'churn') seem to have been going to recent immigrants, rather than British workers. Part of that is necessary; unless the employment rate among British workers is rising – and British workers are being drawn from non-employment or unemployment – then foreigners *have* to take the new jobs. (The native employment rate has remained more or less static for a decade or more, aside from the downward blip in 2008.)

There is potential displacement even when there is a growth in jobs, but mainly through making it harder for the unemployed to get back into work. When, as in recent years, the total number of jobs is falling and foreign labour is more attractive than its domestic equivalent then more displacement is likely to occur. In some sectors employers appear to have acquired a 'foreigner bias' when it comes to new hires, finding them better motivated and with lower wage expectations.[1]

In an analysis of more than forty-five studies between 1982 and 2007, Simonetta Longhi et al. found the immigration effect on employment was small but it did show that immigration discouraged workless natives from re-entering the labour market. And a paper by Massimiliano Tani and Timothy

---

1. See the survey of small employers in the hospitality and agricultural sector in 'Trends in A8 migration to the UK during the recession', *Population Trends*, vol. 145, by D. McCollum and A. Findlay.

Hatton found that foreign immigration into a region leads to less migration from elsewhere in the UK, so northerners are less likely to come south to take jobs.[1] According to the government-appointed Migration Advisory Committee, between 1995 and 2010 there was some displacement, with one British worker displaced for every thirteen immigrants. The 'illiteracy' that Legrain refers to is the so-called 'lump of labour' fallacy, the false idea that the demand for labour is fixed. It is true that immigrants themselves create extra demand for labour through the incomes they spend and the taxes they pay. Polish builders create new jobs for locals – in supermarkets, at builders' merchants and for interior designers; at least they do so as long as they are expanding the market for building work and not just displacing natives or sending most of their income home. But there is often a time lag between the jobs they take and the jobs they create, and the new jobs may also be in different places to the lost jobs.

And because much of it is concentrated at the top and bottom, immigration often reinforces inequality and can reduce social mobility for domestic workers. As the 2008 House of Lords report on the economics of immigration vividly puts it: 'The City of London illustrates this range of occupations, where immigrants are widely found among the staff of the restaurants serving financial executives, many of who are also immigrants.'[2]

One third of all graduate jobs in London are now taken by people born outside Britain, which may be one factor behind the apparent slow-down in social mobility in recent years.[3] There is less room at the top for existing citizens from low- and middle-income backgrounds. Indeed, if a country pursues a 'global talent' policy at quite a broad level there is likely to be some crowding-out effect for the resident population – bright and inventive natives, whatever their background, are going to get somewhat less good jobs if they have to compete with the very best in the world. In some cases the arrival of

1. Simonetta Longhi, Peter Nijkamp and Jacques Poot, 'Meta-analysis of empirical evidence on the labour market impacts of immigration', *Région et Développement*, no. 27, 2008. Timothy Hatton and Massimiliano Tani, 'Immigration and inter-regional mobility in the UK 1982–2000', *Economic Journal*, vol. 115, no. 507, November 2005.

2. The Economic Affairs Committee of the House of Lords report on the Economic Impact of Immigration, April 2008.

3. Figure from Professor Ian Gordon, LSE London and Spatial Economics Research Centre.

skilled foreigners can boost the overall jobs market for skilled people; the City of London is probably an example of that. But not all the new jobs will be complementary to domestic workers and there is bound to be some demotion effect. There are many excellent British footballers who are playing in the Championship and not in the Premier League because they are competing against the best in the world. We may welcome that in football because it makes the Premier League so exceptional, and the negative effect on a few hundred British footballers, who are in any case successful and highly paid, is not a matter for concern. But do we want the same thing to apply across the range of professional and highly skilled jobs?[1]

So, what about wages? As with employment, all the studies suggest no great effect either positively or negatively on native workers. But while wages 'overall' may not be significantly depressed by mass immigration or even slightly boosted, there is strong evidence that the bottom layer of workers are hurt. (The leading American immigration analyst George Borjas believes that the economics of immigration turned negative for most native US workers as early as 1970.) Christian Dustmann and others (2008) found that immigration overall had led to a small increase in average wages but also to a small reduction in the wages of the bottom 20 per cent in Britain.[2] Stephen Nickell and Jumana Saleheen (2009) found that the effect of a 10 percentage point rise in the proportion of immigrants working in semi-skilled and unskilled sectors like care homes, bars and shops led to a 5.2 per cent reduction in overall pay in the sector.[3]

There is also the 'opportunity cost' for native workers, meaning the higher wages that they would almost certainly have enjoyed, at least in some sectors, if not for the big inflows in recent years. The enthusiasm of the Treasury for

1. The relative decline in the number of British post-graduate students as the foreign post-graduate numbers increase sharply is beginning to worry some business leaders who say that we do not have enough home-grown talent; see *Postgraduate Education*, an inquiry by the Higher Education Commission, October 2012.
2. Christian Dustmann, Albrecht Glitz, and Tommaso Frattini, 'The labour market impact of immigration', *Oxford Review of Economic Policy*, vol. 24, no. 3, pp. 477–94, 2008.
3. Stephen Nickell and Jumana Saleheen, *The Impact of Immigration on Occupational Wages: Evidence from Britain*, Spatial Economics Research Centre, Discussion Paper 34, October 2009.

mass immigration in the 1990s and 2000s was partly based on the assumption that it did indeed hold down real wages.

Given that nearly 750,000 extra workers arrived between 2004 and 2011 from Eastern Europe alone – and that figure does not include the large number of self-employed East Europeans – it is perhaps surprising that the downward pressure on native wages has not been as marked as it seems to have been on employment. East Europeans represented almost 10 per cent of the unskilled workforce in 2007, higher in certain areas, and one in five of all low-skilled workers in Britain is now foreign born.[1] The immigration effect on the low-paid and low-skilled would have been much sharper but for the introduction of the minimum wage in 1999. (The majority of East Europeans who arrived after 2004 have been working for around the minimum wage.)

It is often said that immigrants are needed to do the jobs that local workers won't do. That is sometimes the case but not generally so; in those parts of the country where there are not many immigrants local people will fill the vacancies. It is true that workers in welfare states usually have a strong sense of their worth – a welcome product of a civilised society – and will not do certain jobs *at the wage rates or conditions on offer*. Immigrants, from poorer places, will often do those jobs instead.

A keen young Latvian graduate who is here for two or three years on a working holiday to improve his or her English and have some fun is more attractive to employ in a pub or a care home, and has lower wage expectations, than a local youngster with a clutch of poor GCSEs and a bit of attitude.

Workers in rich countries with welfare states can sometimes be lazy or difficult or poorly educated (Britain has a particular problem with literacy and numeracy among the bottom 20 per cent), and a keen, well-educated foreigner who speaks good English will often seem preferable from the point of view of an individual employer. But to have millions of long-standing residents sitting at home on benefit while poorer foreigners come in and take the jobs that they should be doing makes no sense for the country as a whole; it creates a kind of 'Saudi Arabianisation' of the labour market. The number of British citizens on out of work benefits has fallen from a peak of about

1. See 'Non-UK born workers', Office for National Statistics, 26 May 2011.

6 million in the early 1990s but even in the long boom it never then fell below 4.5 million. Moreover, Britain now has an especially acute problem with the unemployment of younger people which may be exacerbated by the fact that a disproportionate number of East European immigrants have been in the 18–34 bracket.

And the notion that labour market competition with foreigners will cause British workers to buck up their ideas seems quite implausible. If a local unemployed worker sees local employers using agencies specialising in East Europeans providing whole shifts for factory work, as is common in food manufacturing or the agricultural and horticultural sector, it is likely to make them even more disenchanted with the system and push them deeper into welfare dependence.

At the more skilled end of the labour market, immigrants are often helpful in plugging temporary skill shortages. But they can also discourage investment in education and training. The classic example of this was medicine, which for many years was over-dependent on luring doctors from third world countries because Britain didn't train enough of its own.

The same pattern of employer 'addiction' to skilled foreigners is visible in many other sectors. Indeed Martin Ruhs of the Migration Advisory Committee argues that the historic institutions and policy assumptions of British economic life – low levels of labour regulation, non-existent employer collaboration on training – make this country particularly vulnerable to over-dependence on foreign labour.

The construction industry, for example, is highly fragmented and does very little training, relying instead on project-based labour, informal recruitment and casualised employment. By contrast, many European countries have proper training and apprenticeship programmes, producing workers with a wide range of transferable skills. It is often these workers who are doing jobs in Britain. There are fewer British skilled construction workers now than ten years ago, despite a big construction boom through much of the last decade. Most of the skilled construction jobs on recent large projects – for example the Olympic sites – were filled by non-British citizens.[1]

1. The data on this is disputed, but to qualify as a local worker on the Olympic sites all you needed was a National Insurance number and a local address. Some construction industry

Social care is another sector that has an in-built bias towards foreign workers, in this case not so much because of their skill but because of their readiness to work long and antisocial hours for low pay in an often physically and emotionally demanding job. Because of the constraints on the local authority budgets that pay for social care, about two-thirds of care assistants in London are immigrants, though the number is lower in other parts of the country and the picture is changing because of recent immigration restrictions.

One big and simple point is often lost sight of in this debate – immigration has a more positive economic impact when there is full employment than when there is a big stock of long-term unemployed and hard-to-employ natives as in most rich countries today. Importing cheap and motivated foreign labour in effect shelves the problem of how to get the difficult natives back into work. It has, as Fraser Nelson, editor of the *Spectator*, argues, 'broken the link between more jobs and less dole'.

Supporters of large-scale immigration will argue that this is too pessimistic an account. Immigration is not a zero sum game; the right kind of immigrant labour is a kind of yeast that helps to swell the economic brew both for the incomer and the native. And it is true that some employers who have been hiring East European labour would have hired *no one at all* if the foreign labour was not available. It is not clear, however, that recent immigration in Britain created any significant extra income growth per head for existing citizens once the immigrants themselves are removed from the equation.

In 2004 Tony Blair made a speech defending the government's immigration policy and said that growth would have been almost one-half per cent lower in 2001–2 without immigration. But most of the immigration-induced increase of 0.4 per cent of GDP came from growth in the immigrant population itself. A major paper a couple of years later by the National Institute of Economic and Social Research (published in the *National Institute Economic Review* in October 2006) was greeted as an endorsement of the benefits of immigration, but it actually showed that while immigration in the years 1998–2005 had boosted

---

insiders put the proportion of non-British skilled workers as high as 70 per cent.

growth by 3 per cent it had also increased the population by 3.8 per cent so immigration had *reduced* GDP per head.[1] And a more recent National Institute paper (April 2011) found that the arrival of more than 700,000 East European workers since 2004 has raised output by merely 0.4 per cent, meaning a small fall in GDP per head of the resident population.

So, even on wages, employment and economic growth it is a mixed picture. But what about the more generic claim about diversity and dynamism? It is a commonplace of the immigration debate to say that Britain has benefited in the past from inflows of dynamic outsiders – perhaps most significantly the small Jewish inflow of the late nineteenth and early twentieth century and the smaller East African Asian inflow of the 1970s. Britain continues to attract creative and inventive foreigners and should, of course, go on doing so – immigrants are twice as likely to start a business as natives, both corner shops and bigger businesses too, and about 25 per cent of Britain's Nobel Prize winners have been foreign born.

The 'immigrationists' make much of how immigrants see things differently and are more determined to succeed. But one could also argue that in a complex knowledge economy companies increasingly operate with high levels of implicit understanding that are only easily available to those raised in the same culture; this certainly seems to be the case in Japan and South Korea. In any case the idea that if net immigration is reduced to 80,000 a year Britain will gradually become economically stagnant is absurd. The country has a vast amount of diversity stored up already thanks to the immigration of the last sixty years. It needs time to absorb it and make the best use of it.

1. Partly thanks to the work of the government's Migration Advisory Committee (established by Labour in 2007) led by Professor David Metcalf there has been a more appropriate focus on economic benefit to the resident British population in recent years.

Immigration Now, British Hubs and Caps

I want now to come closer to the present day and consider what is happening with the Conservative-led Coalition government's concerted attempt to bring immigration down to more normal levels. The aim is to bring annual net immigration below 100,000 a year by 2015, down from an average of close to 250,000 in recent years.[1]

Managing such a step change is harder than when this was last attempted in the late 1970s and 1980s, partly because the flows are much larger, movement within the EU (which cannot be controlled) has increased, Britain's hub economy and especially its higher education sector is more dependent on big inflows and immigrants have greater legal protection than in earlier decades.

To understand the current policy dilemmas we need a quick snapshot of the flows and the various routes people arrive through. First the raw numbers. Since about 2004 the number of people coming to live in this country for a year or more (the technical definition of an immigrant) has hovered just below 600,000 each year, while the number of people leaving the country has fluctuated around the 350,000 mark. This produces an annual net inflow of around 250,000; strip out the comings and goings of British citizens and the annual net immigration figure is closer to 300,000 (because more Brits are leaving than returning).

In the year to December 2011 non-British net immigration was just below 300,000, and contrary to popular opinion more than two-thirds of it came from outside the EU. Most of the rest came from the new EU countries (40,000), and the old (30,000).

The four main channels of the gross inflow in 2011, with rough numbers attached, were study (230,000), work (180,000), family reunion (80,000), seeking asylum (20,000) plus other residual categories (50,000). The only category in which people from outside the EU were not the overwhelming majority was work.

It is often stressed how much more varied in country of origin (and place

1. Technically this pledge is not part of the Coalition agreement between the Conservatives and the Liberal Democrats, but the Conservatives have behaved as if it is.

of destination in Britain) the post-1997 wave of immigration has been. There is some truth to that, but there is also more overlap with the post-colonial wave than is sometimes recognised – about half of the non-EU gross inflow in 2011 came from New Commonwealth countries (mainly Africa and the Indian subcontinent) and most came to study.

That means, again contrary to the common assumption, that most contemporary immigration *can* be controlled. If governments want to screen out most immigrants and keep a door open to only a small number of the 'brightest and the best' they can. The main constraints being not so much the EU free-movement rules but the moral and legal constraints relating to asylum and family reunion and the perceived needs of British business and, above all, the higher education sector.

Some countries, such as Canada, have been highly selective throughout the post-war period. It was harder to be selective in Britain because of the country's colonial and post-colonial obligations. In the second great wave of post-war British immigration, beginning in 1997, it was supposed to be different. This was no longer a question of imperial obligation but 'managed migration', in the language of Labour ministers, for the benefit of Britain.

In practice, however, immigration was not especially managed in the late 1990s and early 2000s, partly because the political priority was to move people from the rising asylum route to more legitimate work routes (see Chapter 5, 'Labour's Greatest Legacy').

In the mid-2000s Labour began designing its Points Based System or PBS (borrowed from the practice in places like Canada and Australia of ranking potential immigrants by their economic desirability) which reduced the number of routes for non-EU migrants from eighty to just five: tier one, highly skilled people without a job offer; tier two, skilled people with a job offer; tier three, low-skilled workers; tier four, students; and tier five, temporary and domestic workers.

Labour's PBS did not in itself reduce numbers, it was merely a sorting mechanism and a self-categorising one too. Indeed, the inflow hit the new high plateau of almost 600,000 a year in 2004 (including returning British citizens) and has stayed close to that number ever since. But the nature of the inflow did begin to change. The number of non-EU people arriving through the work route was halved between 2004 and 2009, falling to 55,000 mainly by reducing the numer of work permits for low-skilled workers. But in the meantime there was a sharp rise in the East European inflow and in student numbers, which have trebled in the past decade from 80,000 in 2001 to 230,000 in 2011. (Study hit a peak of 273,000 in 2009 when it also overtook work as the most common reason for coming to Britain.)

After the 2010 general election the new government began to implement its more restrictive immigration policy, one of the Conservative Party's most popular election pledges. The immigration 'cap', introduced in April 2011, is a rather technical matter which directly impacts on only a very small proportion of the total annual inflow.[1] Far more important than the cap itself is that related pledge to reduce net immigration to the 'tens of thousands' by 2015. This is leading to downward pressure in all the main areas of inflow and the beginning of a break with what used to be the semi-automatic link between coming here to work or study and the eventual right to settlement after a certain number of years' residence (currently five).

Critics of the cap, and of stricter controls more generally, complain that the current arrangements are driving away some of the more popular and desirable immigrants from outside the EU – high-skilled workers, academics, artists and students – while still allowing in less productive, and often hard to integrate, immigrants who continue to arrive through the family reunion and other routes.[2]

The government is, however, bearing down hard on the family reunion route too, especially the bringing in of spouses, by requiring that they pass an

---

1. The details of the first 2011/2012 cap are this: tier one was replaced with a new quota of 1,000 people a year with exceptional talent in science and the arts, and the tier two of skilled workers with a job offer was 'capped' at 20,700 a year, though as a result of business lobbying intra-company transfers remained outside the cap. In 2009 there were about 50,000 non-EU people coming through tiers one and two; it is now down to about 40,000 (including intra-company transfers).

2. They also point out that by choosing a 'net' immigration target the government has exposed itself to the vagaries of emigration, including the emigration of British citizens (to retirement homes in Spain for example). If British emigration drops for whatever reason, say a weaker pound sterling, there will have to be ever more downward pressure on inflows. But in 2011 emigration of British citizens nudged up a bit to 150,000.

English language test and also insisting that the sponsor has an annual income of at least £18,600 so as to prevent welfare dependency.[1] Both measures are being challenged in the courts under European Convention on Human Rights Article 8, the right to a family life; an earlier attempt to raise the minimum age of a spouse from 18 to 21 has been successfully challenged already.

This policy brings the government into direct conflict with much of liberal Britain and more significantly with some of the post-colonial, and especially South Asian, minorities which continue to have strong family links and obligations to their ancestral homes. But there is a powerful double rationale for it: not only bringing down inflows to more moderate levels but also reducing the number of Pakistani and Bangladeshi subcontinental arranged marriages, which tend to slow down the integration process.

There will be argument too over any attempt to further reduce asylum inflows. Asylum claims (including dependants) in recent years have been running at around 20,000 a year. Rather less than one third of cases are accepted as genuine, which is higher than many other European countries, but there continue to be serious difficulties in removing the large backlog of failed asylum-seekers – both because of the legal constraints and the reluctance of many countries to take them back. (For more on asylum flows see Chapter 5, 'Labour's Greatest Legacy'.)

There have been some teething troubles with the cap on skilled workers from outside the EU. But in its first year of operation in 2011/12 it worked in one very obvious sense: the non-EU skilled worker category, which is the only stream that the cap covers, under-filled its 20,700 quota by more than half.[2]

But the biggest challenge – in the context of trying to sharply reduce numbers without doing economic damage to the country – is students. Students are not covered by the cap (though some academics are), but by dint of the sheer size of the student inflow they are the main target as the government tries to reach its 'tens of thousands' goal.

1. About 40 per cent of all spouses currently come from the Indian subcontinent and it is estimated that about half of those South Asian families fall below that income threshold.
2. There might be room in the future to bear down on other non-EU workflows that are currently uncapped such as intra-company transfers, now running at about 30,000 a year and, rather bizarrely, 16,000 domestic servants.

The student question also raises the broader connection between short term 'churn' and longer-term settlement. And that in turn raises big questions about whether we have a border control bureaucracy that can adequately police the dividing line between the two – in other words make sure that short-termers such as students, short-term workers and visa-controlled visitors leave when they are supposed to.

The way we classify immigrants also has a bearing on this. The way Britain gathers its immigration statistics has been the subject of criticism for many years. The main source remains the international passenger survey, a basic clipboard survey stopping people at ports and airports and asking them how long they are coming for and for what main purpose. The annual immigration sample is only 2,400 people and for emigration it is just 2,000. (But the immigration numbers are supplemented and refined with many other sources such as work and student visas, asylum numbers, family reunion permissions and so on.)

There is also no attempt in the immigration figures to distinguish between long-term and short-term movements. Because every one of the roughly 1,500 people a day who say they are coming to Britain for more than a year is classified as an immigrant, a lot of short-term movements – people coming to work for eighteen months, or for a two-year college course – get swept up into what sound like longer-term movements of people.

Carlos Vargas-Silva of the Oxford Migration Observatory has estimated that more than 70 per cent of current immigrants stay for less than five years. But even if the short-term flows are stripped out there remains one big immigration fact: since 1997 about 2.2 million people have been granted settlement in Britain. Through the 1970s, 1980s and 1990s the annual settlement figure was around 50,000. The figure then began to rise sharply in the late 1990s reaching a peak of almost 250,000 in 2010, partly thanks to a backlog of asylum claims. The figure was down to 166,000 in 2011 and is now likely to fall quite sharply.

Around 80 per cent of people accepted for settlement still come from developing countries, mainly from Asia and Africa – in 2011 more than 30 per cent came from the Indian subcontinent alone. Apart from students those who come and go tend to be people from other rich countries both inside and outside Europe who do not need British citizenship for a secure and comfortable life.[1]

There are two main categories of people who are granted settlement. First there are those who have come here to work and have done so for five years or more, at which point they become eligible to apply for settlement, and are normally granted it so long as they have been of 'good character' – though from 2016 there will be a demanding minimum annual income requirement of around £35,000.[2] Second, there is family reunion, people who already have settlement rights bringing in relatives, mainly spouses. In 2009, when nearly 200,000 people were granted settlement, 81,000 came through work and 72,000 through family reunion. But if you look at the figures more closely it turns out that almost 133,000, around 70 per cent, are dependants of one kind or another.

This does not look like a very selective immigration policy, though presumably the dependants of high-skill workers are themselves more likely to be skilled and educated (or likely to become so). But it does show that there is more room for manoeuvre in reducing numbers than is often supposed.

Britain is drifting towards the idea that almost all non-EU immigration should be temporary and therefore should not confer rights to bring in family members. Other countries have various forms of immigration which time-limit stays in the country, prohibit the bringing in of dependants and limit access to public services. Such arrangements can still be of mutual benefit to immigrant and host country: for the immigrant there are remittances returned and experiences gained. They are generally disapproved of, however, by human rights lawyers for creating different classes of citizen; and human rights legislation seeks to minimise the distinction between citizen and non-citizen. Rights legislation also makes it harder to prevent short-term stayers such as students, temporary workers and holiday-makers turning into permanent residents.

It is possible to imagine returning to something like the low levels of

1. A study in the journal *Population Trends* in 2004 found that 57 per cent of Australians and New Zealanders leave within five years compared to just 15 per cent from the Indian subcontinent.
2. Students cannot settle unless they switch to the work or family route or are continuously resident for ten years.

settlement of the early 1990s but accompanied by high levels of the temporary migration required by business and higher education. In an age of mass transit this does, however, depend on a well-functioning border and immigration bureaucracy to restrict 'leakage' to a minimum.

The UK Borders Agency has had a poor reputation for efficiency, and it has certainly not been a fashionable destination for top civil service talent. It has seen several public disputes between officials and ministers and was accused by John Reid, when Labour home secretary, of being 'not fit for purpose'. But there are mitigating circumstances, and recently its record seems to have improved.[1]

One problem for UKBA is that there are very few internal checks on someone's status – there is no substantial labour inspectorate, and professionals in the health and education and housing systems are reluctant to play a migration policing role. You can even get married without anyone checking your right to be in the country. Also, the Points Based System is a box-ticking system which removed a lot of discretion from UKBA entry clearance officers (though that is now being partly reversed).

More generally the UKBA's difficulties in the Labour years stemmed, in part, from the fact that it was often asked to face two ways at once. Labour wanted to appear as if it was clamping down, especially during the asylum spike of the late 1990s. But at the same time it introduced several liberalising reforms such as the repeal of the 'primary purpose rule', which had restricted the importing of spouses from the Indian subcontinent, and in 2000 it introduced a right of appeal when family visitor visas (running at about 60,000 a year) were rejected.

Above all, it passed the Human Rights Act in 1998, which has made it harder to deport people and has given rights to people who manage to stay for even a few months in the country. The European Convention on Human Rights Article 8, the right to family life, has probably had the biggest impact on immigration cases. It is a 'qualified right' in the legal jargon, and the government is entitled to argue where it should be overridden but in practice

1. It has no doubt helped the UKBA to have had since 2010 a reduction target of net immigration of 'tens of thousands', though with a budget of only £1.2 billion (about 0.25 per cent of UK public spending) it has often been stretched.

has not done so. So we have ended up with a human rights policy and an immigration policy that are in conflict with each other.

Even more significantly, under both Labour and the previous Tory government the bureaucracy of counting people in and, more important, counting people out, was dismantled. This will be reversed soon when the new 'e-borders' system is finally introduced in 2015: the latter will identify people who have not left but it will not tell the authorities where they are or remove any of the legal obstacles to deportation and may just make abuse of the system more visible and politically contentious. (It might also revive the argument for ID cards, at least for short-term visa-controlled immigrants.)

Currently the UKBA issues about 2 million visas a year for those countries that we require them from, mainly in the developing world (about 20 per cent are refused). One internal estimate is that about 20 per cent of people on visas – for work, study and visits – overstay. That is 400,000 people every year, though many of them presumably leave a year or two after they were meant to.

There is some pressure to relax visitor visa requirements, the largest category of visa, especially on the new rich of China and India. It is very unlikely that the government would drop them completely (and China and India still require visas for all visitors), but there might be ways of speeding up or simplifying the process for the 'big spenders' that the London hotel and retail sectors are so keen to attract.[1]

The question of illegal immigrants is less significant in Britain than in the US (which has a long land barrier with what is in effect a third-world country, Mexico). But it is likely to move up the political agenda if legal migration is thought to be brought under control, and it is a bigger issue in London than elsewhere in the country – about two-thirds of illegal immigrants are thought to be in London. The total stock of 'illegals' was estimated at 618,000 in 2007 by the Greater London Authority, though some experts believe it to be much higher.[2]

---

1. According to Sebastian Wood, the British Ambassador to China, Britain issued nearly 200,000 visitor visas in mainland China in 2011, an increase of 28 per cent on 2010 and about one quarter of the visas issued for the whole Schengen area of the EU.
2. There are three main types of 'irregular migrant': those who have entered the country

So, will the government reach its target of net immigration of 'tens of thousands' by 2015? This brings us back to the central issue of student numbers. In 2011 the student immigration number was around 230,000; about half of that was university students and the other half was a combination of lower-level colleges, language schools and private school pupils.

It seems pretty clear that some of the trebling of the student inflow since 2001 has been a backdoor route to settlement, mainly for people from poor countries outside the EU. But the education sector, and especially higher education, has also from the late 1990s made a big international marketing push to attract (full fee) students from abroad. According to Eric Thomas, vice-chancellor of Bristol University, the value of foreign university students alone is £5.6 billion a year, set to grow to £16.5 billion by 2025.[1]

This is a significant 'export' industry in which the country has big historical advantages, and it has helped to cross-subsidise the expansion of British higher education. Only the US attracts more foreign students, and the Department of Business, Innovation and Skills calculated the total value of Britain's education exports at £14.7 billion in 2010. This industry is also said to provide 'soft power' benefits to Britain as graduates return to their countries with friends and connections here.[2]

But not all of the roughly 450,000 foreign students currently studying in British universities are elite students at elite universities whose connection to Britain will be of advantage in the future. There are still a lot of very average colleges with immigrant teachers teaching immigrant students, say, business

---

illegally; those who entered the country legally but are no longer legal (either because they were refused asylum or because they have over-stayed a legal visa); and children born in Britain to illegal parents. The main Home Office estimate from the mid-2000s was a range of 310,000 to 570,000; the more recent GLA analysis (including children) is 417,000 to 863,000.

1. There is some scepticism about Eric Thomas's figures, and his projection of income would imply an increase in the stock of foreign students to about 640,000 in 2025, according to Andrew Green of the lobby group Migration Watch.

2. Global connections are not always a great advantage. Britons of Indian descent are the largest minority in the country and yet our trade with India is lower than with Sweden and lags behind many other European countries without significant Indian-origin groups. India has also shown no special affection for Britain in recent years over defence contracts and other commercial links. (Tesco was refused a licence to operate in India.)

studies courses. Is this really to Britain's advantage, any more than it is to bring in entirely foreign labour forces to pick strawberries that could be just as easily imported?

This also raises the question of whether the British higher education experience remains distinctly British enough and whether, as well as drawing in foreigners, it is also fulfilling its various national functions. The post-graduate field, for example, is too geared to attracting full-fee foreign students, according to a report by the Higher Education Commission published in October 2012. Britain now has the smallest proportion of its own citizens doing post-graduate work of any comparable economy, while foreign post-graduates are up 200 per cent since 1999. The report suggested that Britain had become the 'educational outsourcing capital of the world' but was not providing sufficient home-grown talent for British companies.

This is not, however, a good reason to close down those unglamorous business studies courses. They are still a benefit to the country, providing jobs and incomes, so long as the vast majority of students do return to their countries as their visas require. In recent years 25 per cent of non-EU students – about 40,000 – have been staying on legally after study, mainly to work and marry, and probably about half that number have been qualifying for settlement every year. According to the Home Office[1] about 20 per cent of students are still legally in Britain after five years.

To prevent the wrong kind of leakage the government has been clamping down on 'bogus colleges' which were just acting as immigration businesses.[2] It has also increased the English language requirement and stopped all but postgraduate students from bringing in dependants. More controversially, in April 2012 it removed the automatic right to stay on after a bachelor's or master's course for two years to look for a job. Students can still work twenty hours a week during term and without limit during holidays and can stay on

1. *The Migrant Journey*, Home Office Research Report 43, September 2010.
2. It is said to have closed down about 500 colleges in the last few years, mainly small operations. More controversially, it revoked London Metropolitan University's right to attract foreign students in August 2012 when irregularities were found with about one third of the foreign students (there were around 3,000 of them, about 15 per cent of the student body). This caused a great outcry, as was presumably intended by the UKBA, which wanted to send a 'get tough' warning to the whole higher education sector.

for three years after completing courses, with a possible two-year extension, but only if they have an appropriate job and sponsor. That is making Britain a less attractive destination for some Indian students who cannot afford to come without the work opportunity but the numbers of Chinese and African students continued to rise in 2012, and total applications for English universities from students from outside the EU were up slightly half way through 2012. The total foreign student number will probably be just below 200,000 in 2012, but a higher proportion – up to about two-thirds – are in higher education, probably reflecting the government's clamp-down on lower-level colleges many of which were just immigration businesses.

A statistical change will improve the picture too. Currently it is impossible to produce a proper 'net' figure for the annual student flow – in, subtracted by out – because the international passenger survey asks people who are leaving what they are going to do in their country of destination, not what they have just been doing in Britain. Former foreign students in British universities are likely to say that they are leaving to take up a job, so they are not classified as a leaving student. Starting next year the survey will ask people what they have been doing in Britain, so it will be possible to produce a proper net immigration figure for students.

Once the various restrictions above have taken effect, a clearer 'net' measure for foreign students might give a figure as low as 20,000 or 30,000 a year even while the number of university students continues to rise quite fast. And so long as one can in the future be confident that almost all students are leaving when they should, there might be a case for counting in the immigration figures only those students who stay after their course is completed. The current Tory pledge of reducing net immigration to 'tens of thousands' was made on the basis of the existing statistical system, so the government must stick to the current method. But there is no reason why it should not publish additional parallel figures every quarter with students stripped out.

At the end of 2012 it was looking unlikely that the government would reach its tens of thousands target by the 2015 election – the latest annualised net immigration figure was still 183,000 in early 2012. But after a great deal of policy attention, and investment, in recent years there is a sense of far greater control of immigration from outside the EU. And once some of the recent measures on students and family reunion and work have taken effect, that net immigration figure is likely to start falling quite sharply.[1] If the government can cut the net total to around 120,000 or 130,000 by 2015 it can claim to have roughly halved annual net immigration in five years in which case it is unlikely to be punished politically for missing the target. And it may have found a way of ending Britain's 'irrational exuberance' over immigration without harming an important new wing of the education sector.

1. The first sign of this came at the end of November 2012 when the annualised migration figures to March 2012 showed a fall in net immigration of a quarter to 183,000 down from 242,000 the previous March. On the danger side for the government there could be an upward blip in net immigration when Romanians and Bulgarians are allowed full access to the labour market in 2014.

CHAPTER 2

The Way We Live Now: How Are Britain's Minorities Doing?

Life in Merton

Large-scale immigration has created a new urban England that is increasingly full of mysterious and unfamiliar worlds just around the corner. Or, in this case, a few tube stops away. On a sunny December morning in 2011 I sat listening to a distinguished-looking elderly man preaching. Hadrat Mirza Masroor Ahmad is not any old preacher. In fact, to a couple of million Ahmadiyan Muslims he is the holiest man on the planet. They are a heretical sect, shunned and persecuted by mainstream Sunni and Shia Muslims, because they believe that Islam has had its second coming, its Mahdi – he was a man called Hadrat Mirza Ghulam Ahmad, who lived in British India between 1835 and 1908.

The Mahdi, unlike the original prophet, had a relatively conflict-free succession. The current leader of the faith, or Khalif, is fifth in line to the founder, and when I saw him he was preaching to a congregation of about 2,000 men, of mainly Pakistani background, many in Pashtun dress, in a giant mosque in the London suburb of Merton.

The mosque, which opened in 2003 after a long battle over planning permission, is the European headquarters of the Ahmadis (as they are usually called). It dominates its neighbourhood, though as part of the planning deal no call to prayer rings out from the tall minaret. It replaced an Express Dairies bottling plant which provided a few hundred skilled and semi-skilled manual jobs for local people and, of course, lots of milk bottles – an icon of an earlier, more homogenised age. The large, traditional pub that used to be just up the road from the mosque has also gone and been converted into a Sunni Islamic cultural centre.

The symbolism is not lost on the mainly white older residents. When I walked about near the mosque, just up the road from the Merton council offices, with Stephen Alambritis, the Labour leader of the council (himself of Greek Cypriot background), local people did not seem to be embracing diversity with the enthusiasm he would like.

But Merton is a good place to take the pulse of multiracial Britain. The unassuming south-west London borough of about 200,000 people is divided between affluent Wimbledon and dowdier Mitcham and Morden. Like Barking and Dagenham, Morden is at the end of the tube line and so combines access to employment all over London with relatively affordable private housing – as a result it has been a magnet for new immigrants in the past two decades.

The change in population has not come as sharply as it did in Barking and Dagenham, which remained almost entirely white until the mid-1990s. Merton was also less industrial, with no equivalent of the giant Ford factory in Dagenham and the secure, high-wage employment it provided for more than two generations. So, although Merton did see some BNP activity in the late 1990s – focused on the pleasant St Helier 1930s LCC council estate of houses with gardens – it has not become a symbol of conflict and white working-class alienation like Barking and Dagenham or the former mill towns of northern England.

This is not to say that everyone in Merton is happy with the changes. Not so long ago the poorer part of the borough was 'white van man' country, full of plumbers and small builders; back in the 1970s and 1980s, when hardcore Chelsea fans had a reputation for violent behaviour, the young men up before the courts would often come from Mitcham or Morden. But, if you count in the minority category Australians and white South Africans who mainly live in affluent Wimbledon, Merton's minority population has risen from about 10 per cent in 1980 to almost 50 per cent today. In Mitcham and Morden the minority population is well over half. Merton primary schools which were still majority white as recently as 2003 are now 64 per cent ethnic minority. Merton has become, in the jargon, 'super diverse'.[1]

As in many parts of high-immigration Britain this has been an accommodation rather than an integration. The white population in places like Merton has more or less reluctantly shuffled along the bench and allowed others to sit down. There is no dominant minority in Merton, which helps to make the changes feel less threatening, but there is not much evidence of a common life being built together either. With the exception of the African Caribbeans, who have often set up home with white people, and the richer parts of Wimbledon, where the shared interests of middle-class London professionals trump ethnic difference, this is mainly enclave living.

You can see it in action at weekends in the small park, Mostyn Gardens, about five minutes from Morden station. On a sunny day the park is usually full but divided along ethnic lines: large groups of Pakistani women picnicking with young children, Polish guys drinking beer, young Indian men playing cricket, Africans playing basketball.

Merton is certainly not as residentially segregated as Bradford or parts of Birmingham and Leicester. In only five wards out of twenty is the white population in a minority. No secondary school is more than 80 per cent white or 70 per cent minority, though one third of primary schools are now over 70 per cent minority. Unusually, black Africans seem to live more separately than South Asians – 65 per cent of black African Mertonians live in just five wards.[2]

But this is one of London's 'landing' boroughs with a high degree of population 'churn', which, by definition, makes it harder to establish stable communities. There is quite a large East European group in Merton which tends to keep itself to itself. Several of the more entrepreneurial communities,

1. Merton had the second highest proportionate increase in ethnic minority pupils of any local authority in the country between 1999 and 2009, an increase of just under 20 percentage points; only Barking and Dagenham was higher.
2. Data on Merton is drawn mainly from 'Merton Community Cohesion Strategy 2012–2015' and Merton Council's 'Analysis of Housing and Social Exclusion Issues Amongst Merton's Ethnic Minorities', plus the Institute of Community Cohesion paper 'The Merton Story'. All can be found on the Merton website.

such as the Indians and Tamils and Iraqi Kurds, create jobs, but they invariably go to members of their own community.

Some minorities import historic feuds: orthodox Muslims in the area are suspicious of the Ahmadis and think that they buy themselves favours with the council; Tamil youths fight among themselves, as do Somalis; and the historic black (both Caribbean and African) versus Asian antipathy is also played out on some of Merton's streets.

Nevertheless, 84 per cent of Mertonians told the last government Citizenship Survey that people of different backgrounds get on well together (which is around the national average). The figure for Barking and Dagenham was 48 per cent. The political leadership of Merton deserves some credit for this.

Local political leaders, as in all areas of high minority settlement, have no choice but to celebrate the new diversity – though they will often privately admit to concerns and conflicts too. And from their vantage point things do often look more integrated than they really are, for at the gatherings they attend there will usually be a cross-section of the local minority elites mingling happily together and sharing the same interests and concerns. (It has sometimes been cynically noted that the places where the deepest common life is being forged between the new and the old tribes of urban England is in the local political class and the drug gangs.)

Economically, many minority Mertonites are doing pretty well in their enclaves; and as in the national picture the white British are somewhere in the middle, though with poor whites doing worst of the lot.

The Indians and Chinese of Merton are doing best of all in school and in jobs, also reflecting the national story. They are closely tracked by two minorities with less of a national presence – Koreans and Tamils. Koreans are a significant factor in New Malden, the town that straddles Merton and Kingston-upon-Thames. Tamils, who began arriving as refugees in the early 1980s, have been expanding fast. As with some of Merton's Somalis, a second wave of Tamils has been arriving in recent years from other European countries, believing Britain offers a better life.

Tamils, like many other minority groups, are divided by class and levels of aspiration. There is a middle-class group, usually part of the first wave of Tamil immigrants, who live in West Barnes ward and send their children to the selective grammar schools of nearby Sutton and Kingston. There are other Tamils, more recent arrivals, who are concentrated in the three poorer eastern wards of Graveney, Figges Marsh and Colliers Wood, many of whom speak poor English and are welfare dependent – a sore point with the Tamil Tory councillor Logie Lohendran.

In the middle of the range in terms of schooling and employment come the white British, Pakistanis and some black Africans and Caribbeans, but the bulk of blacks and Bangladeshis are bringing up the rear. Merton's 10,000 Pakistanis are, unusually for British Pakistanis, mainly from urban, educated backgrounds. This may reflect the fact that about half of them are Ahmadis, who are usually in middle-class and professional jobs or running their own businesses.

To many poorer and older white people who haven't been able to move out to Biggin Hill or similar places there is a sense of loss. 'We don't like it but we don't have much choice, do we?' as the owner of a hairdressing salon said in response to the optimistic suggestion of Stephen Alambritis, the council leader, that he didn't mind the competition from an Ahmadi hair-cutter who had set up shop two doors along.

London is not the happily colour-blind multiracial city that many people imagine or that one might think from wandering around in the centre of the city. If you were to travel home with a black or Asian Londoner you might well find that they live in some of the most minority-concentrated parts of Britain – Tower Hamlets, Newham, Southall, Hounslow, parts of Haringey and Lambeth – or in minority enclaves within predominantly white parts of town. There are, of course, many other London stories of unselfconsciously mixed-up living in places like Hackney, Brent and the more affluent suburbs like Harrow in the north-west or Redbridge in the north-east.

If you accompanied a Ghanaian you might end up on the Pollards Hill estate in Merton. It is rather a dreary post-1945 estate of about 1,600 semi-detached houses with gardens, about half now privately owned. Over the past fifteen years it has become nearly half black African, mainly Ghanaian.

According to one local councillor there has been some friction. 'The Ghanaians are mainly hard-working and doing well enough but they do have a different attitude to life – and many of the older residents complain that they are noisy and messy,' he says.

The Pollards Hill residents' association used to be all white, then it went all black, and currently it is white again. White residents I spoke to talked about misuse of public money by the Ghanaians. But there is little overt racism, and younger white people having grown up with a mixed population are largely oblivious to it – though there is some rivalry between black African and African Caribbean youths.

Juliana Owusu, a Ghanaian nurse who was until recently head of the residents' association, has lived on the estate for twenty-five years and says she has only experienced persistent unfriendly behaviour from one family. But she also says that white people in general have not been particularly welcoming or keen to mix with the newcomers.

Owusu is typical of an earlier generation of aspiring, professional West African immigrants who are increasingly outnumbered by poorer black Africans who have arrived since the late 1990s and are more likely to be working as cleaners than lawyers. Twenty years ago her barrister husband was murdered by a black youth in Brixton when he went to the aid of someone being mugged. But Owusu, who has two nursing jobs, has invested ferociously in her four children's success. She has put some through private school and all seem to be well set at college or in professional careers. Her small sitting-room is adorned with pictures of her smiling children, two of them at graduation ceremonies.

By contrast, poorer working-class whites in Merton, as in many similar parts of the country, have mainly opted out: they seldom vote and a lot of the younger people are 'Neets' – not in employment, education or training. A generation ago the Labour political establishment that now runs Merton would still have had remnants of the old white trade union elite; now most of the twenty-nine Labour councillors are either middle-class incomers or minorities – and the most reliable voters are the minorities.

The minority population of Merton is concentrated in the poorest eastern wards but most of minority Merton has a sense of momentum. Sixty-two per cent of sixteen to twenty-four-year-old minority Mertonites are in full-time education compared with just 30 per cent of whites. (Interestingly

Morden was not affected by the 2011 riots though they reached nearby Colliers Wood.)

For many of the white people who have remained in Merton as its personality has changed, the disappearance of familiar mental and physical landmarks has happened too fast – symbolised by that giant Ahmadiyan mosque with its capacity for 10,000 worshippers (plus six smaller, mainstream mosques in the borough).

The Ahmadiyans are model immigrants in many ways. They preach an ecumenical form of Islam and are grateful to be given refuge in this country – they even took out posters on London buses congratulating the Queen during the 2012 Diamond Jubilee. But to many locals that's not the point. As one man – described as White Heritage Elder Male in the jargon of race relations – told a Merton council focus group: 'We've lost this place to other cultures ... it's not English any more.'

Minorities Making Their Way

In this section I want to try to paint a picture of multiracial Britain today – of Merton writ large. How are Britain's different minorities doing at school and at work? How separate or mixed in are the lives they live? Which are the places where immigration has worked well for natives and newcomers, where minorities are thriving alongside the white majority and the level of mixing between people from different ethnic backgrounds is generally high? And which are the places where it has not worked well, where there is division and mutual resentment? And what about the in-between sort of places, like Merton?

To do this, I will draw on both the statistics available and my own observations and conversations on visits to places of high minority settlement including Leicester, Oldham, Bradford, Luton, Birmingham, Slough, Leeds, Dewsbury, Wolverhampton, Manchester, Redbridge, Walthamstow, Newham and Tower Hamlets.

I want to try, too, to make a judgement about how much racial disadvantage there still is in Britain. Few people would deny that overt racism in

Britain has declined sharply in recent decades, but how much discrimination do minorities still face?

To understand where we are today on these big issues one obviously needs to know some historical background – on the history of immigration itself and its management in the early post-war decades. I will touch on that where relevant in this chapter, but I explore it in greater depth in later chapters on the history of post-war immigration and on multiculturalism.

Instead I want to begin here with the basic data on minority performance today in education and employment. But before looking at the figures it is worth bearing in mind two big background historical facts. First, in the long history of immigration to Britain it is only in the past fifty years or so that an overt promise of equality – of equal rights and opportunities and equal access to public resources – has been made by the host society. This is as it should be in a liberal society, but it raises expectations that are sometimes hard to fulfil, especially as equality has a 'felt' as well as a formal dimension.

Second, one reason the expectations have been hard to fulfil is because the majority of Britons who arrived in the first wave of post-colonial immigration from the Caribbean, Africa and the Indian subcontinent between 1948 and the early 1990s were not only from poor countries but often from relatively poor, traditional places within those countries. (There are, of course, many individual exceptions to that rule, but the main larger-scale exceptions were doctors and academics from India, students from West Africa and many East African Asians arriving in the 1960s and 1970s.)

And yet, despite the general assumption of minority disadvantage, most of the larger settled minorities do reasonably well relative to the white average with the exception of a few 'stuck' groups. There is also enormous divergence between different minority groups, in relation both to each other and to the white average. Taken together this suggests that Britain is a more open society than is normally assumed.

In the academic and 'race industry' worlds there is some discomfort about this divergence because it complicates the simple story told since the 1960s of a racist Britain blocking the progress of all minorities. There is still a tendency to see any departure from the proportional representation of minorities in, say, professional jobs as evidence of racism, yet if you take starting point and qualifications into account the gulf in outcomes usually largely disappears.

Even allowing for some 'ethnic penalty' still affecting *all* minorities, why do Indian and, above all, Chinese pupils do much better than white ones on average? And why are 43 per cent of Indian Muslims in professional/managerial jobs compared to 26 per cent of Pakistani Muslims?[1] Even though they may live in similar-looking urban environments and go to similar schools, people who live inside very different cultures at home – say Hindu Indian and Turkish – often end up with very different capabilities and aspirations.

Anti-racist academics and activists tend to shy away from cultural explanations and often argue that cultural 'essentialism' is just a new form of racism (even though multiculturalism is based on the idea of preserving those cultural 'essences'). They often dislike drawing attention to the formative power of inherited cultures – of class, ethnicity, religion, national origin – because it seems to absolve the host society of responsibility for minority failure.

One of the unhelpful paradoxes of modern multiculturalism is that it both accentuates ethnic/cultural difference while also denying it. It justifies people living apart from the mainstream in the name of cultural preservation. But it is reluctant to accept that culture can have a bearing on group outcomes in British society – when, say, Bangladeshis are under-represented in elite universities it presumes that this must be the result of handicaps imposed by British society rather than, in part, factors internal to British Bangladeshi culture and to the starting point of most Bangladeshis.

I can, perhaps, be accused of the opposite inconsistency – I want colour-blind outcomes in which ethnicity plays as small a role as possible in the distribution of life chances in Britain and yet as a means to that end I want us to be *more* culture and colour conscious. But this is no different in principle to a reformist approach to social class: anyone who worries about the fact that social class has too great an influence on people's chances in life will first want to study and highlight the role of class in order to reduce it.

It is part of the universally accepted common sense of our society that the child of aspiring and well-educated middle-class parents is far more likely to

1. The number of Pakistani Muslims in such jobs is considerably higher for those born in Britain.

succeed than the child of poorly educated and unaspirational working-class parents. (And parental attitude here is even more important than income.) People on the left will happily accept that social class can be a sufficient explanation for success or failure but are far more suspicious of ethnic-cultural explanations – yet these things are inherited by young children in exactly the same manner as social class.

Many factors – socio-economic position, parental interest, ethnic traditions (which may have a bearing on parental interest), role models and cultural confidence, language spoken at home and so on – feed into the performance of both individuals and large groups. And though there is great variety within ethnic groups and many individuals will buck the trend, some minority cultures evidently help people to flourish in this society more than others. Indeed, British people and institutions can often seem barely relevant when it comes to minority outcomes, as cultural traits inherited over centuries in other parts of the world play themselves out in our schools and offices.

The data is clear.[1] Ethnic differences in GCSE results are starting to narrow, except at the top, where Chinese and Indian students are pulling away. In England about 58 per cent of pupils achieved five GCSEs at A to C grade, including English and maths, in 2010/11. White British students were almost exactly on that average figure, 80 per cent of Chinese students and 75 per cent of Indian students achieved it. Bangladeshi students have put on a recent spurt – thanks to a disproportionate improvement in London schools where they are over-represented – and now just outperform the white average. Black African students are almost on the average. The only two big groups to lag behind the white average are Pakistanis and Caribbeans, and they too have been catching up in recent years. Among poorer children who qualify for free school meals, all the main minority groups now do better than white children.

These results are particularly remarkable when you consider that all the big minority groups, with the exception of the Chinese, lag behind the white

1. Most of the data on ethnic performance in this chapter is taken from the *Equality and Human Rights Commission Triennial Review 2010* and *An Anatomy of Economic Inequality in the UK 2010* (the report of the LSE national equality panel).

British when they are first tested at age six or seven. This means that with the exception of black Caribbean pupils, all ethnic minority pupils substantially gain relative to white British pupils throughout primary and secondary schooling.[1] The main explanation is that a majority of pupils of Chinese (64 per cent), Indian (54 per cent), Pakistani (62 per cent) and Bangladeshi (78 per cent) origin come from homes where another language is spoken.[2] Their English improves rapidly during their years at primary and secondary school (this is with the help of a substantial public investment in teaching English to those who do not speak it at home).

Some minorities, above all Caribbeans, have historically suffered from the low expectations of white teachers. And as recently as the early 1990s the mainly Bangladeshi Central Foundation girls' school in Tower Hamlets was explicitly teaching for D grades in GCSE, according to one former pupil.

But in the London area children who have English as a second language now, on average, outperform native English speakers. Whites are also less likely than people of Indian, Pakistani, Bangladeshi and black African backgrounds to stay on at school at sixteen, as we saw in Merton. There is a sense of momentum and aspiration among almost all minority groups that is much less strong for lower-income whites. This is especially true for minority young women, who do better than young men in all groups but significantly so in some: about half of British Pakistani/Bangladeshi girls have A levels by the age of nineteen, compared with 29 per cent of boys (though only about 20 per cent of the girls go on to university, way below the female average).[3]

According to the analyst of school segregation, Simon Burgess of Bristol University, just under 60 per cent of low-income white boys' parents want

1. See 'Ethnicity and educational achievement in compulsory schooling' by Christian Dustmann, Stephen Machin, Uta Schönberg, *The Economic Journal*, vol. 120, issue 546, February 2010, p. 3.
2. Figures taken from the 2009 Labour Force Survey, people of sixteen or over including those born here and abroad.
3. Paper by Philip Lewis of Bradford University: 'The Civic and Religious Incorporation of British Muslims: Whose Incorporation, Which Islam?', p. 12, citing Cambridge Muslim College paper 'Proposed Fellowship in Critical Islamic Education', 2011.

their sons to stay on at school compared with 90 per cent of Indian, Pakistani, Bangladeshi and black African parents across all income levels.[1]

Adult educational achievement shows the same broad pattern, with some ethnic minorities catching up and overtaking the white average while others lag behind. A generation ago British universities were almost entirely white; now almost 20 per cent of British students are from minority backgrounds, slightly higher than the minority proportion of the 18–24 age group. Almost all the large minority groups have a higher proportion at university than their share of the 18–24 population; and most, even including Pakistanis and Bangladeshis, have a higher proportional representation at university than the white British. It is true, however, that many minority Britons are more likely to go to local, less prestigious former polytechnics and to continue living at home (less than 10 per cent of black students are at Russell Group universities, compared with 25 per cent of white students and *half* of all British Indian students).[2]

Just under 20 per cent of white British people have first or higher degrees, compared with around 30 per cent of black Africans and Indians and around 40 per cent of Chinese men and women (some of these degrees were acquired abroad). At the other end of the spectrum more than 40 per cent of Bangladeshi and Pakistani men and women have no qualifications above basic education (though Pakistani men are also slightly more likely to have a degree than white British men). One in six British adults is said to be functionally illiterate, with that number rising to more than a quarter for black Caribbean and black African men.

The white British population occupies the centre of the educational bell curve, having a smaller proportion of people both with degrees and with no or low qualifications than minority Britons. Employment outcomes tell a similar

1. Simon Burgess asked fourteen-year-olds in English schools: 'What do you want to do when you are 16?' Only 85 per cent of white girls said they wanted to stay on at school, compared with 95 per cent for South Asians and black Caribbeans and 99 per cent for black African girls; for white boys the number was 73 per cent, compared with 81 per cent for Black Caribbean boys and over 90 per cent for South Asian and black African boys.

2. See *Race into Higher Education*, published by Business in the Community, 2010. The figure of half of Indian students being at Russell Group universities comes from the British Indian peer Lord Popat.

story to education. Some groups shoot ahead of the white average while others struggle.

Most groups are more successful if they are born and raised here – including most Muslims, Sikh Indians and black Africans; some, including the Chinese, do slightly worse. But overall, second-generation minority employees (allowing for age and qualifications) are just as likely to be in professional and managerial jobs as white people.[1] About 45 per cent of the white British are in professional and managerial jobs compared with around 60 per cent for Chinese and Hindu Indians, 55 per cent for Sikh Indians and 51 per cent for black Africans thanks to a strong performance from Nigerians (all numbers refer to British born). But perhaps more remarkable is the fact that even groups that are thought of as struggling – Caribbeans, Pakistanis and Bangladeshis – all have comparable representation in professional and managerial jobs to the white British (between 40 and 45 per cent), at least for those born in Britain.[2]

There remains a small 'pay gap' for minority people doing the same kind of jobs as whites, but it is, for most groups, now just a few percentage points. Comparing a white British man in his early forties working in a skilled but non-professional job with similar workers of minority background, it has been discovered that there was no significant difference in pay for Hindu or Sikh Indians or black Caribbean men, though Chinese, Pakistani, Bangladeshi and black African men did suffer some penalty.[3]

Unemployment rates are slightly higher for most minorities (significantly so for Bangladeshis, Pakistanis and young Caribbean males) and somewhat higher in the second generation, partly perhaps because of higher expectations and less readiness to take the first job that comes along.

I will return to the job market later in this chapter when I address the question of the persistence of racial discrimination. But here I want to focus on what other factors may be causing minority divergence from the white

1. An Anatomy of Economic Inequality in the UK: report of the National Equality Panel, London School of Economics, John Hills et al. (January 2010), p. 225, citing Heath and Cheung.
2. It should, however, be remembered that professional/managerial is a big category which contains within it a wide range of levels of pay and prestige, for example both nurses and doctors count as professionals. People who work in small family businesses are also categorised as managers.
3. An Anatomy of Economic Inequality, p. 228.

average (either for better or worse) and from other minorities. Some things are obvious: levels of education and knowledge of English that people arrive with, the social networks they have or can establish plus the job prospects and quality of life in the places where they settle in Britain.

We know, for example, that people of East African Asian background have usually done well because they arrived as relatively high-status individuals: they were urbanised, usually spoke English well, were often quite highly educated or had highly marketable intellectual or business skills, invested in their children's progress and had no 'myth of return', knowing that they had to make life in Britain work. Moreover they settled in, or swiftly moved to, relatively prosperous places in the northern and western London suburbs and Leicester.

By contrast, Somalis, another group who like East African Asians came mainly as refugees, arrived often from rural areas and with generally low levels of education and poor or non-existent English – the result is that fewer than 30 per cent are employed and Somalis have the highest welfare dependency of any significant immigrant group.

Similarly, people of rural Pakistani background arriving sixty years ago from Kashmir, in the north-west corner of Pakistan, had little or no education (indeed were often illiterate), spoke little English and were unable to invest in their children's progress. And they took jobs in the factory economy of the North and Midlands that within a generation had largely disappeared.[1] It is hardly surprising that two generations later most people of East African Asian background are thriving in professional careers while more than a quarter of Pakistani men drive taxis or work in shops.[2]

Leaving aside the obvious advantages and disadvantages that individuals arrive with, there is also the invisible cultural stitching that prompts people to make certain choices rather than others. These cultural factors can help either to transcend or to reinforce the short-term immigrant disadvantages of poor language skills, lack of education and lack of networks.

1. Most British Pakistanis have roots in the Pakistani-controlled region of Azad ('Free') Kashmir, and most of them come from a single region called Mirpur, but I will refer to them as Kashmiri Pakistanis.
2. An Anatomy of Economic Inequality, p. 231.

One way of observing the power of culture is to look at two groups with similar starting points but rather different outcomes. For example, Indian Sikhs and Pakistani Muslims often arrived in Britain in the 1950s and 1960s from similar backgrounds as small farmers in different parts of the (partitioned) rural Punjab and Kashmir, and came mainly to do basic manual jobs in British factories. The Sikhs were often slightly better educated, and more of them landed in the generally prosperous south-east of England, but why have they done much better on most conventional measures than the Pakistanis?[1]

Religion made many Muslim Pakistanis of the pioneer generation feel ambivalent about British life and people, while the Biraderi system of family and clan connections meant strong diaspora links to Kashmir. But something similar was true for many Sikh families too. Both groups also often looked for marriage partners from outside Britain. But where Pakistanis sought, and often still seek, non-English-speaking spouses from their extended family in Pakistan, Sikh marriage partners, if they come from outside Britain at all, are more likely to be from the English-speaking Sikh diaspora. Sikhs also had the advantage of a cultural self-confidence derived from their role in the British empire and from being part of a worldwide immigrant network; moreover, the Sikh religion promotes self-reliance and does not discourage women from working.

There is another important difference concerning language. Sikhs are expected to work with two languages: Punjabi, a written language which is also the language of their sacred scriptures, and English; this contrasts with Pakistanis (from Kashmir), who are expected to operate across four languages: Mirpuri Punjabi at home, an oral language not generally available in written script; Urdu, the language of Islamic preaching and high Islamic culture in South Asia; English; and Quranic Arabic. Moreover, although both religions are similarly rooted in collective ritual, Sikhs will usually expect their children only to attend a gurdwara on a Saturday morning for religious education. Many Pakistani children, especially in the north of England, are expected to spend two hours a day five days a week for six years from the age

1. Roger Ballard makes this comparison in Chapter 10 of *South Asians Overseas: Migration and Ethnicity*, Cambridge University Press, 2009.

of five or six in a madrasa after school, and most of this time is spent learning Quranic Arabic by heart. As Andrey Rosowsky, a Rotherham-based English teacher, has explained: this means that primary schoolchildren are spending more time learning Quranic Arabic by rote than English.[1]

People from both backgrounds often faced similar discrimination when they arrived in Britain. With little help from the authorities, both were thrown back on their own extended family networks and religious institutions. But while Pakistanis drew a defensive shield around themselves (especially when families and women arrived) that both protected and limited them, many more Sikhs by contrast began to battle their way into British society, so that today they are better represented in the professional and managerial class.

One test of who has been upwardly mobile and who hasn't can be found on the British high street – in the corner shops and restaurants run by people of Indian, Pakistani, Bangladeshi and Chinese background. All four of those groups were over-represented in self-employment on the high street in the first generation. Today, rates of self-employment have fallen quite sharply for those of Chinese and Indian background, as the next generation have gone on to become lawyers, accountants and teachers – living the British dream – while many Pakistanis and Bangladeshis remain in low-status self-employment.

Minorities, including recent immigrants, tend on average to have a slightly lower employment rate than the white British, but South Asian Muslims are way below the average (second only in recent years to Somalis). Taking Pakistani – and Bangladeshi – background adults together, less than half are in conventional paid employment. That is partly because men are disproportionately in self-employment, part-time work or unemployed. But far and away the biggest reason is that only about 25 per cent of women from these backgrounds work outside the home.

The main reason for this is not because women are being excluded from the labour market but because for religious and cultural reasons women focus on family and child-rearing (and still tend to have significantly larger families than the white average). This is starting to change among younger women but remains very powerful, even for those who are getting good qualifications.

1. Andrey Rosowsky, 'Decoding as a cultural practice and its effects on the reading process of bilingual pupils', *Language and Education*, vol. 15, no. 1, 2001.

The generally low earnings of the men and the usually non-existent earnings of the women means that Pakistani and Bangladeshi households are hugely over-represented in the poverty and welfare figures. According to IPPR research published in 2007, Pakistani-born immigrants are three times more likely to be on income support and twice as likely to be on disability benefit as their British peers. About three-quarters of all Bangladeshi children are classified as poor. Indeed, as I have already pointed out, minority households are twice as likely to be poor as white households and that higher figure is driven by Pakistanis, Bangladeshis and Somalis with a contribution from other black Africans and Caribbeans.[1]

After this brief summary of outcomes for Britain's main minority groups in education and employment it is clear what a rough league table of relative success and failure looks like, at least for the main post-colonial groups. At the top are those of Chinese and Hindu Indian background and East African Asians of all religions. In the middle are the white British and Sikh Indians, with black Africans and East Europeans lagging behind a bit. And at the bottom are people from rural Pakistani and Bangladeshi backgrounds, Somalis, African Caribbeans, most people of black mixed race background, Turks and Romanies/Irish travellers (and from the majority population the bottom part of the white working class).[2]

Such a simple categorisation fails to capture the randomness of individual experience and also occludes lots of smaller stories from within the different groups. For example, the relative success of Caribbean women. Despite the fact that more than 65 per cent of Caribbean households are led by a single parent (usually a single mother), Caribbean women are more likely to be in full-time work than any other group of women, including white British. They are also twice as likely to have degrees and to work in professional or management jobs (usually in the public sector) than Caribbean men. This underlines

1. Peter Kenway and Guy Palmer, *Poverty among ethnic groups*, New Policy Institute and Joseph Rowntree Foundation, March 2007.
2. The rough numbers for the main British minorities are: Chinese, 500,000; Hindu Indian, 750,000; Sikh Indian, 350,000; black African, 850,000; East European, 1 million; Pakistani, 1.2 million; Bangladeshi, 400,000; African Caribbean, 600,000; people of mixed race background, about 1 million.

the special problems of Caribbean men, something I will address later in this chapter.

As one might expect, there are also pockets of relative failure in otherwise successful groups and vice versa. A significant minority of both Hindu and Sikh Indians live in poverty. The Chinese can be subdivided into mainland, Hong Kong, Taiwanese and Malay, with varying levels of success in Britain. And there is a group of mainly urban Pakistanis who, partly because of that urban and more educated background, far outperform the numerically dominant rural Pakistani group. Similarly, Gujarati Muslims, mainly from East Africa, do far better than rural Pakistani and Bangladeshi Muslims.

There is also some movement up and down the league table. Second- and third-generation Bangladeshis, especially girls, have sharply improved their educational performance in recent years but it remains to be seen whether this translates into superior employment outcomes.

The story of black Africans (excluding Somalis) is one of relative decline and sharp regional and national differences. Back in the 1960s and 1970s tens of thousands of black Africans, mainly from newly independent Ghana and Nigeria, came to study in Britain. They were usually from middle-class backgrounds and had a confidence and self-esteem in the face of discrimination that the more working-class African Caribbeans often lacked. Caribbeans had come to make a new life here; most Africans were passing through to improve their qualifications in order to help build a new country back home.

For those who ended up staying, life was not always easy and they routinely had to take jobs below the level of their qualifications. But they tended to invest heavily in their children's education and many of the second generation went to good universities and into the professions.

Juliana Owusu in Merton is a good example. The Bonsu family of Cheetham Hill in Manchester is another. Henry Bonsu, the Oxford-educated broadcaster who helped to set up the black-led radio station Colourful Radio, is the son of Ghanaian-born John Bonsu. John came over to Britain in the 1960s, like thousands of other Ghanaians and Nigerians who were encouraged by their respective governments to get qualifications.

After getting a banking diploma in Leeds he went to work for National Westminster Bank in Manchester in 1970, only to be told by his boss that he would never get a job at a level appropriate to his qualifications. So he began work as a stock controller at the local automotive parts company Don International, ending up staying twenty-three years – and still managed to put two of his four children through private school.

When I met him in the small front room of his house in the now mainly Asian area of Cheetham Hill, he talked eloquently and without bitterness about the racial conflicts of the 1960s and 1970s and how he preferred factory life and colleagues to the snobbery and competitiveness of office life.

Both Henry Bonsu, now in his mid-forties, and his father agree that the black African generation after Henry has generally been less successful. One reason for that is clear. The post-1997 wave is from a wider spread of Sub-Saharan African countries including Zimbabwe, the Congo and Uganda, and has included poorer people from the countryside. Africans who used to come as students or doctors are now more likely to come to work in care homes.

There is another, less quantifiable, reason: many young black Africans have got sucked into a white working-class/Caribbean street culture which is about street credibility, transgression and consumption; the African educational ethos has found it hard to compete. The result is a complex picture, with Africans from Henry's generation well represented in professional and managerial jobs but about half of those classified as black Africans living in poverty.

Of course, Britain still has some barriers for those from ethnic minority backgrounds, but the bleak picture painted by some activists of reflexive and persistent discrimination by teachers and employers is untenable.

Indeed, continuing to look at these issues mainly through the lens of minority victimhood simply fails to capture the complexity of real life. A much more useful framework was the one coined in the 1920s by the American sociologist Robert Park, who talked about the immigrant group-host society relationship going through a three-generational pattern: the 'avoidance' of the first generation, who lack the linguistic and cultural skills to engage with the host society, and are in any case often met with closed doors; the 'engagement' and conflict of the second generation, which demands the opening of host society doors; the 'accommodation' of the third generation.

It then becomes possible to ask why some minorities move with ease through the three stages and why others seem to get stuck. And here another useful concept is that of 'cultural protection'. The hypothesis, which I have borrowed from Trevor Phillips, former head of the Equalities Commission, is that a successful immigrant community needs just the right amount of protection *from the host society* in order to better integrate into it; too much cultural protection and you remain trapped in an 'internal colony' unable to join mainstream society, too little and you are likely to lose what is of value in your own traditions and thus the ethnic support mechanisms that help to ease the transition into a very different kind of society.

Groups that tend to have too much include those from traditional rural Muslim cultures in South Asia, which, as I have argued in the case of the Pakistanis, have reservations about the materialism and individualism of western liberalism and also extended family connections that co-exist uneasily with the idea of individual choice.

But there are also groups that have too little protection. The leading case here is African Caribbeans (with some spillover into black Africans). The pioneer generation – English-speaking, Christian, westernised, individualistic – came with high hopes of the mother country, and the desire, and attributes, to fit in, but often met rejection and, in many cases, a downward assimilation into the rough end of working-class culture.

The in-betweeners who have flourished best – such as Hindu and Sikh Indians – have had some protection in the shape of strong families, ancestral languages, distinct religious institutions and marrying 'in'. But those protections have not locked them away from mainstream British society, and their cultures have placed a high premium on educational and material success, like Jews before them.

Nor do they suffer the self-inflicted cultural wounds of some groups. For African Caribbeans it is single parenthood and the 'baby father' (the father who takes no responsibility for his children), and a stereotype of street disaffection that many young men actively embrace. For British Kashmiri Pakistanis it is the continuing pattern of importing spouses from Pakistan – which means that children seldom start school speaking decent English and educational success and integration become harder to achieve.

So some minority children, especially young Muslims, will suffer a triple handicap: poverty, parents unable to support them at school, and a culture that may mean not just a different language spoken at home but a sense of distance and even dislocation from British society.

It is worth noting here that different immigrant groups can establish different profiles in different countries. The most famous example is Muslims in America, who are much more middle-class and more Middle Eastern in origin than British Muslims and tend to have an occupational stereotype (doctors, lawyers) that is closer to Hindu Indians in Britain. The different outcomes are not very surprising but they are a useful reminder that the problems experienced by Muslim groups in Britain and the rest of Europe have little directly to do with Islam itself and more with the cultures within which it is embedded.

Less well known is the much greater success of Caribbeans in America than in Britain from a relatively similar starting point. That seems to be the product of a different history, which has produced a different collective reputation and different role models. Caribbeans have been established in the US since the late nineteenth century and have long been associated with business success (owning nearly 20 per cent of the businesses in Harlem in the 1920s). There is also a long line of Caribbean American success in public life: Shirley Chisholm (the first black Congresswoman), the political activist Stokely Carmichael, the singer Harry Belafonte, the soldier Colin Powell. Caribbeans seem to behave more like classic immigrants in the US: they cluster together, marry 'in' and are famous for hard work and getting on – they have, it seems, just the right amount of cultural protection.

This last example is a reminder that minorities are not just pawns acted upon by the host society. They are agents, both individually and collectively, with their own histories, strategies and goals – goals which may in some cases differ from those of mainstream British society.

In Alison Shaw's anthropological study of the small, tightly-knit Pakistani community in Oxford she describes an able young man called Mahboob whom she encouraged to take exams to become a social worker. He liked the idea but decided that he would be more useful to his family working in the family shop, where to her dismay Shaw found him when he should have been taking his exams. But, she later reflected, Mahboob's decision to study to be a social worker was not just a matter of weighing up the advantage to his career, he also had to consider the interests of his extended kin group both here and in Pakistan. She wrote: 'My misunderstanding of Mahboob's reasoning was for me a salutary reminder that even for a researcher who thinks she knows a group of people well it is difficult to abandon "western" assumptions.'[1]

Conservative South Asian cultures often have very different notions of success, especially for young women, compared with the liberal mainstream of British society. And although this can lead to generational conflict within families, these different goals are sometimes accepted and even embraced by the women themselves.

This section has been a story of statistics and relative performance but behind them are real lives, with frictions and expectations and disappointments and choices. Choice is always constrained by history, culture and personality, and people tend to see themselves more as the authors of their own destiny than they really are. But people do choose and can choose failure over what British society regards as success, or segregation over integration.

Thinking about Integration and Segregation

How does the performance of Britain's main minority groups map on to the separate but related story of minority integration into, or segregation from, British life? Are minorities becoming more or less separate from the mainstream? The simple answer is that some minorities (usually but not always the more successful ones) and places are becoming more integrated and other minorities (or parts of minorities) and places are becoming more segregated. But we know less about this than you might expect, partly because integration is something that is hard to both define and to measure.

After a bruising few decades in which Britain, both officially and in everyday life, seemed indifferent or even hostile to its visible minorities, the story today is much more benign and varied. In some of the prosperous suburbs of London and Manchester or Wolverhampton, Leicester, Slough and Reading, whites and non-whites (usually Asians) live together in the same

1. Alison Shaw, *Kinship and Continuity: Pakistani Families in Britain*, Taylor and Francis, 2000, p. 2.

neighbourhoods and streets quite unselfconsciously. It is the same story in some of the rougher parts of inner-city Britain – where whites and Black Caribbeans or Africans share streets and schools and work, and, if they are young, a minority-led youth culture.

But in the former industrial towns of the North and the Midlands – in parts of Birmingham, Oldham, Stoke, Blackburn and many other towns – it is a less happy story, with high degrees of segregation between the white majority and the (usually South Asian Muslim) minority communities, and between different minorities too – with at least some of this segregation apparently chosen by both sides.

Today integration is generally regarded as the happy medium between separation on the one hand and assimilation (in which minority identities and traditions are abandoned) on the other.

A high degree of separation was the norm in the early days of post-war immigration; it was forced on the newcomers whether they wanted it or not. Workplaces were often crudely segregated, with semi-official colour bars and quotas commonplace until the 1970s – at the Cowley British Leyland plant there was an unofficial ban on black and Asian workers until 1965.

Residential segregation was engineered by estate agents or, later, local authority housing officials directing minorities to 'their' areas. In parts of London, Birmingham and the North, immigrants usually congregated initially in the slum clearance areas, where the cheapest accommodation was to be found, which often overlapped with areas of historic Jewish or Irish immigration.

Moreover, until the mid-1960s there was almost no official support for immigrants or protection from overt discrimination. This meant that people in the first decades were almost entirely dependent on their own networks of friends and family for protection and support, which in turn tended to reinforce separation.

But how do we measure the progress towards integration that has been made since then? First there needs to be some sort of rough definition. One academic has described integration as a 'treacherous' idea.[1] Those who are

1. Michael Banton in 'National Integration in France and Britain', *Journal of Ethnic and Migration Studies*, 2001.

suspicious of the idea – and there are many in the race world who are – question what there is to integrate into. In a complex, liberal, open society there is of course no simple 'thing' for people to join. But that doesn't mean to say that there is nothing. It just means it is hard to express.

Strong multiculturalists argue that integration of minorities is not necessary at all and a good society can accommodate many different groups with radically different goals and values; all that matters is the absence of conflict. More broadly, integration sceptics tend to stress only one side of the integration contract – the readiness of the host society to remove obstacles to full participation for newcomers. They also tend to insist that the work of integration has to come equally from the white majority as it does from the new minorities. That is like saying that existing citizens have no special rights in relation to newcomers, and it treats the majority as if it was just a rather larger minority. But citizens in modern democracies have 'squatters' rights'; beyond treating newcomers fairly there is no obligation on them to change. It is the immigrant who has freely chosen to join an already existing society and must carry the burden of any adaptation that is necessary for a fruitful life (see my argument in Chapter 4, 'What's the Big Idea?').

The other argument of the integration sceptic is to point to the segregation and separateness of social class. But class is somewhat different: members of different social classes share a language, a history and to some extent a culture, and have long-established patterns of mutual recognition and conflict. Moreover, part of the progress of the last sixty years has been about breaking down rigid class barriers; to erect a whole set of new barriers hardly represents progress.

The most simple way of looking at integration is in terms of the characteristics of migrants and natives converging. As the political scientist Shamit Saggar has put it: 'How far and how fast are they becoming like us.' This is complicated by many different kinds of convergence and the different parts of the 'us' it is possible to converge with. Many Caribbean males have, as I have argued, integrated all too well with the bottom of the white working-class in recent decades. While, as we have seen, Indians and Chinese, happily for them and for the country, often fail to converge on the

British average by comfortably surpassing it. Perfect integration might be defined as a society in which objectively measured life chances are randomly distributed by ethnic background. But that would require a degree of behavioural and lifestyle homogeneity that is surely incompatible with a properly diverse society. Perhaps a more useful way of thinking about integration in a liberal society is in terms of *convergence of life chances without convergence of lifestyles*.

The latter definition would allow for some freely chosen 'clustering' and a degree of cultural and ethnic variety while insisting that the key choices that people take about where they live, where their children go to school, where they work, where they socialise in their spare time should be 'unconstrained' by ethnic background. But this also means acknowledging that some lifestyle difference can be an obstacle to life-chance convergence.

And while convergence in outcomes is obviously an important part of the story, this 'performance' integration needs to be supplemented by something else for it to become meaningful – what one might call 'lived' integration. The common-sense version of this I have heard several times, from white Britons, is 'buying the local paper and supporting the local football team'. That is too specific and prescriptive but captures the spirit of it. To put it more abstractly, it is about becoming comfortably part of the common life and conversation of wherever you live – and through that the country as a whole.

This is about neighbourhoods and workplaces, about common spaces and language; it is not about being represented to 'official' Britain through your ethnic community leaders. It therefore depends on repeated interaction with the mainstream, something that is obviously harder to achieve if you live in an ethnic enclave immersed in the institutions of your own minority.

In a liberal society people cannot be forced to integrate. And they do not need to in all areas of life. Integration is not an all-or-nothing thing. Individuals and groups can be quite separate in one area of life and part of the mainstream in another. Sikhs and Jews, for example, tend to be quite residentially segregated (the least white ward in Britain is Southall Broadway, in West London, which is overwhelmingly Sikh) but this does not damage their life chances, as it might do for some other groups, because they are usually well integrated in the workplace and the culture more generally, in a hyphenated Sikh-ish and Jew-ish sort of way.[1]

For integration to have any meaning it must require participation in the mainstream in at least one big area of life – neighbourhood, or workplace or leisure time (perhaps sports or hobbies); and it clearly requires a good grasp of English.

There is no correct level of integration; but 'parallel lives' on a significant scale does tend to lead to lower trust and a reduced willingness to share (see Chapter 6, 'Progressive Dilemmas'). Like most other social and political processes, integration is a journey – made possible by an open society ready to extend equal treatment to newcomers and the readiness of newcomers to join in and feel a commitment to their new country. But it is not a panacea. As we have seen, partly thanks to the paradox of cultural protection, *more* integrated groups can sometimes be less successful than *less* integrated groups.

So what does the data reveal about integration and segregation? First, that they are surprisingly difficult things to measure. Even something as apparently simple as residential segregation and the direction in which it is heading provides material for a bitter argument within British social science.

Getting a rounded picture is difficult because it involves making a judgement about how much weight should be given to various aspects of human existence: where someone lives, where their children go to school, where they work, where they worship, what language they speak at home, who their friends are. Which forms of segregation matter and which don't?

There is also the subjective and objective dimension. When I visited Bradford in spring 2011 to write about the tenth anniversary of the northern mill town riots of 2001, I spoke to Ludi Simpson, an academic expert on integration and segregation. He told me that the town had become less residentially segregated since 2001.[2] But almost everyone I spoke to in the town,

---

1. A good example of Sikh hyphenation is 'Punjabi Wolves', the Sikh supporters club of Wolverhampton Wanderers Football Club, who have organised themselves into the most popular and well-funded ethnic minority football supporters club in the country.
2. Ludi Simpson and Nissa Finney, *Sleepwalking to Segregation? Challenging myths about Race and Immigration*, Policy Press, 2009.

both white people and members of the dominant Pakistani minority, said that the Pakistani areas *felt* more separate than they did ten years before, partly because more people were wearing traditional Kashmiri dress on normal working days.

A more politically polarised town will feel more segregated than a less polarised town even if the numbers living in minority enclaves are lower. At an ethnically mixed focus group in Oldham arranged for me by Maxine Moar, a local community worker, an elderly white woman spoke about her regret that the town no longer felt like a single entity. She said she felt no animosity towards the South Asian Muslims, indeed had a few Asian friends, but if possible she would always avoid walking through an Asian area to avoid what she acknowledged was the small chance of getting involved in some sort of incident. 'It might be one of their special days, you don't want to take the risk,' she said.

In some of the most divided towns in Britain, like Oldham and Bradford, 'territorialism' is commonplace among younger men, white and (usually) Pakistani, who mark out areas as 'ours' and 'theirs.' Some of this territorial gang mentality and the attempt to 'ethnically purify' certain areas seems to have been one of the factors behind the 2001 riots, especially in Bradford.

There is also the question of whether there can be good segregation and bad segregation, as Ceri Peach, the leading authority on minority Britain, has argued.[1] Many people say that 'clustering' or 'congregating' along the lines of ethnicity or class or occupation can be 'good' when it is voluntary. By contrast, bad segregation is involuntary and 'the result of inequalities and discrimination'. But most people feel intuitively that there is something wrong with the gated communities of the rich, even if they are voluntary. And just because some South Asian groups are living together voluntarily as if they were still in Kashmir or Sylhet does not automatically make it a good thing.

Debates about multiculturalism often use the space metaphor; the multicultural idea is partly about giving people from minority backgrounds the psychological and physical 'space' to be themselves. Some groups have

1. 'Good Segregation, bad segregation', *Planning Perspectives*, 11, 1996.

used the separate space that multiculturalism offers to launch themselves confidently into modern Britain, secure in their hybrid identities, while others – especially Muslims from rural backgrounds, Somalis, ultra-orthodox Jews and some Chinese groups – have often used it to barricade themselves away from modern Britain.

In the segregation debate the same distinction applies, only here we are talking about real spaces, not metaphorical ones. Jews, Sikhs and Hindus still live disproportionately alongside other Jews, Sikhs and Hindus but there are seldom invisible walls around these places, and with some exceptions members of all three groups march out every morning to take their place in the wider society. In conservative Muslim communities there is often a thicker institutional structure of halal shops, mosques and madrasas and a sense of a whole separate way of life and even career structure on offer.

Every minority community experiences absorption into Britain differently because of their different traditions but also because of when they came – it's a very different place now than in 1950. But there are also historic patterns. The standard success pattern is to arrive, live in the poorest part of town and form a protective enclave; after a generation or two the immigrant family moves out to a better, usually suburban, area where there are more members of the host community. In generational terms the first generation still lives culturally back home and is torn between wanting their children to fit into Britain and retaining their ancestral culture; the second generation is duly torn, socialised here but with some commitment to their parents' world; the third generation is usually wholly British – though often fiercely aware of belonging to a minority if they are visibly different – with the world from which their grandparents came largely a mystery to which they feel only a distant connection.

Some groups have pursued a strategy of assimilation and others of hybridisation. The assimilationists shed their ethnic culture completely (like many Irish) and disperse into British society, while others hold on to it to a greater or lesser extent and create hybrid identities (Jews and South Asians).

And within the second group, some are more separate than others. The Pakistani Muslims in the North and Midlands, the Bangladeshi Muslims in Tower Hamlets and elsewhere, the Gujarati Muslims in Leicester and the

Somalis in London, Leicester and Bristol often live in enclaves and lead 'parallel lives'. The more successful among them tend not to move out to more middle-class suburbs, at least not at the same rate as other groups.

That was the basic finding of the Ouseley report into racial conflict in Bradford (published just after the 2001 riots), the Ritchie report on the Oldham riots of 2001 and Ted Cantle's report into all of the 2001 mill town riots.

As Cantle put it: 'Separate educational arrangements, community and voluntary bodies, employment, places of worship, language, social and cultural networks, means that many communities operate on the basis of a series of parallel lives. They do not touch at any point, let alone overlap and promote any meaningful interchange.' But this is contested territory. It was the Cantle report in particular which triggered the recent academic 'segregation wars'. In 2004 Ludi Simpson responded to Cantle with a detailed analysis of residential patterns in Bradford and declared that growing segregation was a 'myth'. So what do we actually know?

The most developed field of research on integration/segregation is about where people live. The main measure of residential segregation used by academics is called the 'index of dissimilarity'. It is a complex formula which shows what percentage of any given group would have to move house to achieve an even spread across a district. A figure of below 30 per cent for any group is low segregation, 30 to 60 per cent is moderate, and over 60 per cent is high segregation.

Using the census data for 1991 and 2001, Ludi Simpson and others worked out that the index had *fallen slightly* for all ethnic groups – the standard dispersal to the suburbs is happening, they argued, both nationally and in high-settlement places like Bradford.

A noisy argument broke out at the annual conference of the Royal Geographical Society in 2005, when a paper by Mike Poulsen said that segregation in Britain was in fact getting worse and that in Bradford, Leicester and Oldham it was now almost as bad as the worst parts of the US. Poulsen claimed that on another conventional measure of segregation, the 'index of isolation' (which measures the extent to which minority members are exposed only to one another), segregation had increased for Pakistanis and Bangladeshis between 1991 and 2001 in the following sixteen cities: Bradford, Leicester and Oldham, plus London, Birmingham, Leeds, Sheffield, Liverpool, Manchester, Coventry, Bristol, Wolverhampton, Luton, Blackburn, Oxford and Slough.

Poulsen's arguments were echoed by Trevor Phillips, then head of the Commission for Racial Equality, in a speech titled 'Sleepwalking to Segregation' just two months after the 7/7 bombings of 2005. Phillips presented a range of evidence to support his intuition that segregation was getting worse in some places and briefly gave the academic debate a national profile.

Phillips and Poulsen have a point. Just looking at minority percentages at ward level in 2001, in Leicester almost half of the minority population, and in Bradford 42 per cent, lived in areas where minorities formed more than 67 per cent of the population (the technical definition of a ghetto). And even if the index of dissimilarity is moving in the right direction for the country as a whole, it is still very high nationally, in the low 60s, for Pakistanis and Bangladeshis.

There appear to be two diverging trends at work. In many parts of the country and with many different minorities the standard suburbanisation and dispersal story is happening. And there has also been a sharp reduction in the number of almost completely white parts of the country, partly thanks to the wider spread of the post-1997 immigration wave – every region of the country, even the whitest areas like Wales and the North-East and the South-West, now has a non-white British population of at least 7 per cent.

But in certain urban centres, including London, Slough, Leicester and Luton – all of which are now majority-minority – and parts of Birmingham, Oldham, Bradford, Bolton, Blackburn, Rochdale, Burnley and a few others, the ethnic enclaves are getting bigger: the relatively young minority population is growing quite rapidly and people are dispersing only slowly.

Leicester is often held up as a multicultural model, and it clearly has many strengths, but this is how it is described by long-term resident Ibrahim Hewitt: 'Leicester is a series of interconnected and loosely connecting ghettos. There are the middle-class areas, the white working-class estates surrounding the city, and in the inner city the Somali area, the Hindu area, the Muslim Gujarati area and so on.' Hewitt is a white convert to Islam so not someone predisposed to scepticism about Leicester's successful multicultural image.

Leicester is perhaps, rather like Merton, neither a success nor a failure – an in-between sort of place with a story of accommodation rather than integration. It changed very quickly with the arrival of tens of thousands of East African Asians in the 1970s, too quickly for most of the existing population. But unlike the equally rapid transformation of Tower Hamlets by the Bangladeshi population, Leicester had three important advantages: there was no dominant minority, the newcomers were mainly well educated and entrepreneurial and were able to visibly contribute from the start and they had arrived in a prosperous English industrial city. There was some protest and violence in the 1970s but levels of conflict have subsequently been low, and though Leicester is not, as Hewitt says, a very integrated city, the mild form of multiculturalism that has been practised by the ruling Labour Party, and current directly elected mayor Peter Soulsby, has ensured a successful accommodation.[1]

But overall the segregation/integration story can be seen as another dimension of England's North–South divide. Seventeen of Britain's twenty most segregated towns – according to the index of dissimilarity – are in the North and North-West, mainly the Pennine towns of West Yorkshire and east Lancashire.

Why has this happened? It has been an unfortunate coincidence that the most integration-unfriendly large minority of the post-war period – the rural background, mainly Kashmiri, Pakistanis – are generally the dominant minority in the old industrial towns of the North, and to a lesser extent the Midlands, places that have been in headlong economic decline for decades.

As one senior academic said to me, anonymously: 'Let me be frank, some of the most difficult and declining towns in Britain attracted some of the

1. Some of the greatest emblems of Leicester's success can be seen in its suburbs, in places like Oadby, a leafy country suburb, where I met a successful Indian medical consultant, Gautam Bodiwala, who was the first British Asian in Oadby twenty-five years ago and says that it is now at least half Asian. A less affluent satellite town is Braunstone Town, which was a pocket of hostility to multiracial Leicester a couple of decades ago and now has a settled Asian population of about 20 per cent.

most difficult-to-integrate immigrants – the left-behind white working class and inward-looking Muslim minorities now glower at each other resentfully across no-man's-land, it has not been a happy marriage.'

Several developments in the past two or three decades have reinforced parallel lives: the factories closed and removed the one area where the men mixed together; as Kashmiri numbers rose to 15 per cent or more in some towns they came to completely dominate some neighbourhoods, and in the 1980s and 90s schools in those areas 'flipped' to become almost 100 per cent minority; a more separate 'diaspora' existence has also been made possible by technology – television, radio and internet can connect you to your homeland and your ancestral tongue and cheap travel makes it more feasible to return frequently, sometimes for long periods. But what if the Pakistanis of Bradford had integrated more with the local white working class on the outer ring estates? It might have made for a less polarised town but it would not necessarily have helped either group to superior education or employment outcomes.

Bradford is a place with a certain battered Yorkshire charm, but more than any other town in Britain it has become the emblem of these divisions. It has had further to fall than most. Just after the First World War it is said to have had more Rolls-Royces per head than any town in the world, and in *The Waste Land* T. S. Eliot refers to the moneyed assurance of the Bradford millionaire. After losing 80 per cent of its textile jobs between 1960 and 1990, it is now more famous for statistics of ethnic separation. More than one third of primary and secondary schools are overwhelmingly minority – meaning Kashmiri Pakistani – and 43 per cent of Bradfordians speak a language other than English at home. I have already mentioned the madrasas and the multiple-language issue for Kashmiris, but the most vivid statistic concerns the 5,500 babies born each year in Bradford, nearly half of whom are born to parents of Kashmiri Pakistani background. According to the pioneering 'Born in Bradford' cohort study based at the Bradford Royal Infirmary, fully 85 per cent of third- and fourth-generation Kashmiri babies have at least one parent who was born in Pakistan – the 'first generation in every generation' issue. Moreover, the 'Born in Bradford' study finds that 63 per cent of Pakistani mothers are married to cousins.

Factors such as these have contributed to the story of accommodation and co-existence rather than integration in declining parts of the North. But the story is generally happier further south. Seventeen of the twenty-six cities with the lowest spatial segregation figures are in the south or east.

The Joseph Rowntree Trust has looked at the seventy-eight local authorities in Britain with above-average non-white populations and discovered, perhaps unsurprisingly, very low levels of isolation in most London boroughs (with Hackney and Brent having the lowest level of all at 1.2, with 1 being completely mixed and 10 completely isolated). By comparison, at the high social isolation end it is the usual suspects from the North: Oldham and Burnley both score over 8 and Kirklees (Dewsbury and Huddersfield), Bolton, Bradford, Pendle, Blackburn, Rochdale and Hyndburn are all in the range of 5 to 7.7.

The most remarkable North–South comparison is between two pairs of towns with similar minority levels: Reading and Oldham, and Northampton and Burnley. Reading and Northampton have an isolation reading of 1.5 and 1.6 respectively. Oldham and Burnley are 8 and 8.7.

London is a special case in the integration/segregation story. It has been the main centre of post-war immigration for many of Britain's minorities, has a visible minority population of about 43 per cent (23 out of 33 boroughs are already majority-minority and another three are close to it), and has a self-image as a thriving, liberal, multiracial success story.

But as the portrait of Merton suggests, London is also a more segregated, and even polarised, place than it looks. Mark Rusling, a Labour councillor in Waltham Forest, puts it like this: 'The streets might be very mixed but the schools are often much less so. There seems to be an element of "pick-and-mix" integration going on, people living their lives together in some ways but not in others.' In America this is called 'Sundown Segregation', people mixing during the day but then going home to quite separate neighbourhoods.

Recent opinion polls reveal that London is the region of Britain that has the lowest number of people who think that immigration is a big or a very big problem (61 per cent) and the highest number of people who would consider voting for the BNP (24 per cent). As presumably relatively few minority Britons would vote for a far-right party, that suggests that more than 40 per cent of the white population of London would consider casting a protest vote for the far right.[1] And of the roughly 51,000 racist incidents that were recorded by police in England and Wales in 2010/11, a somewhat disproportionate number, almost 10,000, or 18 per cent, took place in London.

Parts of London, like the northern mill towns and parts of Birmingham, are also very poor – of the twenty places in Britain with the highest levels of non-employment or unemployment, ten are in London. It is, however, harder to be completely cut off from mainstream society in London than it is in, say, Bradford or Oldham. 'You can always just jump on the tube and step out in a completely different place, which is harder to do up north,' according to one Pakistani-background professional from Walthamstow, who developed an interest in design as a teenager partly through visits to the V&A museum.

As mentioned in the introduction, the White British are now a minority of just 44.9 per cent in London (down from 60 per cent in 2001), one of the big surprises of the 2011 census. Whites, including non-British whites, are still about 57 per cent of the London population but the experts seem to have underestimated the level of White British outflow from London; it was 600,000 over the 2001 to 2011 period. The White British are now less than one third of the population in Tower Hamlets, Harrow, Ealing, Brent and Newham (where they are just 16.7 per cent of the population). There are many reasons why the White British might be leaving London in such numbers but discomfort with the rapid change in the ethnic composition of a neighbourhood – 'white flight' – is probably one of them; indeed the sharpest fall in the White British population in London in this period was the troubled district of Barking and Dagenham, where it fell by 40,000 or almost one third in just ten years.

If parts of London have trouble creating anything like a stable common life between people of different backgrounds it is partly because, as we saw in Merton, it is the landing pad for so many new arrivals into Britain – the high 'churn' problem. The 2007 Commission on Integration and Cohesion,

1. Peter Taylor-Gooby, 'Background note 1: immigration and diversity', 18 August 2011, citing P. John and H. Margetts, 'The latent support for the extreme right in British politics', *West European Politics*, vol. 32, issue 3, 2009.

led by the former local government official Darra Singh, was relatively optimistic about diversity but pinpointed a few places that had reacted badly
to unexpected immigration surges, mentioning the Wash and Boston in
Lincolnshire (the focus of an East European inflow) and some of the outer
London boroughs.

And London schools are often highly segregated. Although about 75 per
cent of London's black population live in majority white areas, less than half
of black primary school pupils attend a majority white school. Similarly,
although about 60 per cent of the South Asian population live in majority
white areas, only about one third of South Asian primary school pupils are in
white majority schools.[1]

What about school segregation more generally? Many schools in areas of
quite high minority settlement reached a tipping point in the 1980s or 1990s
and went from being quite mixed to overwhelmingly minority dominated.
Indeed, academics now work on the assumption that schools tend to be more
segregated than the communities they serve.

Researchers at the University of Bristol have worked out an index of
dissimilarity for schools and found that Bangladeshi, Pakistani and black
Africans are in the most segregated schools. Data on the ethnic background of
pupils has only been collected since the early 1990s, so there is little historical
perspective available, but in sharp contrast with the debate on residence there
is much more consensus among academics that the schooling of minorities
has become more, not less, segregated in recent years. Primary schools tend to
be more segregated than secondary schools, partly because they have smaller
catchment areas, but also because the minority population is larger the lower
down the age cohort you go.

Oldham, again, has the worst record of all on school segregation. But
Bradford might be catching up, as the number of primary schools that are 75
per cent or more minority has risen from thirty to fifty in the past ten years.

The picture is not entirely bleak. According to Simon Burgess, school
segregation seems to be reducing for Indians and Caribbeans – and in parts

1. See Richard Harris, *Sleepwalking Towards Johannesburg? Local Measures of Ethnic Segregation
Between London's Secondary Schools, 2003–2008/9*, Centre for Market and Public Organisation
working paper, Bristol University.

of London, Manchester and Leicester – although it may be getting worse for Pakistanis in the northern towns. Also, segregation in Britain has a much less negative impact on test scores than it does for blacks in the US.

Over half of primary pupils in London do not have English as their mother tongue, which may be a factor in school segregation there as whites seek to escape schools where they fear their child will be held back by non-English speakers.

And what about language more generally? Speaking good English is clearly one of the keys to living a fulfilled and successful life in Britain – most good jobs are unavailable to you if you cannot speak the language at close to a native level, leaving aside the ability to take part in social and cultural life. According to the Labour Force Survey, South Asian households are still mainly speaking a South Asian language: 78 per cent of Bangladeshis, 62 per cent of Pakistanis and 54 per cent of Indians. About one third of black African households speak an African language (or French), and nearly two-thirds of Chinese households speak one of the Chinese languages.

There are now 1 million schoolchildren who come from homes where English is not spoken as the first language, though in many cases the children will be semi-bilingual when they start school. According to the 2011 census nearly 3 million people in England and Wales live in households where no one has English as a first language – about one third of the visible minority population. There is one London borough, Newham, where more than half the adults speak a language other than English at home.

In principle it is clearly a benefit to speak more than one language, and a country that is notoriously monoglot should be encouraging bilingualism. But there are still far too many people – especially South Asian women – whose lives are more restricted than they might be because they do not speak decent English. One friend of South Asian background has a mother who never learnt to speak English, partly because his father never encouraged it, and my friend now regrets that he did not do more to encourage her. 'Without the English language my mother lives in a smaller world and has a cruder and more stereotyped view of this country,' he says.

It is estimated that £184 million has been spent in the past three years on translating official documents and hiring translators for those, including those in long-established minorities, who do not speak English adequately.[1] Some local authorities in areas of high minority settlement are also funding minority language lessons – Bengali lessons in Tower Hamlets and Somali lessons in Camden. This makes no sense, especially where the people taking these lessons cannot yet speak good English. In any case it is an activity that should be paid for privately.

The Chinese outcomes underline how speaking a foreign language at home is not necessarily a disadvantage in education or professional life, and as noted there has recently been a sharp improvement in exam results among Bangladeshi children in Tower Hamlets who mainly speak Bengali at home.[2] Indeed, some of the most successful and best-integrated minorities live in a bilingual or even bicultural world, with an ancestral language spoken in the private sphere of the family but English spoken at work, when socialising with English speakers and in the public world more generally.

But for some other groups – notably Kashmiri Pakistanis – language ability does seem to be a limiting factor. Phil Lewis, an academic based in Bradford who has made a close study of the Kashmiri community there, says that poor language skills are a big factor holding back Kashmiris, young men in particular. 'The trouble is that in many cases they are semi-lingual in three or even four languages. They often speak none of them well and get frustrated at their inability to express themselves,' he says.

The government does subsidise language lessons for some recent arrivals, but free or heavily subsidised lessons ought to be far more easily available. Passing an English test is now required for citizenship and also for certain kinds of immigration – both student and spouse – but the level of English required to qualify for a spouse or a student visa is still relatively basic.[3]

One thing that can hold back linguistic and cultural integration is immersion in television and radio from 'back home'. Information on this is patchy,

1. *Sunday Times*, 23 October 2011.
2. In 2011, Tower Hamlets had the second most improved GCSE performance in the country, with 61.4 per cent of students getting at least five A to C grades, including English and Maths, despite 70 per cent coming from homes where English is a second language. Overall in London, pupils with English as a second language now outperform native speakers.
3. ESOL classes (English for Speakers of Other Languages), provided mainly by further education colleges, are now subsidised for very few immigrants.

but in the past two decades there has been an explosion in satellite television and radio channels from Pakistan, India and, to a lesser extent, Africa, available to minority Britons from those places. Most of them can be picked up on digital television. Some of the channels are mainly entertainment like Zee TV – based in Mumbai in India – or Star Gold, the Hindi movie channel. Others, like PTV Global, broadcast by the Pakistan Television Corporation, are more news-dominated.

There is also a large domestic electronic media industry aimed specifically at British minorities, usually but not always in English, including the BBC Asian Network. The Sikh Channel operates from a studio in the Aston area of Birmingham. But the largest section is the specifically Muslim electronic media. There are several television channels serving the 400,000-strong Bangladeshi community alone, the best known of which are Channel S and Bangla TV.

The most popular Muslim channel is the Islam Channel, which claims that it is watched by more than half of British Muslims. Although based in Britain, these channels usually have a global Muslim perspective (and British Muslims are involved in setting up similar channels in other countries). These stations came to be more closely monitored after 9/11 in relation to extremism, and one – the Iranian-based Press TV – has had its licence to broadcast revoked. The Islam Channel has attracted controversy over breaking the rules of political balance during elections, Islamic sectarianism and illiberal views about sex and marriage.

In some households these channels, either foreign or Britain-based minority channels, will be an additional source of information and entertainment on top of mainstream domestic channels, while in others it is the main source. The media experience has become more fragmented for everyone in Britain in the past two decades but it remains an important part of the collective experience and conversation – X Factor finals, big sporting events, news programmes during crises or elections still attract audiences of 15 or 20 million. According to OFCOM, minority households spend less time watching the mainstream BBC and ITV channels than white households, at 16 per cent compared to 23 per cent.

There are many confidently bicultural households that are part of that national conversation but also draw on other cultural and linguistic traditions in their media consumption. On the other hand, total immersion in foreign media, unless it is just for a transitional period, seems like the rejection of a common life in Britain and part of a tendency to see the place as just a legal or economic convenience. And for some young Muslims, television and radio, as well as the internet, have made the Ummah – the global community of Muslims – a living reality in a way that it would not have been thirty years ago, more real in some ways than the country they are living in.

For minority Britons who are born here the language barrier is usually not an issue, whatever language might be coming out of the television in the sitting-room. That does not automatically mean a high degree of mixing between groups. In parts of the country that are overwhelmingly white, or that are highly segregated, young people may never have mixed with, let alone become friends with, people from a different ethnic group – until they go to sixth form college or on to further or higher education. In Huddersfield the mutual ignorance among white and Pakistani children about each other was summed up by one primary school headteacher who heard a Pakistani child expressing surprise to have discovered that white children 'liked pizza as much as we do'.

Travelling around the country talking to young South Asians in quite seg-regated places like Bradford, Oldham, Dewsbury and even London, I have often asked them whether they had white friends when they were growing up. Invariably the answer has been 'No, but I do now I go to college.' Colleges and universities play an important role in this mixing process – as factories once did. And although as pointed out earlier there is some under-representation of minorities in Russell Group universities, there is now a significant ethnic mix at a growing number of British universities.[1]

So, finally, what do we know about this most vital but hard to capture aspect of the majority-minority integration story – the extent of human contact both shallow and deep: how far we have any or regular contact, friendship, relationships, partnerships, marriage and so on across ethnic boundaries?

1. There are sixteen universities that are majority minority, including the School of Pharmacy at UCL, Brunel, Queen Mary, the University of East London and Aston.

Easiest to quantify is marriage/partnerships. This is the story of a Caribbean embrace and South Asian reticence, though less well known is the high level of 'outmarriage' by Chinese women and black Africans. Almost half of Caribbean men are in relationships outside their ethnic group. For Caribbean women it is 34 per cent.[1] As a result the fastest growing minority group is people of mixed race white-Caribbean origin – and the 2011 census found 12 per cent of all households (with at least two occupants) had people from more than one ethnic group in them.[2]

As recently as the 1970s, growing up mixed race was often more of a disadvantage than growing up black or Asian; and it sometimes led to an exaggerated identification with the minority half of one's background. There is now not only strength in numbers but also a certain social cachet associated with the idea of a benign mixing of different races.

Chinese women also partner outside their group at a rate of 39 per cent, although Chinese men were rather lower at 17 per cent. Black African men partner out at a rate of 25 per cent and women at 18 per cent. The figures for South Asians are strikingly lower. Indian men partner out at a rate of 8 per cent, and women at 7 per cent. Pakistanis were 6.8 per cent for men and about 5 per cent for women, and Bangladeshis lower still.

These differences reflect what the integration expert Ceri Peach has called the Irish and the Jewish trajectory. In the past 150 years Irish immigrants have generally just assimilated into British society after a generation or two – their residential patterns, socio-economic profiles and marriage patterns have mirrored those of the population as a whole. The Caribbeans are somewhat more gradually doing the same today. Jews, on the other hand, have remained more residentially and culturally separate and have achieved above-average economic success – which looks more like the path being pursued by Indian Hindus and Sikhs. Pakistani and Bangladeshi Muslims seem to be following

1. Lucinda Platt, *Ethnicity and Family. Relationships within and between ethnic groups*, Equality and Human Rights Commission, 2010.
2. Mixed race has only been a category in the census since 2001, so there is less data on people from the main mixed categories – white and black Caribbean, white and Asian, white and Other, and white and black African – than for other minority groups. But in terms of educational and employment outcomes mixed race people generally follow their minority side, albeit more mildly, than their white side.

a more separate version of the Jewish trajectory but without the economic success – at least not yet.

South Asian marriages in Britain are often still arranged unions between two families, not just two individuals. Marriage is usually within the same caste and region, and in the case of Pakistanis and Bangladeshis the same families (in Britain more than half of all Pakistani couples are married to cousins). This extended family bonding lies at the root of the higher segregation of South Asians, and especially South Asian Muslims. This tends to be reinforced when the arranged marriage is a transcontinental one with someone from an ancestral home usually in the Indian subcontinent. No one knows precisely the extent of transcontinental marriage, and whether it is declining or not, though Katharine Charsley at Bristol University estimates that about half of British Pakistani spouses and a quarter of British Indian (mainly Sikh) spouses come from abroad.[1]

And, as usual, in Bradford cousin marriage is even higher. As I have just noted, the 'Born in Bradford' study reports that 63 per cent of Pakistani mothers there are married to cousins. Cousin marriage is much more common in diaspora marriages, and two generations or more of repeated cousin marriage enormously increases the risk of damage to children. Nuzhat Ali, a British Pakistani woman who has studied the problem, says that nearly 30 per cent of Pakistani children suffer from either mild or severe genetic disability as a result, and a disproportionate number have special needs at school. Nationally, Pakistanis are ten times more likely than other ethnic groups to suffer these genetic disabilities.[2]

Apart from marriage and formal partnerships, what else do we know about relationships across ethnic boundaries? The truth is not that much. For the past decade or so the government has been publishing a bi-annual Citizenship Survey (now being replaced with a Community Life Survey), asking people about their attitude to their local community and how

1. Katharine Charsley, *Marriage Migration and Integration*, paper for a Department of Communities and Local Government seminar, September 2012.
2. Bradford Royal Infirmary estimates that nearly half of Pakistani children have special needs at school.

people get on: 'Do people from different backgrounds in your area get on well together?'

In the 2009–10 survey the average number of people saying that people from different backgrounds in the area get on well together rose to an all-time high of 85 per cent, but this is not a very meaningful figure as almost everyone likes to feel that they live in a decent area. It was below 60 per cent in just ten out of 387 local authority areas: Stoke (58 per cent), Thurrock (57), Boston (38), Burnley (53), Fenland (57), Great Yarmouth (58), Pendle (53), South Holland (58), Barking and Dagenham (48), Oldham (54).

Some of the surveys have asked more specific questions about contact and friendship across ethnic boundaries. One such question is whether you have mixed socially in the past month with people from different religious or ethnic backgrounds. The overall positive response to that question was 81 per cent, 79 per cent for white people. Though the figure is brought down to earth somewhat by the fact that the most likely place for this 'meaningful interaction' to take place was the shops (61 per cent), with college close behind. The number who said the interaction took place at home was 32 per cent.

People were also asked whether they had friends from other ethnic groups. An impressively large total of 53 per cent said that they did, including 49 per cent of white people. People from ethnic minority backgrounds are obviously, because of much greater exposure, more likely to have friends from other ethnic groups and 81 per cent said they did, although somewhat lower, at 71 per cent and 73 per cent for Pakistanis and Bangladeshis.

It is surprising that this 49 per cent figure for white people is not better known. It may be that officials and researchers regard the Citizenship Survey numbers as implausibly high given how many parts of the country are still overwhelmingly white, and also given other data on the subject including the 'meaningful interaction' part of the Citizenship Survey.

But even if all the figures are halved – allowing for a weak definition of friendship and people giving the answer that they know is officially preferred – that is still quite an impressive bank of friendship across the ethnic divide for the British dream to build on, and is no doubt one factor in the sharp decline in racial prejudice over the last generation.

There are a few other interesting snippets that emerge from the Citizenship

Surveys. South Asians are far more likely than other groups to say that they belong strongly to their neighbourhood, all above 80 per cent, but that is maybe because they live in very heavily South Asian areas. By contrast only 60 per cent of Chinese people strongly belong, mixed race 68 per cent and black African 71 per cent. Also, when asked how more mixing could be encouraged, white people mainly suggested sport, hobbies and going to the pub, while black and Asian people were more likely to suggest something more 'official', such as fêtes, fairs and community centre events.

But however optimistic a big picture the Citizenship Surveys paint, the ordinary human contact is often simply not there in the 'bad' immigration places where it is needed most, in the segregated parts of the North, the Midlands and east London.

I have been told by quite liberal-minded white people in Beeston, the suburb of Leeds famous for being the home of three of the four London 7/7 bombers, that Pakistani Muslim neighbours will not talk to them. Tariq Rafique, a young Pakistani Muslim youth worker in Oldham, told me in 2011 that in the street he had recently moved into in the suburb of Lees there were seven houses where the people had been friendly to their first Pakistani neighbour and five where they had not returned his hello's.

In researching this book I have heard these sorts of stories dozens of times. Both sides in towns like Bradford and Oldham think the other is stand-offish, or, worse, has contempt for them. According to a nationwide YouGov poll, 39 per cent of the white population (and 29 per cent of the minority population) believe there are 'no go' areas in Britain as a result of immigration.

The social psychologist Miles Hewstone, Britain's leading exponent of 'contact theory', makes the commonsensical point that diversity without contact can lead to the flourishing of stereotypes and suspicions and eventually to conflict. Encouraging the right kind of interaction is one of the simplest ways to overcome ethnic suspicions, though it is easier said than done.[1]

Some differences just fall away when understood better. For example, the

---

1. Contact theory goes back to Gordon Allport's 1954 classic, *The Nature of Prejudice*. There are many papers by Miles Hewstone on contact theory and practice. For a good overview see *Intergroup Contact: A strategy for challenging segregation and prejudice*, paper for a Department of Communities and Local Government seminar, September 2012.

idea that the Asian areas of Bradford in the 1980s were 'smelly and messy' was partly true but – at least according to the Barratt report into the 1995 riots – it was the consequence of Asians cooking more with fresh produce and their bins then getting turned over by animals in pursuit of the waste. But there are also genuine differences in lifestyle that can be a source of conflict and cannot just be wished away: some groups, for example, are more public and collective and noisy and nocturnal, which can easily alienate neighbours who are none of those things.

Much of the 'community cohesion' work by local and national government over recent years – the twinning of white-dominated and minority-dominated schools, the duty on schools to promote cohesion, funding for events that bring people together – is based on the idea that regular contact can change attitudes. But the experience is usually too formal or too brief to make a difference to entrenched suspicion. People live more by anecdote than public policy.

Hewstone points out that there are many different kinds of contact, direct and indirect, and the quality and quantity and context all matter. Even fleeting contact with a friendly Asian shopkeeper can help reduce the prejudices or anxieties of a white person, or the fact that a friend of his has an Indian girlfriend even if he has never met her. And the more deprived people are of direct contact, if they live in a rural area for example, the more important indirect contact becomes through a non-white newsreader or an ethnic minority character in The Archers.

When I met Hewstone at the end of 2011 he was working on an educational experiment in Oldham, where an almost entirely Asian secondary school (Breeze Hill) and an almost entirely white school (Counthill) are being merged on a new site called the Waterhead Academy. Alun Francis, principal of Oldham College, a further education college and sponsor of the Waterhead Academy, is aware that this process needs enormous care, and time, to work. Attempts to overcome school segregation with similar mergers in Leeds, Bradford and Burnley have not worked well, and Francis allowed at least eighteen months of preparation before the full merger took place in autumn 2012.

Oldham over many decades has become one of the most segregated places in Britain and it acquired mainly monocultural schools in the 1990s.[1] Even in Oldham College itself, which is about half white and half Asian, and where most students have liberal views about race, they still overwhelmingly socialise in their own groups and cluster together in the canteen. (One youth worker told me that the young clubbers of Oldham were far more likely to meet across the ethnic divide in Manchester than in Oldham itself.)

Few people, either majority or minority, have actively chosen the segregation that has emerged in some places over recent decades. Surveys show that a large majority of white people do not have a preference for living in a homogeneous white area, and only 6 per cent of people say they would not want a person of another race as a neighbour. But if people prefer to live in mixed areas and send their children to mixed schools, why don't they?

The work of American academic Thomas Schelling in 1950s Chicago explains how in certain circumstances only quite a mild preference to live in a familiar neighbourhood with a preponderance of people like yourself can, without anyone wishing it, turn into an almost all-white or all minority enclave. Schelling's work is also associated with the idea of a tipping point: the idea that once an area reaches a certain level of minority population, anything between 10 per cent and 40 per cent, it 'tips' into becoming an overwhelmingly minority area. White people, in other words, are happy living in mixed-race areas so long as they are not too mixed.[2]

This raises the question of 'white flight' on the one hand and minority 'self-segregation' on the other – in some places, despite a genuine desire to live in more mixed neighbourhoods, there are other priorities that in practice override it. Even if white people hold individually liberal views about race, they may regard the arrival of a significant number of non-white people in an area as the start of a demographic shift which will lower house prices and lower school standards. And it is an unusually uncaring or an unusually liberal and confident white parent who does not worry if their child faces the

1. The 2012 *Oldham Chronicle* 'Pride in Oldham' awards included not a single Asian person.
2. One exception to this rule is the gentrifying London inner city areas. See the work of Eric Kaufmann at Birkbeck College, London University. Schelling's most famous essay on this subject is 'Models of segregation', published in the *American Economic Review* in 1969.

prospect of becoming a minority at school, especially if many of the majority pupils do not speak English as a first language.

Similarly, British Pakistanis or Bangladeshis may regard some white majority parts of town as unsafe, and may also want to be close to the institutions of their community and want their children to go to a school which has a Muslim ethos and understands Muslim issues (even if it is a state school).

Many people who have lived with segregation in the northern towns have come to see it as a normal and even desirable state of affairs. Phil Riley, a leading figure in the Blackburn Labour Party, calls it a 'benign separation' at home and school, with people mixing at work and in the town centre. Charlie Parker, the chief executive of Oldham Council, told me segregation was a sign of people feeling comfortable about their identities. And his opposite number in Burnley, Steve Rumbelow, also says that people can live separately and still rub along: 'no one says the middle class are segregating themselves.'

There is a new view in academia, based partly on Swedish experience, that homogeneous neighbourhoods are not antisocial so long as they lie *within* more mixed communities. But it is hard to see how the creation of stronger internal solidarity within groups ('bonding capital', in the language of the American political scientist Robert Putnam), is going to produce the meaningful connection to people from different groups. And without that connection how is it possible to create a sense of mutual interest based on a common public space?

Collective action is obviously easier when people share at least elements of a common culture and ascribe to common norms – surveys show white people, as one might expect, hugely in favour of integration measures such as learning English.[1] When people instead see the public space as a mess of competing interest groups, including ethnic ones, social distance is likely to grow and with it reluctance to support the welfare state. There is some evidence that this is exactly what is happening now (see Chapter 6, 'The Flight from State Welfare').

The problem of segregation is compounded by the loss of what are sometimes called 'third places', safe places where people can meet easily that are

1. Almost 90 per cent of British adults think that immigrants should be made to learn English, according to an Ipsos MORI poll for the Borders Agency.

neither the home nor work. Pubs used to be one, though they are rapidly disappearing, and are in any case no good for observant Muslims. The internet and social media worlds tend to reinforce existing connections and relationships and are less good at establishing new ones.

Community centres, where they exist, are often divided by ethnicity – part of what is called 'single-identity funding' which was criticised in the Cantle report on the 2001 mill town riots but still continues in many places. Cantle is also critical of the delivery of ethnic-specific welfare – Caribbean elder care, youth services delivered through mosques and so on.

This separateness is often regretted by older members of minority groups too, especially South Asian people who remember fondly 'when we were all just Asians together'. On a visit to Slough in 2011 the then Sikh mayoress Sukhjit Dhaliwal, daughter of the first Asian to become a councillor in the town in 1976, told me with regret: 'Life was much more mixed in the 1970s and 1980s than it is now. Sikhs and Hindus and Muslims were all in and out of each other's houses, but now we've become lonelier in our own cultures.'

A Sikh former mayor of Newham, Sukhdev Marway, also told me that 'we are much more separate than in the 1970s and 1980s, we used to mix together in the pubs but no longer'. In his case, he also voiced a common Sikh complaint that 'the Muslims get special treatment'.

The relationship between integration, mobility and economic success is not straightforward – all three exist to some extent independently of each other. But there are certain 'stuck' groups – above all the three major groups from traditional, rural Muslim roots (Pakistanis, Bangladeshis and Somalis) – which tend to do badly on all three spectrums, and others, such as black Caribbean males, which have a more mixed profile. The pattern of relative failure is often as specific as the pattern of success, but, as we have seen in this section, there also seem to be a few general conditions that apply to the most stuck groups.

First, stuck groups are usually people (or their children or grandchildren) who come from poor parts of poor countries, often with little or no education. Second, they then often end up in poor, undynamic parts of Britain doing routine, badly paid work or none at all. Third, they are often over-protected by a traditional culture and its family and clan connections and have few networks that draw them into white society; in the case of traditional Islamic cultures they are especially likely to be ambivalent about women working and western liberalism in general. Fourth, discrimination and stereotyping can restrict both how people in stuck groups are seen and how they see themselves – for example the 'badness' and transgression of black street culture; the lack of role models on both the national stage and within families is also a problem. Fifth, some stuck groups are adept at the 'capture' of local political institutions; this can help to 'lock in' traditional practices and world-views which hold British society at arm's length.

In the final chapter I will sketch out some ideas about how, even in liberal societies, it is possible to lean against the forces of separation. And there are some countervailing factors. The culture of the professional middle class is increasingly colour blind; consider an affluent home counties village like Langley, near Slough, or a suburb of Leicester like Oadby, or parts of north-west London. There is some 'reverse white flight', with young, usually middle-class white professionals moving into edgy minority-dominated parts of the inner city. And there is a global youth culture which transcends race and ethnicity. In many areas of high minority settlement, however, Britain is increasingly open but still apart.

How Racist is Britain Still?

Is Britain really an increasingly open society where segregation, so far as it exists, is substantially chosen? Or is there still a significant amount of racial exclusion? Despite the apparent decline in racist attitudes in recent decades, is there a persistent problem for minorities? (I will consider whether there is a distinct issue for Muslims, and if so whether that is down to Islamophobia, in Chapter 5, 'The Muslim Question'.)

On the face of it, white Britain has gone through a radical change of attitude on race in the past forty years. If you had told people in 1972 that in forty years' time less than 2 per cent of the white population would admit to being very prejudiced, that mixed relationships would be common, that proportionately more members of ethnic minorities would go to university than white Britons and that several sizeable minorities would have higher representation in the professional/managerial class (per head) than white Britons, the liberal-minded among them would have been pleasantly surprised.

The decline of prejudicial behaviour, partly through law and politics, partly just through contact and experience and the passing of time, has been an important part of the British story in the past couple of generations.

Opinion poll numbers are not wholly reliable but are striking nonetheless. According to the self-reported prejudice data in 1987, 5 per cent of whites reported themselves very prejudiced against people of other races, 34 per cent a little prejudiced and 60 per cent not prejudiced at all. By 2001 that had fallen to just 2 per cent admitting to being very prejudiced, 23 per cent a little prejudiced and 73 per cent not prejudiced at all.

The more informative 'social distance' data tells a similar story. The percentage strongly objecting to a non-white boss fell from about 12 per cent in 1983 to below 5 per cent in 1996. Similarly, those strongly objecting to a non-white person marrying a close relative fell from over 30 per cent to about 12 per cent over the same period. These numbers are not non-existent, and the proportions expressing *some* objection are considerably larger, but the levels of objection are vanishingly small for the cohort born in 1970. Racists are dying out.[1]

In a paper analysing this data the political scientist Robert Ford stresses two big background factors. First, the collapse of belief in any kind of white superiority with the end of empire, and a cross-party political consensus in the last three decades in favour of action to promote racial equality, so that even mildly prejudiced comments can cause a national scandal. Second, the relative success across the national culture of people from black and Asian backgrounds, and the much greater likelihood of daily contact with a black or Asian person.[2] This is surely the positive effect of direct and indirect contact theory writ large. As the sociologist Paul Gilroy has put it: 'Nobody post-Lenny, Lennox and Linford, Scary, Denise and Naomi could doubt that

1. Thank you to David Aaronovitch for this observation.
2. Robert Ford, 'Is Racial Prejudice Declining in Britain?', *The British Journal of Sociology*, 2008, vol. 59, issue 4.

there is, after all, some kind of black somewhere in or rather underneath the Union Jack.'[1]

Both of those factors will have stronger effects on younger generations, as will rising educational standards, numbers in higher education (which is strongly associated with more tolerant views), and a general liberalisation and feminisation of British society. The racism of British society in the early decades of post-colonial immigration must be seen in the context of a society that was, by today's standards, remarkably violent, intolerant and chauvinistic: most people believed in corporal and capital punishment and the criminality of homosexuality, Protestants and Catholics seldom married, slums and extreme poverty existed everywhere and pubs in the rough parts of town would routinely witness violent brawls.

As that Britain has faded away, so too has overt racism. But the fact that racism, and racist language, no longer has any public legitimacy does not mean the attitudes have completely disappeared, and nor do people stop being prejudiced just because they think they have. As the anti-racism activists remind us, racial attitudes – particularly those of white people towards black people – are deeply embedded in Britain's subconscious and its imperial history, and indeed in the history of the world.

There continue to be pockets of racial hostility, and being the only non-white in certain places and social situations can, by many accounts, still be intimidating. The police service, particularly the Metropolitan Police, has its own special history of conflict with minorities – Caribbeans above all – which continues to rumble on. And poorly educated whites with little contact with minorities are a group that often still shows high levels of prejudice (those that do have contact with minorities are often the least prejudiced and are the most likely to be living with non-whites).

It would be absurd to say that skin-colour racism has been completely

---

1. Surprisingly, Gilroy mentions no black footballers yet football has been one of the main crucibles of racial conflict and acceptance, especially in working-class life, over the past thirty years. Now that about 25 per cent of professional footballers and, typically, about one third of any England team are black the question of acceptance has been long resolved (though there is still an issue of black under-representation among managers). But there has, of course, been a long history of strife, at club and national level, associated with names like Viv Anderson, John Barnes and Ian Wright.

abolished. But it is equally incredible to say that racism today is the same as it ever was, just better concealed. Yet this is exactly the argument of some respected activists and academics. Consider this from a recent book, *Understanding 'Race' and Ethnicity*, from some of the leading academics in the field: 'Recent migrants face similar prejudice and discrimination to that experienced by the newly arrived migrants of 40 years ago.' Or this from Omar Khan, one of the leading thinkers in the racial justice lobby group the Runnymede Trust: 'Racism isn't a scourge from the past, it is just enacted in different ways.'[1]

It is hard to see how that judgement can be made consistent with the evidence above about minority performance. The truth is that poorly educated minorities are concentrated in low-paid jobs, while highly educated minorities are concentrated in high-paid jobs.

But there is a long charge sheet of evidence that points to continuing racial disadvantage. The place most cited is the criminal justice system. On average black people are five times more likely than white people to be imprisoned in England and Wales, where one in four of all prisoners is from an ethnic minority. Black and Asian defendants are more likely to go to jail than white people when convicted of similar crimes, and they serve longer sentences. In 2010, 23 per cent of white defendants were sent to prison for an indictable offence, compared with 27 per cent of blacks and 29 per cent of Asians. Stop and search is seven times higher for blacks than it is for whites.

Clearly there is stark disproportionality here and prejudice must play a role, but there are qualifying factors. Young people and poor people are more likely to commit crime, and blacks, and some Asians, are more likely to be both of those. Moreover, some groups – above all young black males – *do simply commit more crime*. This is not because they are inherently more criminal but rather because they have less invested in society and are attached to subcultures of disaffection that have grown out of a particular Anglo-Caribbean history.

There is clearly a particular issue with the sub-culture of young Caribbean males in Britain (though it has also been picked up and adapted by some

1. See *Understanding 'Race' and Ethnicity*, edited by Gary Craig, Karl Atkin, Sangeeta Chattoo and Ronny Flynn, Policy Press, 2012, p. 5. Omar Khan article in the *Guardian*, 13 October 2010.

South Asian sub-cultures). This stems partly from their families' absorption into the roughest end of British society back in the 1950s and 60s, the breakdown of the Caribbean two-parent family and the limited number of 'bad' ghetto stereotypes that seem to be available to them. The hardcore end of a US-dominated hip-hop culture which tells them that white society is a racist stitch-up, and the only honourable path is violent rejection, has exacerbated the problem.[1]

Lindsay Johns, the mixed-race writer and volunteer mentor to young people in Peckham, describes it like this: 'This is a culture of extreme anti-intellectualism and instant gratification, where reading and learning are not perceived as cool and where education as the route to success is not on the whole valued. It's summed up by a phrase which I hear countless times from boys, when asked if they like reading: "Nah, bruv, reading's a long ting." It's a culture of absent fathers and "babies having babies", where positive, cerebral (as opposed to physical) male role models are chronically lacking.'

Some of this is common to other youth cultures too, including young whites, but it is expressed in particularly acute form by Caribbean youth. Is Britain to blame for this nihilism? The brutalisation that many Caribbean men suffered, both in the education system, in police cells and on the streets, in the early decades of immigration is certainly a stain on Britain's conscience, and it has left a twitchy instinct of hostility and grievance in relation to authority figures such as teachers and policemen. Every time a young black man is brusquely treated by a police officer or excluded from school it resonates in a collective memory and confirms and reinforces a stereotype.[2]

That stereotype of oppression is carefully preserved in black street culture and – to some – justifies transgressive behaviour. The fact that the stereotype is, by and large, no longer justified by the attitudes of *today's* teachers and police officers has not been enough. It may take several more decades of largely positive experiences to eradicate the bad memories and the righteous

---

1. British hip-hop has been a positive, creative force too and has become the idiom of choice for many of the most popular white singers like Mike Skinner and Plan B.
2. Caribbean boys are excluded from school at a rate of 23 per 10,000, that is nearly twice the rate of white boys and six times the rate of Asian boys, though the absolute number was only 210 in 2010/11.

aggression. It probably also requires many more black teachers and police officers. The number of minority police officers is still only about 5 per cent, about half Asian and the rest black or mixed race, though the number in the Metropolitan Police is almost 10 per cent and the number of community support officers – who often go on to become police officers – nationally is now about 20 per cent.

So there are perfectly rational historical explanations for black criminal sub-cultures, just as there are reasons why largely white Glasgow has the highest level of knife crime in Britain. But it remains a fact that young black people do commit proportionally more of certain kinds of particularly visible crime, so you would expect them to be over-represented in prison. Ministry of Justice figures for 2007/8 show that while 2.2 per cent of Britons aged ten or above are black, 14 per cent of criminal cases tried in a crown court involve black suspects. More than a quarter of all the people arrested for robbery in England and Wales are black, according to Home Office data. In London the numbers are even more striking, though the black population is also larger.[1] Almost 8,000 black Britons are in prison, about 10 per cent of the British population in prison – roughly three times higher than the black proportion of the population – and of those about 5,000 are thought to be of black Caribbean background.[2]

The police have obviously come a long way from the days of 'nigger hunting' in the 1960s.[3] The Scarman report after the Brixton riots, the 1984 Police and Criminal Evidence Act which introduced more external monitoring of police

1. Figures are taken mainly from the Ministry of Justice and the Home Office. According to the Metropolitan Police in 2009/10, 54 per cent of those proceeded against for street crime in London were black, 59 per cent of those proceeded against for robbery, 67 per cent for gun crime and 32 per cent for sexual offences. At Feltham Young Offenders Institution in London in the mid-2000s, 42 per cent of the inmates were black.
2. Contrary to popular myth there are not more young black Caribbean men in prison than at university, in fact there are at least twice as many at university. Both black Caribbeans (31,000) and black Africans (82,000) are well represented at British universities, though it is true that only one third of the Caribbean students are male and only a few hundred of them are at the elite Russell Group set of universities; so it probably is true to say that there are roughly ten times more Caribbean males in prison than at Russell Group universities.
3. Cited by Ben Bowling, Alpa Parmar and Coretta Phillips, 'Policing ethnic minority communities', in Tim Newburn (ed.), Handbook of Policing, Willan Publishing, 2003.

action when dealing with suspects, and the Macpherson Inquiry of 1998 into the mishandling of the murder of Stephen Lawrence in 1993 have all nudged police behaviour in a more publicly respectful direction. Another measure of improvement is the decline in the number of deaths in police custody – it is now down to about fifteen a year from an average of over fifty in the 1990s, and the number of ethnic minority deaths is only slightly disproportionate.[1]

And black perception of the police seems to be improving. The respected British Crime Survey in 2009/2010 asked whether the police were doing a good or excellent job – 56 per cent of whites agreed, 60 per cent of blacks and 62 per cent of Asians. Asked whether the police would treat you with respect – 75 per cent of blacks agreed, 84 per cent of whites and the same number of Asians.

The high level of stop and search remains a sensitive issue, especially among black Londoners, in whose city about half of it takes place. Operation Trident, the attempt by the Metropolitan Police, at the urging of black Londoners, to clamp down on gun and knife crime, is one reason for the high levels; but it is now officially acknowledged that stop and search should be done 'less but more effectively'. Similarly stop and search under the Terrorism Act has disproportionately focused on young South Asians, but rather less disproportionately than one might expect given the overwhelmingly South Asian Muslim source of Al-Qaeda-inspired terrorism in Britain.

Attacks and harassment are also cited as an area of persistent racism. Reports of racist 'incidents' (including crimes) have fallen slightly in recent years but have risen sharply since the early 1990s – the latest annual figure is 51,000, up from 11,000 in 1993. But it does not seem plausible that the actual number of incidents has increased almost five-fold. The reason for the increase is partly definitional – a racist incident is defined as one if the victim, or any other person, perceives it to be so (this is one of the legacies of the Macpherson Inquiry). But it is also because people are positively encouraged to report such incidents – and perhaps more confident about doing so – and the police are obliged to record them.

1. According to the Independent Advisory Panel on Deaths in Custody, there were 294 deaths in police custody between 2000 and the end of 2010; black men accounted for only sixteen of the deaths, a bit more than 5 per cent.

Another, and perhaps slightly more encouraging, perspective on harassment comes from the Citizenship Survey for 2009/10. About 7 per cent of people perceived harassment on grounds of race or religion to be a problem in their area but only 4 per cent had actually experienced harassment in the previous two years, rising to 18 per cent for black Africans. The nature of the harassment was verbal in 73 per cent of cases, with much smaller proportions mentioning damage to property, threats and physical attack. It is estimated that there have been ninety-six racially motivated murders since the death of Stephen Lawrence in 1993, which is around half of 1 per cent of the total.

Minorities continue to be under-represented in key power centres such as law, politics and the media. But again we must be careful about jumping to conclusions about discrimination, as most elite professional jobs are occupied by older, highly educated people. Until about twenty-five years ago most minorities were either too poorly educated (if first-generation) or too young (if second generation) to be in contention for these jobs. People from white working-class backgrounds are sometimes as, if not more, under-represented in some of these places, but their whiteness makes their absence invisible.

There is also the factor that minority students, especially from South Asian backgrounds, tend to concentrate heavily in vocational subjects – law, accountancy, medicine – rather than the humanities subjects that are usually the route to the very top in the media and politics. But Shamit Saggar describes as 'bitter sweet' the experience of many people from minority backgrounds who enjoy successful careers but do not quite reach the level they think they deserve and feel there is a white charmed circle that will always exclude them.

Some progress has been made in the law in recent years; there are only two non-white senior judges but about one in ten barristers now come from an ethnic minority. The former broadcaster Samir Shah says that top jobs in the media too have become more open since the day in 1987, just after he had taken over as head of current affairs at the BBC, when a secretary mistook him for a mini-cab driver. Shah says that the problem today is 'cultural cloning', not racism – the tendency to recruit in one's own image. This may be one reason for the surprisingly poor record of local authorities in recruiting minorities to the top jobs in town halls – only one of London's thirty-three local authorities (Lambeth) currently has a non-white chief executive.

The number of young people from ethnic minority backgrounds being accepted into the civil service 'fast stream' increased to 12.3 per cent in 2010, but, shockingly, there was not a single successful black African or Caribbean or Bangladeshi candidate.[1]

Parliament has been making progress, slowly, from a figure of zero minority MPs before 1987 to twenty-eight today. This represents a bit less than 5 per cent of all MPs, less than half of where it should be – and bear in mind there are now about twenty-five majority-minority constituencies. The under-representation is even sharper in local government, where there were over 500 councillors in the mid-1990s, a figure which briefly rose to 800 in the early 2000s and has now fallen back to about 650. This represents a bit less than 4 per cent of the total but there are factors that help to explain the discrepancy: nearly half of all white councillors are retired and relatively few have caring responsibilities. Both are factors which make it much easier to be a councillor and both are factors which are much less likely to apply to minorities because of their relative youth.

Most minorities have a high degree of respect for and trust in Britain's political institutions – the major exception, perhaps not surprisingly, is African Caribbeans. Most minorities in recent decades have become more likely to vote than the white majority, and several are also more likely to provide party activists. In some places, notably Bangladeshis in east London and Kashmiri Pakistanis in some of the northern towns, this has led to a partial 'takeover' of the local party (usually Labour) machine. (See Chapter 4, 'How Multiculturalism Changed its Spots' for a discussion of the ethnic bloc vote.)

Minority British political representation is often unfavourably compared with African American representation in the US. Nearly 10 per cent of Congressmen and women in the US are black, which is only slightly less than the 12 per cent black population of the country. One reason for that is the residential concentration of African Americans; the ghetto does at least produce

---

1. *Sunday Times*, 19 August 2012.

a power base. The size and visibility of the black British middle class too is often compared unfavourably with the US. But this overlooks the relative success in Britain of black Africans and Caribbean women, not to mention the rapid rise of an Asian middle class; the real black under-representation in the middle class – in higher education and in professional occupations – is Caribbean males.

There is also the question of minority employment or recruitment in more everyday centres of power and authority like the police, the teaching profession and the armed forces. We have already looked at the low, but improving, recruitment of minorities to the police. Teaching has risen from a very low level twenty years ago to 6.3 per cent of all teachers in state schools and 2.3 per cent of headteachers being from minority backgrounds. Similarly, the armed forces is now 6.8 per cent minority but only 2.4 per cent in the officer ranks.

The final charge on the discrimination charge sheet takes us back to pay and jobs. Overall, the evidence suggests that the pay gap is small to disappearing for people with the same qualifications.[1]

It is true that all the big minorities have a higher percentage of people in the poorest income quintile than the 18 per cent of whites who are there. Even Indians have 27 per cent in the bottom quintile, though they also have 19 per cent in the top quintile, almost the same as the white figure. Pakistanis and Bangladeshis have virtually no one in the top two quintiles. But these figures mainly reflect less favourable starting points and qualification levels.

What about the question of economic ghettoisation? Going back to the 1960s and 1970s, there were racial exclusions and 'colour bars' all over the British economy. There may be some echoes today in the forced specialisation that created; there are certainly minority concentrations at both the top and bottom of the labour market.

Overall since 1979, minority Britons have experienced a huge decline in factory work and a big increase in employment in public services (especially

1. There are a few small anomalies: second-generation Hindu Indian men on average are paid 13 per cent more than white British men, but that figure was 3 per cent less than would be expected from their qualifications. Similarly, in 2006 actual pay for Chinese men exceeded that of white British men by 11 per cent, but taking education levels into account that amounted to a pay penalty of 11 per cent.

health), finance and, at the bottom end, in retail, restaurant work and taxi-driving. About 25 per cent of Londoners born in Turkey work in the wholesale or retail trade. Around 50 per cent of male Bangladeshis either work in or own restaurants (compared with less than 2 per cent of white British males). But in what sense is this the product of discrimination? It has been an immigration route into the country and is an area of comparative advantage for a group with generally low qualifications who tend to prefer employment within extended families. (Though the pay and conditions are often poor, it is far from a backwater of the British economy: Indian restaurants now have an annual turnover of £3 billion and employ about 70,000 people, more jobs than in the steel, shipbuilding and coal industries combined.)

East Europeans tend to cluster in certain sectors such as the meat and poultry processing industry where about one third of the permanent workforce and 70 per cent of all agency workers are immigrants. According to an Equalities Commission report some companies segregate shifts or production lines by nationality and language.[1]

At the top end of the labour market, more than one in twenty Indian men is a medical professional (about ten times the national average), about 60 per cent of members of the Royal College of Pharmacy are from minorities, and, taking health employment as a whole, about 15 per cent of Indians and 18 per cent of male black African immigrants work in the sector compared with 4 per cent of the white British. A remarkable 41 per cent of NHS doctors are from ethnic minority backgrounds – and 31 per cent of consultants – and 20 per cent of all qualified nursing, midwifery and health-visiting staff.

There is a strong American and white 'old' Commonwealth – Canada, South Africa, Australia and New Zealand – representation in financial services because of their historic ties, good qualifications and similar financial systems. By contrast, white East Europeans are overwhelmingly concentrated in low-skill jobs, often below their qualification level.

So, sectoral concentration is not necessarily the result of discrimination and nor is the fact that some ethnic groups are over- or under-represented in professional and managerial jobs. Overall, as we have seen, second-generation

---

1. Inquiry into Recruitment and Employment in the Meat and Poultry Processing Sector, Equality and Human Rights Commission, March 2010.

ethnic minority men and women in work have similar chances – after allowing for age and qualifications – of working in professional and managerial jobs to white British people.

The sixth Citizenship Survey of 2009–10, which focused particularly on race and discrimination, and included a big extra sample of minority adults, found that perceived levels of discrimination at work were relatively low. Seven per cent of people said they had experienced discrimination seeking work in the previous five years, and in the same period 6 per cent of people said they had been discriminated against regarding a promotion. (Perceived discrimination was especially high among black Africans and Caribbeans.) A survey by the Understanding Society unit found that race was given as a reason for being turned down for a job by around 6 per cent of people from most minority groups, rising to 16 per cent only for Caribbeans.

As we saw earlier for Pakistanis and Bangladeshis, the low qualifications of men and the high level of women not working (and larger families) are the main factors behind their low employment levels and relative poverty. Minority unemployment rates do tend to be a few percentage points higher than for whites, but when region and skill levels and age are accounted for the difference narrows. There are three exceptions to this: black Britons, Pakistanis and Bangladeshis – in all three cases about 20 per cent of households are workless, compared with an overall British average of 12 per cent. Black Britons do particularly badly, especially young males. In 2012 unemployment among black men aged sixteen to twenty-four hit 50 per cent, about twice the level for white youths. It was far lower for black graduates but at 15 per cent still twice the white graduate level – though the discrepancy there is partly explained by the fact that whites are more likely to go to higher-status colleges and study subjects like science and engineering that lead to secure employment.

The most apparently egregious workplace discrimination is found in job applications. A 'CV test' experiment found that sending CVs in response to real job advertisements got a positive response in 10.7 per cent of cases with an apparently British name and only 6.2 per cent with an apparently ethnic minority name, though the gap has been narrowing over time. There was much greater evidence of bias in the private sector that in the public sector.

But the CV test does raise the bar quite high. At least for smaller organisations, an employee is almost like a member of an extended family and a high premium is placed on fitting in. In the mind of the boss of a small office there will be a question about whether someone who might be a recent immigrant speaks English fluently and has absorbed British norms of workplace behaviour, and also whether an ethnic boundary will be a source of tension and embarrassment, at least initially.

Where do we draw the line? In many areas of life we accept that people will generally give preference to, and feel more comfortable being around, people they are familiar with. Such sentiments are certainly regarded as legitimate for minorities – indeed modern multiculturalism is partly built around the idea that it is legitimate for minorities to remain immersed in their own cultures. However, there has to be some asymmetry here between majorities and minorities; if the majority was to consistently 'stick to its own', any multiracial society would be a disaster of segregation and exclusion – as it was in many places in the early years of post-war immigration and still is in a few pockets today.

Not only the success of a multiracial society but the idea of equality before the law even in a monoracial society requires that people are able to transcend, or set aside, their 'in-group' loyalties to friends and family at least some of the time. But it is not wrong that they have these preferences in the first place; indeed as group-based primates it is part of our nature. In a racially mixed society with a fair degree of interaction many people's idea of the in-group will change and expand to include people who look different to them and might even have somewhat different values. The history of racial conflict and tension in post-war Britain, and its subsequent decline, would seem entirely rational and predictable to a social psychologist. (See Chapter 6.)

In a modern liberal society with a settled official view that overt racism is illegal and morally unacceptable it will largely disappear, and it has. That does not eliminate all forms of in-group bias or preference for the familiar.

It is not surprising to find that the two places where prejudice appears to persist most are in selection for the relatively intimate workplace 'in-group' and in the police force, an institution which has been on the front line of conflict with minorities and which has remained until recently almost a protected employment sector for lower-status whites where 'out-group' stereotypes have flourished.

Further progress will be made in both areas but it begs the question of how far it is possible to go. Can there be a truly post-racial society? Is there some irreducible level of preference for one's own group which will never be eradicated, at least when thinking about large groups of people? And does this matter?

I do not know. But I am confident that an anti-racism that registers the progress made in recent decades and acknowledges the persistence of some degree of human 'clannishness' will be more appealing and successful than the righteous, censorious kind that makes the best the enemy of the good.

When I was a child Robertson's marmalade had golliwogs on the pot, children read *Little Black Sambo* and millions watched *The Black and White Minstrel Show* on the television. As recently as the early 1990s racial abuse at football matches, both of players and of non-white fans, was commonplace. All of that has changed, partly because 'political correctness' helped to change common sense and common language. When did you last hear an Irish joke?

As the British Pakistani writer Munira Mirza has said: 'Of course racism still exists, but things have improved to a point where many ethnic minority Britons do not experience it as a regular feature in their lives. But as a society we seem unable to accept this decline in racism for fear of underestimating the problem.'[1]

Or as historian Robert Colls has put it, we have evolved from being a somewhat racist society to being an intensely racialised one. Instead of making race increasingly banal we are in danger of creating new layers of anxiety around it. Older white people or those who have little contact with minorities often struggle to use the right language and come to fear their own responses. To them a non-white person is no longer a threat but a potential source of embarrassment.

A combination of race and class and geography is still important in determining life chances. But class is usually now the most decisive factor. You are far more likely to succeed if you are born into a middle-class Indian family in

1. Munira Mirza, 'Rethinking Race', *Prospect*, October 2010.

Harrow than a white working-class family in Oldham. Belonging to a minority race as such is not automatically a major factor of disadvantage, even if belonging to a particular race might be.

Many race activists argue that this view is too complacent. All minorities still suffer various ethnic penalties. Racism, they argue, now operates through a thousand tiny exclusions, often unconscious, which together produce some of the discrepancies I have listed above.

But this pessimism can itself be a barrier to progress. Which is the more useful myth for a young black man growing up in Tottenham – the idea that the cards are stacked against him by a still racist Britain, or that this is essentially a decent society struggling to make good on its offer of equality and that you can get on if you make the effort? And if the young Bangladeshis of Tower Hamlets believe they will never get jobs up the road in the glass palaces of the City or Canary Wharf, it becomes a self-fulfilling prophecy.

Liberals point to the 'false consciousness' of poorly educated white people who sometimes believe damaging myths about the ethnic minority population. But there is also a minority 'false consciousness' which sees racism around every corner.

The reasoning of some of the most prominent anti-racist activists is bleak and dogmatic. Lee Jasper, a former race adviser to Ken Livingstone, and Joseph Harker, a senior editor at the *Guardian*, both argue (more or less in the tradition of Malcolm X and Franz Fanon) that black people can't be racist and white people have to be. Racism, they argue, is prejudice combined with power. Globally white people are the dominant group, so they are the only ones who can impose a prejudice about their own innate superiority born from hundreds of years of dominance.

Clearly the distribution of power over the globe in the past 500 years means that white racism has been the dominant form. Moreover, power and self-confidence *are* relevant factors in the experience of racism. The Ghanaian-born John Bonsu described to me how, in the 1960s and 1970s, racial slights from customers in his bank or junior fellow workers in his factory just washed off him, while more subtle put-downs from an educated or more senior person stung him. He also described how his own generation of black Africans were more immunised against racism than Caribbeans, especially those born here, because the Africans had a sense of self-worth developed in another place and were also free of the psychological curse of slavery.

The idea of unconscious prejudice is not absurd either, but the assumption that it cannot be controlled by conscious political and moral behaviour – or indeed by law – is deeply pessimistic. Equally the idea that non-white people can't be racist towards white people or other non-white people is true only if you twist the definition of racism to fit the thesis. But it flies in the face of all evidence to the contrary and would not survive thirty minutes of listening to people talk in Africa or Asia, or Lozells or Lambeth for that matter. Just because white racism has been dominant does not mean that other races aren't racist at least in the everyday sense of having a negative presumption about someone based on their race.

Moreover, to focus the blame for the relative failure of some minorities almost exclusively on racial disadvantage not only attributes too much power to racial thinking but also implies too easy a solution to the problem of unemployed young black men in Tottenham or Pakistanis in Bradford. Removing whatever continuing racial disadvantage they do face will not automatically transform their lives for the better.

The final problem with the race pessimists is their over-use of the word racism itself. In fact this is part of a more general problem of the impoverishment of our language to describe a whole spectrum of feelings and attitudes towards 'others' – and the impoverishment of language itself reflects a narrowness of thought.

There is a big conceptual blank between racism at one end of the spectrum and complete colour blindness at the other. Most people live somewhere in between – they will often have strong affinities to the people they have been raised among and initial unease about outsiders, especially if they live in poor, embattled communities and feel they are having to compete with large numbers of newcomers. But the grey area in which most people live remains undescribed.

The word racist is used to describe everything from surprise at seeing a black face on a Cornish beach, through the suspicion that an Asian man with a holdall on the London tube might be a bomber, to the Holocaust and ethnic cleansing. The word has become a portmanteau term of opprobrium, devalued through overuse and inaccurate use. We need to unpack it and call some of the things that are currently rolled up in it by different names.

There is racism proper, which comes in two, usually related, forms. There is the belief in the inherent superiority of one race over another, of, say, Jews over Arabs or white Europeans over black Africans. The other form of racism is just straightforward antipathy to a particular race or to all races other than your own, without any necessary hierarchy of superiority. Both beliefs are normally associated with anxieties about racial purity and a general tendency to think that, as Disraeli put it, 'race is all'.

Then there are other attitudes for which we need a different vocabulary. Some expressions of community attachment and resistance to change or to newcomers are better described as clannishness or 'in-groupism'. In recent years this has been directed in some places as much at white East Europeans as at non-whites. Words like nativism or xenophobia are sometimes used to describe such strong in-group loyalty, but they have merely become racism substitutes.

There are many ways in which people separate or exclude – think of the gated communities of the rich or white working-class housing estates – and racial division is just one sub-set of a common human impulse to classify and judge; yet through its association with the violence of colonialism and the Holocaust – and indeed early post-war Britain – it has been turned into a uniquely evil and incomprehensible prejudice. Northern Ireland has been the site of the most persistent and violent ethnic conflict in the British Isles since the 1960s, but because it doesn't involve race it is seen as a regrettable but normal part of life.

Then there is the problem of stereotyping and typecasting – that is the tendency to make an automatic connection between membership of a certain group or race and certain forms of behaviour and abilities. This is probably the commonest sense in which the word racist is used in everyday life today. And some kinds of stereotyping do deserve the word, even if it involves no antipathy towards the race in question. The kind of stereotyping that is based on, perhaps unconscious, ideas of European superiority and will not respond to any evidence to the contrary deserves the label of racism.

But most stereotyping is not about racial superiority or inferiority but rather about extrapolating from limited experience. And many stereotypes are partly true. Jews are more likely to be successful financiers than Pakistanis, African Caribbeans are more likely to succeed in sport or popular culture than Chinese people (in Britain at least), some groups are generally harder-working or more family orientated than others. But stereotypes by definition do not apply to every member of a group, and rational people adjust in the light of experience.

In the case of limited information about the person you are dealing with, rational people also discriminate in order to protect themselves from risk. The example used in the US is that a cab driver might decide not to pick up black customers at night (even if he is black himself) because, statistically, they are more likely to mug him. This is the problem of collective reputa-tions – belonging to a group that has a good one (say East African Asians) can pull you up even if you are a below-average performer, and conversely belonging to a group that has a bad one (African Caribbean young males) will pull you down even if you are a star performer.

Collective reputations are not immutable but they take time to change. In the meantime people will inevitably draw upon them as they classify the world about them. If you are on the wrong end of stereotyping it is frustrating and limiting but *is not necessarily racist* – so long as people, particularly those in authority, make an effort to treat everyone as an individual and respond to evidence that challenges stereotypes.

Many individuals escape the dominant ethos of their ethnic group or social class, but as my analysis of minority outcomes in education and employment has shown, group cultures are as real as the chair I am sitting on. To point to the existence of these patterns is not racist; it becomes so only when the explanation for a cultural trait becomes racial rather than historical. Nor is it racist to assume that one member of a group is likely to share the common characteristics of the group. Bangladeshi men do often work in curry houses; to assume that every Bangladeshi man you meet is a cook or a waiter is impo-lite stereotyping, it is not racism.

In trying to compensate for our racist past we have ruled out a proper spectrum in our thinking about prejudice, from the harmless that should be shrugged off to the harmful that should be damned, and if necessary punished. And a dogmatic, zero-tolerance anti-racism has made it harder to distinguish between the ignorant and the malicious. It can also place the majority in a double bind: 'Do not judge me by my background, but never forget where I have come from.'[1]

People are not going to stop noticing racial differences, it is not in our nature to. Indeed, people of all races will go on generalising about members of other minority groups, consciously and unconsciously, just as we do about national traits and social class behaviours. But linking such ordinary low-level stereotyping so casually in our language to real racism and ethnic cleansing is damaging and confusing. The threshold for the use of the word racism has fallen too low in the past two decades. A more discriminating language that more carefully captures the gradations of human behaviour could make a far-reaching contribution to defusing tensions and misunderstandings about race.

1. This idea, like quite a few others in this book, comes from Paul Scheffer's book *Immigrant Nations*, published by Polity Press in English in 2011 from the original Dutch edition, published in 2007.

Part Two

How Did We Get Here?

CHAPTER 3

The First Great Arrival 1948–92

Early Years 1948–62

The story of post-war British immigration can be divided into two great movements. First, the post-colonial wave from the late 1940s until the early 1990s, mainly bringing non-white, non-European people here from the Caribbbean, Africa and South Asia. Second, the post-1997 wave, which has been considerably larger in terms of the inflow, has affected a wider area of Britain, and, as well as fresh flows from Africa and South Asia, has also brought in many people without colonial connections to Britain, a large minority of them white East Europeans.

These two big waves can also be further subdivided into four distinct flows and ebbs: an initial open door from 1948 to 1962; a gradual closing of the door at least to primary immigration, though numbers did not fall very much because of secondary immigration (mainly family reunion); a partial reopening of the door in 1997, which brought historically unprecedented inflows; and the current Coalition government's attempt to bring numbers sharply down again.

In this chapter I will sketch an overview of the first two periods from the late 1940s to the early 1990s (I will look at the post-1997 period in Chapter 5). Who came and why? Where did they go? How did the people of Britain and their governments respond? What were the political milestones and crises, from the 1948 Nationality Act to Enoch Powell's 'rivers of blood' speech in

1968, to the East African Asian controversy of the late 1960s and early 1970s and the Rushdie affair in 1988?

In 1948 the non-white population of Britain is estimated to have been around 30,000 – mainly people from the colonies who had settled in Britain after the First or Second World War after serving in the armed forces or the merchant navy. Many of them lived in cities that had small but long-standing African and Asian communities, in a few cases stretching back a few hundred years. These were mainly in London or in port cities like Liverpool and Cardiff. The 'lascar' sailors from Bengal, who had worked on East India Company and then merchant navy ships, were one such group in east London.

By 1962, and the first attempt to control inflows, the 'New Commonwealth' numbers had risen to 500,000. They came overwhelmingly from the Caribbean, India and Pakistan. The Caribbean provided the biggest single group, with about 300,000 by 1962. They settled where there was work, usually in a factory, or where they knew a friend or family member or in districts that had been home to earlier immigrant inflows, especially Irish. Already in the 1950s the districts that were later to become synonymous with non-white immigration had begun to be settled by new arrivals – Handsworth in Birmingham; Notting Hill, Brixton, Tottenham, Southall, Hounslow and Ealing in London; Cheetham Hill in Manchester; Chapeltown in Leeds; Manningham in Bradford; St Paul's in Bristol; Highfields and Belgrave in Leicester, and so on. Many of those areas were centres of Caribbean immigration – some still are – but others have been settled by more recent waves as the pioneers moved on. (In some places this has involved tension and conflict, for example, between Somalis and African Caribbeans in Bristol and elsewhere.)

Why did people come? For a mix of reasons, including personal ambition, economic incentive, persecution, family connection and government policy and legal status – an intertwining of geography, colonial history and individual biography – that mainly comes down to 'for a better life' (and for older pioneers 'for a better life for the children'). That was certainly true of the first big non-European group, the African Caribbeans, though 'to escape war and destitution' might be more accurate in the case of the last big non-European settlers, the Somalis.

But talking to the now elderly first-generation immigrants from around

Britain about their experience here in the 1950s or early 1960s, they will invariably state that they came because they were invited 'to help rebuild Britain after the war' or some such formulation.

There *were* labour shortages, not least because as many as 750,000 people are thought to have emigrated from Britain between 1946 and 1950. But the truth is that Britain's new black and Asian citizens were not invited, at least not in any formal sense. There are some exceptions to this generalisation. Certain industries, especially textiles, were so desperately in need of night-shift and weekend workers that they advertised in newspapers in India or Pakistan or sent invitations by word of mouth – the 'Ali get Ali' scheme, as it was known in Bradford. London Transport and the British Hotels and Restaurants Association both recruited in Barbados and there was some limited NHS recruitment of nurses, generally from the Caribbean, and doctors from India in the 1970s.[1] Fewer than 50,000 people – less than 10 per cent of those who came between 1948 and 1962 – were invited in any meaningful sense.

The Attlee government had considered recruiting colonial labour but decided against it in the late 1940s, and all the relevant Whitehall departments (with the exception of the Colonial Office) were opposed to the idea throughout the period, partly on grounds of race. This is an extract from a letter sent by a group of Labour MPs to Clement Attlee in 1948: 'An influx of coloured people domiciled here is likely to impair the harmony, strength and cohesion of our public and social life and to cause discord and unhappiness among all concerned.'[2] This was typical of one strand of thought in Westminster and Whitehall at the time.

Moreover, although Britain had full employment and, as we have seen, some sectors were hungry for hands, the British economy did not require rebuilding to the extent of the big continental European economies. And, in any case, there were other European sources of labour with fewer citizenship rights who were also therefore easier to control and deport if necessary.

The Polish Resettlement Act 1947 gave settlement rights to Polish soldiers who had fought under British military command, and about 120,000 took

1. Probably the biggest scheme was London Transport recruiting almost 5,000 people in Barbados between 1955 and 1961.
2. Quoted by James Hampshire in *Citizenship and Belonging*, Palgrave Macmillan, 2005, p. 63.

advantage of it. There was also a European Voluntary Workers Programme for a few years after the war, which recruited former prisoners of war and displaced persons, mainly from the Ukraine and Italy (many Italians ended up working in the brickworks in Bedford and Peterborough). And, finally, Britain had always called upon the Irish as an industrial reserve army based just a few miles away; about 50,000 a year were arriving in the late 1940s and early 1950s joining an Irish community of about 700,000, and more could and would have come if the labour demand was there.

It is understandable that the pioneer generation of colonial immigrants should regard themselves as invited, even if for the vast majority it was not the case. The myth of invitation provides a psychological advantage in relation to the 'host' society. If you are invited into someone's house they have a duty to treat you well, and if they don't treat you well they are in your moral debt and require your forgiveness.

Even if most immigrants came for a better life, they usually came *here* because of a historic connection. The post-colonial minority refrain, 'We are here because you were there,' is true. People often came because they had some special connection to Britain, beyond simply living in British colonies or recently ex-colonies. The men had, perhaps, been in the British Indian army (this was especially true of Sikhs) or the merchant navy during the war or, like some Caribbeans, had worked as RAF ground crew. They had discovered a bigger world in the war and often did not want to return to their pre-war worlds. In the case of the Kashmiri Pakistanis from the Mirpur district, they often came because they had resettlement money after being displaced from their homes by the great Mangla dam, funded by the World Bank and completed in 1967 – about 110,000 people were relocated from the late 1950s to the mid-1960s.

But they mainly came because they could, and they could earn some decent money – in many cases at least twenty times more than they could earn at home. There was at the time essentially free movement within the British empire, much as there is within the European Union today. And that free movement for 400 million people was reinforced in 1948 by a new Nationality Act which granted colonial subjects (and ex-colonial subjects in recently independent India and Pakistan) exactly the same national status as native Britons – Citizen of the United Kingdom and Colonies (CUKC). In retrospect it was one of the most extraordinary pieces of legislation in recent British history. Britain acquired a large, non-European, minority population, like it acquired an empire, in a fit of absence of mind.

The 1948 Act was passed by a Labour government but it represented the last gasp of the idea of the imperial family. Yet it was not really about African and Asian people at all. We tend today to think of empire as being about the subjugation of black and brown people. But to most ordinary British people in the first part of the twentieth century the empire mainly meant 'the white Dominions' – Australia, New Zealand, Canada and to a lesser extent South Africa; these were places where they were more likely to have relatives and with whom they shared a language and, up to a point, a culture.

The Dominions, or the Old Commonwealth as they came to be known, had just helped Britain and its empire emerge victorious from two world wars at the cost of about 150,000 Dominion dead in the First World War and 90,000 in the Second. (The New Commonwealth of Caribbean, African and South Asian countries had also played a smaller but significant part in both world wars, although their contribution did not come to be recognised until much later; see later in this chapter.) As the writer and historian of immigration Randall Hansen puts it: 'The Old Dominions were central to the United Kingdom's economic and foreign policy; they contributed to its international prestige and influence; and they ensured the flourishing of the English language and British culture in the international arena.'[1]

It is this commitment to the Dominions that lies behind the 1948 Nationality Act. The British political class wanted to hang on to the idea of a British subject status which would apply to all people in Britain itself and throughout the empire and Commonwealth, old and new, even including the citizens of the newly formed republics of India and Pakistan. Some of the Dominions, Canada in particular, were not so sure about this and in 1946 began to look for a way of distinguishing Canadian citizenship from British imperial subjecthood. They came up with a plan that broke with the idea of

---

1. Randall Hansen, *Citizenship and Immigration in Post-War Britain*, Oxford University Press, 2000, p. 17.

the imperial family by seeing British subject status as flowing from Canadian citizenship and not the other way round.

A 1947 conference confirmed the idea that all Commonwealth states would create national citizenship legislation prior to British subjecthood. But Britain itself decided in the 1948 Act not only to retain the idea of free movement within the empire and Commonwealth but to formally give citizenship rights to all its people, creating the category of Citizen of the United Kingdom and Colonies. The result, as we now know, is that policy-makers accepted the transformation of Britain into a multiracial society as the price of reinforcing ties between Britain and the white Dominions, a reinforcement that the Dominions themselves were sceptical about.

Of course they did not know they were doing that at the time. As Randall Hansen has noted, not a single speaker in the lengthy debates in the Commons and the Lords on the 1948 Act mentioned the possibility that colonial subjects, particularly African and Asian ones, might take advantage of their right to turn up in the mother country to live and work. Even if they had stopped to think about it they would not have been unduly worried because they would have assumed that the 'coloured' people who would have turned up were the ones who had always turned up, members of the emergent ruling classes and middle-class students.

Instead, as we noted above, in the space of fourteen years about half a million people came from the Caribbean, India and Pakistan – and most of them were from 'working-class' or from rural, small farmer backgrounds in the case of most Pakistanis and many Indian Sikhs too.

By chance the *Empire Windrush*, an old German troop carrier, arrived at Tilbury docks in June 1948 with 492 Jamaicans on board while the Nationality Act was going through its final committee stage in Parliament. The *Windrush*, which has subsequently come to symbolise the start of post-war immigration, was not welcomed by the authorities but could not be turned away.

And so began the Anglo-Caribbean tragedy – or the original sin of British post-war immigration. The story is too well known to rehearse in detail here, but talking to elderly Caribbeans or reading fiction (such as Andrea Levy's *Small Island*) or non-fiction (Mike and Trevor Phillips's *Windrush*) you can still feel the pain and disappointment of that initial encounter decades later.

The Caribbean islanders had come with what now seems like extraordinarily naïve expectations of the mother country. They were generally not well educated, but some had been in Britain during the war and many more had an emotional investment in the country.[1] As Mike Phillips put it: 'Back in the Caribbean the migrants had been brought up to perceive British power as part of the natural order of things, but they had also believed that British citizenship made them part of the show. After a few months in Britain it was impossible to maintain that illusion.'

Many of the Caribbean arrivals knew the towns, industries and Kings and Queens of England from rudimentary schooling, yet they didn't really know the country at all and had probably never met an ordinary British person. They had an idealised view of a country peopled by cultured gentlemen and women and were, famously, shocked to see white people doing dirty manual jobs. Unlike India, the Caribbean had never been garrisoned on any scale and Caribbeans were unlikely to have met working-class people from Britain.

The empire may have been a family but it was a very hierarchical one; the white British were at the top of it and the Caribbeans soon discovered that they were at the bottom. Almost as painful as the open racist slurs and hostility was the simple ignorance of who they were or where they had come from. Consider this from Andrea Levy's 2004 novel *Small Island*:

Let me ask you to imagine this. Living far from you is a beloved relation whom you have never met. Yet this relation is so dear a kin she is known as Mother. Your own mummy talks of Mother all the time. 'Oh, Mother is a beautiful woman – refined, mannerly and cultured.' Your daddy tells you, 'Mother thinks of you as her children; like the Lord above she takes care of you from afar' ...

Then one day you hear Mother calling – she is troubled, she need your help. Your mummy, your daddy say go ...

The filthy tramp that eventually greets you is she. Ragged, old and dusty as the long dead. Mother has a blackened eye, bad breath and one lone tooth that waves in her head when she speaks. Can this be that fabled

1. Throughout this period all the West Indian islands were still British colonies. Jamaica and Trinidad became independent in 1962, the other islands following soon after.

relation you heard so much of? This twisted-crooked weary woman. This stinking cantankerous hag. She offers you no comfort after your journey. No smile. No welcome. Yet she looks down at you through lordly eyes and says, 'Who the bloody hell are you?'[1]

There was discrimination everywhere in jobs and in housing. Council housing was still reserved for the respectable white working class and excluded outsiders (not just non-whites). New arrivals were forced into rented accommodation in the poorest parts of towns, often in slum clearance areas that had not been cleared and where normal rent controls did not apply.

Even in these areas it was often hard to find private landlords who would rent to immigrants. Paul Rachman, the infamous west London landlord, was one of the few who did rent to Caribbeans, but he charged them inflated rents for squalid, tiny flats in west London and also used them to drive out older white residents whose flats he could then buy at knock-down prices.

Second World War veterans from the Caribbean often had to set up their own British Legion clubs because the existing ones wouldn't let them in (and it was not until the 1980s that the Caribbean and Asian veterans were properly recognised on Remembrance Day). Many churches, even, closed their doors to these often piously Christian people, who had to set up their own black churches – a lost opportunity to reverse the slow decline of the Anglican Church.

Then there was the violence. It is true Britain was a much more violent place in the 1950s than it is today. But racial violence was routine. In Nottingham and many other cities black people operated a self-imposed curfew – it was simply too dangerous to be out on your own after dark. It was Nottingham where the first serious race riot took place in August 1958, after a small group of black men decided to strike back against the violence and humiliation they had been subjected to, which in turn quickly attracted a white crowd of about 1,500 young men who went on the rampage in the St Ann's Well Road area, where many black people lived.

But it was the much bigger Notting Hill riots of late August and early September that year that really shook the country and the political class and

1. Andrea Levy, *Small Island*, Headline, 2004, p. 139.

helped to tilt the argument against a continuing open door to all colonial subjects. The riots themselves are said to have been triggered by an argument in the street between a black man and a white woman; a group of Teddy boys came to the aid of the woman (who was Swedish) only to discover that it was a lover's tiff and the woman turned angrily on the white youths.

The riots raged for several days and hundreds of people were injured. But no one was killed (although a young Antiguan carpenter, Kelso Cochrane, was stabbed to death a few months later), and it was a minor affair compared with the American Watts riots in the late 1960s or even the Brixton riots of 1981. According to Mike Phillips, it had the unexpected effect of giving

dence to black Britons.[1] They had taken the worst
ow at them and survived, and become more united
-class Africans often resented being associated with
).

Britons the riots underlined the racial anxiety that
storic European racial stereotypes of the childlike,
fused with more contemporary fears about pressure
a sense of losing control of historic working-class
aper stories about the immigrants that had started
quickly came to focus on black people as a source of

en involved in the anti-black violence were of Irish
ave been used to fighting their own corner against
ic sentiment from other whites. (Right up to the
was common in parts of London, the Midlands, the
, where there were big Irish communities.)
e and exclusion. One Caribbean interviewee in the
indrush, remembering the late 1940s, estimated that
'imperialist', meaning presumably chauvinistic and
ly interested in 'whether Arsenal won on Saturday',
ice'.
est in and admiration for the Caribbean arrivals.

carnival celebration of Caribbean life grew out of the riots.

The clubs and dens of west London became a magnet for white bohemians and even some high-society figures. (These mixed signals from the host society became even more acute in the 1960s and 1970s, when young black men were being excluded from school and beaten by the police on the one hand, yet also lionised within the counter-culture for their rebelliousness and apparent authenticity.)

It is easy with hindsight to say that the authorities should have done more to support and integrate people and provide extra funds for the areas where the newcomers congregated. But because there was an open-door policy, nobody knew how many would come – the number from the Caribbean, for example, rose sharply after the McCarran Walter Act of 1952 made it much harder for them to settle in the United States, which had been the preferred destination of most.

Moreover, talking to immigrants of the pioneer generation, almost all recall thinking that they were going to stay for a few years, earn some decent money and then return home. The fact that most of them didn't return home had something to do with subsequent immigration restrictions and related complications of moving back and forth, but it is also a sign that for all the prejudice, and even violence, in the first decades of post-colonial immigration, the newcomers also thought of Britain as a decent enough place to live and raise families and make their permanent home.

It was always incredible that a country of 50 million souls would continue to remain completely open to 400 million colonial subjects from Dhaka to Vancouver – especially as, unlike in the case of nineteenth-century and early twentieth-century immigration, Britain was now a proper democracy in which public opinion counted and also had a welfare state, meaning that access to Britain conferred valuable social as well as political and legal rights.

There was some sympathy for 'keep Britain white' sentiments on the Conservative back benches, and from Labour MPs, who mainly represented the areas of high immigration. There were also plenty of voices in Whitehall expressing racial anxieties about the arrival of non-Europeans, and the cabinet committee on colonial immigrants appointed by Anthony Eden in 1956 worried about 'miscegenation', especially among those groups where many more men than women had come. There were several attempts to keep numbers down by placing administrative obstacles in the way of would-be immigrants and persuading the high commissions in India and elsewhere not to issue too many passports.

But there was also strong resistance to the idea of excluding people from Britain on grounds of race. The Labour home secretary, James Chuter Ede, said this after the docking of the *Windrush* in 1948: 'We recognise the right of the colonial peoples to be treated as men and brothers with the people of this country.' The Colonial Secretary, Alan Lennox-Boyd, threatened to resign in 1955 after some Tory cabinet members moved to apply restrictions only to New Commonwealth countries. Lennox-Boyd said he would accept controls on the whole Commonwealth or no controls at all. (He was a believer in the imperial idea rather than racial equality and ended his career as a leading light of the right-wing Monday Club.)

The Colonial Office was the voice of the colonies within Britain, so it is perhaps no surprise that it remained in favour of openness. But in a striking example of how stereotypes can change rapidly, Randall Hansen found official Colonial Office documents that are full of praise for industrious, reliable and talented West Indians compared with the lazy and feckless Indians.

The pressure for restriction had, however, become overwhelming by the early 1960s – both from ordinary citizens as channelled through MPs and from party activists (especially Tory) and from within Whitehall itself – and immigration control legislation was drawn up. In 1961 there was a 'beat the bar' surge and net New Commonwealth immigration rose to 136,000 – the highest inflow in one year until the post-1997 immigration wave – West Indian numbers rose to 66,000, Indian to 24,000 and Pakistani to 25,000 in a single year.

The Commonwealth Immigrants Act was finally passed in 1962. In the same year the country applied to join the European Community. The two steps taken together marked the beginning of the end of imperial ties. The white Dominions had already started to envisage their futures in regional rather than Commonwealth alliances, and Britain too was reluctantly seeing its own future as a European rather than a global power.

But the 1962 Act did not mark a clean break with the past. It was considered too difficult to create a new form of British citizenship, so instead the old form of imperial subjecthood – Citizens of the United Kingdom and Colonies – remained; but there was no longer an automatic right to come and live and work in Britain unless your passport had been issued in London, as it would have been for most British people. But the change did remain broadly colour-blind. Whether a passport was issued by the colonial governor in Nairobi or the high commissioner's office in Ottawa, it was equally subject to the same restriction.

Historians of immigration point to the surprising ease with which the British government ended primary immigration, and indeed squeezed it down further over the next three decades, in a way that was not replicated in continental Europe, where popular objection to similar levels of immigration was just as strong. They attribute this to the fact that at that time, unlike today, Britain had neither an activist judiciary nor the equivalent of a bill of rights to confer extra rights on actual or would-be immigrants.

Back in the early 1960s, what was perhaps most surprising to the layman was how little the numbers fell after 1962 – indeed, in the fourteen years after the 1962 Act the number of net immigrants from the New Commonwealth was actually a little higher than it had been in the open-door fourteen years. (According to the 1981 census, 75 per cent of Asian immigrants had arrived after the 1962 restrictions.)

The reason for that increase was, at least initially, a liberal issuing of work permits (about 60,000 were issued to New Commonwealth citizens in the two years after the Act, with preference given to those who had served with the British forces) and family reunion. For many years after 1962 about 75 per cent of New Commonwealth immigration was women and children. Family reunification has always been considered a basic right in liberal societies, although there are intense arguments – including today in Britain – about who should be included under that catch-all phrase, and what conditions a receiving society is entitled to place on those coming in.

So far I have concentrated on the African Caribbean story, which was the most important immigrant tale right up until the early 1980s and even beyond. Why has the African Caribbean story been so influential, arguably too influential? Caribbeans were the largest single minority group until overtaken by Indians in the late 1970s. Their number, about 600,000, has barely risen since then (if you exclude mixed-race people with one African Caribbean parent) and they are now only Britain's fifth biggest minority, behind black Africans.

The fact that Britain behaved especially badly to its Caribbean minority confirms a story that became pervasive in the 1980s, at least in liberal Britain, of a racist host society and victim minority groups. And, as we have seen, Anglo-Caribbean conflict has left scars that are still raw today in various aspects of black failure, in the sensitivity of black-police relations, and in a sometimes confrontational black street culture.

Another reason the Caribbean story has remained so influential is because black Caribbean people came to be especially culturally visible, in music and sport above all, and partly because the American civil rights movement turned black Caribbean immigrants, who were also descended from slaves, into similar symbols of both oppression and liberation.

There are various reasons why newcomers from the Caribbean had such a rough time. Partly it was just that they were the pioneers. They were the first big group to arrive in an exhausted, bad-tempered Britain and felt the full blast of ordinary people's prejudice before law, time and manners were able to do their work. And they came, as we have seen, with high expectations, so had further to fall. Also people from the Caribbean were westernised and out on the streets in a way that many South Asian immigrants in the early days were not. There was more contact and therefore more opportunity for conflict.

In the 'avoidance, conflict, accommodation' typology of American sociologist Robert Park, African Caribbeans seemed to miss out the avoidance phase and went straight to conflict. And as I argued in Chapter 2 they had *too little* cultural protection. They came to Britain as westernised, Christian, English speakers. Coming from a largely agrarian economy they did not fit into Britain's class schema, but many of them nonetheless felt *downwardly* mobile into the white working class.

Meanwhile, there were other, less visible South Asian immigrant stories unfolding in that period both before and after 1962 – most notably the Kashmiri Pakistanis who started arriving in Birmingham and the northern mill towns. Some Indian Muslims had worked in munitions factories during the war, so there were connections. There was a big pull factor from the well-paid factory work and, in the case of the Kashmiris from Mirpur who had lost, or were going to lose, their homes thanks to the Mangla dam, there was also a push factor provided by relocation money.

It was the textile mills of Bradford, Oldham, Blackburn, Dewsbury, Burnley, Huddersfield and elsewhere that were a particular magnet for the Pakistanis, who came mainly from the rural parts of Kashmir and the western Punjab. In 1959 the textile industry, with an injection of public money, invested heavily in new equipment in a final, failed, attempt to remain competitive against new rivals in Hong Kong, Japan and the Indian subcontinent itself.

That meant more of the night shifts and weekend shifts that were unpopular with the native workforce, which at that time had the choice of better pay and conditions in other industries. Progressive social legislation from the late nineteenth century which banned women from working night shifts also increased the demand for foreign workers. Women traditionally performed certain functions on the textile machinery, and because the native male workers refused to cover 'women's work' on the night shift outsiders had to be found – Poles, Ukrainians and, by the late 1950s and early 1960s, Kashmiris.

For the rural Kashmiris, many of whom were illiterate, travelling halfway around the world to a place like Bradford was a huge wrench; but merely moving to urban Pakistan would have been a big move too – and as wages were many times higher in Bradford it seemed a sensible step. And, of course, as with most of the Caribbeans, everyone thought it was a temporary arrangement that would last just a few years.

Sher Azam, a leading figure in the Bradford Council of Mosques who was later to play a leading role in the Rushdie affair, recalls the mole-like existence of the young Kashmiris. 'We worked the night shifts and did as much overtime as we could, so it meant we didn't see very much of normal Bradford. Also we couldn't speak any English, we shopped by pointing at things, we couldn't even read the place names on the front of the buses.'

As with many other pioneer immigrants, they rented houses in the cheap part of town and shared the house with perhaps ten or fifteen other men, some men sleeping while the other men worked in the factory and then swapping around – a 'hot bedding' system. Azam tells one poignant story of how they understood so little of the system that a group of them one day went to lobby the lord mayor of Bradford over various housing and welfare problems – they assumed the mayor with his chains and big black car was the 'big man', only to discover that it was a largely ceremonial position. There was no Kashmiri middle class who spoke the language well and understood the culture to intercede on their behalf.

For the South Asians this was the 'guest worker' period – mainly young men on their own who assumed they would return home. (The African Caribbeans had a more even gender balance.) In Bradford in 1961 there were nearly 4,000 Pakistani men and just eighty-one women. Later on, when the women, families and imams came over in the mid- and late 1960s or even the 1970s, life changed completely. The tradition of purdah required that women should be protected from contact with male strangers, and there was a conscious effort to recreate the kin networks of village life in Kashmir, known as the Biraderi system.

The migration pattern for rural South Asians was generally a few male pioneers from a particular village, followed by 'chain migration' of more male workers from that and neighbouring villages and then finally wives and children. The retailer Anwar Parvez, who pioneered late, and seven-day-a-week opening at his London supermarkets in the 1970s, arrived in Bradford aged twenty-one in 1958. He told a BBC radio documentary about the Pakistani Biraderi system how when he first arrived that system had helped him to find a place to live and work and how he then felt it was his duty to help others to come to Britain.

'I felt my first job was to bring the people here. First I brought my brother-in-law. Then another brother-in-law. Then my own brothers and my uncles... Then slowly and steadily I started calling friends as well. So first I looked after my immediate family, then very close friends... then I began to look further afield within my area... Yes, proudly I can say I helped my whole area to come here.'[1]

When the men were here on their own in the 1950s and early 1960s there was a brief period of semi-integration. Life was not easy, as Sher Azam makes clear, and there was plenty of prejudice to deal with, but the young Pakistanis worked in factories with white people and often established friendships so far

1. Quoted in Philip Lewis, *Young, British and Muslim*, Continuum, 2007, p. 17. The BBC radio documentary produced by Navid Akhtar, *The Biraderi*, was first broadcast on 26 August 2003.

as language allowed. They joined trade unions, went to the pub, sometimes had relationships with white women (I have met several British Pakistanis with white grandmothers from this period). Something of this more liberal spirit continued well into the 1980s before Muslim piety snuffed it out in many places.

The story of 'hot-bedding' in run-down parts of town, of well-paid factory work and a rough-and-ready sort of integration, is common to many of the other South Asian immigrant pioneers in industrial Britain. But the story of that limited integration then going into reverse and the creation of enclaves all over the northern towns and the Midlands is particularly true for the Kashmiris, the numerically dominant group among British Pakistanis. The 'separating out' was further exacerbated by the closure of many of the factories that had brought the men here in the first place in the 1970s and 1980s, but that is to jump ahead.

The other big group in this pre-1962 pioneer phase were Indians (Hindus and Sikhs), who settled a swathe of west London. Ealing, Southall, Hounslow, Neasden, Wembley, Harrow and Brent had a significant Indian presence by the early 1960s – and Heathrow airport had already become a big employer of Sikhs in particular. Sikhs and Hindus were also to be found in Slough, east London, Leicester, Birmingham, Walsall and Wolverhampton. And there were significant Sikh settlements in Bedford and Gravesend.

Many Indians came from rural Gujarat, while other Hindus and Sikhs came from rural Punjab, one of the most highly developed parts of India but also one that suffered severe disruption in the partition of the country, with the western part of the state ending up in Pakistan. Sikhs and Hindus from the Punjab shared a common culture and language and often lived in the same areas. The Hindus were generally better educated, and a few were from business, medical or academic backgrounds. The Sikhs were less well educated, though mainly literate, and were often small farmers from three districts in the Doaba region.

As with other groups, the places they ended up were determined either by family connections or availability of work. Sikhs often ended up doing physically demanding jobs, such as foundry work in the west Midlands, and quickly became known for their work ethic. More middle-class Hindus often had to take jobs below their qualification level, unless specifically recruited, such as the doctors (trained in British-built medical schools in India) who came to fill jobs in the expanding NHS.

Both Hindus and Sikhs have gone on to establish themselves as two of Britain's more successful big minorities, helped in part by the arrival a decade later of co-religionists from East Africa. They are two groups for whom the imperial connection may have had some genuine advantages. The Hindus often spoke reasonable English, something that was not true of most Sikh or Muslim arrivals from the subcontinent. The Sikhs, however, had a long tradition of military prowess, and as the 'favoured sons of the empire' who had fought for the Crown during the Indian Mutiny were recruited in large numbers into the British Indian army, along with Muslims from the Punjab. This knowledge of their military contribution must have given them some resilience and self-belief in the face of prejudice and setbacks in their adopted country.

The role of the British Indian army in both world wars, indeed the con-tribution of non-white colonial subjects in general, has only recently begun to feature in the public memorialising of both world wars. But in the First World War the British Indian army had 1.4 million volunteer troops under arms, of whom nearly 50,000 died, some of them in France in 1914 where they were the first empire troops to see action (they also fought at Gallipoli and in East Africa). That cannot compare with the 5.7 million troops from the British Isles, of whom 670,000 died, but in terms of the numbers of dead the Indian sacrifice almost matches that of Canada or Australia.

In the Second World War the British Indian army was even larger. With 2.5 million men under arms, it is said to be the largest volunteer army in history. The force lost about 40,000 men during the war, fighting mainly in Burma against the Japanese. There were also significant contributions from Africa and from the West Indies, most notably the 5,000 RAF ground staff and 300 aircrew. The colonies contributed with labour and goods too.

The amnesia about the colonial role in both wars reflects not just a fail-ure on the part of white-majority Britain to acknowledge the sacrifice of non-white troops but also a reluctance on the part of the former colonised countries to celebrate this aspect of empire. Even at the time there were complex cross-currents of both solidarity and racial conflict, and some colonial troops were radicalised by the experience: for example, 20,000 Indian troops swapped sides and joined the Japanese before the fall of Singapore.

In 2002 the Memorial Gates on Constitution Hill were finally opened by the Queen, commemorating the roughly 5 million volunteers from India, Africa and the Caribbean in two world wars and inscribed with the names of all the winners of the Victoria and George Cross from those places.

I attended a small ceremony in Slough, in 2011, celebrating the Sikh role in the British Indian army. But today there are only eighty people of Sikh background serving in the British army. A positive story about empire which inspired some of the first wave of post-colonial immigration became in the 1970s and 1980s a much more complex one of guilt and recrimination; though this in itself reflects a more egalitarian presumption on the part of the majority and a greater political self-confidence of ex-colonial minorities.

To conclude this section: the pre-1962 phase of the post-war immigration story is a dramatic one and it set some patterns that have lasted to this day. The first and most obvious pattern is the extraordinarily laissez-faire way in which Britain both acquired and then managed, or rather didn't manage, a whole new population.

It is often said that the importation of people from the Indian subcontinent to work in textile mills that were soon to close, partly thanks to competition from India and Pakistan itself, was a poor piece of social engineering. But the whole point was that no one really engineered it, with the partial exception of the textile employers – it just happened. Ishtiaq Ahmed, a leading figure in Bradford's Council of Mosques, recalls that his father only ended up in Bradford because he bumped into some fellow Kashmiris at Heathrow airport who told him there would be familiar faces and jobs in the town.

Caribbean immigrants came to Nottingham after 1948 because there had been a big West Indian servicemen's camp there in 1944. A lot of Sikhs moved from Gravesend to Southall because a former officer in the British Indian army owned a factory there, the Woolf Rubber Company, and invited them to come and work for him.

'For most migrants early social life in Britain was like a commune in which relatives supported each other and villagers grouped their resources in the first steps towards a community,' wrote Gurharpal Singh and Darshan Singh Tatla in their book about Sikhs in Britain.[1]

To the extent that Britain did manage this first wave of post-colonial immigration it was with an odd mix of racial exclusion and liberalism. There was a 'communalist' assumption, derived from the experience of colonialism, that minorities would want to live in their own areas – much as Britain's social classes did – with a sense of what the anthropologist Geoffrey Gorer called 'a distant cordiality' towards the host society. But there was also a liberal assumption that the country should apply to immigrants the same 'live and let live' approach that it applied to everyone else, so no attempt was made to prevent minorities congregating together.

Yet by the 1960s Britain was also a welfare state composed of a dense set of communities and social contracts that combined to create some sense of a common, cross-class interest. Indeed, as the sociologist Geoff Dench and others have argued in the book The New East End, the first wave of post-colonial immigration came just as the British working class felt that it was coming into its welfare inheritance as a reward for decades of deprivation, depression and sacrifice in two world wars, and many people were reluctant to share this hard-won reward with newcomers who they felt had not been part of the national contract.[2]

And some help with fitting in would have been useful. It was naïve and neglectful to assume that Britain was an easy place to join. It was also asking quite a lot of the insular working-class communities of industrial Britain to open their doors to large numbers of strangers from distant, non-European cultures. And the immigrant ways of life *were* different, often alarmingly so: the newcomers were noisy and boisterous (especially Caribbeans) and brought with them unfamiliar smells (South Asians) and different attitudes to hygiene and tidiness. (As I noted earlier in relation to Bradford, the mess associated with some immigrant areas was partly the consequence of different kinds of cooking.)

1. Gurharpal Singh and Darshan Singh Tatla, Sikhs in Britain: The Making of a Community, Zed Books, 2006.
2. Geoff Dench, Kate Gavron and Michael Young, The New East End: Kinship, Race and Conflict, Profile Books, 2006.

One of the paradoxes of immigration is that the good, strong communities that people on the political left admire, with high levels of stability and mutual support, are, by definition, communities that are quite hard for outsiders to join. Resistance to immigration has a legitimate community preservation aspect as well as the more obvious xenophobic dimension, and the two are often impossible to disentangle.

Clearly racial prejudice and acute awareness of racial difference were commonplace in 1950s Britain. Just after the Second World War many, perhaps most, British people had markedly chauvinistic views about the superiority of themselves and their empire over all others in the world, with the possible exception of America. In relation to non-whites there was often a further layer of prejudice and assumed superiority to contend with.

Much of the academic literature on this period contemptuously judges the past by the standards of the more liberal present. One of the debates concerns whether the racism of this period was predominantly top-down or bottom-up. Evidently it was both, but rawer from the bottom.[1]

Among the political and intellectual elite there was already an enlightened minority which actively campaigned for racial equality, as well as many ordinary white people who were already living it in practice.

One reason for the largely laissez-faire approach to the management of the new communities – and the lack of preparation of native Britons – was that notion of the imperial family. It was the idea that had held open the door to potentially 400 million people, and it was the same idea that told politicians and officials, notwithstanding racial anxieties about the non-white arrivals, that nothing special needed to be done for them. After all, through the experience of empire they knew Britain and Britain knew them; we were in a sense already integrated by mutual knowledge and respect.

The trouble with this idea is that it was not true, or at least worked only at the elite level. And to the extent that it was true that the Christian, English-speaking Caribbeans did know about us from books, 'we' – in the case of

---

1. Robert Winder in his book *Bloody Foreigners* (Little, Brown, 2004) sums it up well: 'Britain's working-class culture emphasised the manly, the loyal, the muscular. Fortified by drink it could be aggressive and uncouth. Caribbean islanders in London or Birmingham moved through a daily barrage of four-letter words and physical intimidation.'

working-class Britain – did not, as we have seen, know them. The Indians from the Punjab and Gujarat knew little about Britain and few of the Sikhs spoke decent English, while many of the illiterate rural Kashmiris did not even consider themselves part of Pakistan, let alone the British empire.

But it was this damaging idea of the imperial family that set the pattern for Britain's very light-touch approach to integration. As we will see again in the discussion of multiculturalism and national citizenship, this has not always been a bad thing; at its best it has allowed minority Britons to find their own way to a new identity which is the stronger for not being forced upon them.

Yet as the story of the Bradford pioneers and their children illustrates, many people were confused and adrift in the back streets of Britain and the authorities did little to help them. 'We were just left to get on with it. It was assumed that people from the colonies knew the mother country, and perhaps we thought we did know it, but it wasn't as we had imagined,' says Ishtiaq Ahmed from Bradford.

Having allowed the night-shift Bradford 'moles', and their equivalents elsewhere, into the country, Britain should at least have provided them with language lessons and some idea of the country that they were to make their home. The failure to do this drove people deeper into their protective family and clan networks and has contributed to the segregated communities today in places like Bradford, parts of central Birmingham, Tower Hamlets and elsewhere.

To repeat, and to be fair to the authorities, prior to 1962 few people expected the pioneers to stay more than a couple of years – few deep roots had been laid down, and especially among the South Asians there were few women and children to lay them.

The word 'integration', already in use in the mid-1960s, seemed to mean mainly arranging conversations between local authorities, church groups and immigrant representatives. Intriguingly, however, Edward Boyle, when Conservative education secretary in 1963, did float the idea that no school should have a minority population of more than 30 per cent. Looking back from today it seems like a missed chance. But then it probably seemed unnecessarily dirigiste for the small number of schools that might have been affected – an idea ahead of its time.

To the extent that there was a fair amount of mixing between natives and newcomers it happened in factories – or the factory equivalent like the giant Post Office sorting office. Factories are good for integration, especially for people who may not understand the language or culture well – the skills required in manual labour are not usually linguistic. There was, of course, conflict and prejudice within factories too, and trade unions could exclude as well as include, though it was generally in their interests to ensure that the foreigners did not undercut their own members while at the same time often making it hard for them to progress into the higher-status, higher-paid functions.

But at least back in the 50s, 60s and 70s when the Caribbeans or the men in their turbans and even women in saris were pouring out of the factories in the late afternoon it was very obvious that they were here for a good economic reason. Older Pakistani and Bangladeshi men today, especially in the post-industrial North, are more likely to be self-employed or to work in taxi companies or curry houses with their fellow South Asians than to work alongside white people.

Finally, this pioneer period was when racism was overt and almost innocent. Many white people barely knew it was wrong to treat visible minorities like second-class citizens. It just seemed natural. And some of the exclusion, from council housing for example, was simply because the rules were not designed to include outsiders. More directly prejudiced and hurtful was the exclusion from parts of the private rented sector – those famous signs 'No blacks, no Irish, no dogs'.

Yet the prejudice was not all one way, especially among South Asians. Describing growing up in the 1970s in her book *Shame*, Jasvinder Sanghera writes about her Sikh mother: 'We weren't allowed to mix with white people because Mum said they didn't have any morals or self-respect. She said whites were dirty people with dirty ways. That's what all the women I called Aunty thought too, and everyone else in our community.'[1]

Moreover, the picture of an unremittingly hostile welcome is also false. New arrivals often threw themselves on the mercy of ordinary people and

1. Jasvinder Sanghera, *Shame*, Hodder & Stoughton, 2007.

generally got a helpful response. Consider this description of quiet consideration from several natives towards a young Kashmiri who landed at Heathrow
in the mid-1950s with just £5, an address in Bradford, and barely a word of
English.

> I collected my bag and came out of the airport. I wanted to get to London,
> so I started showing the address and the £5 note to anybody and every-
> body hoping they would help me. A police officer saw me doing that so
> he took me to a bus stop. I got on the bus and gave the driver the full £5,
> he took the fare and gave me change. The bus took me to King's Cross.
> The driver came out and handed me over to a porter. The porter took me
> to a ticket office, took my money, bought my ticket and gave me the right
> change. He then made me sit down on a platform. It was very cold, I was
> hungry, and most of all I was very scared. I wish I had stayed home ... I
> tried getting on a train but the porter prevented me. I thought I had been
> arrested ... Finally the right train came. The porter went round until he
> found a person in uniform (a naval officer). They made me sit near the
> window. Now I was convinced I had definitely been arrested. Eventually
> the train pulled into Bradford and the naval officer helped me get a taxi
> and took me to Arcadia Street, where Babu's brother opened the door. I
> ran towards him shouting 'Hide me, hide me, they have arrested me.' He
> laughed. I rushed upstairs, from where I saw the officer get into the taxi
> and drive away.[1]

There was no official system of mentoring but many immigrants from
the pioneer generation do recall being taken under the wing of a considerate
white person. It sometimes happened in schools too, with kindly teachers
spotting and nurturing minority talent.

The dominant fact of the mid-1960s was the increasing rootedness of the
immigrants. Families arrived, children were born, or started going to school –
there was no turning back. And however hard life in Britain sometimes was
for the pioneers, there was now a good reason to stay and make whatever
sacrifices were necessary: for a better life for the children.

1. From an interview in *A Postcolonial People, South Asians in Britain*, N. Ali, V.S. Kalra and S.
   Sayyid (eds), Hurst, 2006, p. 33.

The housing conditions of the newcomers were often appalling. One leading academic recalls visiting Moss Side in Manchester in 1960 and finding the small front room of a two up/two down occupied by two different families from Jamaica, with a curtain dividing the room in two. As noted, many immigrants lived in the slum clearance areas of large cities, usually renting, sometimes clubbing together to buy properties at knock-down prices. Pakistanis in the North and the Midlands usually rented and then bought inner-city Victorian terraced housing. Indians did the same, though sometimes in slightly leafier suburban parts of town. This period laid the roots of residential segregation, which was usually both chosen by the newcomers and reinforced by informal 'racial zoning' by estate agents and local authorities.

The shift from the pioneer period to the middle period of the story of post-war immigration – from the mid-1960s to the mid-1980s – is the shift in Robert Park's terminology from 'avoidance' to 'conflict' as the second generation fought for the rights they had been promised. The second generation felt much less deferential than their parents, partly because they did not compare their lives to the lives back in Mirpur or Jamaica that they might have been leading. They were born in Britain and compared their lives to their white compatriots'. This is the era of Powellism, of the rise and fall of the National Front, of set-piece confrontations in many big cities which have gone into radical and minority folklore.

Conflict and Accommodation 1962–92

Before the 1962 Act ended free movement from the colonies (and ex-colonies) to Britain, the people from those colonies had been treated in a legal sense not as immigrants but as extra-territorial citizens. And, as we have seen with the African Caribbeans, many of them did indeed feel like citizens of the British empire, especially those who had been involved with the British armed forces during the war or who had come with the idea that they were needed to help rebuild the mother country. But most people in the mother country evidently did not include Caribbeans, Africans and Asians in their picture of

Britain – the idea of the imperial family did not resonate in the back streets of Nottingham or Wolverhampton.

For the story of post-war British immigration the year 1948 has a double significance – as the year of the 1948 Nationality Act and of the *Windrush*. But it is a totem year in one other respect too – it was also the year of the UN Declaration of Human Rights. Thanks in part to the declaration, the old, often religious idea of human equality across races as well as classes – the idea that each human life was as intrinsically valuable as any other – came to be absorbed into the mainstream politics of the liberal democracies of the rich world. But it was not yet part of the common sense of most ordinary people, especially in a country like Britain where for many generations people had been encouraged to feel that they were superior to colonial people, albeit in a decent, Christian way.

Indeed, by the mid-1960s a gap had opened up on immigration and racial equality between popular opinion – as captured in polls, journalistic reportage and indeed street violence – and much educated and political class opinion, which came to accept, at least in theory, that idea of human equality as demanded by the UN Declaration and by the emerging civil rights movement in the US. (The gap between elites and masses on racial justice has partly closed over the last fifty years; the gap on attitudes to immigration has not.)

The 1964 election was the first in which race and immigration played a significant role. In Smethwick in the west Midlands, which had attracted both Sikhs and Caribbeans to work in the factories and foundries, the Tory candidate Peter Griffiths won a safe Labour seat from a senior Labour figure, Patrick Gordon Walker, with the slogan 'If you want a nigger neighbour, vote Liberal or Labour.' Race also played a role in Perry Bar in Birmingham, Southall in west London – where a lot of Indians had settled – and the pro-immigration Labour MP Fenner Brockway lost his Slough seat by four votes against the national swing.

Labour had opposed the 1962 immigration restrictions, but despite its internationalist, anti-colonial and anti-racist traditions (at least on the left of the party) it realised that opposition to uncontrolled immigration was not practical politics and when it came to power in 1964 it made no real change to immigration policy. The majority of MPs and both front benches were now more liberal on race and immigration than most voters, with a few exceptions, mainly in the Tory party. But two irresistible forces had ended free movement within the empire – first and most important was the public opposition to non-white immigration, to which the politicians had to respond, while the second was Britain's gradual reorientation away from the empire and Commonwealth towards Europe.

Out of this emerged a new political consensus which on the one hand pledged to keep, or even tighten, the restrictions on immigration but on the other hand pledged to protect Britain's new minorities with anti-discrimination legislation. The new Labour home secretary, Frank Soskice, called it a 'package'. The first part was the restriction of 1962 – reinforced in 1968 and 1971 – and the second part was a series of anti-discrimination laws starting with the 1965 Race Relations Act.

The first part of the package was certainly delivered; although, as noted, after 1962 there was a big increase in family members (secondary immigration) and overall numbers actually rose somewhat through the 1960s and 1970s. But the restrictions did eventually start to effect numbers: in 1972 immigration from the New Commonwealth was around 70,000 and represented about three-quarters of the 93,000 total inflow – by 1992 it was down to 27,000 and represented only a bit over half of the 52,000 total.

The second part of the package was harder to achieve. Drawing on the example of the anti-discrimination initiatives of the civil rights movement in the US, the first Race Relations Act in Europe became law in July 1965. It was not a powerful piece of legislation and probably did little to change behaviour or attitudes – overt racism remained commonplace for at least another twenty years – but it was a start. The legislation strengthened the Public Order Act to include racial incitement and made discrimination an offence in places like hotels, restaurants and hospitals – though instead of criminal sanctions there would be conciliation through a Race Relations Board. In a separate piece of legislation there were also the first proposals to encourage integration, including extra funds for local authorities with large numbers of New Commonwealth immigrants and the creation of the National Committee for Commonwealth Immigration (NCCI).

So the 'race industry' was born. And one of its first jobs, encouraged by the new reforming home secretary, Roy Jenkins, was to give itself greater powers. Anthony Lester, one of Jenkins's political lieutenants, recalls his thinking at the time: 'We took US experience as a warning that racial injustice and unrest would occur if an indigenous non-white population ... were permitted to be treated as inferior. We believed that Britain was at risk of creating a black underclass unless effective measures were taken before patterns of segregation and discrimination became entrenched. That is why Roy Jenkins devoted so much political energy and skill to achieving effective civil rights legislation.' (See Jenkins discussion in Chapter 4, 'What is Multiculturalism and Where Did it Come From?')

But it was a sign of the toothlessness of the 1965 Act that it didn't even outlaw the notorious 'No blacks, no Irish, no dogs' sign in boarding houses because it did not apply to private housing. In 1968 the Act was strengthened to apply to employment, housing and education but not to the police force. And in 1976 it was strengthened again to include indirect and unintentional discrimination, and the bolder Commission for Racial Equality replaced the old Race Relations Board and Community Relations Commission.

The decade of the late 1960s to the late 1970s was perhaps the most dramatic in the history of post-war immigration. The 'young men' phase of post-colonial immigration, which was dominated by single men, here to work and return home, turned into the 'family' phase, in which minorities established roots and started to demand space and recognition – and council flats and school places – and so began to compete directly with local whites for public resources. Most large towns also began to experience the benefits of late-opening corner shops and Indian restaurants – around 2,000 by 1970.

The first great drama of this decade of upheaval was the Kenyan Asian crisis of 1968. At the end of 1967 the 'Africanisation' policies pursued by the Kenyan government were starting to make life unpleasant for the 200,000-strong Asian minority in the country. They had arrived there mainly from Gujarat in the late nineteenth and early twentieth century to help build the railways – the local Africans were regarded as insufficiently disciplined for the job by the British – and had subsequently become the dominant force in business and the civil service, occupying a space above blacks and below whites in the racial hierarchy. Believing that they had a right to settle in Britain, about 2,000 a month started to arrive here in late 1967 and early 1968. But on 22 February the home secretary, James Callaghan, announced that the Kenyan Asians would not have automatic right of entry to Britain, beyond an annual quota of 1,500. The Kenyan Asians should have been caught by the 1962 restriction, which declared that only passports issued in London, and not in colonial capitals, attracted full rights of British citizenship. But for various reasons they were not and Jim Callaghan moved to decisively close the loophole, aware of how hostile public opinion would have been to such a relatively large inflow.

Many people on the left, already dismayed by Labour's acquiescence in a Tory-led restrictionist immigration policy after 1964, were horrified by Callaghan's decision. But according to Kenneth Morgan, Callaghan's biographer, immigration for him was 'an issue to be handled in a way attuned to public opinion, rather than on the basis of abstract liberal political theory'. It may have been the last time that blue-collar, socially conservative Labour won such a decisive policy victory.

A few weeks later Enoch Powell delivered his inflammatory 'rivers of blood' speech to Conservative Party activists at Birmingham's Midland Hotel – and the extraordinarily positive reaction to it suggests that Callaghan's instinct was politically attuned. Technically Powell's speech did not do much more than spell out the reasons for the restrictive Conservative policy on immigration, but it included a highly emotional, even apocalyptic, picture of multiracial Britain. He quoted one man as saying that 'in this country in 15 or 20 years time the black man will have the whip-hand over the white man' and stated himself that 'We must be mad, literally mad, as a nation to be permitting the annual inflow of some 50,000 dependants ... It is like watching a nation busily engaged in heaping up its own funeral pyre ... As I look ahead, I am filled with foreboding. Like the Roman, I seem to see "the River Tiber foaming with much blood".'

There was also a passage in which he talked about a white woman pensioner being intimidated by the increasingly dominant black population on her street in Powell's constituency in Wolverhampton. 'Windows are broken.

She finds excreta pushed through her letterbox. When she goes out, she is followed by children, charming, wide-grinning piccaninnies. They cannot speak English, but one word they know. "Racialist," they chant.'

Clem Jones, the then editor of the *Wolverhampton Express and Star*, whose friendship with Powell was ended by the speech, says that he tried and failed for many years to track down the Wolverhampton pensioner and believes she was probably invented by Powell, albeit from amalgamating various stories he had heard or letters he had received (though others claim that she did exist). What is not in doubt is the popularity of the speech. A national opinion poll soon after it found only 15 per cent disagreeing with it and 74 per cent agreeing. The numbers were probably even higher in the west Midlands and Jones admits that the enormous mailbag he received about the speech was overwhelmingly pro-Powell.

The speech caused Powell to be sacked from the front bench by the Tory opposition leader, Edward Heath, but there was a huge upsurge of support for him. Dockers marched in his defence and 69 per cent of the public disapproved of his sacking. He was a lightning rod for mainstream anti-immigration feeling and has cast his shadow over British politics, and the immigration debate in particular, from that day in April 1968 to this.

The immediate impact of the speech was undoubtedly to make life more uncomfortable for Britain's visible minorities. There appears to have been a marked rise in overt hostility and violence in the subsequent weeks and months. This was particularly true in Powell's home town of Wolverhampton itself, which in 1968 already had a minority population of about 15,000 (out of a total population of around 150,000), about half from the Caribbean and half from India, mainly Sikhs and Hindus from the Punjab.

Many older Asians remember the speech all too well. When in December 2011 I met a group of mainly elderly Wolverhamptoners of Hindu and Sikh background, including the first Asian mayor of the town, Bishan Dass, they recalled the bad old days vividly: not being allowed to wear turbans; the battle of Queen Street against the National Front in 1971; but also how the Powell speech created a sense of unity among the town's minorities.

One beneficial consequence of Powell's speech is that Wolverhampton itself has tried harder than most towns to defy him and become an example of the British dream, with some success. One younger Labour councillor in my group said the town had been transformed for the better in his lifetime. He also remembered an underlying confidence in the decency of the average white person when his mother had said to him as a boy in the 1970s, 'If you are being chased by a skinhead, just knock on anyone's door and ask for help.'

Other younger participants in our discussion were more likely to stress the obstacles of caste than of race. And another sign that Powell's dystopian vision has not come to pass in his home town is that at the 2010 election his old seat of Wolverhampton South West was won by a Tory of East African Sikh background, Paul Uppal.

But in almost all other respects Powell and Powellism were a setback for Britain. Just when a discussion should have been starting about integration, racial justice, and distinguishing the reasonable from the racist complaints of the white people whose communities were being transformed, he polarised the argument and closed it down. He put back by more than a generation a robust debate about the successes and failures of immigration. Powell also made it far harder for liberal and centre-left Britain to start thinking about a modern, post-imperial national identity which could unite both the majority and the minorities in a new shared account of the country.

The tacit agreement between the leaders of both the main political parties not to stir the beast of public opinion became even more deeply entrenched; people were told that a few immigrants would not change anything very much and the subject of race was in effect removed from democratic politics.

Decent people avoided the issue and no vocabulary was developed to talk about it sensibly beyond whether someone was a 'racialist' or not. Why did Britain not have a white paper on minority integration policy in the 1970s, possibly even a ministry of immigration and integration, given the importance of what was happening to the country? There are many historical reasons for Britain's offhand approach to minority integration, but Enoch Powell certainly reinforced it by making it seem slightly indecent to think rationally about borders, immigration, race, integration and national identity.

If one reads the memoirs of Britain's political leaders over the next twenty years, when Britain was being transformed into a multiracial country, there is hardly a word on the subject.[1] The dominant liberal wing of the Tory party and after Roy Jenkins most of the Labour leadership too ended up subcontracting the management of minority politics to local government, the liberal professions, the young left and minority leaders themselves. At the 1981 Tory party conference, soon after the Toxteth riots in Liverpool, Michael Heseltine was still having to tell his party that black Britons were here to stay even though many of the second generation were already young adults.

It was increasingly the 'rainbow coalition' left, whose members had often come into politics to challenge Powellism or the far right, that came to lead the public debate on the issues of race and minority politics. And after Powell the default position of the left was generally to support whatever minority leaders wanted.

One should be wary of attributing too much power over events to one man. But Powell can claim to have had a significant influence on the election of Margaret Thatcher, the rise of the multiculturalist left in the 1980s and 1990s and even, indirectly, Labour's new immigration opening in 1997 – after Powell the one cause that liberals and the left could agree on was that they were against Powell and in favour of immigration and immigrants.

The Tories won the election in 1970, and another Immigration Act, the 1971 Act, was soon being drawn up which effectively ended the remaining privileges – such as the work permit scheme that operated between 1962 and 1971 – for Citizens of the United Kingdom and Colonies (the CUKC category created in 1948). The CUKCs were now treated the same way as other foreign nationals: they could come only as a family member or with a specific job offer. There was still no attempt to create a new post-imperial form of national citizenship, that was to come later in 1981, but a new category of 'patrial' continued to enjoy automatic access to British citizenship so long as a parent or grandparent had been a British citizen.

This clearly had the effect of privileging white people from the 'old Commonwealth' of Canada, Australia and New Zealand and was attacked as racist for that reason, though most forms of national citizenship around the world allow for some ancestry connection even if they are otherwise largely

---

1. I owe this observation to Randall Hansen.

based on place of birth and colour-blind, as is the case with British citizen-ship. (Moreover, the argument that a citizen of India should be treated in the same way as a citizen of Canada or Australia with a British mother or grand-father is implicitly based on the surely reactionary idea of the colonial family. In any case the family had clearly broken up by now and consisted mainly of independent states which did not swear allegiance to the Crown, so why should their citizens enjoy the full rights of British citizens?)

Powell and Powellism probably helped to push both political parties in a somewhat more restrictionist direction on immigration. But as one door closed, another opened. For Edward Heath's dream of taking Britain into Europe – the European Economic Community as it then was – was finally made reality in 1973, giving EEC nationals the right to live and work in Britain just as Britain was making it harder for people from the former colonies. But just before that fateful step was taken, Ted Heath had to handle another East African Asian crisis, this time in Uganda.

As with the Kenyan Asians a few years before, the Asians of Uganda were threatened by a policy of 'Africanisation', in this case from the new populist leader of Uganda, Idi Amin. In August 1972 Amin announced without warning that all 73,000 of them had to leave within three months. A few days later the British government said it would accept full responsibility for all those, about 50,000, who had British passports.

Coming just a few years after the Powell outburst and the intense hostil-ity to immigration among many rank-and-file Conservatives, it was a brave and liberal decision by the Tory cabinet.[1] The far right National Front organ-ised a series of protests against the decision, the most famous being by the Smithfield porters in London, who marched on the Home Office chanting, 'Enoch is right,' and the Tory leadership faced some pressure from the right at its party conference in October. Heath's action has been compared favourably to Jim Callaghan's decision to block most of the Kenyan Asians. But to be fair to Callaghan, there were about four times more Kenyan Asians and they were not facing such an immediate threat as the Ugandans. (Most Kenyan Asians who wanted to come to Britain did eventually get here.)

1. In 1969, 327 out of 412 Conservative constituency associations wanted all 'coloured immi-gration' stopped indefinitely.

After successfully appealing to other countries to accept some of the flee-
ing Ugandan Asians, Britain in the end gave sanctuary to about 28,000. Many
of them found a home in Leicester, despite the government's attempt to disperse them around the country and the city council taking out advertisements
in the Ugandan Asian press saying that Leicester was 'full'. Forty years on,
the East African Asians, mainly entrepreneurial Hindus or Muslims originally
from Gujarat, or well-educated Sikhs, have proved (at least in financial terms)
the most successful non-European minority group in post-war Britain and
have also helped to make Leicester the relative success story that it is (see
Chapter 2, 'Thinking about Integration and Segregation').

In 1974 Labour returned to power but (again) did not attempt to reverse
the Tory immigration legislation. Roy Jenkins returned, briefly, to the Home
Office, but aside from raising the Kenyan Asian quota to 5,000 a year and
producing a new race relations act in 1976 his impact was small, certainly far
less than in his reforming heyday in the 1960s.

New Commonwealth immigration was running at roughly 50,000 a year
through the 1970s, on the way down to roughly half that through the 1980s,
and the total ethnic minority population was about 1.5 million by 1980.[1] By
today's standards the numbers seem small but for the white population in the
centres of settlement like parts of London, Birmingham, Wolverhampton,
Leicester, Bradford and Leeds it had often been life-changing.

Immigrants arriving in the 1950s, 60s and 70s had little or no access to
the most desirable public housing: the philanthropic housing associations,
the pre-war council estates built on the periphery of many big cities, the new
post-war estates, and, indeed, the new *towns* that began to spring up in the
1960s. But that gradually began to change in the mid-1970s.

Public housing became an emblematic issue in some areas as minorities
demanded their social entitlements, increasing the white sense of competition. A national NOP poll found in 1978 that 85 per cent of the population
thought there were too many immigrants in Britain.

In Tower Hamlets in east London in the late 1970s, the rapidly expanding Bangladeshi population gradually battled its way into the GLC-owned

---

1. Alongside the main post-colonial groups were smaller inflows from Hong Kong, Sri Lanka,
Cyprus and Malta; the Maltese attracted attention with their Soho gang wars.

public housing estates that were in some cases half empty. Similarly, African Caribbeans and Africans started to move into the hard-to-let estates in south London and elsewhere. By the early 1990s about half of the African Caribbean and Bangladeshi populations were living in council housing. Legal reforms – in the 1976 Race Relations Act and the 1977 Homeless Persons Act – helped to break open public housing by effectively abolishing the 'sons and daughters' informal inheritance rights and making housing 'need' the main criterion for housing allocation. This led to privileging those with the biggest families, the worst health and the poorest housing conditions, which often meant recent immigrants. At the same time it became relatively harder for an affluent working-class couple to qualify for a new let. The better-off white working class was in any case often moving out to private housing estates – in the case of Londoners to Essex and Kent – but they often did so feeling they had been driven out by the newcomers.

Right-wing extremism often plays too large a part in accounts of post-war immigration, especially in that decade after 1968. Powellism was a far more significant pressure on politicians than the far right, and the great bulk of British people, though sceptical about mass immigration and anxious about race, never considered voting for a far-right party. And according to the Eurobarometer opinion surveys, from the 1970s to the turn of the century Britain was squarely in the European middle on attitudes to race and immigration.

Those marches, flags and set-piece battles between far right and left (the latter organised under the umbrella body the Anti-Nazi League, established in 1977) provide a vivid backdrop to the decade for television documentary makers – as the riots do for the 1980s – but they probably involved no more than 100,000 activists on both sides. The biggest conflicts were mainly in London: Lewisham 1977, Brick Lane 1978 and Southall 1979 (where the teacher Blair Peach died after being struck by a policeman).

Mike Phillips in *Windrush* sees the battle in Lewisham as a particular turning point: 'Whites fought whites viciously in defence of blacks. Families split, and the racists who had ruled the street corners only a decade previously were challenged and harassed everywhere they appeared. Britain was still riddled with racist values, but it was now obvious that the migrants no longer existed on the margins. Instead, black people had become part of the moral and social landscape in which young Britons grew up.'

Young black British style, mainly Jamaican, was admired on the streets and in the clubs by young whites – ska, soul, reggae, Rastafarianism. Caribbeans like Lenny Henry and Jazzy B started to break through into mainstream popular culture. The Notting Hill carnival became a national event, though it was often marred by violence, most notably in 1976. Trevor Phillips became the first black president of the National Union of Students in 1978. Black was still trouble but, also, beautiful.

The National Front had briefly fizzled into life in the 1970s, mainly in areas of high immigration or nearby. But with its Hitler-loving leaders, who were always falling out with each other, it was never going to be more than a street rabble. The NF was feared, and perhaps admired too, far beyond its peak of 15,000 members. But it never came close to an election breakthrough and never won a single council seat. The NF's best national election result was 16 per cent in a West Bromwich by-election in 1976.

Britain was saved from more powerful extremist voices partly by the electoral system but also by the arrival of Margaret Thatcher. A liberal consensus has usually united the two main parties on race and immigration from the mid-1960s to the present, but from time to time it has become a 'wedge' issue between them, and it became one briefly in the run-up to the 1979 election. In a famous *World in Action* interview in January 1978 Thatcher, then opposition leader, said that immigration was too high and that 'the British people were rather afraid that this country might be rather swamped by people with a different culture … we do have to hold out the prospect of an end to immigration, except, of course, for compassionate cases'.

The Thatcher governments are now, of course, associated with the free market modernisation of Britain, breaking the power of the unions and a big increase in inequality. It is often forgotten that Mrs Thatcher herself had at least been a fellow traveller of the Powellite right of the party and may have won the 1979 election with the help of some Powellite themes. When elected she was true to her word on immigration, though she rarely spoke about the subject. The number of work permits was cut further (they averaged 10,000 to 20,000 a year from 1973 to 1989), and even the automatic right to bring in a foreign spouse was curtailed by the 'primary purpose rule', in which the husband or wife to be (mainly from South Asia) had to prove that the main purpose of the marriage was not to gain access to Britain.

Randall Hansen puts it thus: 'Like many people, Margaret Thatcher had only good to say about actual immigrants, and nothing good to say about immigration.'[1] Mrs Thatcher's own views on immigration, as spelt out in her memoirs, are rather eloquent:

> It was part of my credo that individuals were worthy of respect as individuals, not as members of classes or races ... I felt no sympathy for rabble rousers, like the National Front, who sought to exploit race ... at the same time, large scale New Commonwealth immigration over the years had transformed large areas of Britain in a way which the indigenous population found hard to accept. It is one thing for a well-heeled politician to preach the merits of tolerance on a public platform before returning to a comfortable home in a tranquil road in one of the more respectable suburbs, where house prices ensure him the exclusiveness of apartheid without the stigma. It is quite another for poorer people, who cannot afford to move, to watch their neighbourhoods changing and the value of their house falling. Those in such a situation need to be reassured rather than patronised ... The failure to articulate the sentiments of ordinary people ... had left the way open to the extremists.[2]

She is right. Being tolerant about post-colonial immigration was an abstract thing for most of upper- and middle-class Britain. For parts of working-class Britain there was real change and real people to accommodate. And after some grumbling they were accommodated, and in some cases even embraced.

Finally, two years into the first Thatcher government, Britain repealed the Nationality Act of 1948 and joined the modern world by defining citizenship to the exclusion of its former colonies. The 1981 British Nationality Act formally ended the absurdity of offering British nationality to a large minority of the world's population, in theory if no longer in practice, and decoupled

1. *Citizenship and Immigration in Post-War Britain*, p. 210.
2. *Margaret Thatcher: The Path to Power*, HarperCollins, 1995, pp. 405–6.

nationality law from immigration. Anyone born in the UK is now automatically a citizen if one of their parents is a citizen or a permanent resident – a combination of jus soli and jus sanguinis, citizenship based on 'soil', where you are born, and citizenship based on descent or 'blood'. Some people complained about the abandonment of a pure 'jus soli' rule but Britain's citizenship regime remains one of the most liberal in the world, more liberal than France's for example, and a passport is relatively easy to acquire if you don't get it automatically – candidates apply for permanent residence after five years of living here (and for citizenship a year later). And it is easy to combine with other citizenships too; Britain has never had a difficulty with dual or multiple citizenships.

As the 1970s gave way to the 1980s, immigration gave way to race relations. The story was no longer about who should be allowed into the country and in what numbers, but how they should be treated when they were here.

First-generation immigrants, especially from the Indian subcontinent, did not usually expect immediate equality. It was not in any case a realistic prospect for an illiterate peasant farmer from Kashmir or Sylhet. As Sher Azam, of the Bradford Council of Mosques, puts it: 'When you are a guest, expectations are lower. But when you are born here and you are a citizen, then expectations rise. But just as this was happening in the 1970s and 1980s the mills started closing, and then we started getting conflict.'

But in the early 1980s it was still the African Caribbean community that was writing the main script for minority Britain, although by this time it had lost its numerical supremacy to British Indians (about half Hindus, one third Sikh and 15 per cent Muslim) and Pakistanis too. The hard time that Britain had given to these most integration-willing Caribbean migrants rebounded in an often angry and troubled second generation – too many were discarded by the education system or harassed by the police, and they rioted their way into the public consciousness.

The roll-call of the early 1980s riots and disturbances is the roll-call of African Caribbean areas of settlement. St Paul's in Bristol in 1980. Brixton, Toxteth, Moss Side, Chapeltown, Handsworth in 1981. Broadwater Farm (Tottenham), Brixton, Handsworth in 1985.

The riots were mainly against the police. Young blacks felt they were being victimised by the police or were not being sufficiently protected from racists. The extensive use of the 'sus' laws, which allowed police officers to arrest people without any evidence of wrongdoing, and the brutality of units like the Special Patrol Group, were among the triggers. The Brixton riot was preceded by 'Operation Swamp', in which 120 plain-clothes and uniformed officers stopped nearly 1,000 people over a four-day period.

Another preface to the wave of riots was the New Cross fire in January 1981 in south London, in which thirteen young blacks were killed by a fire that swept through a party in a crowded flat. It was widely believed that it had been a racist arson attack, though no evidence for that was ever found. But what really prompted the biggest wave of organised political protest yet by black Britain was the belief that white Britain simply didn't care. A few weeks after the New Cross fire a similar fire at a disco in Dublin provoked a wave of grief and messages of condolence from the Queen and the Prime Minister. There was not a word for the grieving families of the New Cross thirteen.

Various local and national black organisations including the Black Parents' Movement and the journal *Race Today* (edited by the leading radical Darcus Howe) came together to organise a march and demonstration in London in early March. It was reported as a riot by some sections of the press, but it had succeeded in giving expression to a sense of injustice and increased the political confidence of black Britain.

The police justified the tough stance they took towards black youth by pointing to levels of drug use and criminality that could not be ignored. A vicious circle was established on the streets of black Britain – which remains in weaker form to this day: brusque and sometimes racist policing created disaffection and criminality which justified the continuing vindictiveness of the policing.

In the zealotry of the police to prevent criminal 'no go' areas, the evidence for police racism was overwhelming, and shocked even conservative, law-abiding Caribbean parents. One would expect the police to reflect public opinion as a whole, but researchers in the 1980s found far higher levels of racism and more negative stereotypes of black people than in the population as a whole.

After the Scarman report on the Brixton riots, money was invested and police practice and attitudes gradually changed. Most significant of all was the Police and Criminal Evidence Act, which placed behaviour inside police stations under greater formal scrutiny, including the tape-recording of suspect interviews, which made it harder for police officers to beat confessions out of people.

The two other big stories of the 1980s were the rise of a more activist multiculturalism (which spilled over in some communities into separatism, see Chapter 4, 'How Multiculturalism Changed its Spots') and the emergence of South Asian Britain into the spotlight. And the two stories are strongly connected.

By the end of the 1980s the minority population had risen to about 3 million, or 6 per cent of the population – with a big jump in the numbers born in Britain and numerical supremacy now claimed by South Asians.[1] Around half of the minority population lived in London and most of the rest in the west Midlands, the former mill towns of Yorkshire and Lancashire, and other towns including Leicester, Bristol, Manchester, Leeds, Nottingham, Slough and Luton.

The pioneer groups of the 1950s and 1960s – African Caribbeans, Indians and Kashmiri Pakistanis – had been joined in the 1970s and 1980s by others: black Africans; Bangladeshis mainly from the Sylhet region, who started coming in quite large numbers after their war for independence from Pakistan in 1971; more Greek and Turkish Cypriots arrived after their civil war of 1974, there were also Turks from Turkey itself and all three groups settled overwhelmingly in north London.

Minority political activism was now supported in London and elsewhere by a new young white left who were pushing aside what they saw as the reactionary old white working-class trade unionists in local councils and in Parliament, many of whom had in any case fallen with the Jim Callaghan government in 1979.

Paul Boateng, who went on to become part of the first intake of black MPs in 1987, recalls lying in bed in 1979 and turning on the radio to hear

1. In 1988, the Commission for Racial Equality decided to stop using the term 'black' to refer to all non-white minorities.

Bob Mellish, an old-school Labour trade unionist MP, saying (in Boateng's words) to black people who were complaining about housing conditions in Southwark, 'Don't push your luck.'

For young leftist lawyers like Boateng and his white allies the equal rights policies of the 1960s and 1970s were failing. The 'soft' celebration of difference – steel bands, saris and samosas – was not enough. What was required, some people argued, was the positive promotion, and funding, of separate minority identities. Encouraging autonomous organisation would increase minority confidence – instead of a women's centre, a Sikh women's centre, an African women's centre, a Muslim women's centre and so on.

The new identity politics worked up to a point and certainly helped to create a more confident minority elite. But it weakened the integrationist pulse, especially coming at a time when rising numbers and satellite dishes were making it easier for some minorities to live increasingly apart from mainstream society. Some minorities became more like diasporas: Kashmiri-Pakistanis and Bangladeshis in particular would often return 'home' for a few months every two or three years; this had been unthinkable in the 1950s and 1960s, when families often couldn't afford to return home for important marriages or funerals.

At a time when national politicians should have been leaning against the drift towards more segregated communities, for the most part they had nothing to say at all. The Conservative government had other priorities and the legacy of Powell discouraged intervention if it could be avoided. And Tories did not, on the whole, know about or understand what was going on in minority enclaves because they did not represent the industrial and inner-city constituencies where most minority Britons lived.

The intriguing argument of both Geoff Dench and Trevor Phillips is that white radicals, and the growing meritocratic elite that was beginning to dominate the higher levels of the expanding public sector, needed a new victim class to sponsor and represent, and they found it in minority Britain. It also gave liberal Britain a new post-imperial cause – to prove to the world that it could produce a successful multiracial society.

'With the decline of socialism and the old working class, radicals needed a new rallying cry and they found it in race ... and in the first half of the 1980s the left sort of outsourced its anger to ethnic minorities. I was symbolic of that too, I became president of the National Union of Students in 1978 and the fact that I am black played a big part in it,' Phillips said to me for a BBC radio Analysis programme on black politics.[1]

Meanwhile, South Asian Britain was now starting to eclipse black Britain not only numerically but also in terms of political attention. From the 1950s to the mid-1980s, with the partial exception of the East African Asian crises, Asians had kept a lower political profile than African Caribbeans. And, of course, there was no such thing as a single 'Asian' community, although until well into the 1990s most people of South Asian background – Indian, Pakistani, Bangladeshi, Sri Lankan – were lumped together in this way.

Through the 1960s, 1970s and into the 1980s all South Asian communities shared certain things in common: they tended to be more religious and family-oriented than the white majority (and to have larger families), but they were also marked by national and caste divisions. Indians were doing better than Pakistanis both in education and employment, although one thing they increasingly shared was home ownership.

The Asian political identity in the 1960s and 1970s had been – along with black Britain – a largely secular, political one, about combating racism and equal rights, typified by the Indian Workers' Association, founded in Southall in 1957, or later by the Southall Black Sisters, founded in 1979, or the Asian Youth Movement in Bradford in 1978. One struggle that combined the equal rights of the 1970s with the identity politics of the 1980s was the successful Sikh legal battle in 1976 to be allowed to wear turbans on motorcycles, and later on building sites.

Into the 1980s paths began to diverge and the Asian 'bloc' began to dissolve into its constituent parts as numbers rose, Britain became more accommodating, and multiculturalism encouraged the promotion of separate Asian identities. In 1983 Sikhs were legally classified as an ethnic group (unlike Hindus and Muslims). There was also some conflict between different South Asian groups, sometimes driven by politics back in India. The militant Sikh struggle for more self-governance within India, the crisis at the Golden

1. *A New Black Politics?*, BBC Radio 4, first broadcast 31 October 2011.

Temple at Amritsar in 1984 and the subsequent murder of Indira Gandhi by her Sikh bodyguards led to a small new wave of Sikh immigration to Britain to escape retribution.

But the biggest shift of all within the Asian community was the emergence, especially at the end of the 1980s, of a more demanding and political Muslim identity. Some Muslims from India, from East Africa and from urban Pakistan had been progressing with some success in British society. But, as we have seen, more than two-thirds of British Muslims had arrived from rural, traditional communities in the subcontinent – the Kashmiris from northern Pakistan and the Sylhetis from Bangladesh – and were doing far less well than other South Asians. And it was mainly from Kashmiri Britain that a conservative Muslim sensibility forced itself on to the public stage in the late 1980s in the Salman Rushdie affair.

The Rushdie affair did not come out of nowhere. The dominant minority in Bradford, the Kashmiris, had entered politics tentatively in the 1970s and early 1980s, requesting that Muslim majority schools adopt more Islamic ways, an end to school bussing and the provision of halal meat in schools. In 1981, the local authority established the Bradford Council of Mosques, which gave a louder voice to the Muslim minority. There were some stirrings connected to the Muslim revival triggered by the 1979 Iranian revolution, but there were, as yet, few signs of political Islam.

With the benefit of hindsight, however, it seems neglectful that national governments took so little interest in this growing sub-culture. There was no attempt to control the importing of imams from Pakistan, or to prevent the Saudis from funding many of the new mosques that began to spring up in Muslim areas, or indeed to offer English lessons for the women at home.

Muslims lived mainly in Labour areas, so became the beneficiaries of the politics of identity and recognition promoted by the young new left. Their introversion and piety was endorsed and supported despite the patriarchal and often illiberal behaviour of community leaders. Mothers rarely worked, and seldom spoke English. Men were often unemployed too, after the rounds of factory closures in the 1980s and 1990s and the only slow opening of public sector jobs to South Asians, which gave the mosque an even greater social focus. There was no sizeable middle class or role model for success in a

British society which, with its growing secularism and assumption of female equality, often seemed at odds with their own ways. And many South Asian Muslim families were tense generational battlegrounds between British-raised children caught between love or fear of their parents on the one hand and the pull of western freedoms and wanting to fit in with white friends on the other (well described in Zaiba Malik's memoir of growing up in Bradford, *We Are a Muslim, Please*).

This was the context for the Rushdie affair of the late 1980s. Salman Rushdie's book *The Satanic Verses*, with its unflattering portrayal of the Prophet Mohammed, was published in September 1988. At first it was not noticed. But then various conservative Islamic organisations in northern England saw an opportunity to register a public complaint about the attack on Muslim sensibilities. The first protest was organised by Deobandi religious groups in Bolton, and attracted about 7,000 people. But Bradford soon became the centre of the anti-Rushdie cause. The protesters say they tried letters, marches, petitions, but no one took any notice until they were advised to burn copies of the book, and Britain's media (soon followed by the world's) suddenly sat up and took note. In February 1989 came the Fatwah from Iran calling for Rushdie's death and the dispute escalated.

The Rushdie affair revealed the extent of separateness that had grown up in some of Britain's biggest cities and also contributed to a further deepening of it. There was a sense of bewilderment on both sides. Millions of Britons watching the Rushdie dispute on the television news must have wondered why these men with flowing beards and robes were so agitated about something written in a novel. On the other side of the divide were those Kashmiri 'moles' who had arrived thirty years before to work in the mills. After that first period of mixing when they were here on their own they had, in many cases, turned inward and lived a quiet life centred on family, clan and mosque. Now they came blinking into the political limelight for the first time to demand that someone in authority acknowledge their pain. Were they not citizens too? Did the blasphemy laws not offer protection to Christian feelings? Did their feelings not matter?

This did not happen spontaneously. It happened because the leaders of Britain's half a million Muslims organised it to help restore what they feared was their dwindling authority, particularly over the next generation of British-born children. And the more separatist multiculturalism of the early 1980s helped to boost the confidence of a Muslim leadership that had lacked the education and cultural know-how to make its presence felt in local or national politics. Now they were playing on a national stage and establishing themselves as a distinct minority force with demands and grievances.

Although Kashmiris were the biggest single group in Muslim Britain, there were others too: urban Pakistanis from Rawalpindi, Lahore and elsewhere, Indian Muslims from East Africa (often originally from Gujarat). The non-Kashmiris tended to be better educated and more middle-class and often provided the Muslim leadership even in towns where Kashmiris were numerically dominant. But increasingly a Muslim identity came to shade out ethnic and national origin identities.

Between 1981 and the end of the 1990s it was the birth rate that was the most important source of growth for Britain's minorities. But the last big, late-arrival group of the post-colonial period was the Bangladeshis, who like the Kashmiris were mainly Muslims from conservative, rural roots. The main centre of Bangladeshi settlement was London, and especially Tower Hamlets in east London – numbers there grew from only about 3,000 in 1971 to nearly 70,000 by 2001 (overall numbers grew from 22,000 to nearly 300,000 over that period). There were other significant centres of settlement too, in Birmingham, Oldham, Luton and Bradford, and there are small Bangladeshi communities all over the country thanks to their domination of the 'Indian' restaurant business.

How come so many Bangladeshis were able to enter Britain after primary immigration had ceased? For generations there had been small communities of 'lascar' sailors, who served on the East India shipping lines and then in the merchant navy, living unobtrusively in port cities, particularly London, though some Bangladeshis also went north to work in textile mills.

It is often said that the population expanded swiftly in the early 1970s because of a severe cyclone in 1970 and then the civil war that led to the creation of Bangladesh out of East Pakistan in 1971. The civil war may have had some effect on numbers, but the cyclone did not affect Sylhet, the main source area for British Bangladeshis. In fact there had been a big inflow of young men in the late 1960s, through a chain migration system based on job offers from friends or relatives in the textile and restaurant businesses. That then led to a wave of family reunion in the early and mid-1970s as the men brought in wives and children.

By the beginning of the 1990s Muslims had begun to dominate the story of minority politics – but they still represented rather less than one third of the total minority population in Britain, much less than in most of continental Europe where Muslims were (and are) usually in the majority.

More overt piety, partly inspired by the Muslim example, also rubbed off on other groups. Hindus and Sikhs had in the 1980s begun to define themselves in more religious terms. There were more Sikh religious processions than political ones through the streets of Southall as the 1980s progressed. Hindu revivalism was on the rise in India and this inevitably spread to Britain. Both Hindus and Sikhs came to resent the extra noisiness of Muslim Britain and its supposed political influence after the Rushdie affair, and the more conservative religious forces in both groups also tried to mimic and exploit the Rushdie effect.

But the relative success in British society of Hindus and Sikhs also placed strict limits on radicalism. The children of the first generation were generally doing well at school and starting to rise into the middle class. There were still conflicts over discrimination, but the distinct cultural practices of Hindus and Sikhs only rarely clashed with mainstream Britain, and even then in rather technical or exotic matters such as open-air cremations for Hindus or carrying swords on special occasions for Sikhs. And, unlike most Muslim families, Hindu and Sikh women generally worked, helping both with household income and with integration.

South Asian 'melas' or festivals became an established part of the calendar in many towns with high Asian settlement, and Asian youth culture and Punjabi-origin Bhangra music started in the 1990s to rival black culture for coolness.[1] The lack of an alcohol prohibition for Sikhs or Hindus meant mingling with white friends in pubs and clubs was easier than for Muslims.

1. Hounslow and Southall were, and are, at the heart of British Indian popular culture. Channi Singh, the 'Godfather of Bhangra', comes from Hounslow and the comedy show *Goodness Gracious Me* has its roots there too.

Black Britons were also finding a more comfortable place. After the trauma of rejection and the street battles and conflicts of earlier decades, Caribbeans of the second and third generations had become a familiar, and accepted, sub-culture – often compared with the Irish in the first half of the twentieth century. Caribbean performance in education and the job market was still poor, and the community was marked by a very high rate of fatherless families and high crime and imprisonment rates, but Caribbeans gradually came to be seen as part of the 'us', another tribe of modern Britain.

With the eras of avoidance and conflict at least partly behind it, Britain was entering the era of minority accommodation. Two generations of familiarity with the minority presence, plus the effect of laws and political activism – both of the liberal establishment and the more aggressive leftist and anti-racist movements – had decisively changed Britain. Minorities had become increasingly visible throughout the national culture as writers, musicians, newsreaders, politicians, actors. Television dramas such as *Love Thy Neighbour*, with stereotypical minority characters, had been replaced with more truthful portrayals, and films such as *Bend it like Beckham* celebrated the mingling of South Asian and British life.

The behaviour of football crowds was one very public measure of the change. As recently as the early 1990s racist chanting, making monkey noises at black opposition players and even throwing bananas on to the pitch was relatively common. By the end of the 1990s such behaviour had largely disappeared, thanks to organisations like Kick Racism Out of Football and a much tougher line taken by the football authorities – but mainly just through a change in what was socially acceptable. Not coincidentally, by 1997 around 15 per cent of all professional footballers were black.[1]

There was a small breakthrough in minority political representation when in the 1987 election three black MPs were elected to Parliament, all for London seats – two of Caribbean background, Diane Abbott in Hackney and

---

1. An emblematic moment of mutual acceptance came at a warm-up England game in Morocco for the 1998 World Cup. When the recording of the national anthem music could not be found three of England's black players – Ian Wright, captain Paul Ince and Sol Campbell – led the rest of the team, and the travelling supporters, in a hearty unaccompanied rendition of the anthem for which they were hailed as national heroes in *The Sun* newspaper.

Bernie Grant in Tottenham, and one of mixed-race Ghanaian background, Paul Boateng in Brent. By the early 1990s there were also about 500 minority councillors, mainly Labour.

Another symbol of this period of accommodation was John Major's elevation to prime minister in 1990. Margaret Thatcher's world-view was formed before post-war immigration had begun to change Britain, and she remained provincial and Powellite in many of her instincts, but John Major had been marked in a very different way by immigration as a young man growing up in Brixton. His experiences as a councillor in Lambeth turned him into a liberal Tory on racial equality issues and prefigured the more self-conscious Tory liberalisation under David Cameron.

So, in the period just prior to the second great wave of post-war immigration, which began with Labour's election in 1997, there was a sense of the culmination of a journey. Net immigration was more or less flat, even the gross annual inflows were only around 50,000, and in 1995 the total minority population stood at about 4 million or about 7 per cent of the British population. Of course that proportion was very much higher in the main centres of immigrant settlement, where there often remained a sense of displacement on the part of white working-class communities. But overall there was a feeling that after a period of sometimes painful adjustment in the 1960s and 1970s the Powellite heresy had been vanquished and a modus vivendi was being reached. Official and liberal Britain was beginning to think that the country had, indeed, set the world an example not only in the manner of shedding an empire but also in absorbing some of that empire back home.

It is true that minority Britain often faced various obstacles not faced by white people, but the more successful minorities – Indian Hindus and Sikhs, Chinese and some black Africans – had bypassed those obstacles with relative ease. There were the two conservative Muslim communities, the northern and Midland Pakistanis and the mainly east London Bangladeshis, who lived more apart seemingly by choice. Meanwhile most second- and third-generation minority Britons were establishing hybrid identities and often being absorbed by – and even dominating – the powerful currents of a generic, western youth culture. At the same time many minority Britons, not just Muslims, continued to eschew the godless individualism of modern Britain in favour of stronger family ties and religious beliefs, as the giant Hindu temple in Neasden or the mega-black churches in Walthamstow – and their equivalents all around the country – bore witness.

So, as the first great wave of post-colonial immigration drew to a close in the 1990s, Britain had established neither a theory nor a practice of integration, nor had it written a new post-imperial national narrative. But laissez-faire multiculturalism seemed to work in a patch-and-mend sort of way. It appealed to both a stand-offish and a 'live and let live' aspect of the British spirit – Geoffrey Gorer's 'distant cordiality' – while at the same time conforming to a liberal idea that in some vague sense all cultures were equal and that minorities could both remain true to their own traditions and fit into Britain's.

CHAPTER 4

The Multicultural Odyssey

Sabeen and Yasmin

Sabeen is a charming and successful young woman whose family came to Britain from Sylhet in Bangladesh when she was seven years old in 1982. Her father had already been in Britain for a few years, working for a cousin in a small textile factory. The family lived in Tower Hamlets, where Sabeen attended local schools. Against expectations she got to Oxford and is now a highly paid legal professional. She is proud of her Bangladeshi background, speaks Sylheti with her parents and wears traditional dress on special occasions – though she is only a semi-observant Muslim and does not wear a hijab. She is also thoroughly immersed in the life and language and culture of her adopted country, and the majority of her friends are white. A multicultural model, one might say.

Sabeen has a sister called Yasmin, who is seven years younger and started school at the other end of the 1980s. A lot had changed in that short time. When Sabeen attended school there were plenty of other Bangladeshi girls but they were not quite the majority. By the time Yasmin was at school, the Bangladeshi population of her part of Tower Hamlets had reached a critical mass which allowed for almost complete self-sufficiency in cultural life and education and employment. The 'separating out' which often seems to happen at a certain point – even in places where it is not the strong preference of either the majority or the minority populations – had reached the schools of Tower Hamlets by the late 1980s, and Yasmin attended schools where almost everyone was Bangladeshi. Yasmin has also had a successful career – she is a financial controller working for Tower Hamlets council – but almost all of her life has been spent within the boundaries of her culture and, indeed, her borough – she admits to not knowing the mainstream culture of Britain very well and has not a single close friend who is white. She is a devout Muslim and always wears a hijab. Yasmin is a consequence of another strand of multiculturalism.[1]

Why has Tower Hamlets turned out in the way it has? One of the characteristics of the Bangladeshi arrival, described briefly in the previous chapter, was how swiftly it happened. The Bangladeshi population of east London rose from two or three thousand in the late 1960s to over 30,000 in the course of the 1970s.

Whole communities established themselves very quickly, with families from certain districts of Sylhet migrating to particular neighbourhoods in Tower Hamlets, recreating their kin networks and establishing their own shops, cafés and mosques. To this day Bengali councillors, even those born in Britain, often identify themselves as being from a particular village in Sylhet.

The arrival of a whole community almost en bloc inevitably had a disruptive effect on the white working class of the East End. Until this point they had felt unthreatened by the single Bengali men, who generally kept themselves to themselves. The attitude now changed and a minority of whites took the law into their own hands to, as they saw it, defend their communities from an unwanted, and unexplained, encroachment. The disappearance of the inner London docks over this period – the symbol of East End labour – made matters worse; decline began in the 1950s and the last yard closed in 1981.

The twenty years, from the mid-1970s to the late 1990s, saw some of the worst racial violence of the whole post-war period – the British nightmare. Some of this was organised from outside by the far right, but most of it came from local people. In 1978 a twenty-five-year-old clothing worker called Altab Ali (who now has a park named after him) was murdered in a racial attack,

---

1. Sabeen and Yasmin are real enough but do not exist; they are patched together from several people who do exist.

and later in the same year the 'battle of Brick Lane' saw one of the biggest far right v. anti-racist confrontations of the era.

In alliance with parts of the white left, the Bangladeshis learnt how to organise and fight back. They also joined the squatting movement, centred in Spitalfields, led by a celebrated radical called Terry Fitzpatrick. Most Bangladeshi families were living in poor private accommodation and were still excluded from public housing by 'sons and daughters' policies that favoured long-standing residents. One of the squatting organisers was Helal Abbas, who later became Labour's first Bangladeshi councillor and then council leader.

The Bangladeshis were not without friends in white Britain. Parts of the local Labour Party, particularly the younger activists, took up their cause. And national legislation, notably the 1977 Homeless Persons Act, gave priority to need in public housing rather than length of residence. Starting in Spitalfields, a growing number of council estates gradually became Bangladeshi-dominated.

The language of British Bangladeshi politics was largely secular in the first couple of decades, reflecting the domination of the leftist Awami League in Bangladesh itself. Despite that, there was little common life being forged in the East End across the ethnic divide, with the exception of the Labour Party itself and parts of youth culture. Most Bangladeshi adults did not speak English well, especially the women, and the men were usually employed by other Bangladeshis in restaurants or sweatshops so did not generally mix with white people at work. Marriages or relationships between whites and Bangladeshis were, and remain, rare.

Younger people did mix in schools and colleges, at least before the schools became almost completely mono-ethnic, but there was often wariness in the playground too. And the racial conflict served to reinforce the institutional separateness of Bengali life and therefore the power of conservative elders, who were happy enough to have only minimal contact with a host culture many considered godless and corrupt.[1]

1. This is how one successful, professional British Bangladeshi woman described her Tower Hamlets school years in the 1980s: 'I didn't have white friends when I was growing up, the white girls were not interested, we were too different. I wouldn't say that's racism, it's just

That habit of separate organisation – even in youth clubs and football leagues – persisted after Tower Hamlets had, by the mid- to late 1990s, become generally safe for Bangladeshis. But there was now another reason for separation: bit by bit through the late 1980s and into the 1990s the power of an Islamic identity, and increasingly a political Islamic identity, became more manifest – particularly among younger Bangladeshis born in Britain. (Nationally, Bangladeshi numbers rose to about 200,000 at the end of the 1980s to today's figure of around 400,000.)

There was no significant attempt on the part of local or national politicians to challenge any of this or offer an alternative. Indeed all three parties locally were complicit through the 1980s and 1990s (and to this day) in fitting their candidates to match the racial profile of an area. And there was a sort of polite apartheid in housing, with the west of the borough increasingly Bangladeshi while the east remained white and mainly hostile to the new settlement. And once the lines were drawn they became self-reinforcing, so that any attempt to create more mixed housing in the east often ended with Bangladeshi families being driven back out.

The Liberal Democrats briefly won power on Tower Hamlets council in the late 1980s and early 1990s by giving voice to white grievances. Labour meanwhile was split between an old right which also sympathised with those white grievances and a younger left which wanted to engage with the Bangladeshis, especially after the election of a BNP candidate, Derek Beackon, on the Isle of Dogs in 1993. Labour hegemony was re-established under Michael Keith in the mid-1990s partly by striking deals with the Bangladeshi community, in effect trading generous regeneration funding and Bangladeshi-centric policies for their votes. This was the time of lucrative dockland redevelopment schemes, which the local authority got its share of. (It also marked the arrival of 'Yuppies', middle-class professionals who often worked in the City and renovated some of the eighteenth- and nineteenth-century housing stock.)

Bangladeshis were increasingly addressed and dealt with – colonial style – through their ethno-religious leaders, and the major mosques in the borough

how kids are; anything not familiar is strange and hostile. Integration for me seemed to be easier with middle-class households than working-class ones. By the time I went to FE college I had lots of white friends but they tended to be middle class.'

became ever more central to politics (and even, more recently, in the delivery of some public welfare functions). In the last decade this religious/communalist politics has led to the triumph of political Islam in Tower Hamlets.

It is probably best understood as a three-generation model: a first generation still very focused on life back home; a second generation who mainly came here as young children who were politicised through the secular left and the racism battles; and a third generation politicised by 9/11 and Iraq, who gravitate towards Islamist politics.

A stroll through Whitechapel market, often used as an emblem of multicultural Britain, reveals far more women wearing full Arab burkas or hijabs than a decade ago. More, in fact, according to Bengalis, than in Bangladesh itself. The same is true of Roman Road in Bow, the cultural heart of jellied eels, cockney London until a few years ago.

The young women at the Queen Mary University campus, in their designer headscarves, will tell you that their outfits represent a new feminism among Muslim women. That may be so, but what they also represent is the influence of the East London Mosque in Whitechapel, a mosque linked, through the Islamic Forum of Europe, to the radical Jamaat e Islami movement, which strives for an Islamic republic in Bangladesh.

The rise of the East London Mosque is itself the result of the defeat of the Awami League in 2001 by the more Islamic Bangladesh Nationalist Party (in alliance with Jamaat e Islami). It is also the result of some sophisticated targeting of disaffected British Bangladeshi youth. Islamic politics has learnt to speak the language of the street and has been designed to appeal to the sort of kids who might follow the Tower Hamlets-based hip-hop band the Asian Dub Foundation (or its current equivalent).

There is still a leftist and anti-western strand to the ideas but it sees Islamic brotherhood as a more powerful tool to combat poverty and discrimination than conventional politics. There is no evidence for the success of this strategy, but it has created a beleaguered sense of empowerment. Or as Claire Alexander, author of *The Asian Gang: Ethnicity, Identity and Masculinity*, has put it: 'Islam stands as a psychological barricade behind which ... Bangladeshi young people (usually men) can hide their lack of self-esteem.'

Political Islam in Tower Hamlets scored its first major victory with the election to Parliament of George Galloway as the Respect candidate in the May 2005 election in Bethnal Green and Bow, riding a protest vote against the Iraq war. Respect also won some seats on Tower Hamlets council. And in October 2010 the lawyer Lutfur Rahman became Britain's first directly elected Muslim mayor, crowning the Islamic shift of the past twenty years and confirming the political 'capture' of Tower Hamlets by one strand of Bengali–Islamist politics. He defeated the Labour establishment that he had once been part of and, in doing so, was backed by the East London Mosque, Respect and the Islamic Forum of Europe. Lutfur was elected on a turnout of 25 per cent.[1]

The increasingly elderly white working class, which is still a substantial minority in parts of the borough, has largely opted out of politics – squeezed, as they see it, between the Bangladeshis and the Yuppies. When Ray Gipson, a popular old white working-class councillor, lost his seat in Bow in 2006, many of his former white voters told him there was no point in voting 'because they don't care about us'.

As documented by Ted Jeory, the former East London Advertiser deputy editor, Lutfur's cabinet is all Bengali and some of them cannot speak good English. Public money is directed to organisations like the Osmani Trust, a charity that combats gangs, crime and drugs among young Bangladeshis and has some links to the East London Mosque. Public money is also, controversially, spent on Bengali lessons often for people who do not speak English well.[2]

Tower Hamlets, the fastest growing borough in Britain, now more than half Bengali and where twenty-nine of the fifty-one councillors are Bengali, has become the apotheosis of a politics of inverted ethnic favouritism. This was brutally illustrated by the Labour group decision in 2010 to bring back a 'sons and daughters' policy for public housing, once denounced as racist, at the request of the now numerically and politically dominant Bangladeshi community. The policy – combined with more four and five bedroom social housing – means that fewer Bengalis will have to move away from the community to Redbridge or other parts of suburban London.

1. Many of the local Respect leaders are people with, to put it mildly, colourful pasts. Religion and politics has offered them redemption.
2. See Ted Jeory's blog on the mysteries of Tower Hamlets politics, 'Trial by Jeory'.

One sign of progress is that school results in Tower Hamlets have improved sharply in recent years, especially for Muslim girls, and there is evidence of much higher aspirations for third- and fourth-generation Bangladeshis. But it seems quite possible that this will not lead to a big increase in good professional jobs, because living in the Tower Hamlets ghetto means young Bengalis lack the networks and 'soft skills' to get such jobs – unless, like Yasmin (described at the start of the chapter), they work for the council itself.

There is an ingrained expectation that the world outside Bangladeshi Tower Hamlets will be a hostile one. One young woman, Ayesha Qureshi, who has lived in Tower Hamlets all her life and works as a lawyer at one of the most prestigious City law firms, fears that the insularity of the place will prevent many following in her wake. 'We had a group of Bangladeshi girls here at the office recently from my old school and they were astonished to discover that I'm working in a corporate environment wearing a headscarf, and that I got paid the same as the men, and that my husband "allowed" me to work and travel abroad alone. We've got a long way to go.'

What is Multiculturalism and Where Did it Come From?

People talk past each other in many modern political disputes, none more so than in the debate on multiculturalism. Supporters and detractors have loaded the word with great emotional charge but they are usually talking about completely different things.

The word 'multiculturalism' could be used in a neutral, descriptive sense to simply mean the presence within a country of many distinct cultural, religious, ethnic or racial groups and ways of life. In this sense pretty well all societies have been multicultural since humans stopped being hunter-gatherers and developed a more complex division of labour; European societies, with their historic class and religious divides, have been multicultural for many hundreds of years.

But nobody calls Tudor England multicultural. The word, in today's usage, has come to refer to the arrival of non-European, 'visible' immigrants in western countries in recent decades and their political and social interaction with the majority society. But unlike the more objective 'multiracial' or 'multi-ethnic', the term 'multicultural' also implies a favourable and accommodating attitude to the arrival on the part of the majority society. The word first came into common usage in Canada in the early 1970s after Pierre Trudeau's Liberal government endorsed a report granting French-speaking Quebec greater linguistic and cultural autonomy (in order to head off full independence). It spread to America and Britain in the 1980s, where it came to be associated with the active pursuit of minority rights and in particular the right to be different and the space in which to enjoy that right. From the start it had little pretence at conceptual precision or neutrality and became a 'badge' word instead. The badge read 'I celebrate difference.'

So multiculturalism came to mean both the simple reality of a growing minority presence in western countries and an optimistic account of how that presence was best managed by allowing difference to flourish – it was a description combined with a prescription. That explains why the critics of multiculturalism still often find themselves on the back foot by appearing ambivalent about the very existence of a multi-ethnic, multiracial land.

But most of the mainstream sceptics of multiculturalism, myself included, are quite comfortable with the principle of a multiracial country. They just fear that the multicultural invitation to newcomers – 'You can remain unchanged and still fit in' – waves away the problem of integration but does not solve it. It also sets up a potential conflict with modern liberal ideas of individual rights and sex equality which are not accepted in the conservative cultures of some minority groups.

So what exactly constitutes the practice of multiculturalism that emerged in Britain from the late 1960s to the early 1980s in response to immigration from the Caribbean, Asia and Africa? It is usefully subdivided into a thin and a thick version or a soft and a hard, or perhaps best of all a liberal and a separatist form. Liberal multiculturalism is more or less coterminous with modern, colour-blind equality. It has been the official position of government, Whitehall, and all mainstream parties at least since the late 1960s (even if the word itself did not arrive for another decade or so) – a belief in equal rights, anti-discrimination legislation and reform of institutions to stamp out prejudice and abuse of power. Colour-blind liberalism is one part of the post-Second World War 'universalist shift' (see Chapter 1, 'Nations and People') which saw the breakdown of many hierarchies, including racial ones, and the acceptance, at least in theory, of human moral equality – 'the human rights revolution'. Britain was opening up to this change in the 1960s and 1970s, with the legalisation of homosexuality, the abolition of capital punishment, greater ease of divorce and so on – and multiculturalism in its liberal form can be seen as the racial aspect of that bigger change.

The liberal multiculturalism that dominated debate and official practice until the 1980s was more flexible than many of its radical critics allow. It is an undogmatic doctrine that accepts that it is reasonable for people to hold on to aspects of their ancestral culture and that minorities do sometimes need special recognition and support: for example, the observance of minority holy days, or religious routines, or the 'rule and exemption' liberalism that exempted turban-wearing Sikhs from having to wear protective headgear on motorcycles, or even the 'affirmative' promotion of black and Asian faces at the BBC so that members of minorities can see themselves reflected in the public space. The problem with liberal multiculturalism is not that it drew a false picture of the world or came up with inadequate solutions, rather that it was never sufficiently practised. Liberal multiculturalism was the presiding ideology through the 1960s and 1970s when much of Britain had not yet embraced the idea of racial justice.

Liberal multiculturalism overlaps with harder or more separatist multiculturalism at certain points, as we shall see. But there is a crucial difference. It is prepared to extend special treatment to minorities but only when this helps to integrate them better as equal citizens into mainstream society. And liberal multiculturalism wants to accommodate newcomers and treat them fairly *within an already existing culture and political system*. Immigration to modern Britain is freely chosen (even refugees usually have the choice to go somewhere else) and people are aware that they are coming to a place where things are done in a certain way; until separatist multiculturalism told them otherwise, newcomers expected, and usually wanted, to fit in, especially in the public sphere. Liberal multiculturalism respects minority rights but it also recognises the existence of a majority, and the majority's right to stability and continuity in everyday life and political arrangements. And the rights of majorities and minorities can sometimes conflict – consider the arguments about banning alcohol in public places so as not to alienate Muslims, or the more serious dispute over free speech raised by the Rushdie and Danish cartoon affairs.

One of the most persistent clichés of the race/immigration/multiculturalism conference circuit is that integration into Britain must be 'a two-way street' – in other words, the host society and not just the immigrant must adjust. But what is the relative adjustment expected of the newcomer and the host society? Liberal multiculturalism places the overwhelming onus on the newcomer. One cannot be British on one's own exclusive terms or on a highly selective basis. That does not, of course, mean, as the standard riposte maintains, that pious Muslims must give up their religion and get drunk on Saturday nights. But it does mean that Muslims must adjust to a society dominated by Christian and secular humanist values, which places a high degree of stress on individual freedom and the rights of women. And they must accept that their minority rights must co-exist with and sometimes concede to majority rights, especially in the public sphere.

At some point in the late 1970s and early 1980s, in response to the persistence of racism and the relative failure of some minority groups, liberal multiculturalism came to seem inadequate to some activists and mutated into something else – partly this was a matter of using the state more aggressively to enforce liberal multiculturalism, but it also involved a shift in principles. It was pioneered at local government level at the GLC in London and in Birmingham, Bradford and Leicester, but soon spread to most of the other areas of high immigration in the Midlands and the North.

But before looking more closely at how exactly Britain's liberal multiculturalism changed its spots, some historical background, particularly relating to the empire, is required.

The lived experience of today's non-European immigrants – whether for Kashmiri Pakistanis in the terraced streets of Blackburn in northern England or Algerians in the Paris *banlieues* or Turks in the tenement blocks of Berlin – has more in common than one might suppose when listening to experts talking about Europe's different models of migration and integration. All three are deeply rooted in the west, but also remain semi-detached from the society around them and live in areas dominated by a pervasive minority culture (and at least in Blackburn and Berlin are likely to speak a minority language at home).

But those different national models have made some difference to the outcomes in different European countries: France with its assimilationist aspiration to turn all newcomers into French republican citizens, Germany with its odd mixture of conservatism about granting citizenship and official liberalism towards foreigners and Britain with its 'live and let live' multiculturalism.

These models are bequeathed by history and, at least in the case of Britain and France, grow directly out of our respective colonial stories. Britain ruled most of its colonial territories with a relatively light touch, dividing and ruling and often governing indirectly through local elites, like Nigerian emirs and Indian maharajahs. The British colonial elite had a racialised view of the world, as did almost everyone in the nineteenth century, but at least in the mature phase of empire it did not generally want to transform the existing group identities and practices it found in Africa and Asia – unless these interfered in some way with imperial goals. Unlike the French, it did not try to turn everyone into a black or brown version of a Briton.

This British approach, as perhaps with the multiculturalism story in general, was a mix of reactionary and progressive. Some accounts of empire see this apparent indifference to changing the lives of colonial subjects as a racial apartheid, compared to the more universalist, interventionist French.[1]

But British colonial administrators also often admired the cultures they discovered and worried about how to protect them from the interference of the modern world. In today's language we would say that British colonialism embraced 'difference', albeit in the context of a hierarchy that placed white Europeans at the top.

British colonialism was based on a feeling of civilisational superiority and the higher calling of British political and legal institutions and the Christian religion, but not, generally, on the idea of simple racial superiority – though

---

1. One example that is sometimes cited is how in eighteenth-century New Orleans if a British merchant had a child with a slave woman the child remained a slave, while if a Frenchman did the child was free.

there was a late nineteenth-century interest in 'Anglo-Saxon' race theory. Even the idea of civilisational superiority was tempered by a kind of equality at the very top end of the class system. And all subjects, even if they never became British, would be protected in a disinterested manner by the empire regardless of race or religion – the idea of Civis Romanus Sum.

The extent to which British colonialists mixed with the local population and the extent to which they interfered in local politics and culture did, of course, change over time and in different places. In the first part of the nineteenth century a strong sense of a Whiggish 'civilising mission' in the colonies was expressed by Thomas Babington Macaulay, James Mill and others. But the principle of benign non-intervention generally won the argument. This was often for the practical reason that the British empire did not have the manpower or resources to be more interventionist.

In India after the 1857 Mutiny a form of multiculturalism became official policy. This was partly because the Mutiny itself had been triggered by a casual disregard for the religious sensibilities of Muslim soldiers. Patrick French describes it like this: 'Providing a community did not engage in open revolt, it could continue with whatever obscure social and religious practices it liked. In the half-century leading up to the rebellion, English evangelical Christians had promoted the abolition of practices like sati, the burning of supposedly willing widows who did not wish to live without their husbands ... Now, on the instruction of Queen Victoria, the natives were free to follow whatever they declared their customs to be.'[1]

Queen Victoria's proclamation read as follows: 'Firmly relying Ourselves on the truth of Christianity, and acknowledging with gratitude the solace of Religion, We disclaim alike the Right and the Desire to impose our Convictions on any of Our Subjects. We declare it to be Our Royal Will and Pleasure that none be in any wise favoured, none molested or disquieted by reason of their Religious Faith or Observances; but that all shall alike enjoy the equal and impartial protection of the Law.'

Compare that with this proclamation of French colonialism from Gentry de Bussy, one of the French rulers of Algeria, in 1834: 'Is it up to the French to

1. Patrick French, *India: A Portrait*, Allen Lane, 2011, p. 338.

civilise the Arabs or the Arabs to civilise the French? But the French are further down the road of civilisation, it is therefore up to them to lay down laws and regulations.' Is it any wonder that 150 years later France has laid down the law on the Islamic veil, banning it from schools and public offices, and Britain has not even considered it, merely grumbling a bit about the full-face coverings of the niqab and the burka?

Britain's imperial elite often saw itself as standing above the nation, including its own, with its role to manage relations between different groups. And members of the elite often used language that today would be considered multicultural. Consider this from the Scottish novelist John Buchan, who as Lord Tweedsmuir was governor general of Canada from 1935 to 1940: 'Races should retain their individuality and each make its contribution to the national character ...'

Many modern-day proponents of multiculturalism admit that the idea has, so far, flourished best within empires.[1] The imperial authority – whether in the Ottoman, Austro-Hungarian or British empires – granted protection and rights to various minorities in return for allegiance to the imperial power. The Ottoman empire's 'millet' system, allowing different religions to exist within their own jurisdictions, was the most developed. This system worked as an impediment to the rising tide of national democratic sovereignty that was eventually to sweep away the empires, and in some cases the minority rights too.

If modern multiculturalism has one important 'right-wing' root in the management of difference in colonial societies, it has another 'left-wing' root in cultural relativism and anti-racism. The work of early twentieth-century anthropologists like Franz Boas, which stressed the equal value of all cultures, was partly a reaction against nineteenth-century colonial racism. He influenced the theorist Horace Kallen, often described as the intellectual father of American multiculturalism, who placed ethnic identity at the centre of social relations and opposed the idea of the melting pot.[2]

1. 'In the past, multicultural societies have tended to only flourish under imperial rule,' says Tariq Modood, a leading British multiculturalist.
2. 'Men,' he said, 'may change their clothes, their politics, their wives, their religions, their philosophies, to a greater or lesser extent: they cannot change their grandfathers.' A new

A further strand of thought came through black thinkers like Franz Fanon and Malcolm X, whose pessimism about overcoming white European racism and the psychological inheritance of slavery led them towards various kinds of black separatism. In the US in the 1960s many black activists broke away from the main civil rights movement to promote black identity, 'a recognition of those things uniquely ours which separate ourselves from the white man', according to the Black Power activist Julius Lester.

In post-war Britain there was a fusion between the colonial and the left-ist strands of nascent multiculturalism. As we have seen, colonial Tories or people from colonial backgrounds such as Alan Lennox Boyd spoke up for the 'imperial family' and rejected attempts to discriminate in immigration policy between white and non-white members of the family.

On the left, Richard Titmuss, one of the intellectual fathers of the post-war welfare state, wrote about 'our genius for colonisation' and about a British empire 'which with all its faults still shines with the lights of our gifts to mankind and still glows with the quiet patient courage of the common people'. A younger generation, such as Eileen Younghusband (daughter of imperial adventurer Francis Younghusband), rejected the racial domination of empire. She, along with many other children of colonialists, developed an acute sense of racial justice at a young age and a special interest in the rights of ethnic minorities at home. Younghusband was a founder of modern social work and influenced early discussions of multiculturalism in the 1960s and 1970s.

What both left and right 'noblesse oblige' multiculturalists had in common was a belief in the centrality of 'thick' ethnic identities and a relative lack of interest in integrating people into a British national culture, one that they often felt only a rather distant connection to themselves. Ken Livingstone embodies this fusion with his networks of minority patronage in London. In his reluctance to criticise even illiberal ethnic minority behaviour he has more in common with a post-1857 British colonial administrator than he realises.

---

country like America could become a 'community of communities', a 'democracy of nation-alities, co-operating voluntarily and autonomously through common institutions ...' Kallen also coined the phrase 'cultural pluralism'.

What we would later call multiculturalism was evident in the benign neglect that accompanied the first wave of post-colonial immigration from 1948 to 1962. 'We know these are good people, loyal to the British Empire, and that Britain will benefit from their presence,' seemed to be the optimistic view of the liberal colonialists.

The empire functioned as a labour market transmission belt, shifting people around the world according to where their skills and aptitudes would be most useful to British interests. After 1945 and the early years of colonial and post-colonial immigration to the imperial centre, it was as if Britain itself became just another destination on this map of labour market mobility – you might say that Britain's rulers came to treat their own country in the kind of instrumental manner that they had treated the colonies. And the native white working-class tribe of Britain were no more consulted about the new arrivals than black Africans in East Africa had been consulted about the arrival of thousands of Indians in the nineteenth and twentieth centuries.

As we have seen, some people in Whitehall and Westminster, indeed throughout British society, began expressing misgivings about non-European immigration as soon as it began with the docking of the *Windrush* in 1948, and various attempts were made to close the open door.

But those racial misgivings must be set alongside another story that I mentioned in the last chapter. Sociologist Geoff Dench describes the emergence of a new post-imperial idealism that was popular with the post-war liberal elite: 'Borrowing Whig pride in Britain's imperial legacy of tolerance and respect for indigenous cultures, Labour devised a new world role for Britain. Empire imposed on other nations had been wrong. But Britain could still show the world how to foster a peaceful, multicultural and open metropolitan society. Roy Jenkins' definition of a liberal nation converted a growing problem into a potential asset. A progressive national mission was drafted around a new empire that would atone for the old ... Britain's national interest now required cosmopolitanism and disdain for narrow expressions of identity or destiny. What was truly British now was to be global and inclusive.'[1]

1. 'Britain's Internal Empire', unpublished paper.

The celebrated Nigerian writer Wole Soyinka has a similar view: 'It's part of the British character ... Colonialism bred an innate arrogance but when you undertake that sort of imperial adventure, that arrogance gives way to a feeling of accommodativeness. You take pride in your openness.'

How Multiculturalism Changed its Spots

The distinction I made earlier between liberal and hard or 'separatist' multiculturalism is not always obvious, and is a disputed one. But I believe three themes can be identified as central to the separatist variant. First, it is 'ethnicist': it privileges minority identities over common citizenship, if the two conflict, and insists that ethnic and religious belonging are the most important thing about a person's individual and political identity. Second, it wants to positively promote and fund ethnic difference: all groups in a society have equal claims to public recognition and financial support and that should be reflected in policies to protect and promote minority cultures through exemptions, public funding and varieties of affirmative action; moreover, groups can have rights as well as individuals (which can be bad news for minorities within minorities). Third, separatist multiculturalism regards a core national culture as either non-existent or illegitimate and regards society as a kind of federation of groups – a 'community of communities', in the phrase of the Parekh report on multiculturalism of 2000 – and it therefore rejects the duty of integration.

For some of the historical reasons I have sketched out, Britain is often thought of as a multicultural country, especially by foreign observers, with a laissez-faire attitude to minority integration and a liberal attitude to difference. But, perhaps in a rather typically British way, it is not spelt out anywhere, in either its liberal or separatist forms. Along with our unwritten constitution, there is no explicit national multiculturalism policy.

Multiculturalism – of either the liberal or the separatist kind – has no canonical texts nor white papers nor government policy statements. David Cameron, in a famous speech in February 2011, criticised 'state multiculturalism', but to the extent that multiculturalism has generated policies it has been at the level of the local state, the professions and big organisations. It still remains more of an attitude of mind than a political philosophy, summed up in phrases like 'You can come here and still be yourself' or, in Tony Blair's more balanced formulation of liberal multiculturalism, 'The right to be different, the duty to integrate'.

The closest that Britain comes to having a multiculturalism manifesto is a speech by the Labour home secretary Roy Jenkins in May 1966. Here are the relevant three paragraphs, the first and third of which are often quoted.

> Integration is perhaps rather a loose word. I do not regard it as meaning the loss, by immigrants, of their own national characteristics and culture. I do not think we need in this country a 'melting pot', which would turn everybody out in a common mould, as one of a series of carbon copies of someone's misplaced vision of the stereotyped Englishman.
>
> It would be bad enough if that were to occur in the relatively few in this country who happen to have pure Anglo-Saxon blood in their veins. If it were to happen to the rest of us, to the Welsh (like myself), to the Scots, to the Irish, to the Jews, to the mid-European, and to still more recent arrivals, it would be little short of a national disaster. It would deprive us of most of the positive advantages of immigration, which ... I believe to be very great indeed.
>
> I define integration, therefore, not as a flattening process of assimilation but as equal opportunity, accompanied by cultural diversity, in an atmosphere of mutual tolerance. That is the goal. We may fall a little short of its full attainment, as have other communities both in the past and in the present. But if we are to maintain any sort of world reputation for civilized living and social cohesion, we must get far nearer to its achievement than is the case today.

Although eloquent in its way, the famous Jenkins quote is also part of a *de haut en bas* problem of British multiculturalism – grand liberal statements made by people who know little about what is happening on the ground. (The speech was actually written in the chapel of King's College Cambridge, where Jenkins was the guest of Noel Annan, a leading member of the liberal establishment.) Although Jenkins represented the Stechford constituency of

Birmingham (now Hodge Hill and more than half minority, mainly Pakistani), the only non-European immigrants that he knew at all well were intellectuals and politicians from colonial or former colonial countries.

He seems to have just taken for granted an integrationist framework and a high level of similarity between the majority and minority culture. Hence what now seems his rather bizarre conflation between a Welsh-born member of the British elite like himself and 'more recent arrivals' such as an illiterate peasant farmer from Kashmir.

Jenkins would undoubtedly have been a liberal not a separatist multiculturalist, but one reason that the speech still resonates is because of the way it blurs the distinction. The speech is claimed by the liberal multiculturalists by placing the stress on integration and equal opportunity and by the separatist multiculturalists by placing the emphasis on cultural diversity and the rejection of the 'melting pot'. (Despite his protestations, Jenkins, the son of a Welsh mining union official, who via grammar school and Oxford joined the elite, was himself the embodiment of the best of the British melting pot.)

But what of the actual policies associated with multiculturalism in its liberal and more separatist forms? The first phase of liberal multiculturalism from the 1960s to the late 1970s is mainly associated with anti-discrimination legislation – above all the 1965, 1968 and 1976 Race Relations Acts – pursuing a colour-blind equality between races that today seems utterly uncontroversial (though it was not always so at the time, especially as the laws gradually became tougher).

There were also some ad hoc attempts at integration policies at this time. This is the path not taken in the British immigration story. When immigration controls were first introduced in 1962 there was an explicit understanding that this should be accompanied by fairer treatment for those minority Britons who were settling here permanently. The Labour Party and liberal Britain had seen the controls as a regrettably necessary sop to populist opinion, but intended to compensate for the restrictions not only with race legislation but also with the establishment of Community Relations Councils and special 'Section 11' spending on minorities by local authorities.

Alongside this there were some more explicitly integrationist ideas and experiments, especially in the field of education. The Commonwealth

Immigrants Advisory Council recommended compulsory English language teaching and the dispersal or 'bussing' of non-white pupils. Edward Boyle, who was Secretary of State for Education in Harold Macmillan's government, proposed in 1963 – partly in response to the protests of white parents in Southall – that no school should have more than 30 per cent minority pupils.[1]

The idea was not taken up but neither did it completely disappear. In 1965, after Labour had been returned to government, the Department of Education recommended the dispersal of immigrant children in Circular 7/65: 'Up to a fifth of immigrant children in any group fit in with reasonable ease... if that proportion goes above one third either in the school as a whole or in any one class, serious strains arise.'[2] The department recommended adjusting school catchment areas to avoid minority concentration and if that proved impossible then adopting a dispersal policy.

Large-scale bussing did take place in Ealing (including Southall) and Bradford and on a smaller scale in Leicester, Bristol and Luton. But it was never very popular with minority parents and a court ruling in 1975 found that it was in breach of the 1968 Race Relations Act. In Bradford I was told by Ishtiaq Ahmed, spokesman for the Council of Mosques, that bussing was unpopular with the Pakistani minority and was one of the first things that was abolished when the Muslim community started to find its political voice in the 1980s. Ahmed himself had been bussed to a majority white school outside his own neighbourhood and admitted that it had helped to integrate him and give him confidence in dealing with white society.

The path that *was* taken was, if anything, the opposite of an integration strategy. The shift to a more separatist multiculturalist stance happened mainly in an unplanned way at local level. One of the most visible and iconic policies associated with separatist multiculturalism was the idea that newcomers should be able to continue to live within their own cultures even to the extent of not learning English – with important official documents and even street signs to be translated into the relevant languages. Of course, few people would object to documents being translated for a transitional period

1. See Hansard, 27 November 1963, Schools (racial integration).
2. Circular 7/65 quoted by Vicki Butler in Bussing in the UK during the 1960s and 1970s, Runnymede Trust.

while people learn adequate English, but the strong multicultural position went beyond that to embrace a multilingual society.

Meanwhile, the late 1970s and early 1980s also saw the establishment of special race bodies, at Ken Livingstone's GLC and elsewhere, to monitor the progress of and promote the interests of minorities. Some of this more focused pursuit of equality was welcome and innovative. The GLC, for example, drew up equal opportunities policies and demanded contractors comply with them. And its Ethnic Minorities Unit invited in minority groups and handed out grants to them. (By the mid-1980s the GLC was handing out £77m a year to minority organisations; Leicester Council something comparable.)

On a small scale such grants were hardly revolutionary and many of them were used to do valuable work. But with the benefit of hindsight one can see that the late 1970s to early 1980s was a watershed. Multiculturalism began to change its spots, in two rather different ways. On the one hand, it just became more impatient and more aggressive in pursuit of equality and combating discrimination, but on the other hand, it began to redefine racism. As the writer Kenan Malik describes it: 'Racism now meant not the denial of equal rights but the denial of the right to be different. Black people ... should not be forced to accept British values or to adopt a British identity. Rather different peoples should have the right to express their own identities, explore their own histories, formulate their own values, pursue their own lifestyles.' At the GLC both of these strands of multiculturalism were pursued and supported.[1]

In the 1960s and 1970s most immigration and minority issues were looked at through the prism of discrimination and deprivation – equality at work or access to public housing (or to jobs on public transport in the case of the Bristol bus boycott of 1963). The Urban Programme of the late 1960s targeted deprived inner cities, not particular ethnic groups. And the national organisations that sprang up to deal with immigration-related issues – such as the National Committee for Commonwealth Immigrants – talked for all immigrants, not just Muslims or Caribbeans or Sikhs.

Some of the new ideas had floated across the Atlantic from the black radicals in the US who had broken away from the integrationist civil rights

1. Kenan Malik, From Faith to Jihad: The Rushdie Affair and its Legacy, Atlantic Books, 2009.

organisations to set up separate organisations to promote black identity. Municipal anti-racism was also part of the cultural turn of the young, white left in the 1970s and 1980s in which a 'rainbow coalition' of the dispossessed, led by ethnic minorities, would be the new driver of change now that affluence had blunted working-class radicalism.

In response to the harsh economic consequences of the early Thatcher years, Labour was soon piling up huge majorities again in local authorities in London and big industrial cities – like Birmingham, Sheffield, Manchester and Leeds. Many of those elected were young rainbow coalitionists. Bill Bush, who was right-hand man to Ken Livingstone at the GLC and a Brent councillor, recalls one example of the experimental and sometimes plain daft politics of that era. 'The Brent council Labour group imposed a 50 per cent ethnic minority quota on itself for council seats, but there simply weren't enough experienced people to go round and it often ended in a complete mess. One African woman ended up defecting to the Tories when we refused to fund one of her pet ethnic projects.'

Funding systems encouraged separate ethnic organisations. Instead of single tenants' associations or women's groups there would now often be separate Sikh, Hindu, Muslim and African organisations.[1] Also, in 1986 the Housing Corporation invested heavily in the promotion of separate ethnic minority managed housing associations nationwide – at one point there were forty-four black managed associations – creating new career opportunities for minority activists as well as more segregated housing.

Education, too, was fertile ground for multicultural initiatives – some motivated by a proper sensitivity to difference, others that tipped over into an active promotion of separation. This meant in Muslim areas more segregation between the sexes and the introduction of halal meat. It could also mean playing down British history and national traditions in favour of a greater emphasis on the culture and the history of minorities. Separatist assumptions also touched central government in publications like the 1985 Swann report 'Education for All', which talked about 'assisting the ethnic minority communities in maintaining their distinct ethnic identities'. By 1989, half of

1. Roger Hewitt has written about the tension caused by the establishment of separate ethnic minority tenants' associations for council estates in Eltham in the 1990s.

the 108 local education authorities had multicultural policies in place. Special units produced ethnic materials for schools and some local authorities with big South Asian populations provided library books in Urdu and Punjabi.

The new more activist multiculturalism was mainly funded through local authorities, but there were also national funds from the Commission for Racial Equality, and after the 1981 Brixton riots and the Scarman report the urban aid programmes started channelling more money towards groups that were organised along ethnic lines. Soon it became commonplace to see dedicated minority voluntary bodies, arts centres and radio channels.

Up to this point religion had played only a small role in minority politics. The politics of race and immigration was avowedly secular and had become an arm of the British left (the banner of the Indian Workers' Association was a familiar sight at big trade union protests). One of my own first experiences of political demonstrations as a left-wing student was attending the Grunwick picket line in 1976, where a group of Indian women in west London had gone on strike for union recognition; they were backed by the elite mass picketers of the trade union movement, led by Arthur Scargill's Yorkshire miners.

While Sikhs often led these political and industrial battles, the Pakistanis of the west Midlands or the northern mill towns did not generally join in. The kin networks of village life, the Biraderi system, helped to insulate people from ordinary British life, and often subordinated the individual to the extended family and the clan. The outside world took little interest in this conservative world and through the 1960s, 1970s and into the 1980s tended to see British Muslims as a politically quiescent group of Asians – 'Pakis', in the language of the street.

All that changed with the Rushdie affair at the end of the 1980s. If the Brixton riots and the subsequent Scarman report defined one of the high-water marks of an integrationist race politics – the African Caribbean community wanting to join society and demanding fair treatment – the Rushdie affair marks the shift towards a more separate identity politics. A secular conflict over equal rights turned into a struggle for more separate space within British society, and that space was often religious. Many supporters of racial justice felt uneasy about this new direction but had no intellectual means of challenging it, and no alternative. As Kenan Malik has put it, the rise of identity politics in the 1980s and 1990s helped to create a Britain that was 'less racist but more insidiously tribal'.

In Malik's book *From Fatwa to Jihad* he describes visiting Bradford during the Rushdie crisis and meeting somebody who vividly embodied the change in British minority politics. Hassan, an old friend of Malik's from the London left, had been a hard-drinking, chain-smoking, rock-music-loving, Arsenal-supporting, girl-chasing, Jack-the-lad. When Malik bumped into him by chance in the Bradford Council of Mosques office he was wearing traditional dress and had rediscovered Islam, explaining that he had 'lost a sense of who he was and where he'd come from'.

The Rushdie affair helped to bolster, at least for a while, the power of parents and elders. Sher Azam, one of the leaders of the anti-Rushdie movement in Bradford, declared: 'Rushdie has been good for us Muslims. We've found ourselves as Muslims. Our children were growing up hating our culture, they were being drawn to western values and western lifestyles.'

British Muslims, led by the Kashmiri Pakistanis of northern England, had marched on to the national stage with a big demand: change your free speech tradition to accommodate us. Most other large minorities had merely demanded that Britain live up to its existing rules – that young black men not be harassed by the police, that Indian Hindus and Sikhs not be discriminated against at work. The Muslim demand was more intrusive and harder to grant.

Liberal Britain was divided over the demand. Some, including Labour politicians with big Muslim minorities in their constituencies, such as Roy Hattersley and Jack Straw, argued that blasphemy laws still protected Christianity, so why shouldn't they be extended to this pious and powerless minority? But most sided with Rushdie (including Margaret Thatcher) and freedom of expression, especially after the Fatwah from Iran.

What was the legacy of the Rushdie affair? It began to mark out Muslims as a special, and in some ways especially problematic, minority – the minority most at odds with the free-and-easy ways of modern Britain, on women's rights, on free speech, on religious piety. The conservative rural Islam of the Kashmiris, and the growing number of Bangladeshis too, had been an issue in the towns where they lived but had not impinged much on the national consciousness; now it did.

The Rushdie affair, and opposition to the first Gulf War in 1991, also helped to shape a new generation of young Muslim leaders, many of whom were to emerge a decade later in the leadership of the Muslim Council of Britain, the national umbrella organisation established in the mid-1990s – people like Iqbal Sacranie and Inayat Bunglawala. They were the children of the more separate multiculturalism of the early 1980s and were determined that Britain should accommodate their demands for cultural and religious autonomy.[1] The turn towards a 'harder' multiculturalism in the Rushdie dispute came through the assertion of Muslim sensibilities. But, as I have noted, it had been building for some years before in response to the assumed failures of more conventional 'colour-blind' race politics. The separatist ideas generally came from the left, but the power and influence and money often accrued to conservative religious leaders in the 1980s, especially in South Asian Britain. A blind eye was sometimes turned to illiberal and patriarchal practices inside those communities – what one might call 'community elder' multiculturalism.[2]

In Bradford the council helped to establish the Bradford Council of Mosques in 1981 and subsequently started funding a whole Muslim welfare network. Sher Azam again: 'We wanted help from the council to make sure our children were not lost to Islam, we told them the best way to deal with drugs, jobs, fighting was to restore pride in our culture and religion.' The council effectively ended up handing to the Council of Mosques responsibility for the welfare of Muslims in the town. In Tower Hamlets the process has been more contested, but a generation later something similar began to happen at the East London Mosque.

Then there was the Ray Honeyford affair. In 1984 the headmaster of Drummond Middle School in Bradford was denounced, initially by the white

---

1. Inayat Bunglawala, and some of the other MCB leaders who were active in the anti-Rushdie campaign, have admitted their error over calling for the book to be banned. Here is Bunglawala in the *Guardian* on 15 September 2012: 'Of course our demands, which included the pulping of all copies of Rushdie's novel, were in retrospect totally over the top and very embarrassing.'

2. In 1986 the *Bandung File* programme for Channel 4 exposed right-wing Hindu revivalist groups that were being funded by the GLC, and there were many other examples of officially recognised and financed minority groups which oppressed their own internal minorities.

left, for what now seem prescient views (if sometimes offensively articulated) on the dangers for both majority and minority of educational segregation. Honeyford, whose school was 90 per cent Muslim, wrote articles in right-wing publications criticising Pakistani parents for taking their children on long trips to Pakistan during term-time and attacked the corporal punishment culture of mosque schools. Extracts of his work were translated into Urdu, and a campaign by both Muslim parents and local white activists eventually forced him to resign.

White metropolitan liberals and leftists on the network of ethnic minority and anti-racist committees that had sprung up all over the country found themselves setting aside their liberal principles, especially over women's equality, in the name of cultural and ethnic difference. Rather than appealing to Muslims or Sikhs or other minorities as British citizens and trying to draw them into the mainstream political process, local and national politicians came to see them as people whose primary loyalty was to their faith or culture and who could be politically engaged only by their own leaders.

Most minority Britons, then and now, live in Labour seats and tend to be Labour voters. The first step on the mainstream political ladder taken by the more secular leaders in minority communities was often to become a Labour councillor. In the 1960s and 1970s this sometimes involved bitter internal struggles against the old guard in local Labour parties, though by the early 1990s there were about 500 minority councillors, mainly Labour. Black sections in the party and the unions seemed, at least for a period, a necessity.

The idea can still provoke argument. 'What exactly was so wrong with black sections in the Labour Party or the National Union of Journalists?' The question was addressed to me by the former Labour cabinet minister Paul Boateng, as I was interviewing him for this book. I had been trying to explain why I thought the distinction between liberal and separatist multiculturalism was a useful one. But he could hold back his exasperation no longer and wanted to remind me of a bigger historical context.

'You forget how bad it was ... we were combating out and out racism ... we were constantly made to feel ashamed ... It is never completely comfortable belonging to an ethnic minority ... and it certainly wasn't back then.' In that context, he explained, it is understandable that people wanted to organise autonomously and develop a positive idea of 'difference'. Boateng (who was also the deputy head of the GLC's Ethnic Minorities Unit in the early 1980s) continued: 'Turn on the television today and you see many people of colour. Thirty years ago that was not the case, we made a fuss about it and the society responded. You shouldn't be too hard on the people that wanted a black women's centre, people wanted autonomy and that did have some unintended consequences but the main thrust has been positive.'

Herman Ouseley, who later became head of the Commission for Racial Equality, has a similar view. He had worked for the GLC when it was first formed in 1965 and returned in 1980 – before Ken Livingstone's takeover – to find it was still a 'bastion of white supremacy'. More generally he recalls the 'apartheid' that existed in London towards black people in the 1960s and 1970s, which forced them back on self-help, not so much out of choice but of necessity. 'The one institution that you thought might have been welcoming to blacks was the church, but it wasn't. Black churches were set up because the church was not welcoming,' says Ouseley.

Boateng and Ouseley make a reasonable point about the need for some autonomy for ethnic minority organisations at that time. And it is perhaps difficult, especially for a white person, to imagine how bad things were thirty years ago. But two separate ideas came to be confused – a more vigorous pursuit of the struggle to be included in mainstream Britain (associated with black Britain), and the desire for a sort of subsidised separation from it (increasingly associated with Muslim Britain).

The two can sometimes blur. People are often surprised to discover that Britain has publicly subsidised ethnic minority media organisations – most notably the BBC Asian Network. Initially the minority networks were defensive institutions based on the assumption that there was insufficient space in the mainstream media, but now the BBC Asian Network has become a talent nursery for mainstream channels. This arguably represents the successful use of autonomy, to better launch people into the mainstream and to thereby help blur the line between majority and minority.[1]

But a protected space or a special measure could (and can) swiftly lead to

---

1. Though the BBC Asian Network is the most expensive per listener spend of any BBC station and is also in direct competition with various commercial rivals.

a sort of parallel minority world – a particular danger in places like Bradford, central Birmingham and Tower Hamlets where there is an overwhelmingly dominant minority community. In Birmingham after the Handsworth riots of 1985, nine umbrella groups based on ethnicity and faith (the Council of Black-led Churches, the Hindu Council and so on) were established by Birmingham Council to represent the needs of different communities. Most of the organisations represented only themselves but they helped to place ethnicity and faith at the centre of politics.

Kenan Malik argues that it is no coincidence that the 1985 riots saw blacks and Asians fighting together against police harassment and joblessness, but twenty years later the next major riot in the Lozells area was between Asians and blacks, following a rumour that a black girl had been raped by Asians. The ethnicisation of Birmingham politics was partly to blame.[1]

By the 1990s and early 2000s overt racism had become much rarer in Britain and public opinion, particularly among younger people, was by now far more liberal on race and gender (see the discussion in Chapter 2, 'How Racist is Britain Still?'). Some ethnic institutions, those that catered for Caribbeans for example, have mainly died out. Yet in too many local authorities and public bodies institutional inertia, and activist self-interest, has helped to preserve the protective apparatus of an earlier era. One former leader of Camden Council in London told me how hard it was to phase out 'single-identity' ethnic funding because of the bloc vote that some minority leaders can wield come local council elections.

Single-identity funding has been a significant cause of resentment between minorities and the majority, especially lower-income whites in the Midlands and the northern towns. Real single-identity funding is a grant to, say, a Somali group to build a community centre with public funds. This may be justified if it is helping a new minority find its feet, but it should be time limited and linked if possible to mixing across ethnic boundaries. There is also another apparent form of single-identity funding where urban regeneration, or other forms of public spending, is concentrated on one area of a divided town that can make it look like ethnic favouritism when it isn't.

1. See Kenan Malik's Milton K. Wong lecture which is available on his Pandaemonium website.

Special funding has also sometimes been an issue between minorities.[1] Yet despite Ted Cantle's advice, in his report on the 2001 mill town riots, to phase out single-identity funding, it persists in many parts of the country.[2]

At root the problem with separatist multiculturalism lies in all those ways in which minority Britons are encouraged to identify *first* as a member of that minority and only second, if at all, as a citizen. It is continuing to translate rather than teaching people English. It is funding streams in housing and education and other public services earmarked only for particular groups, as well as the minority-only housing associations and tenants' groups. This is not *always* unjustified but the assumption that this should be the norm, especially in areas of high minority settlement, makes it harder to create a common life.

When political power and money is allocated along ethnic or religious lines, more and more people tend to identify themselves in terms of their ethnicity even if it is not their original instinct to do so. As Dilwar Hussain has written about Tower Hamlets: 'The way the state allocates funds by dividing people along faith lines has resulted in increasingly separate lives led by many Bengali Muslims.'

The ethnic 'bloc vote' is a particularly graphic illustration of separatist multiculturalism in the political sphere. Whether it is minority leaders trading votes for policy favours from white politicians, or minorities voting for 'their' politicians in the belief that they will give priority to their concerns, this is about the politics of sectional interests.

In fact most minority voters, like most white voters, have no 'group' political leverage, they are too dispersed spatially and ideologically. And most minority groups are gradually coming to vote more like mainstream Britain, increasingly voting for their perceived economic interest rather than for a perceived ethnic interest. Hindu Indians are already coming close to the majority voting pattern, though Sikhs remain disproportionately Labour

1. In a famous case in west London, Southall's new community centre, built in 1986, was resented by the African Caribbean community which complained that it catered almost exclusively for the more numerous and powerful Sikh and Hindu communities.
2. Darra Singh's *Our Shared Future* report produced by the Commission on Integration and Cohesion in 2007 was also sceptical about single-identity funding.

loyalist, perhaps because they are slightly poorer than Hindus and have a more collectivist religious culture.

Where 'wholesale' politics does prevail – with community leaders trading votes for policy influence and prestige – Labour has been the main beneficiary (though the votes have sometimes been switched to the Liberal Democrats or Respect). But this doesn't make a big difference to political outcomes because minority Britons are overwhelmingly Labour voters anyway, both out of economic interest and because Labour has defended their rights more than other big parties. At the 2010 election Labour got 68 per cent of the minority vote (compared with 29 per cent of the overall vote) while the Tories got just 16 per cent of the minority vote (and 36 per cent of the overall vote).

The two most segregated large minority groups – Kashmiri Pakistanis and Bangladeshis – are as successful and well organised politically as they are unsuccessful economically, and the manner in which they have 'captured' parts of local politics does raise some awkward questions. In the parts of old industrial England or east London where they are concentrated they have come to dominate, or at least have a significant influence on, the Labour political machine – and as trade unions have faded in size and influence they have emerged as the new bloc vote in some areas.

In the case of the British Pakistanis it is the operation of the 'Biraderi' system that lies behind the bloc vote that is the problem. The Biraderi is a clan system which, like an extended family, carries with it an obligation to look after the interests of fellow members. There is also a hierarchy within the Biraderis, like the caste system: the Rajputs, who own the land, and the Jaats, who work it, who would both be considered upper-class; the Gujars, who are herders, and the Arains, who are market gardeners, who are middle-class; and the Kammi, who are the servant class.

The Biraderi has had a significant bearing on chain migration patterns, transcontinental marriage partnerships and business and welfare arrangements. It may have played a useful support role in the early years when the community was establishing itself in a strange and sometimes hostile country, but thereafter the way it operates as a state within a state has generally been in conflict with the principles and assumptions of a modern liberal democracy.

And while it is true that Biraderi collective loyalty probably makes little practical difference to overall voting outcomes, the clan system does have a big influence on the selection of candidates for council, and to a lesser extent, parliamentary seats. The Labour peer Nazeer Ahmed complains that he was blocked from becoming an MP because of it: 'It does not matter what their politics is, when it comes to voting, they will vote for their own. This is what happened during my Parliamentary selection. People said "Well, he's a Jaat so we won't vote for him."'

According to the former Labour MP Shahid Malik, the system of automatically supporting your own Biraderi, with the threat of social sanction if you don't, perpetuates an undemocratic, unmeritocratic clan mentality which also excludes women and younger people. Moreover, in certain areas it has been regularly associated with postal vote fraud and other forms of vote rigging.[1]

The first time I witnessed the Kashmiri Pakistani 'bloc' in action was at a rally for the Labour candidates for the Lozells area of Birmingham before the May 2011 local council elections. The hall in the centre of Birmingham was overflowing with about 200 Kashmiri men, mainly in traditional dress, who were not, if my conversations were anything to judge by, politically motivated. They were there to support a Kashmiri candidate who was a member of their clan. Lozells is the area that became briefly infamous for its black versus Asian riots in October 2005 (which led to two deaths and a huge amount of damage to shops and property), but in the hall there were about three black people, half a dozen white people and two women. This was Kashmiri male clan politics in action.

I felt ambivalent about the event. On the positive side, here was another minority, like the Irish before them, breathing new life into the Labour Party. And here too was the Labour Party helping to integrate an outsider group into the political system, as it had once brought in Irish Catholics and brokered relations between Protestants and Catholics. And the rhetoric from the platform was of a traditional Labour kind – for more public spending, against the cuts – and was not asking for special favours for any minority.

1. This section draws on an unpublished Newcastle University undergraduate dissertation by Ellie Hill, 'Ethnicity and Democracy: A Study into Biraderi'. Also on Navid Akhtar's BBC radio documentary *The Biraderi*, first broadcast 26 August 2003.

Yet there is the danger that ethnic group thinking, or in this case sub-ethnic clan thinking, will take precedence over citizen thinking in politics. There is nothing wrong with minority domination of political parties in areas where they are numerically strong, but there is also the possibility that minority voters will automatically vote for 'their' ethnic candidate and then expect them to look after their interests rather than represent all voters. Something like this seems to be going on in inner-city Bradford and in Tower Hamlets. In Bradford in the nine inner city wards all but three of the councillors are South Asians. In Tower Hamlets, as we have seen, both the directly elected mayor's cabinet and the ruling Labour group on the council are overwhelmingly Bengali, despite the fact that the area is barely half minority.

And in some places the British political parties often just seem to be flags of convenience for the playing out of personal or Pakistani or Bangladeshi political goals. A couple of years ago in Tower Hamlets, for example, one Bangladeshi councillor switched support from the far left Respect party to the Conservative Party.

There is a patron–client element to almost all democratic politics: you vote for me and I will do X for you in return. It can also take a group form where social class interests are invoked. And it is easy to see why the Labour Party in parts of northern England has colluded with the system. Not only is it a reliable vote machine in areas where the party has little money, few activists and a white core vote that seldom votes, but there is also a continuity with the way in which the party has traditionally represented the trade union interest. But it is not progressive politics to foster clan thinking, and it probably further alienates working-class whites from taking part in politics in the former industrial areas where the Kashmiri influence is strong.

In any case, following George Galloway's surprise victory for Respect in the Bradford West by-election in April 2012, partly on the back of a revolt by younger and female Pakistani voters against the 'old boys' network' Biraderi system, it is likely to become increasingly dysfunctional for Labour.

All parties will continue to woo voter 'blocs', including ethnic ones.[1] And

---

1. At the end of 2011 I attended such a wooing exercise towards Somali leaders by a group of Labour MPs, led by Alun Michael.

most of the time this has little bearing on the broader political landscape. Moreover, minorities do sometimes have interests, especially in foreign policy, that differ, at least in intensity, from the majority. And yet the sizeable Muslim bloc vote, and its importance to Labour, did not stop Labour in government embarking on several unpopular wars in Muslim countries. The effective Muslim outcry – and the switching of votes to Liberal Democrats and Respect in some areas – will certainly make Muslim public opinion a factor in any similar action in the future. But there is nothing in principle wrong with that, it is just a form of pressure group politics.

In domestic policy it is different; the idea of significantly different political interests for minority Britons is one of the most malign products of separatist multiculturalism. And in the longer run, especially if the fashion for proportional representation returns, there is a danger that ethnic grievance parties like Respect will establish a foothold in parts of the country and exacerbate division.

A different, but related, issue is how some minorities develop a 'diaspora' mentality and still remain rooted in the political disputes of their country of origin. Modern communication technologies, and the internet, have made it easier for people to live in a diaspora bubble, continuing to see the world through the eyes of their ancestral lands.

The effect of satellite television and other technologies in slowing down or even stopping integration cannot be underestimated. Some who had the best of intentions to integrate slipped back when technology made it possible to return home, at least culturally. Ozlan Keles, the son of an Anatolian chef who was brought up in Palmers Green, recalls his father always watching the evening BBC television news in the 1970s and 1980s as a sort of 'ritual of integration'. And after the news he and his siblings would sometimes translate *Dallas* for their mother. But when in the early 1990s they got satellite television they immediately started watching Turkish news and soap operas, and lived again in a mainly Turkish world.

Cheaper international travel, too, has made it easier to be a kind of 'commuter-immigrant', spending many months a year in your country of origin and perhaps even retiring there, at least if you are a first-generation immigrant with deep roots back home. An increasing number of semi-detached immigrants – most notably Jamaicans, Poles, Pakistanis, Indians and Russians – live both in Britain and in their country of origin.

Faith schools are often included on the list of state-sponsored 'bad' separate multiculturalism but the story is more complicated than that. There is a long history of state-funded faith schools – mainly Church of England and Catholic but also Jewish and now increasingly Muslim too. There has been a significant increase in recent years partly because the Church of England has been the biggest sponsor of academies. Faith schools are popular with parents because they tend to enforce stricter rules and their results are generally better. But many of them, especially C of E, have large numbers of pupils from other religions or no religion – some have a non-Christian quota of 25 per cent. Indeed, Christian faith schools in some parts of the country, especially Catholic, are often the most ethnically mixed in their area. Muslim schools are usually less mixed, but that is true of ordinary state schools in Muslim areas too, and it is impossible to deny Muslims the right to state-funded faith schools when other religions enjoy it. Also, the alternative is a large expansion in Muslim private schools, which do not have to teach the national curriculum and have much lighter inspections.

Perhaps the largest impact of the ideology of separatist multiculturalism that emerged in the early 1980s was not so much what it prompted the political elite to do, but what it prompted it *not* to do. Just at the time when the authorities and the wider public culture should have been leaning *against* all the pressures towards spatial and mental separation arising from larger numbers, instead it was reinforcing them. As we have seen, local authorities like Bradford turned against integrationists like Honeyford and handed power and resources to often self-appointed community leaders.

Separatist multiculturalism was also responsible for something else that didn't happen in Britain in the last quarter of the twentieth century. The country did not develop a new story of Britishness to encompass both old and new citizens. From the mid-1960s to the mid-1980s a confident, liberal national story – of the kind captured by Danny Boyle in the 2012 Olympic opening ceremony – got squeezed between the anti-immigrant right of British politics, which did not want a new story of the nation, and the anti-racism on the left, which had become increasingly anti-national.

And because no clear national identity was on offer to new citizens, inherited ethnic and religious identities filled the gap. The language of citizens and citizenship was not even routinely used until the 1990s.

Separatist multiculturalism may have acted as a conservative force in the minority communities, preserving traditional ways of life, but it was often felt as a radical and disruptive force by the existing white communities in the towns of high immigrant settlement. As Graham Mahony, a former Bradford race relations official, has put it, 'a form of internal colonisation'. Older white people have often been left bemused and confused by the effects of modern multiculturalism – 'They keep themselves to themselves' or 'They don't want to fit in' are the phrases you often still hear.

It is true there is sometimes an element of white hypocrisy in the complaint about people not 'fitting in'; after all, multiculturalism was partly a response to white Britain's refusal to allow immigrants to join in. But times have changed.

And there is another point here. When equality was merely about granting abstract rights to migrants, as it was in the 1960s and 1970s, it was easy enough, at least in theory. But when Muslims, and other groups with strong traditionalist beliefs, started to ask society not only to give them more space but to adapt its own rules to accommodate them it is not unreasonable for the majority to wonder what they are getting in return. If you demand more, should you not contribute more in some way, or at least acknowledge that integration cannot be completely on your own terms?

Indeed, perhaps in addition to the *liberal* multiculturalism of equal rights and the *separatist* multiculturalism of those, like orthodox Jews and pious Muslims, who just want to be left alone to be different, there is a third category – most often associated with Muslims – that one might label *extra-territorial* multiculturalism or reverse integration, where the minority wants the majority society to shift its norms, values and laws to better suit the minority.

So, to summarise the story of multiculturalism so far: it starts with colour-blind liberalism and minorities seeking full membership of British society before switching to a more 'groupist' identity politics and the right to be different, partly because of the perceived failure of the first approach. Separatist multiculturalism sided with the imams against Salman Rushdie in the late

1980s; it encouraged people to wear non-western dress not just on special occasions and to continue speaking an ancestral language at home; it judged the chauvinistic assumptions of many South Asian households by a different standard to that applied to white Britain; it was happy with South Asians going back to the subcontinent for arranged marriages with non-English speaking spouses despite the damage to integration this often caused (and the misery for many young women). It even considered the absence of fathers in African-Caribbean households to be a cultural trait that just had to be accepted.

Separatist multiculturalism preserves in aspic the patterns of life of the first immigration generation and thus slows down integration, making some British South Asian communities seem laughably old-fashioned to their actual South Asian cousins. In its extreme form separatist multiculturalism even indulged or turned a blind eye to practices that were the opposite of the liberalism that inspired it: forced marriage, female genital mutilation, the hounding of gays. How widespread some of these aspects of 'community elder' multiculturalism are is hard to tell. But Jasvinder Sanghera, the co-founder of Karma Nirvana, a charity that supports South Asian women affected by forced marriage and honour-based crimes, receives about 600 calls a month from women seeking her help. One reason the small charity is so busy, according to Sanghera, is because of the reluctance of many white professionals to intervene for fear of causing cultural offence.[1] Sanghera, who ran away from home aged sixteen to escape a planned forced marriage, says that no one can know for certain how many thousands of South Asian women are affected each year, but she points out that the suicide rate among young Asian women is three times the national average.

The original liberal multiculturalism of the 1960s *was* working too slowly against entrenched discrimination and needed a shove. But by making ethnic separateness the basis of this political change – rather than a broader notion of social justice – it helped to harden ideas of 'us' and 'them'. Instead of a common life across ethnic boundaries, in too many places it has produced a rather cold, formal practice of tolerance. In recent years there has been a

1. A similar fear of stereotyping seems to lie behind the slowness to intervene against the sexual grooming of young white girls – regarded as 'fair game' by groups of mainly Pakistani men in Rochdale and other northern towns.

reaction against the more separatist strain of multiculturalism. In the next chapter I will consider the most recent journey of the idea but first I want to take a short detour to see how the multicultural argument has unfolded in the world of ideas.

Multiculturalism, What's the Big Idea?

Academic multiculturalism faces two big intellectual challenges. First, how can its stress on group rights and the primacy of ethnic identities be reconciled with the centrality of individual rights in western liberalism? Second, how can a multiculturalism that wants equal *recognition* for minority groups, and not just minority *rights*, and is hostile to the idea of a dominant culture, co-exist with the idea of democratic national citizenship?

First, the liberalism debate. How universally applicable are liberal ideas and how far should minority groups be able to challenge them on things like women's equality and free speech? To what extent should minority religious and cultural practices be accepted in the name of cultural difference? At the extreme end the practices cited are female genital mutilation, polygamy and forced marriage, but more mainstream practices might include wearing traditional dress (including the burka or niqab) in the school or workplace, Muslim and Jewish forms of slaughtering animals, segregation of the sexes and protecting minority religions from ridicule. The traditional objection to some of the above is made either in the name of universal liberal rights – to female equality for example – or in the name of a core culture, 'That's how we do/don't do things around here.'

The traditional defence of difference or exotic practices is the Millian principle that they should only be stopped if they cause harm to others. But this can be hard to measure. If a neighbourhood suddenly acquires a new population of people wearing the burkha and speaking a foreign language, the original residents may feel an indirect psychological harm. And, in any case, an extreme multiculturalist could justify causing harm to someone – say forcing them to accept an arranged marriage against their will – by arguing on utilitarian grounds that the continued existence of the group culture is a source of happiness to many and depends on the persistence of such practices. As the philosopher Anthony Appiah has pointed out, 'upholding differences among groups may entail imposing uniformity within them ... culture represents not only difference but the elimination of difference'.[1]

There are a few radical multiculturalists who do not believe that western liberal principles, such as female equality, should trump traditional ethnic practices. But most academic multiculturalists – and certainly the three most influential in Britain, Bhikhu Parekh, Tariq Modood and the Canadian Will Kymlicka – are liberals to the extent that they sign up to a minimum number of universal rights and rules.

This means they are not full-blooded cultural relativists. The Canadian multiculturalist philosopher Charles Taylor, in his influential 1992 essay 'The Politics of Recognition', rejects the idea that all cultures should be declared of equal moral worth a priori; instead he argues for a presumption that any culture should be worthy of at least some respect if it has proved meaningful to many people over an extended period of time. Similarly, Bhikhu Parekh writes in his book *Rethinking Multiculturalism* that 'although all cultures have worth and deserve basic respect, they are not equally worthy and do not merit equal respect'.[2]

So most academic multiculturalists are not cultural relativists but they are cosmopolitans, meaning they are on the side of fluidity, hybridity, cultural borrowing and so on. They see ethnic identities as central to human life but also as evolving rather than fixed. Against them are communitarian multiculturalists who do see identities as more or less fixed and worry about boundary maintenance. 'Community elders' tend to be in this camp. Critics of communitarian multiculturalism, such as Amartya Sen, have called it plural monoculturalism or, in everyday language, 'putting people in ethnic boxes'.

But notwithstanding this cosmopolitanism, most academic multiculturalists are ambivalent about liberalism and reject the UN Declaration of Human Rights as too western-centric and secular. Parekh again: 'Although

1. Anthony Appiah, *The Ethics of Identity*, Chapter 4, 'The Trouble with Culture', Princeton University Press, 2007.
2. Bhikhu Parekh, *Rethinking Multiculturalism: Cultural Diversity and Political Theory*, Macmillan, 2000.

admirable, the UN Declaration is not free of defects. It retains a distinctly liberal bias and includes rights which ... cannot claim universal validity: for example, the rights to a more or less unlimited freedom of expression, to marriage based on the "full and free consent" of the parties involved, and to relatively unlimited property.'

Similarly, Tariq Modood seems relatively unworried about the imprisoning aspect of ethnic/religious culture: 'Some forms of abuse of women are disproportionately found in some minority communities (clitorodotomy, forced marriages). Unfortunately feminism has come to be used as a missionary ideology to express the supremacy of the west and the backwardness of the rest.'[1]

Modood is also equivocal on free speech: 'If people are to occupy the same political space without conflict they mutually have to limit the extent to which they subject each other's fundamental beliefs to criticism.' Preservation of diversity leaves less room for a diversity of views, as Kenan Malik has pointed out.

There is a strong anti-western sentiment that runs through much modern multicultural thinking. Indeed, contrary to its modern image, multiculturalism, especially in its harder forms, could be said to represent the concerns and instincts of more traditional, collectivist societies – a revenge of the colonised (leading multiculturalists, in Britain at least, are disproportionately people with family roots in former colonial countries). In his critique of liberalism Parekh makes much of its western bias and its roots in colonial history. The British Pakistani science writer Zia Sardar is also suspicious of liberalism's roots and has put his complaint with characteristic directness: 'Multiculturalism is about dethroning the west, about reminding people that western principles are not universal. And the main beef with liberal secularism is that it narrows the public domain and tends to exclude Muslims.'

But many nineteenth-century liberals were critics of colonialism, and the historical origin of an idea does not in itself invalidate it. Liberalism is a more subtle and accommodating philosophy than Sardar, Parekh and others paint it. For example, the multiculturalist critique of 'monism' – the idea that there

1. Runnymede Trust paper, March 2008.

is a particular way of life or belief system that is superior to others and can be used to measure others against – has long been attacked by philosophical pluralists, many of whom would also call themselves liberals. The best-known figure here is Isaiah Berlin, whose idea that values and cultures are 'incommensurable' – meaning they are not measurable against one another on a single scale – prefigures many modern debates within multiculturalism.

Parekh, as we have seen, believes that societies do need to be governed by some universal principles. He just thinks that liberalism is not equipped for the job because it places too much stress on western ideas like individual autonomy. Multiculturalists like him are often enthusiastic about *group* autonomy, but much less so about *individual* autonomy.

But, as George Crowder has argued, liberalism's alleged 'ethno-centrism' is not proved by pointing to the fact that it can't accommodate every existing culture. 'No political system can do that; some values must always be emphasised at the expense of others. The best a political framework can do is to be as accommodating as possible, consistent with the basic values of the framework.' And on that score, Crowder concludes, liberalism does better than any alternative.[1]

What about the second multiculturalism debate over minority recognition and the idea of a national culture? Multiculturalism, especially in its harder form, has an avowedly anti-national bias. It emerged in part to promote the interests of minorities in an era, in Britain at least, when the left had fallen out of love with the nation state. But things are not quite that simple. For a start the two best-known Canadian multiculturalists, Will Kymlicka and Charles Taylor, argue that immigrant groups should indeed conform to the cultures of long-standing nations, but that is partly because they are sympathetic to the right of the minority nation within Canada, the Québécois, to impose its culture on immigrants. Parekh condemns Kymlicka for this: 'He reflects the long-familiar liberal tendency ... to draw a sharp contrast between ethnic groups and nations and privilege the latter.'

Yet all three of the main multiculturalism theorists claim to be quite enthusiastic promoters of national citizenship. Consider the following from

1. Bhikhu Parekh's, 'Multiculturalist Critique of Liberalism', paper delivered at the Australasian Political Studies Annual Conference 2009

Tariq Modood: 'We cannot both ask new Britons to integrate and go around saying that being British (or English) is a hollowed out, meaningless project whose time has come to an end. This will rightly produce confusion and ... will offer no defence against the calls of other loyalties and missions.'[1]

And Parekh is the most enthusiastic supporter of national citizenship of all: 'Members of a political community share common interests and bonds and make claims and entertain expectations of each other that they do not in relation to outsiders ... Citizenship is not just a matter of rights and obligations, but involves identifying with the political community, seeing it as one's own, accepting responsibility for it and promoting its well-being. In welfare states, citizenship also means a willingness to share one's resources with fellow citizens: an obligation to ensure that others enjoy the basic conditions of a decent life. Furthermore, a political community does not exist merely in the present. It is the product of the countless small and large sacrifices of past generations.'[2]

This might be a liberal nationalist manifesto, except that Parekh does not use the word nation or national. Parekh does not see national rights as stronger than ethnic minority rights and wants to strip the idea of the nation of all meaning that is not purely political: 'the idea of a national culture makes little sense, and the project of cultural unification on which ... all modern states have relied for their cohesion is no longer viable today'. He adds: 'Since it [Britain] has no cultural and moral consensus it is not clear what immigrants are to be assimilated into.' But, surely, there is *some* cultural and moral consensus in modern Britain even if it is looser than in the past.

Multiculturalists want a positive politics of recognition to compensate for what Modood calls the 'demeaned' identity minorities have had to suffer; minority rights for individuals is not sufficient. Moreover, they do not accept that the apparently neutral nation state can provide such recognition because it reflects the interests of the dominant group. As Varun Uberoi, a co-author of Tariq Modood, has written: 'If the state only establishes this culture's religion in its political institutions, teaches only this culture's history, uses only this culture's language ... it is treating minorities inequitably because

1. *Multiculturalism: A Civic Idea* by Tariq Modood, Polity Press, 2007.
2. *Prospect*, September 2005

they too are citizens but their cultures receive no such support.' Instead, multiculturalists want equality in connection 'with the symbolic dimensions of public culture',[1] which means, for example, that they want the state to provide official recognition to all significant religions in the public sphere, not just the Church of England.

Many people, probably most, would be perfectly happy to see religious leaders from other faiths sitting in the House of Lords. And beyond that? You cannot cut up the state like a cake. Lots of things about it must be indivisible, like the rule of law or the national language. Or should significant minorities have their own separate legal/political/linguistic space and even Parliament, like Scotland within the United Kingdom?

Some Muslims would certainly like a 'part Islamification' of Britain, and orthodox Jews too want separate jurisdiction in some fields. That way lies apartheid without white domination. Jews and Muslims, and other religions too, do run their own tribunals on matters of family law and so on, but these organisations operate like private clubs within the overall jurisdiction of British law. Similarly, people should speak the national language to be understood in the public sphere but obviously can speak any language they like at home.

Academic multiculturalism in its rejection of liberal minority rights as inadequate is (again) guilty of underestimating liberalism; majority domination is something that liberalism has wrestled with for a long time. Over several hundred years the principle of Cuius regio, eius religio – meaning the religion of the ruler was the religion of the ruled – gradually ceded to the liberal idea of minority religious rights. Catholics, in Britain for example, first became free to practise their religion at the end of the seventeenth century and then by the middle of the nineteenth century lost all significant social and political handicaps (though they never took the next, multiculturalist, step to demanding equal recognition of Catholicism with Protestantism!).

There are all sorts of anti-majoritarian checks and balances in a modern liberal state, not to mention the private space that minorities enjoy to practise their different religions and cultures. And it is simply wrong – or at least out

1. Varun Uberoi, 'Do Policies of Multiculturalism Change National Identities?', *The Political Quarterly*, vol. 79, no. 3, July–September 2008.

of date – to claim, as Varun Oberoi and Tariq Modood do, that 'the cultural majority often sees the nation as only theirs'.[1] Moreover, majorities themselves consist of many different minorities, often with conflicting interests or values. Modern Britain is not a proto-fascist state with an angry and united majority out to do down minorities.

Academic multiculturalists are also in danger of getting on the wrong side of democracy and of being hostile to a sense of democratic 'ownership'. Britain, of course, does not belong only to the majority. But the academic multiculturalists feel it is reserved too much for the majority and so want to dilute or undermine that sense of ownership. Consider this from Varun Uberoi, Tariq Modood and others in an essay on national identity: 'the English majority are privileged because they are dominant and it is difficult to justify why this dominance should continue'.[2]

This is exactly the wrong way round. Instead of trying to deny the majority its sense of ownership, *the point is to include the minority in that feeling of ownership*. Academic multiculturalism's over-sensitivity to the 'second class citizen' status of minorities leads it to make unrealistic and destructive demands on the political status quo – a sort of multicultural over-reach.

This is another way of talking about multiculturalism's 'two-way street' problem, the belief that too much of the onus of integration falls on the immigrant and too little on the host society. 'Integrationists,' Bhikhu Parekh writes, 'worry if immigrants retain a strong sense of commitment to their country of origin, reproduce its political controversies in their new environment, direct their philanthropic activities there'. This is true. But so apparently does Parekh, who writes: 'a political community requires a common sense of belonging ... a shared collective identity, a degree of mutual commitment and attachment, to underpin and nourish the practice of equal and active citizenship'.

It is often said that a host society cannot demand anything of a newcomer that it does not demand of existing citizens. It is an idea that I would agree with in most circumstances, but it's not always true. In citizenship and language

1. See 'Inclusive Britishness: A Multiculturalist Advance', *Political Studies*, 2012.
2. *Global Migration, Ethnicity and Britishness*, Tariq Modood and John Salt (eds), Palgrave Macmillan, 2011, p. 207.

tests Britain makes special demands on newcomers and it's right that it does so. The act of immigration is, normally, freely chosen. The immigrant has chosen to come to an already existing country with its own laws, history, language and so on. Those need to be respected and understood. The host society must offer equal rights to the newcomer, including the right to be different in a way that does not foster separation. Majorities do then adapt to accommodate minorities but it is a long-term and largely unconscious process, whereas the immigrant's adaptation is shorter-term and more conscious. That is as it should be. But the stress that academic multiculturalists place on the 'two-way street' implies that the immigrant is doing the host society a favour by coming to the country and that its citizens should be grateful; a somewhat eccentric view of immigration, especially of the low-skill kind.

The host society majority are, in any case, largely absent from the multiculturalism story. It is one of the blind spots of most of the academic multiculturalists I have been considering (though Parekh has publicly acknowledged the failure). Multiculturalism encourages, and wants funded from the public purse, the expression of minority ethnic identification, but has been silent about – or hostile to – the expression of majority ethnic identification.[1]

It is often hard being a newcomer in a society, even a liberal one like Britain that offers undreamt of protections and rights compared with earlier eras. But mass immigration makes big demands on host communities too, and if multiculturalism only addresses the concerns and promotes the identity of minorities – what Eric Kaufmann calls 'asymmetrical multiculturalism' – it will not help Britain to adapt successfully to the big demographic changes taking place. A successful integration strategy must engage the attention, consent and sympathy of the majority, particularly in the areas of high immigration, if the formal equalities offered to minorities by politics and law are to become the *felt* equality and acceptance of everyday life.

What, for example, does multiculturalism theory have to say to those elderly white people of the Pollards Hill estate in Merton, in south-west London, many of whom feel displaced and disrupted by the arrival of a large Ghanaian population in recent years? To the local whites the Ghanaians

1. Varun Uberoi and Tariq Modood talk about 'minimising' the dominant culture, see 'Inclusive Britishness: A Multiculturalist Advance', *Political Studies*, 2012.

are not fitting in but imposing their own way of life on the neighbourhood. Similar small battles are taking place in thousands of other housing estates up and down the country.

There is a strong strand of wishful thinking in most academic multicul-turalism – and a reluctance to accept trade-offs. All three thinkers I have been looking at assert, for example, that strong multicultural identities are perfectly compatible with strong national identities, but they provide no evidence for this claim. Common sense would surely suggest that, on the contrary, minor-ity autonomy and feelings of national solidarity pull in different directions.

Modood makes much of the 'ethnicity paradox' that the more you are allowed to be yourself and take pride in your own roots the more likely you are to identify with your adopted country – again, this may be true for some groups, particularly relatively successful ones like Hindu Indians, but where is the evidence? French Muslims who tend to be less pious than British ones identify more with France than their British counterparts.

Indeed the argument could be turned around. The more the *majority* in a modern liberal state has a confident and well-articulated sense of its collec-tive identity and history the easier it is for minorities – both as individuals and collectively – to see themselves as part of the national story. This seems to be the case in Scotland, for example, where many of the South Asian minority are enthusiastic Scottish nationalists. On the other hand, as Lauren McLaren has written, possibly with the English in mind, 'where individuals struggle to define their socio-political community they tend to be more threatened by outside influences. Without knowing who "we" are, we worry about where "they" will fit in.'[1]

Surely the interesting and difficult issue here is the balance: how much separateness in lifestyles, language and so on remains compatible with an idea of strong citizenship? All three theorists just assume that the welcom-ing stance implied by multiculturalism towards newcomers must succeed in incorporating them as loyal citizens. And once this is seen to happen, sceptical natives will no longer view immigrants as a threat to prevailing values and will come to accept cultural heterogeneity as compatible with national cohesion.

1. See the recent work of Christian Joppke.

Will Kymlicka makes a strong case for this in the Canadian story, but Canada is a one-off where multiculturalism has always had a strongly integrationist assumption and where it has become part of the country's identity in the quest to distinguish itself from the US. But it is not obviously borne out by recent history in, say, Britain or the Netherlands.

The work of American academic Jack Citrin shows that differences in multicultural policy regimes between countries make no discernible difference to public attitudes towards immigration or minorities. It is just as plausible to argue that multiculturalism has elevated ethnic identification and group belonging at the expense of a commitment to a common core of norms and experience and that the insistence on difference – in dress, in language and so on – provokes resentment that can easily turn into outright hostility. One Labour MP in a town with a large and quite segregated Muslim minority told me about the suppressed anger he has often observed in his white constituents when passing a Muslim woman in a niqab in the town centre. 'You can see them muttering to themselves and scowling at the woman,' he says. That is just an anecdote but no better evidence is provided for the inherently less plausible claim that celebrating difference encourages minorities to join in and majorities to embrace them.[1]

Because it is hostile to the idea of a core national culture and the idea of the legitimate cultural and political weight of the majority community, academic multiculturalism can end up supporting a very thin notion of national citizenship. And despite the avowed leftism of most academic multiculturalists, they often end up on the same side as liberal individualists and conservatives. 'So long as I pay my taxes and obey the law, society can make no further demands on me' – one can imagine this being said by both a small-state free-market conservative and a separatist multiculturalist.

The minority demand for greater autonomy in the light of the prejudice that was still pervasive in the early 1980s was understandable. But at what

---

1. The opinion poll data also shows no support for a strong multiculturalist position even from minorities. According to Ipsos MORI only 16 per cent of the native born with native parents strongly agree that ethnic groups should maintain their traditions. For EU immigrants the figure is similarly low; it is a bit higher for non-European immigrants – 43 per cent for those who have been here less than seven years and 34 per cent for more than seven years.

point does a 'demeaned identity' cease to be demeaned? And how can the demand for something as nebulous as 'recognition' ever be satisfied? Too much of academic multiculturalism remains stuck in the 1980s. Instead of requiring that long-established liberal democracies tear up the rule book and reshape their political structures to suit minority group rights, something that would surely serve only to alienate the majority, academic multiculturalism should focus on how best to exploit the plentiful space offered to minorities by modern liberalism.

Much of the work of multiculturalist writers is highly abstract, with little attempt to test the ideas against the real world. And multiculturalism in the universities has had no significant internal opposition to bring it back to earth. Yet, as one of the intellectual manifestations of post-war immigration, it has brought some insight, and passion, into old debates on liberalism, pluralism, universalism, relativism, religious freedom and identities. And a few good ideas have emerged over recent years. One example is Parekh's idea of 'operative public values' – how values are often hidden or implicit in national institutions, which then tends to favour insiders who enjoy a kind of implicit knowledge. These values should be made more explicit; indeed, if we are trying to reimagine national citizenship for a more plural but still coherent society, many things must be made more explicit.

But the great advances of recent decades in minority rights and anti-discrimination legislation owe little to academic multiculturalism (despite the claims it sometimes makes) and much to conventional, colour-blind liberalism. Moreover, academic multiculturalism's uncritical championing of minority traditions, its neglect of majorities, and suspicion of integration, its continuing promotion of minority autonomy even after Britain has become a much more accommodating country, has left it politically marginalised.

The broader story of multiculturalism as a 'live and let live' approach to the management of minority-majority relationships can, however, count some successes. There is, indeed, *some* truth in Tariq Modood's 'ethnicity paradox'. By allowing the post-war minorities to find their own way to an understanding of the country and their own hybrid versions of what it is to be British, it has probably ended up binding them into the country more thoroughly than if they had been pushed.

This has worked especially well for those minorities, such as Hindus and Sikhs from India, East African Asians and some black Africans, which have the right level of 'cultural protection' – a benign combination of supportive family networks, a powerful work ethic, a pro-education tradition and a cultural confidence that has also helped them to integrate successfully.

But 'laissez-faire' has worked much less well for those groups such as Kashmiri Pakistanis, Bangladeshis and Somalis who were poor and often illiterate when they arrived and brought with them a conservative, rural version of Islam and family networks that locked them away from mainstream society.

Successful immigrant groups do not need an integration strategy, they already have one in their culture and their socio-economic starting points. Britain's brand of multiculturalism has allowed the well-equipped to succeed and the problem groups to flounder and self-segregate. That is one reason why it is possible to hold apparently contradictory views about the multiculturalism record.

CHAPTER 5

The Second Great Arrival 1997–Today

Labour's Greatest Legacy

The second great phase of post-war immigration, which continues to this day, began with the election of Tony Blair's first Labour government in 1997. And the effect was almost instant. Net immigration to Britain in 1997 was 48,000; in 1998 it increased to 140,000. In thirty years' time New Labour's immigration policy will almost certainly be seen as its primary legacy.

The second wave has been almost double the first post-colonial wave but also compressed into fifteen years rather than spread out over fifty, and it is also proving harder to drive down. The total number of immigrants who arrived between 1948 and the early 1990s was about 2 million (who then had about 2 million children in Britain), overwhelmingly non-white minorities from Asia, Africa and the Caribbean. In the second-wave from 1997 to 2012 the total of non-British net immigration has been around 4 million – the annual inflow, which since 2004 has been averaging close to 500,000 a year, minus the outflow.

It is true that someone who comes to live in Britain for more than one year is classified as an immigrant, rather than a visitor, so plenty of 'immigration' includes short-term stays – a student, say, coming to do a two-year course and then going home. But since 1997 more than 2 million people have been granted permanent right of settlement in Britain, mainly from Africa and Asia, and the number is currently rising at about 150,000 a year, roughly three times the 50,000 annual figure from the 1970s to the late 1990s.

The settled minority population of Britain, including about 3 million white people from places like Poland and Ireland, is now around 11 million. In 1997 nearly half the minority population was British born; that has now slipped back to about one third.[1]

Even if the current Conservative-led coalition succeeds in bringing net immigration back down to 'tens of thousands' a year by 2015, as it has pledged, England and Wales is already 20 per cent minority and will be 20 per cent visible minority by around 2020, with several major cities including London, Leicester and Birmingham likely to be 'majority non-white minority' by then. Britain as a whole will hit the 20 per cent mark a few years later. This is a very big change in a very short period, in fact it represents roughly a trebling of the visible minority proportion of the population in just twenty-five years – from about 7 per cent in the mid-1990s to around 20 per cent in 2020.

Because of this enormous scale the second wave will probably change Britain more than the first wave, but it marks less of a psychological rupture. By the early 1990s Britain had already taken the big step, albeit with some reluctance, to becoming a multiracial society. The resident population had become familiar with visible difference by the early 1990s, especially in the big metropolitan centres. The Powellite cloud had largely dispersed and overt racism was on the wane. Britain had acquired some new tribes in some of its big cities but in most places life went on much as it had before.

Fifteen years later things look rather different. Anxiety about immigration which barely registered in the mid-1990s rose in the late 2000s to levels last seen in the late 1960s, before dropping back somewhat after the 2010 election in the light of the new government's pledge to cut back sharply. But the objections have been mainly about speed and scale of change and pressure on resources rather than about race. That was partly because Britain was more comfortable with racial difference and the fact that racial objections were no longer publicly legitimate; also one of the most publicly visible groups to arrive after 2004 were white East Europeans.

1. According to the ONS in 2011 about 12 per cent of the resident population were born outside Britain, but only 8 per cent of the resident population are not British citizens.

Like the first Great Arrival, the second Great Arrival happened largely by accident. There was virtually nothing about immigration in Labour's 1997 manifesto (or indeed that of 2001 or 2005). If the justification for the first opening was imperial obligation, the second was economic benefit. As the dust settles it is clear, however, that the economic case is not, on its own, a strong one (see Chapter 1).

One of the features of the post-1997 immigration wave is that it doesn't have a face in the way that the post-colonial immigration did. It has been somewhat more mixed in its country of origin and it spread out around the country more. To the extent that it has had a face, it has been a white East European one (though more likely to be a Polish factory worker than a plumber). Roughly 1.5 million East Europeans came between 2004 and 2008, and the number of East European residents in 2012 still stood at just over 1 million. This is the largest short-term movement in peacetime European history.

Most of the East Europeans were, and are, young and quite well educated but prepared to work in low or unskilled jobs. Surprisingly the overall economic impact from this labour market 'shock' seems to have been rather limited, with some benefits at the top end of the labour market and some downward pressure on wages at the bottom. Socially, the picture is more mixed, with East Europeans fitting in well in many places but creating tensions in others.

According to the government's 'Place Survey' (2009) some of the most tense places in the country (those where large numbers of people report that people from different backgrounds do not get on well together) are in areas of high Eastern European settlement, like Goole in Humberside and Boston near the Wash. These are places that had not experienced significant immigration before and where East Europeans are employed in large groups in agriculture and horticulture and often have their own temporary accommodation just outside the town.

One reason for the greater dispersal of immigrants, especially East Europeans, is the operation of employment agencies which can supply, say, 100 workers for six months to a fish-finger factory near Scunthorpe, or a farm in a village just outside Grantham. Dispersal is in principle a good thing, but if it is too 'lumpy', if suddenly 500 Poles turn up in a town of 3,000 people, it can create some of the same problems of minority segregation in big cities.[1]

Some of the loudest complaints against the East Europeans have come from less successful members of established minorities: I have heard complaints from Hindu Indians in Slough, Pakistanis in Peterborough and Caribbeans everywhere. Shaun Bailey, the black Tory politician from west London, notes: 'A lot of people in the black community think that just when we were getting a foothold we have been pushed to the back of the queue again and these white Europeans have jumped ahead.'[2]

However, notwithstanding the visibility of the East Europeans, only about 20 per cent of net immigration since 1997 has come from Europe (east and west). And almost everyone who has been granted settlement has come from outside the EU. About three-quarters have come from the traditional centres of post-colonial immigration in Asia and Africa – in 2011, 19 per cent were from India and 9 per cent Pakistan – with others from places like Sri Lanka, Somalia, Afghanistan and Zimbabwe, and some of the rest from places without historic ties to Britain, from the Middle East, from Colombia and other parts of Latin America, and parts of Francophone Africa such as the Congo.

And the two biggest communities to arrive in the past decade are Poles and Somalis. Neither are model immigrants. Poles are usually hard workers and pragmatic, but they mainly have a guest worker mentality and many have no particular interest in joining British society. Somalis are heavily welfare-dependent and notoriously clannish. I will look more closely at the Polish and Somali stories later in this chapter.

London remains central to the British immigration story – while about 25 per cent of all births in England are to foreign-born mothers, that rises to more than 50 per cent in London (77 per cent in Newham). As we have seen, the White British population of London is now just 44.9 per cent but thanks to the relatively wide spread of the incomers around Britain in the post-1997

1. See the Equality and Human Rights Commission 2010 *Inquiry into Recruitment and Employment in the Meat and Poultry Processing Sector* for evidence of ethnic segregation at work.
2. Conversation with the author in the course of making a BBC Radio 4 Analysis programme *A New Black Politics?*, first broadcast on 31 October 2011.

opening, London's share of the non-white population has remained close to 40 per cent for almost a decade. Still, over two-thirds of the black (African and Caribbean) population, two-fifths of the Indian population and a third of the Pakistani and Chinese populations live in London.

What attracts people to Britain, and London in particular, apart from obvious things like jobs and the English language, is the fact that it is a relatively tolerant place – at least in the sense that people are generally left alone to get on with their lives as they see fit – and it is easy to navigate around. There are fewer bureaucratic obstacles to getting a job or setting up a business, for example. This is one of the reasons that quite a few recent immigrants to Britain, including many Somalis and Tamils, are secondary immigrants from other European countries.

And there are some bigger background factors too that lie behind the surge in immigration that began in 1997: the number of asylum-seekers coming to Britain started to rise sharply in the mid-1990s, thanks in part to the Balkan wars; Britain's economy was booming and creating plenty of jobs; the cost of long-distance international travel has been falling sharply over recent decades; and the networks of agents and contacts (both legal and illegal) able to deliver people to places like London have become more extensive and sophisticated.

Global economic interdependence, and the internal openness of the European Union, means there are greater flows of people temporarily and more permanently across national borders compared with the 1950s and 1960s. The number of individual travellers who pass into Britain every year is now 100 million (including multiple trips) compared with a tiny fraction of that number in 1950. So there is no question that immigration would have risen in the late 1990s whoever was in power in Westminster, but equally there is no question that Labour in power took a number of key decisions that contributed to the sharp increase.

In typical British fashion nobody planned or prepared for this big social change. An accumulation of small decisions led to a mighty big – and pretty unpopular – unintended outcome. So what were the decisions? Between 1997 and 2003 there were four significant ones.

First, there was the abolition of the so-called primary purpose rule, which had the effect of significantly raising the inflow of foreign spouses.[1] (This was a payback to Labour's loyal South Asian voters, who particularly resented the rule, and how it was applied.)

Second, the introduction of the Human Rights Act and a more active judiciary (the very things that were absent in 1970s and 1980s Britain, which had made it possible to close the immigration door) now made it harder to clamp down on the asylum wave and deport those who were not genuine refugees, which in most years was the majority.

Third was a liberalisation of student visas and work permits, both of which more than doubled after 1997. The rise in work permits was partly a response to the asylum crisis that began to hit Britain in the mid- to late 1990s. This started with genuine refugees from the Balkan conflict, but soon economic migrants from all over the second and third world saw the opportunity of slipping into the west. Britain did not have an especially open asylum regime but began to attract more applicants as other European countries, notably Germany, became less liberal. The media and public opinion were hostile, and when the operation of the asylum system got clogged up, the government opened other legitimate channels of entry.

Finally, and most significant of all for the fabric of British life, was the decision taken at the end of 2003 to open the British labour market to the new Eastern European and Baltic EU states, seven years before it was legally required and before any other big EU state did. As is now well known, about 1.5 million East Europeans (including dependants) came after 2004, some to work for a few months or years, others to settle here permanently. Many more came than were expected to, but few people in government believed the official prediction of 13,000 a year. The consensus was that they would be hard-working and culturally compatible and that a booming economy would absorb them to the benefit of the whole country.

All of these, with the exception of the primary purpose rule, had persuasive non-immigration rationales too. Foreign students helped to pay for an expanded domestic higher education system. More permits for nurses and doctors from abroad were vital for the NHS when public spending began to

---

1. The number of wives who came in under the more liberal regime rose steadily from about 14,000 to 24,000 a year between 1997 and 2007.

rise in 1999. Opening to the East Europeans was returning a geo-political favour to those countries for support over the Iraq war. Business lobbied hard for liberalisation, eager to tap a new source of relatively cheap and highly motivated labour, at all skill levels. Whitehall was mainly in favour, and there was an influential lobby of NGOs, liberal commentators and legal campaigners who also pushed to keep the door as wide as possible.

There is one more 'world-view' factor in all this. There was a pro-immigration, pro-diversity assumption in the young, 'Cool Britannia' centre-left Labour circles. Indeed it had become an increasingly important part of progressive identity; as the left shifted rightwards in many areas of economic and social policy, being pro-immigrant and pro-immigration became an even more important badge of metropolitan liberal pride. This was true both of young activists and cabinet ministers who shared a belief that large flows of work and student-based immigration were beneficial to Britain – an important part of its 'modernisation' – and should not be hampered by old-fashioned prejudices.

The assumption was not only found on the political left. A large part of the professional middle class and 'opinion-forming' Britain was culturally comfortable with multiracial Britain and also benefited economically from the new immigration – or at least faced little direct competition. A distinctively New Labour combination of economic and cultural liberalism was the backdrop to Britain's great opening of the late 1990s. Much of the political and administrative class believed that large inflows were now simply a fact of modern life (despite the fact that the net inflows had been tiny as recently as the mid-1990s), and Gordon Brown's Treasury was especially encouraging of the inflows which it saw as boosting economic growth and contributing to wage discipline on domestic workers. The Treasury usually won the Whitehall argument with the more sceptical Home Office and could always rely on support from the Foreign Office and the departments representing business and higher education.

It would be wrong to say that in this most existential area of national policy things were made up on the hoof. In fact there were six major Acts of Parliament under Labour relating to asylum and immigration – and Tony Blair had fifty meetings on bringing asylum under control between 2001 and 2004, second in number only to Iraq.[1] There were also anguished national media debates about immigration and integration and Britishness, led in part by the Labour government, in the light of the 2001 riots in the north of England and, of course, the 7/7 bombings. The mid-2000s brought the introduction of citizenship ceremonies (the first was in Brent in 2004) and citizenship tests and language tests (in 2005) as well as the beginnings of a 'points based' framework for sorting and selecting immigrants from outside the EU.

But at least before 2009, by which time all of the important opening decisions had been made, it seems that there was no general discussion in cabinet about what the country's immigration strategy was.[2] Who did Britain want to let in? In roughly what numbers? And how was the country going to absorb them to ensure that not too much extra pressure was placed on public services and infrastructure, especially in poorer neighbourhoods? Nobody at the centre of government was thinking strategically or even politically about these questions. Labour policy was an odd mix of restriction and frenetic intervention combined with benign neglect on the broader national purpose of mass immigration.

Why? A liberal squeamishness seems to be part of the answer. Ed Owen, who had been special adviser to Jack Straw, home secretary from 1997 to 2001, spoke to me in February 2010 for a BBC Radio 4 Analysis programme about Labour's immigration policy. He said this: 'For some in the Labour party, for perhaps understandable historical reasons, the very notion of having an immigration policy was regarded as rather unsavoury and was dismissed as kow-towing to the right. And so there wasn't enough space, I think in retrospect, for people to think about this issue in a serious way.'

1. See Sarah Spencer, *The Migration Debate*, Policy Press, 2011, p. 56.
2. Matt Cavanagh, who was a Labour special adviser throughout this period covering immigration issues for both David Blunkett and Gordon Brown, describes it like this: 'It was only in early 2009 that immigration itself – rather than asylum or various immigration-related problems – became the subject of serious Cabinet debate. Even at this point, most ministers continued to argue that people weren't really concerned about immigration itself, only about pressure on services, housing and labour markets. But eventually it was agreed – in a split decision, with Gordon Brown on the side of Jacqui Smith and Liam Byrne – that we needed to change our approach and accept that immigration itself was a major issue for voters.' Immigration under Labour, IPPR/*Prospect* essay collection, November 2010.

The idea of a 'secret agenda' to transform Britain through mass immigration is, however, far-fetched. The notion was given some support by an article written by a former Labour adviser, Andrew Neather, who described meetings he attended in the early 2000s in this way: 'I remember coming away from some discussions with the clear sense that the policy was intended, even if this wasn't its main purpose, to rub the right's nose in diversity and render their arguments out of date.'

A more reasonable criticism is that Labour was two-faced; more than is usual in politics. It tentatively made the case for immigration in speeches and seminars to elite audiences, but, aware of the unpopularity of greater openness, it used restrictive and hard-nosed rhetoric for Labour's blue-collar base, especially on asylum. David Blunkett, who became home secretary after the 2001 election, was a symbol of this two-facedness – happy to employ robust, populist language about immigration at times and yet presiding over the largest inflows in British history.

When I spoke to him for that same Radio 4 Analysis programme he continued to defend his actions on grounds of economic growth: 'We needed to fill the jobs that weren't being filled. We'd got as near to full employment as it was possible to get in a modern global economy. We'd got jobs that the indigenous population were unable or unwilling to do. We'd got enormous potential for growth, and the Treasury had swung round to believing that without inward migration we would not be able to sustain that ...'

Blunkett was keen to redirect the asylum flows into legal routes: 'The intention was that people should be here openly, that they should pay tax and national insurance, they should earn entitlement, and that we would clamp down on clandestine entry and illegal working.'

The asylum crunch had come at the end of the 1990s, with the Kosovo crisis and the decision to disperse the welfare-dependent, mainly non-English-speaking asylum-seekers into cheap accommodation in the most run-down towns around the country, where they often met rejection and violence. In 2000 the number entering the country to claim asylum hit 100,000 (including dependants) representing almost half of all net immigration, and Britain briefly overtook Germany as the asylum-seeker's main destination in Europe. At that time the Asylum Processing Unit, an unglamorous backwater of the

Home Office, with fifty civil servants struggling to process more than 6,000 arrivals each month, more or less ceased to function.

Asylum claims rose sharply from the mid-1990s and peaked in 2002 but today are back down to around 20,000 a year, the same level as the early 1990s. Taking the period 1997 to 2010 as a whole, about 700,000 asylum claimants arrived. Less than a third of that total were granted asylum or one of the related categories such as 'exceptional leave to remain', but a total of 77 per cent are believed to be still in the country – half illegally. Only 23 per cent of claimants left voluntarily or were deported – underlying how hard it is to find and remove people once they have been in Britain for a few years.[1]

Apart from reflecting the widespread popular antipathy to that sharp rise in the asylum inflow, most of the media were happy enough to go along with Labour's new openness on immigration in the early years; it seemed to be part of the spirit of the times and most of the losers from the new immigration were weak and politically voiceless.

But as the 2000s progressed, the press picked up on the growing unease about the scale of the inflow and became more sceptical. The tabloid press was full of weird or tragic stories involving asylum-seekers or illegal immigrants, capped by the drowning of twenty-three Chinese cockle pickers working illegally in Morecambe Bay in 2004.

Some people in government too, including Tony Blair himself, thought it was time to slow the pace. Much of the focus at this time was on the flawed machinery of border controls. Yet it seemed unfair to blame the bureaucracy when the government was sending out such mixed signals – making it easier to get in and stay while also wanting to apply greater control (see Chapter 1, 'Immigration Now, British Hubs and Caps').

If liberalism on immigration was an important plank of New Labour's modernisation strategy for Britain it was also a half-hidden one. The mixture of insouciance and obliqueness towards the issue was also evidence of the weakness in New Labour circles of the voice of those most adversely affected by the surge of extra competition in the labour market – the skilled and the unskilled working class. Social democracy had once been about

1. See Migration Watch, *Asylum: the Outcome*, August 2011, and The Migration Observatory, *Migration to the UK: Asylum*, December 2011.

reducing risk and labour-market competition for working people; Labour's mass-immigration policy now seemed to do the opposite. The trade unions, which should have been a source of reasonable non-xenophobic opposition to the new immigration policy, had virtually nothing to say – partly because the unions barely existed in many of the sectors where immigrants were most present but also because the union elite was captured by the same metropolitan liberalism on immigration as the Labour elite.

Towards the end of their period in office many Labour politicians did begin to grasp just how unpopular their immigration policy was with many of their once 'core' voters, underlined by the 2009 European elections in which almost 1 million people voted for the British National Party. Meanwhile, the Conservatives had tried and failed to capitalise on anxieties about immigration in both the 2001 and 2005 elections, but because of their own past record on the issue and a generally more liberal spirit in the country it only served to make them look old-fashioned. By the 2010 election more people were prepared to listen and their immigration reduction policy may have helped push them over the line into government.

Revising the Multiculturalism Story

The years between Labour's election in May 1997 and 2001 marked the high-water mark of official multiculturalism. In that brief period there was a raft of minority friendly initiatives and legislation, including a big surge in the number of minority elected MPs and appointed peers; the setting up and reporting of the Macpherson Inquiry into the murder of Stephen Lawrence with its finding of 'institutional racism' in the police force and a new, more subjective definition of racism; the 2000 Race Relations Act which imposed a duty on public bodies to promote race equality; funding for more faith schools and a promise, in response to Muslim lobbying, to introduce legislation outlawing discrimination on grounds of religion.

Leading Labour figures, including Tony Blair and Robin Cook, made speeches celebrating Britain's ethnic diversity.[1] And in 2000 even the sceptical

1. Robin Cook, then foreign secretary, famously claimed that chicken tikka masala was now

Tory leader, William Hague, bowed to the new liberal consensus by arranging a photo-opportunity at the Notting Hill carnival and declaring Britain to be 'a nation of immigrants'.

I remember attending a couple of international conferences of politicians and journalists at around this time, one in France and another in Germany, and on both occasions the British delegation had several non-white faces, compared with none on the other side of the table. There was a marked spirit of self-congratulation on the British side, a feeling that liberal multicultural-ism had worked and that other European countries had a lot to learn from us.

Then in 2001 the tone changed. It was the year of the nightly bulletins from the Sangatte refugee camp near Calais, the riots in the northern mill towns – Bradford, Oldham and Burnley – mainly involving young Muslim men, and then 9/11 in the US, which increased anxiety about segregation and extremism within the British Muslim minority.

The word multiculturalism was not dropped from the political vocabulary. Minority-promoting initiatives were not abandoned, nor was the idea of giv-ing minorities the space to 'be themselves'; but a much greater political stress on 'community cohesion' and integration began to compete with the idea of minority autonomy. Reflecting this new approach several reports were com-missioned by the government (and written by mainly Labour-friendly figures from local government) – the Herman Ouseley report into Bradford, the David Ritchie report into Oldham, the Ted Cantle report into the mill town riots more generally and a few years later in 2007 the Darra Singh Commission on Integration and Cohesion.[1] Ouseley and Cantle spoke about the problem of 'parallel lives', and Darra Singh captured the new spirit of the time by writing in the introduction to his report: 'As a Commission our vision of society is one where people are committed to what we have in common rather than obsessing with those things that make us different.'

Britain's national dish and a good example of how Britain 'absorbs and adapts external influences', saying that: 'chicken tikka is an Indian dish, the masala sauce was added to satisfy the desire of British people to have their meat served in gravy'. The speech infuriated Tony Blair at the time.

1. Darra Singh's commission's report, *Our Shared Future*, used the language of integration but did not propose any significant change to Britain's largely laissez-faire tradition.

That new emphasis was even more evident after the trauma of 7/7 2005, when four young British-born Muslims killed themselves and fifty-two others in four explosions in central London. It came just one day after London's victory in the competition to host the 2012 Olympics, in which the multicultural image of the city had been played to full effect. The dark side of multiculturalism, the violent hostility to Britain that had grown unchallenged in a few Muslim enclaves, was now on full view too.

The response to the bombing itself was impressively calm. Official Britain rallied round to proclaim one message – that this dreadful deed was not to be laid at the door of Britain's Muslim community. And on the whole it wasn't. There was a small increase in attacks on mosques and individual Muslims, but fewer than expected, and two months after the attacks the Greater London Authority reported that the number, in London, was lower than before 7/7.

The government was keen to have television pictures of Muslim leaders marching into 10 Downing Street to help tackle the problem of extremism. It achieved that initial symbolism but not much else. On 19 July Tony Blair met the then head of the Muslim Council of Britain, Iqbal Sacranie, along with a group of other Muslim leaders, and the next day it was agreed to set up seven working parties on various aspects of Muslim life that might have a bearing on combating extremism – such as the education of imams and giving a voice to Muslim women.

After four months' work the findings and recommendations of the working parties were presented to the home secretary. But everyone seemed disappointed. Some Muslim leaders evidently regarded it as an opportunity to negotiate various 'concessions' from government on a shopping list of Muslim demands, and were disappointed when some of their demands were not met. The government was also dismayed that the Muslim leadership – dominated by the Muslim Council of Britain – appeared not to have the authority or the will to change very much in Britain's complex and internally fractured Muslim world (see 'The Muslim Question', later in this chapter).

The London bombings, led by Yorkshire-born Mohammed Sidique Khan, were the culmination of a post-Rushdie story of how Britain had fostered an often poorly integrated, religiously conservative Muslim community, especially in the declining industrial towns of the North, which had itself sprouted

various extremist offshoots. There was much speculation about a lost generation of young Muslims adrift and susceptible to extremism, a generation who
did not accept their parents' village ways but could not find a comfortable
place in British society either.

'Before 9/11, the government was largely indifferent to Muslims in Britain.
After 7/7 it became obsessed. Councils, panels, working groups and advisory
task forces proliferated. At the same time an alphabet soup of bodies with
representative sounding names emerged, each claiming to speak on behalf
of Brtish Muslims and to stand as a barrier to violent extremism.' So wrote
Shiraz Maher and Martyn Frampton in an influential 2009 think tank report
urging the government not to use non-violent extremists in the battle against
violent ones.[1]

Islamic extremism was seen by some as a product of the failure of separatist multiculturalism, just as the Brixton riots had been seen as a failure of
the more liberal variant. A leading academic of Sikh background, Gurharpal
Singh, quipped: 'British multiculturalism is dead, and militant Islam killed
it off.'

Multiculturalism did not, in fact, go away – it was too ingrained – but it
did evolve. The Cantle report proposal of civic integration measures, such as
citizenship tests and ceremonies for new arrivals, was implemented by Home
Secretary David Blunkett in 2004. Whereas in the past people had merely
received a letter through the post informing them that they been accepted
for citizenship, they now had to pass an exam (and possibly a language test
too) based on study of a book, *Life in the* UK. The test, which was under review
at the end of 2012, has attracted criticism for focusing on the minutiae of
bureaucratic life in Britain – the opening and closing time of post offices, for
example – rather than British history and the important aspects of British cultural life; the fact that few indigenous citizens are able to pass the test is not
a reason for scrapping it but rather suggests it is testing the wrong things.

The ceremonies, by contrast, have been a success despite widespread
scepticism about the idea when it was proposed. Around 1 million people have
now been through such a ceremony, usually in the local town hall. Everybody

1. *Choosing our friends wisely*, Policy Exchange report, 2009.

who is granted citizenship and even right of residence must now attend such a ceremony within ninety days.

These rituals of national allegiance are not particularly significant in themselves but they attracted a lot of media interest in the mid-2000s, as they were becoming established, and for good reason. They did represent a step towards a more normal, European-style national citizenship; a recognition that not only does the national matter more than ever in post-imperial, mass-immigration Britain (and post 7/7 Britain) but it is also not something mystical and ineffable – outsiders can join the club.

In the same year, 2002, that citizenship tests were agreed in principle, citizenship classes in schools became a statutory part of the national curriculum for all 11–16-year-olds. This educational experiment has had rather mixed results so far. But taken together with the citizenship rituals for newcomers it represented a rebalancing, a shift from a post-national 'live and let live' ideal – a minority but influential attitude – to a more national integrationist ideal.

Around this time Gordon Brown began his debate on Britishness, and metropolitan liberals started worrying about multiculturalism's 'asymmetry' – the fact that it had nothing to say to what had become known as the 'left-behind' white working class. Later in 2008, the Goldsmith citizenship review (led by the Labour peer Peter Goldsmith) called for a 'social bond of citizenship' going beyond legal rights and duties, it also recommended a Britishness day annual holiday.

As the American academic Jack Citrin has pointed out, this was all part of a Europe-wide swing. In 1999 no European country had a formal policy of civic integration; ten years later almost all did.[1]

At the intellectual level the strongly pro-multiculturalist (Bhikhu) Parekh report on the future of multi-ethnic Britain, published in 2000, also marked a high tide of influence. Thereafter some significant figures who had once been identified with multiculturalism, most notably Trevor Phillips, former head of the Equalities Commission, and Jonathan Sacks, the Chief Rabbi, began

1. *Are we all now Multiculturalists, Assimilationists, neither or both?*, Jack Citrin, University of California, Berkeley. The political scientist Rogers Brubaker has documented the partial retreat from multiculturalism in several countries.

to question whether it was placing too much stress on promoting minority recognition and not enough on integration.

Writing in *The Times* on 7 February 2011, Sacks warned of a new phenomenon across Europe, that the children of immigrants are more hostile to the host societies than their parents were and that 'for the first time in modern history, Britain was being organised to allow a big group of citizens to lead their lives as if in a foreign culture'.[1] The work of American social theorist Robert Putnam on the relationship in the US between ethnic fragmentation and lower levels of trust also added to the focus on social cohesion.

Perhaps even more significantly, Anthony Lester, the man who had helped Roy Jenkins draw up Britain's 1960s and 1970s race relations legislation, turned against multiculturalism. He had this to say about the Parekh report: 'Much of it ... is written entirely from the perspective of victims, with little to challenge attitudes and practices prevalent among some minorities and their leaders that are difficult to reconcile with the ideas of a liberal democratic society.'

This integrationist shift went hand in hand with further multiculturalist initiatives, including an expansion in faith schools and a new law against religious hatred which Muslim groups had been demanding for years. (The religious hatred bill was passed but only after being watered down in the Lords to protect freedom of expression.)

Indeed, Labour in power continued to respond warmly to many of the wishes of the big religious and ethnic minority lobby groups, especially Muslims (in the latter case partly to compensate for the alienation created by the Iraq war). And despite many cases of forced marriage coming to light, especially in the South Asian communities, Labour was reluctant to make it a criminal offence. Instead Anthony Lester introduced a Bill in the House of Lords to give civil protection to forced marriage victims.[2]

1. Sacks, in the same article, said this about multiculturalism: 'Entered into for the noblest of reasons, it has suffered from the law of unintended consequences. Dissolving national identity makes it impossible for groups to integrate because there is nothing to integrate into, and failing to offer people pride in being British forces them to find sources of pride elsewhere.'

2. Lester was highly critical of Labour's apparent blind eye. This is from an article 'Multiculturalism and Free Speech' in the *Political Quarterly*, vol. 81, issue 1, March 2010. 'It

Similarly, when in 2004 a group of Sikhs stormed the Birmingham Rep stage claiming that Gurpreet Kaur Bhatti's play Behzti was an insult to their religion, forcing the play to be closed and the playwright to go into hiding, not a single Labour minister condemned the action. Indeed, Labour Home Office minister Fiona Mactaggart said that the free speech of the Sikh protesters was as important as the free speech of the artists.

Meanwhile, the multiculturalism story moved on again after the 2010 election. David Cameron, having overseen a further liberalisation of his own party on race – and markedly increased the number of minority Tory MPs and candidates – felt confident enough to speak out against 'state multiculturalism' in a speech in February 2011 in Munich. He said this: 'Under the doctrine of state multiculturalism, we have encouraged different cultures to live separate lives, apart from each other and apart from the mainstream. We've failed to provide a vision of society to which they feel they want to belong. We've even tolerated these segregated communities behaving in ways that run completely counter to our values ... instead of encouraging people to live apart, we need a clear sense of shared national identity that is open to everyone.'

Cameron's 'muscular liberalism' echoed what some of the more integration-minded figures in the Labour Party had been saying for a decade or more; the speech reinforced a shift from 'you can come here and be yourself' to Tony Blair's formulation: 'the right to be different, the duty to integrate'. Cameron was later attacked by many, including liberal Tories, for eliding his

---

was or should have been obvious forty years ago that problems would arise in Britain if public authorities tolerated the exploitation of children and the maltreatment of wives and daughters where such practices are condoned by a particular cultural or religious group. That is what has happened. A misguided approach to equality and respect for cultural diversity has become a cloak for oppression and injustice within the minority communities themselves.'

At the time of writing the Coalition government is consulting on making forced marriage illegal. There is resistance to this among some minority group leaders who say it will 'demonise' them. Chris McCurley, a family law solicitor who specialises in forced marriage, said this in his evidence to the Home Affairs Select Committee: 'A review of the 2005 report on the question of whether to criminalise forced marriage inexplicably recorded that the decision was taken not to criminalise it as black and minority ethnic communities may feel targeted. I cannot think of another criminal offence that has been considered and rejected on the basis that the perpetrators might feel "got at".'

attack on separatist multiculturalism with an analysis of Muslim extremism. It was, however, easier for Cameron to make his point about the limits of multiculturalism loudly and without qualification because his party does not have the same historic connections with minority Britain as Labour.

Poles and Somalis, the Latest Arrivals

In the course of the last ten years Britain has become home to two substantial new minorities – Polish and Somali. Both have some historic ties to Britain and there are small communities from the two countries that have been here for a few generations. But like so much else in the history of British immigration, the huge increase in the size of both communities was largely unexpected and happened, in part, by accident. Certainly neither was sought, at least not on their current scale, by either politicians or the public and might be described as unintentional acts of generosity.

Today there are roughly 620,000 Polish-born immigrants in Britain, making them the third largest ethno-national minority behind Indians and Pakistanis; most have arrived since 2004. It is harder to calculate the number for Somalis, as they are included in the black African category on official forms. They have been arriving in significant numbers since the Somalian civil war began at the end of the 1980s, but the figure is complicated by the arrival of tens of thousands of Somalis in recent years from other European countries (particularly the Netherlands). The Labour Force Survey estimate of the Somali population is less than 100,000 but the most likely figure is around 200,000.

And both groups are here as a result of two pieces of legislation that were designed for very different times and purposes. The Poles are here as a result of the European Union free movement legislation passed back in the 1950s, giving citizens of EU member states the right to settle and work in any other EU state. Throughout most of its history the EU has consisted of countries at very similar levels of development, so the incentive to move has not been large. It was assumed that the law, although more than merely symbolic, would be used mainly by large businesses and certain kinds of professionals operating in more than one EU country. And that is largely how it has turned out (the movement from Spain, Portugal and Greece to northern Europe in the 1960s and 1970s happened before they joined the EU). As recently as 2000 only a few tens of thousands of people a year took advantage of this right.

The law was not designed to facilitate a mass movement from one country, or set of countries, to another. But that is what has happened since 2004. The accession of the East European and Baltic states meant that a bloc of eight countries with a combined population of about 70 million and average per capita income of, initially, around one fifth of the richer EU states acquired the unqualified right to come to live and work in just one of the larger rich states – Britain.

At the end of 2011 there were around 1 million East Europeans living in Britain and 730,000 working. With the benefit of hindsight it is easy to see why so many came. First, there was the underlying incentive provided by the huge disparity in levels of pay and standard of living. Second, it was only Britain, along with Ireland and Sweden, which opened its labour market in 2004, seven years earlier than required, though in 2011 all other EU states had to follow. Third, Eastern Europe is very close and travel costs are very low – it costs only about £25 to fly Ryanair from Warsaw to London and less than that to step on a coach and end up thirty hours later in Southampton.

There were other factors too, like the relative weakness of many of the East European economies in the early and mid-2000s and perhaps also the psychological factor of post-communist people with a pent-up desire to travel and live abroad, something that had only become possible from the early 1990s.

The legal-political story behind the Somali arrival is more complicated. The civil war began in the late 1980s between the Somali National Movement and military dictator Said Barre, and the state collapsed in 1991. The northern region, which had been the protectorate British Somaliland, provided some of the first wave of refugees, but has since forged its own path of reconstruction and state building with some success. Most emigrants have subsequently come from other parts of the former country which had colonial links to Italy not to Britain.

Between 1987 and 2007 about 63,000 Somali nationals applied to be refugees in Britain. Relatively few were granted refugee status under the 1951

Refugee Convention, which requires you to show evidence of persecution; this was hard for them to do because although their lives were often in danger there was no functioning state to formally persecute them. But in Britain those endangered by a civil war or even a natural disaster are sometimes granted Exceptional Leave to Remain, now described as Humanitarian Protection. That seems to have been the case with the majority of the 63,000 asylum-seekers. The number of Somalis in Britain has subsequently been swelled by family reunion, by natural growth and by the arrival of Somalis from Sweden, Denmark and the Netherlands (about 20,000 from the latter).

The story is rather similar to the growth of the Bangladeshi community in Britain. Both substantial communities arrived when Britain was supposed to have had relatively strict controls on entry. But through a combination of small historic communities, based partly on merchant navy connections, civil wars back home and family reunion, they have both established large British diasporas.

Neither group has yet been successful economically and both are heavily welfare-dependent, especially Somalis. And yet no lessons seem to have been learnt from the Bangladeshi experience to inform the Somali story. In both cases the relevant authorities – both political and bureaucratic – seem not to have known or cared very much about the growth of these communities.

A kind of laissez-faire 'communalism' – usually reinforcing the authority of conservative elders – has been the British way once again. Ismail Einashe, a young Somali who came here as a ten-year-old from a refugee camp in Ethiopia, and made it to Cambridge from a council estate in Camden, says: 'A number of families I know are still living much like they did when they arrived two decades ago – many of the parents speak no English and even discourage their children from speaking it at home. Britain has offered material help but has not really demanded anything of us, nor provided us with the means to integrate.' Or as one Walthamstow councillor put it to me: 'Around here we have very few British Somalis, just Somalis.'

Rare Somali success stories like Einashe, or the Olympic champion runner Mo Farah, have only advanced by painfully breaking away from their families and community and finding mentors from within British society – PE teacher Alan Watkinson in Farah's case, a couple of inspirational teachers (with the very teachery names of Mrs Pile and Mr Crabtree) in Einashe's case.[1]

Somalis have a reputation as the most troubled significant minority in Britain and the numbers, even though a bit uncertain, seem to bear this out. Only about 30 per cent of adult Somalis are economically active. About 3 per cent have a higher-level qualification and the majority have no qualifications at all. The second generation are doing badly in school: in 2005 only 22 per cent got five decent GCSEs compared with 46 per cent for Ghanaians and 54 per cent for Nigerians in that year.

On welfare dependency, 39 per cent of Somali households claim income support (easily the highest claim rate for an ethnic minority) and 40 per cent claim child benefit (again the highest for an ethnic minority). And the community has a reputation, even among sympathetic Labour MPs and councillors, for gaming the welfare system. One Labour MP whose constituency has a large Somali population said to me: 'The Somalis who come to see me do often seem to have a disturbingly detailed knowledge of the welfare system.'

Maximising welfare returns may be one reason for the high number of single-parent families in Somali households, thought to be around 60 per cent. There are other factors too, as Einashe explains: 'Our culture is a very patriarchal one and some of the men find themselves confused and stripped of status in Britain. Quite a few of them just sit around all day in the cafés chewing khat and the women get fed up with them and chuck them out of the house. The younger men have no role models and often have discipline problems. Too many of the kids I was at school with have moved on from the standard turf-war punch-ups with rival white or black gangs to serious drug and gun crime. I saw it all happening in slow motion, we could have stopped it.'

There are, of course, reasons why Somalis have proved to be such a difficult minority. Many Somalis arrived in Britain, particularly back in the 1990s, traumatised by war. A high number of older Somalis are illiterate, indeed there wasn't even a written language until 1972, and a whole generation missed out on formal education.

But, according to Einashe, Somalis are also a classic example of a group

1. See Ismail Einashe, 'Mo and Me', Prospect, September 2012.

with too much cultural protection, too much falling back on their notorious clan system, their particular brand of Islam and traditional ways of doing things that are not well suited to a rich liberal democracy. 'Too many have retreated into themselves, rather like many of the Kashmiri Pakistanis, and that means they don't have the networks and connections to succeed here. Migration always means losing something of yourself. That's the price you pay for being somewhere safe and free. We are in a different place now and we must stop looking back,' he says.

Somalis have sometimes been called the 'invisible' minority, and Omer Ahmed, director of the Council of Somali Organisations, and part of a small but growing British Somali political elite, blames this partly on an inability to co-operate. There are more Somali organisations per head than almost any other minority, but they seldom work together to try to deal with the communities' manifest social problems. 'The problem is that each Somali is his own Sultan,' says Ahmed.

There are some signs of progress. There are now five British Somali local councillors (including a former mayor of Tower Hamlets); Somali parents are often aspirational for their children and young women are starting to do better at school; and the entrepreneurial spirit is flourishing in the internet shops and money transfer operations on many high streets in London (where most Somalis live), Leicester, Bristol and other places where they have settled.

So, the Somalis represent an old story of immigrant segregation – partly chosen segregation – and a British society which has been decent enough to let them in but then too indifferent to help them join in, exemplified by the failure to ban the mild narcotic khat.[1]

The Polish experience, by contrast, has been very much simpler and easier. Yet, despite coming from another modern western society, albeit a poorer one, they have largely kept themselves apart too.

---

1. There is a continuing debate about whether khat should be banned, as it is in many other European countries. Those who criticise Britain's failure to ban it point to the fact that it is used almost exclusively by Somalis, and a few other East Africans, and claim that the authorities do not care enough about the damage it is causing. Khat certainly does damage the Somali community, but there is a question about whether criminalising it will just drive it underground.

The Poles are the first large group of 'commuter immigrants' in British history. By the end of 2009 around half of the Poles who had arrived since 2004 had returned home. Many of the rest would count as settled in Britain: they probably have their family here and may have children in school (there are about 50,000 Polish children in British schools, disproportionately in faith schools). But even those who have settled are still often commuters of a slightly different kind: they return to Poland regularly, and when here they speak Polish at home (and often at work too) and generally mix with other Poles and tend to live in small Polish enclaves, usually in the rougher parts of town. A research report that looked at the socialising patterns of all East Europeans in 2007 painted a mixed picture: during the first six months half of them said they had no contact with local people at all and even after two and a half years one quarter of the sample still said they had no leisure-time contact with the local population, and fewer than one in five said they spent most of their time with British people.[1]

This may change more over time, especially as the children of those settled here grow up; some of those children are doing well in school, some quite poorly. And there is also a small but growing amount of co-habitation and marriage between Poles and British citizens.

The Poles – who make up nearly 70 per cent of the arrivals from the eight Eastern European countries that joined the EU in 2004 – generally work in low-paid jobs: in 2007 nearly 90 per cent of East Europeans were paid less than £400 a week compared with 57 per cent of the British-born. Poles, like other East Europeans, are generally over-qualified for the work they do and have lower wage expectations than British workers, both of which makes them attractive to employers.

The largest number of Poles live in London and the South-East but they are also quite widely dispersed around the country. And they have spread out across many different business sectors, from the famous Polish plumber/small tradesman/builder to bars and restaurants. In the industrial sector – especially food processing – they are often recruited by employment agencies, who may also house them and generally look after them. Occupations where

1. S. Spencer, M. Ruhs, B. Anderson and B. Rogaly, *Migrants lives beyond the workplace*, Joseph Rowntree Foundation, 2007.

they are particularly numerous include 'packers, bottlers, canners and fill-ers', where they are 20 per cent of the workforce, 'paper and wood machine operatives' (11 per cent), and 'food, drink and tobacco process operatives' (16 per cent).

The Poles have a reputation for being hard-working and hard-drinking and not big users of the welfare state, which altogether makes them reasonably popular (though there is a pattern of conflict in some areas with Muslims who do not like their public drinking). They are also helping to revive Catholic con-gregations in many places. They are less popular in parts of eastern England, where they have arrived in very large numbers, relative to the size of towns like Boston (Fenland), Peterborough, King's Lynn and Corby. In the long run there will probably be a sizeable Polish 'colony' left, somewhat more visible than, say, the French or the Russian, and less integrated than the post-war Polish generation.

There is also a larger question of who benefits from such a large move-ment of people in such a short period of time. The immigrants themselves have obviously benefited, but according to a May 2011 National Institute of Economic and Social Research review of the inflow the effect on growth was 'insignificant'.

The academic economic consensus also states that there has been little job displacement for natives and only a minor downward pressure on wages at the bottom end of the labour market as a result of the East European 'shock'. That is not what many small tradesmen in London believe; it may be because many East Europeans are self-employed that their impact is not showing up in the figures. And it also seems hard to believe that an increase in the unskilled labour force of about 10 per cent, higher in some areas, does not mean signifi-cant downward pressure on local wages.

To summarise, Britain has acquired two substantial new populations in recent years but it is not obvious that they have contributed to the well-being of the average citizen. That is, of course, not the only consideration that mat-ters in a liberal society, and one with important international obligations, but it still remains a central consideration in a democratic society – especially when citizens have been told that immigration is for their benefit. Moreover, in the case of the Somali arrival it is not clear that the Somalis themselves have benefited beyond the short-term advantage of being safe. It may be that both groups will start to drift back to their country of origin in significant numbers, but that seems unlikely, especially for the Somalis. In which case, as Ismail Einashe argues, it is time we started thinking harder about how to draw them into mainstream British society.

The Muslim Question

The post-1997 period saw the emergence of the Muslim minority as Britain's most awkward, thanks to slow progress economically and socially and a connection to the unstable world of global Islamic politics. Before 9/11 most British people still tended to see Muslims as part of a largely undifferentiated group of 'Asians'. This seems to have been true even in areas of high Muslim settlement. Ted Cantle reports that in his inquiry into the northern mill town riots, just a few weeks before 9/11, hardly anyone – including Muslims themselves – used the word Muslim, preferring Asian and Asian community.[1] (Despite being a reasonably well-educated person I knew virtually nothing about Islam or the British Muslim world before 9/11 – I was not even aware of the distinction between Sunnis and Shias.)

Many Muslims, race activists and academics argue that to the extent that Muslim communities in Britain have particular problems or live apart from the mainstream it is the result of being pushed away by a fearful and hostile non-Muslim Britain – expressing what is now called Islamophobia.[2] There are many problems with this idea, as I will explain, but one central problem is that, at least until very recently, it has underestimated the degree of ignorance among most British people of Islam as a distinct theology and way of life.

It is, however, true that the opinion poll data certainly does show greater reservations towards the Muslim minority on the part of majority Britain compared with other large groups. But does this reluctance to think of Muslims

---

1. In the report on the Oldham riots, by David Ritchie, the word Asian is used 183 times, Muslim 9 times.
2. The term was coined by the Runnymede Trust in a 1997 report *Islamophobia: A Challenge for Us All*.

as a comfortable part of modern Britain stem from irrational anxieties or is it based on a reasonable judgement about Muslim collective behaviour, at least as filtered through the media and public events?

Islam, as Trevor Phillips has put it, does 'present a particular kind of challenge'. Phillips, with an eye partly on Islamic fundamentalism, points to two factors: the manner in which some strands of the religion place the Quran above man-made law and the way in which modern communication technology has made the Ummah, the worldwide community of believers, far more real to Muslims living in Britain than the equivalent concept of 'Christendom' is to British Christians.

But there are other more banal factors that have made the relationship a sometimes difficult one. There are now about 2.5 million Muslims living in Britain, nearly 4 per cent of the population (and half of them are under twenty-five). Most of them live in poor parts of Britain – the East End of London or the former industrial towns of northern England and the Midlands. There is also a significant and growing middle-class group – mainly from urban Pakistani and Indian roots – which often resents being bundled together with the poorer and more ghettoised majority.

No one is a Muslim in the abstract, everyone comes from a particular national or religious tradition. And, as we have seen, about three-quarters of British Muslims are from South Asian backgrounds, mainly from rural corners of Pakistan and Bangladesh, where the religion is embedded in traditional (and patriarchal) tribal and clan systems. It is similar with the growing Somali population, though less so with Turks and with more recent arrivals from North Africa, Bosnia, Afghanistan and Iraq, who often come from more educated backgrounds though still from traditional societies. The most successful significant Muslim minority in Britain are Indian Muslims, mainly Gujaratis, who have a socio-economic profile similar to Hindu Indians. Many Gujaratis were part of the East African exodus, and the largest concentration of them is found in Leicester.

Outside of London and Leicester British Islam is dominated by the Kashmiri Pakistanis – probably a bit less than half the total Muslim population of Britain – many of whom, partly as the result of importing spouses from the area, still have strong family and economic ties to the single district of Mirpur in northern Pakistan.[1]

For pious Muslims arriving in the 1950s and 1960s there was much that was profane and alarming about Britain, especially as the 1960s began to loosen the social and sexual constraints of the pre-war era. This ambivalence about British society was shared by other South Asian groups, but most of all by Muslims, who were particularly careful to protect women from exposure to mainstream society. To this day 68 per cent of all Muslim women are economically inactive, compared with just 35 per cent for Hindus and Sikhs and 30 per cent for Christians.

None of this makes Muslims bad citizens. Indeed, by some measures British Muslims are rather exemplary citizens. In opinion polls they identify as strongly with Britain as white people, and more so than many other minorities. They tend to be well organised politically, as we have seen, and vote in large numbers. They are generally God-fearing, family-oriented and take care of their old people – a reminder to some people of an older and better Britain.

The expression of pride in being British, or sense of belonging to Britain, as expressed in opinion polls is, however, more complicated than it looks.

The opinion poll results could be read as a claim for full recognition by Britain, not so much an expression of allegiance or loyalty to it, though there are probably elements of both. Moreover, if you go into heavily Muslim areas of Luton or Leicester or Bradford or Birmingham you immediately become aware of how connected these communities are to the countries of origin of the minority population – through satellite dishes and frequent travel there. The charitable collections are likely to be for a recent disaster in the subcontinent; the political buzz is more likely to be about the latest twist in a Pakistani political drama than the shifting fortunes of the London government.

The government's Citizenship Survey for 2009/10 found that 70 per cent of Muslims said that faith was very important to their identity, compared with 46 per cent of Hindus, 38 per cent of Sikhs and 23 per cent of Christians. In the

---

1. The BBC correspondent Aleem Maqbool featured Mirpur in a March 2012 report – 'How the city of Mirpur became "Little England"' – in which he estimated that 200,000 British people, mainly from Bradford and Birmingham, visit it annually. The local radio station has listeners in Mirpur and Britain.

same survey respondents were asked to define their nationality, and a larger proportion of Muslims chose 'other' than any other faith group.

And according to the Pew opinion research organisation, British Muslims are also more likely than Muslims in other developed countries to place their religious allegiance before their national one: 81 per cent of British Muslims say they are a Muslim before a national citizen, compared with 46 per cent in France, 47 per cent in the US and 66 per cent in Germany.

More worrying is the polling done among Muslim elites (MPs, councillors, community activists) in several European countries by the Danish academic Jytte Klausen. She found that the British elite were 70 per cent 'neo-orthodox' – a far higher number than in other countries – meaning that they regard liberalism as anti-Islamic and think it is possible 'for Muslims to live separately but as loyal citizens in the West'.[1]

When in the 1980s the Muslim identity emerged from the more elastic Asian identity of the 1960s and 1970s, it was, indeed, to demand separate provision and recognition for the Muslim sensibility – food and dress codes, religious rituals, gender relations, marriage norms and so on. And as the institutions of Muslim life – the mosques and halal shops and madrasas – sprang up, it became more possible to live in a wholly Muslim world with little contact with the wider community.

But, as Tufyal Choudhury has written, this was not just a demand for separation: 'The demand for accommodation indicates affection rather than disaffection; it indicates a commitment to Britain and a wish by the younger generation to make themselves more at home in Britain.'[2] That is true but it also begs the question of accommodation on what terms? On purely Muslim terms, or adapting also to key aspects of British life?

As the 1960s and 1970s turned into the 1980s and 1990s the second generation, mainly born in Britain, was adapting to many aspects of life here. They did not share their parents' sense that this was always a temporary, and

1. Klausen's poll results can be found in her book *The Islamic Challenge: Politics and Religion in Western Europe*, Oxford University Press, 2007. Though it should be noted that the polling was done in the wake of the Madrid and 7/7 attacks and at the height of violence in Iraq, when the community was feeling under unusual pressure.
2. Tufyal Choudhury, 'The role of Muslim identity politics in radicalisation', paper commissioned by the Department for Communities and Local Government, March 2007.

even precarious, sojourn. The streets became less threatening, and the more multicultural 'space' that opened up meant that those streets were sometimes filled with melas and carnivals celebrating minority life.

The two schools of Sunni Islam that dominate in Britain are the Barelwis and the Deobandis – both espouse a kind of social conservatism which combines traditionalism, and even separatism, in lifestyle with allegiance to British institutions such as the monarchy.[1] (I experienced this combination on a trip to Bradford during the royal wedding of 2011. I was visiting the home of an established leader of the Kashmiri Pakistani community, and while waiting for him I sat with his wife, who was glued to the television broadcast of the wedding. I realised after a few minutes, when my attempts at conversation had fallen flat, that she could not speak English.)

Deobandism, in particular, also has a fundamentalist strand which has made it more open to the radical currents swirling through the Muslim world after the Iranian revolution in 1979, and also to support from Saudi Arabia. About half the purpose-built mosques in the country are Deobandi and many were built with Saudi money, which brought with it a preference for a more literal and puritanical form of Islam that encouraged isolation from main-stream society.

In 1988 and 1989 came the Rushdie affair and with it an increasingly domi-nant role for political Islam within Britain's Muslim leadership. Then a few years later came Bosnia, followed by 9/11, the invasion of Afghanistan and Iraq, 7/7 and the Danish cartoon affair, all events – and most dramatically 7/7 – that pitted Muslim radicals against their fellow citizens, and most of their fellow Muslims.[2]

Only a small number of British Muslims sympathised with the terrorists (though between 7 and 15 per cent thought the 9/11 attacks were justified), but these sympathisers drew attention to a second and third generation that

---

1. Both the Barelwis and the Deobandis emerged from the failure of the Indian mutiny in 1857, but Deobandis stressed more the need to return to a pure form of the faith.
2. The significance of Bosnia was not so much western foot-dragging over intervention but the belief that Muslims will never be accepted in European society even after generations of living together. But Muslim activists seldom mention the western interventions, notably Kosovo, to save Muslims from genocide.

were growing up more politically radicalised, and more overtly religious, than their parents.

A poll conducted for a Policy Exchange report into Muslim Britain in 2007 found 16–24-year-olds to be far more fundamentalist in their views than the over-55s. Thirty-seven per cent of the younger group claim they would prefer to live under Sharia law compared with just 17 per cent of the older; on preferring women to wear the veil the numbers were 74 per cent to 28 per cent; on the death penalty for apostates it was 36 per cent to 19 per cent; on admiring organisations like Al-Qaeda 13 per cent to 3 per cent; and only 62 per cent of the younger group thought they had as much in common with non-Muslims as Muslims, compared with 71 per cent of the older group.

Some of these numbers should be taken with a pinch of salt. The last figure is particularly interesting because it is so clearly untrue; not only are younger Muslims completely absorbed into many aspects of British life in a way that their parents are not, but their very 'religiosity' revolt seems a very western phenomenon. They are young people struggling between cultures and trying to find a way of expressing their identity. As the authors of the Policy Exchange report put it, the wearing of exotic Islamic dress, often Arab-influenced, is a bit like having a Mohican haircut once was for white kids.

If you are brought up in a conservative Muslim culture in a segregated northern town with few prospects, it is perhaps understandable why the struggles of the Ummah in faraway places might seem a cool and exciting alternative. Other minority youth cultures, indeed youth culture in general, also express disaffection with both Britain and older generations, but rarely with the same intensity as young Muslims, and for most of them there is no equivalent of the Ummah and the backdrop of a perceived global conflict between Islam and the west.

British Muslims almost all come from countries that were once colonised by Britain, which can further exacerbate resentment and sustain negative stereotypes, on both sides. This also helps to explain why there has been so much anguish about Muslims being killed by western soldiers in recent years, while the Iran–Iraq war of 1980–88, in which nearly 1 million Muslims are thought to have died, caused so little concern. In a survey for the *Dispatches* television programme in 2006, Muslims were asked whether Britain was 'My country or their country?' and only 44 per cent of 18–24-year-olds said 'my country'. And there are important strands of Islamic thought, influential in Britain, such as the Arab scholars Yusuf al-Qaradawi and Muhammad al-Ghazali, who argue that Muslims should create a parallel society. Others, such as Tariq Ramadan, argue for a more integrationist strategy.

There is another factor too that contributes to the cultural distance between more traditional Muslims and non-Muslims and to the generational conflict within Muslim families; that is, the tension between the collectivism of traditional cultures and western individualism.

For many generations now in a country like Britain politics, religion and sex, relationships and marriage have all been regarded as matters for the individual to decide about for him or herself. But in traditional cultures of many kinds, and especially in Muslim ones, these are not individual decisions. Who you have sex with and marry, especially if you are a woman, is not at all your own decision, it is a decision taken by and in the interests of your extended family or clan. Politics and religion are similarly collective enterprises.

Young Muslims find themselves caught, wanting the individual choice of their non-Muslim friends yet not wanting to disrespect their own cultural traditions. Many of them also grow up in areas that are dominated by their own ethnic/religious group and feel oppressively watched over not only by their parents but also by the extended families and social networks of their parents. A 2007 study comparing Muslims and non-Muslims in Newham, Bradford and Birmingham found that more than three-quarters of the Muslims mixed only with other Muslims of the same nationality.[1]

The claustrophobia that this life produces is said to be one of the recruiting sergeants for radical Islamist groups, which often take a western view of personal morality alongside their neo-Marxist Islamist politics. (Mohammed Sidique Khan, the organiser of the 7/7 bombings, had become estranged from his family over his decision to marry for love and came to see his extremist comrades as his new family.) Organisations like Hizb ut-Tahrir, which operates like a religious version of a Trotskyist party, have become expert at appealing to the semi-integrated children of Muslim factory workers.

1. Centre on Migration, Policy and Society, *Immigration, Faith and Cohesion*, Joseph Rowntree Foundation, 2007.

It is perhaps not surprising that non-Muslims in Britain are more wary of Muslims than of any other group. Muslims often live in a more visibly different manner in their own ethnic enclaves, where traditional dress is often the norm. Thanks to the alcohol prohibition they generally do not join in the 'drink after work' pub culture, they are less likely to play contact sports, they are often active in projecting their piety and critical of the more liberal aspects of British life. Women usually don't work and the older ones often do not speak English. According to a survey of 300 mosques in 2008, 92 per cent of imams are foreign-born and only 6 per cent speak English as their first language.[1]

On the public stage they have been associated with violent protests against free speech in the Rushdie and Danish cartoons affairs, and profess a special allegiance to fellow Muslims in international affairs. (Fifty-eight per cent of British Muslims believe that 'many of the problems in the world today are a result of arrogant western attitudes', compared with 30 per cent of the general population.) And, of course, whether they like it or not they are associated with the violence of a tiny minority of Muslims.

Much of this can be, and has been, accommodated by a liberal British society, and Muslims are no less entitled to the equal treatment that any citizen should expect. But it does mean that Muslims – especially the poorer, more ghettoised ones – are likely to live more apart from ordinary British life and norms than any other significant minority. Indeed, as I mentioned in the chapter on multiculturalism, the more aggressive wing of Muslim politics is not just demanding the right to be separate but insisting that the majority society changes its rules and laws to fit in with the minority – a kind of reverse integration.

In this context it is not surprising that the British public returns the ambivalence that they find expressed by many British Muslims towards modern Britain. According to the British Social Attitudes Survey of 2003, which is in line with similar surveys, more than 60 per cent of the population agree that Muslims are more loyal to other Muslims around the world than to their fellow British citizens; a little less than half think that Muslims can never be

---

1. The number of English-speaking imams is now rising quite rapidly.

truly committed to Britain; and one quarter would feel unhappy if a relative married a Muslim.

In the more recent British Social Attitudes survey of 2008, analysed by Lauren McLaren and Matt Goodwin, the number who agreed that nearly all Muslims living in Britain want to fit in was smaller (though only slightly) than the number who disagreed. The attitude to a large mosque being built in the community was more hostile, with 57 per cent being bothered a little or a lot by it.[1]

Notwithstanding this suspicion of Muslims, there is little evidence for the systematic discrimination against them implied in the concept of Islamophobia. After both the 9/11 and the 7/7 attacks there was only a small and temporary rise in recorded attacks on Muslims. And the response of the media and all public authorities was exemplary, with the constant repetition of the message that Islam is not a violent religion and that the terrorists were wholly unrepresentative. The national anti-Muslim violence group 'Tell Mama' recorded 140 incidents of harassment, mostly verbal abuse, in five months in 2012, which does not seem like an epidemic.

The writer Kenan Malik analysed the figures for stop and search under the Terrorism Act in 2004 at a time when Muslim organisations were complaining about its unreasonable extent. He found that a total of 21,577 from all backgrounds were stopped, the majority white and about 3,000 Asian (of which about half were probably Muslim). This is not significantly out of line with the proportion of the Asian population in London where most of the stops took place.

Nonetheless the sometimes rather clumsy handling of the government's post 7/7 anti-terrorism 'Prevent' strategy managed to feed rather than challenge the story of Muslim victimhood, while at the same time leaving other minorities and majority Britain with the sense that Muslims were 'benefiting from the bombs', as one Sikh politician described it to me. Prevent did combine 'cohesion' issues with 'extremism' issues in a way that made many Muslims feel that they were all being stigmatised or even spied upon as potential bombers.

1. Lauren McLaren, David J Cutts, Matthew Goodwin, *What Drives Anti-Muslim Sentiment?* APSA 2011 annual meeting paper.

But Muslim leaders in the main made matters worse with a defensive and oppositional stance, reflecting the historic lack of a confident and well educated British Muslim elite. And the Muslim establishment was not able to properly challenge the extremists partly because its own beliefs were often just a non-violent version of the same story: religiously inspired hostility to British foreign policy; ambivalence about western liberalism; a paranoid belief in state-sanctioned Islamophobia.

The Muslim Council of Britain, established at the urging of the then Conservative government in 1996, is itself dominated by political Islamists; many of its leaders are supporters of the Muslim Brotherhood or the radical Jamaat-e-Islami (based in the Indian subcontinent). But its main problem is not so much its radicalism as the fact that it tries to reflect almost every corner of Muslim opinion; for that reason, for example, it cannot be critical of the Taliban in Afghanistan. Instead of constructing a new mainstream Muslim consensus in Britain, it continues to hand a veto to sectarian groups that then entangle it in self-defeating rows such as its boycott of Holocaust Memorial Day (now dropped). Labour in government eventually lost patience with the MCB and the whole strategy of using non-violent radicals to tackle violent ones and decided, after 2009, to channel funds to less influential but more overtly integrationist Muslim groups.

What about the economic and social evidence for Islamophobia? There is some evidence of a 'Muslim penalty' in pay and jobs but once low qualifications are taken into account it is not large. Poorly qualified males, plus women who usually don't work and have relatively large families, means Muslims are significantly over-represented in the poverty and welfare dependency figures. Those that are better qualified, such as more urban, middle-class Pakistanis and Indian Gujarati Muslims, do correspondingly better and are, if anything, over-represented in the managerial and professional class, though a greater reluctance to be mobile especially on the part of young women may prevent them reaching the very top.[1] Half of Muslims aged 18–30 are now in education compared with 38 per cent of the general population, and almost all Muslim

1. A senior executive in a major retail company told me that his group has many Muslim shop managers but very few want to become regional managers because it usually involves moving home.

groups – including Pakistanis and Bangladeshis – have a higher proportion of young people at university than the white majority.

Meanwhile, the last two decades have seen big political and legal advances. Muslims have long complained about their lack of protection from specifically religious discrimination. The crime of blasphemy that used to protect only Christianity (and was one of the issues behind the *Satanic Verses* conflict) has now been abolished. But many Muslims still regard criticism of Islam as a form of discrimination against them as individuals, which it is not; at least no more than the treatment of Jesus in *Jerry Springer the Opera* constitutes discrimination against Christians.

Labour in power after 1997 opened up Westminster and Whitehall to Muslim voices and introduced various measures in direct response to Muslim lobbying – a religion question in the 2001 census; state funding for Muslim faith schools; and a Race and Religious Hatred Act in 2006 that made incitement to religious hatred an offence (though the latter was watered down in Parliament). The political representation of Muslims is better than almost any other minority: there are seven Muslim MPs (including three women), 15 members of the House of Lords and about 300 councillors.[1]

The evidence for sustained discrimination against Muslims is hard to find. Despite the semi-detached status chosen by many British Muslim communities and their unavoidably poor political image in the light of recent events – reflected in a generally negative media emphasis on extremism – Muslims continue to enjoy better protection and freedom than anywhere else in Europe, which is perhaps why there is a steady flow of Muslims arriving here from continental Europe.

And yet the perception of victimhood is pervasive: a Channel 4 NOP poll in 2006 found that 58 per cent of Muslims thought that severe religious persecution of Muslims was likely, 23 per cent very likely and 35 per cent fairly likely. Even among educated and accomplished British Muslims the sense of victimhood is ubiquitous.[2]

1. John Denham, when secretary of state for communities and local government in 2009, was surprised to discover that his department kept no information on the British Bangladeshi community as Bangladeshis, they were simply categorised as Muslims.
2. Consider the 2002 report *Muslims in Britain* by Humayun Ansari OBE, a respected Muslim

A strong sense of victimhood can, as with other minority groups, become a self-fulfilling prophecy, and combined with relatively segregated lives it creates the danger that the relative lack of upward mobility of British Muslims will be sustained longer than necessary. To succeed in Britain requires some confidence, and a Muslim who expects to be discriminated against at every turn is unlikely to have confidence in dealing with mainstream society.

One antidote to negative attitudes towards Muslims is, as one might expect, friendship with a Muslim. And in their analysis of the 2008 British Social Attitudes survey, Lauren McLaren and Matt Goodwin found that 12 per cent of the non-Muslim population say they have a close friend who is a Muslim. Positive role models of young Muslims succeeding in the mainstream – such as the television presenter Konnie Huq or sportsmen Amir Khan and Mo Farah – are also becoming more common and are promoted in places like Emel, a lifestyle magazine aimed at affluent young Muslims.

The City Circle group in London, which brings together young professional Muslims to debate current issues, is another sign of a more confident, integrated British-born elite emerging. There is still, however, a dearth of young Muslims studying humanities subjects – history, literature, political and social sciences – opting instead for vocational courses such as law, accountancy and medicine. Yet a humanities degree is not only often the route to the top jobs in the media and politics, it is also usually the route into becoming one of the teachers, social workers and counsellors who could be helping young Muslims deal with the challenges of British life.

The relationship between Britain and its Muslim minority will continue to be a difficult one partly because it is so directly affected by global events – the largest group of British Muslims are of Pakistani origin and that country will remain a mess of conflict for decades – but also because of the rootedness of the belief in an Islamophobic Britain and the relatively small, but now growing, Muslim middle class.

Among Pakistanis there is some evidence of the weakening of the Biraderi

---

academic and director of the Centre for Ethnic Minority Studies, Royal Holloway, which tries and fails to paint a picture of Muslim misery, and complains at one point that 'some Labour MPs support Israel'. The report is published by Minority Rights Group International.

clan system but arranged marriages with spouses from Pakistan remain common: up to 70 per cent of all Pakistani marriages according to some estimates. The system is sustained by various vested interests including – according to some insiders – the British Pakistani mothers who feel they have had to suffer the system and believe it is their right to now have an obedient daughter-in-law at their beck and call.

Some Muslims, especially Pakistanis, worry about a growing north/south divide in their community and believe that places like Bradford and Oldham are getting left behind. Meanwhile in the rest of the country the Muslim middle class is likely to grow rapidly – it is already well represented in London and Manchester, as well as Leicester – as more Muslim graduates pass through the system and into higher-status jobs: and they will, with luck, act as a collective role model, showing that it is possible to be a devout Muslim and a successful, well-integrated British citizen.

What about the White Workers?

The story of post-war immigration is not just a story of arrival, it is also a story of adjustment, resistance and accommodation for those who were already here: in the main the working-class communities in London and the industrial towns of the Midlands and the North, where most black and Asian people came to settle in the great post-colonial arrival.

The working-class communities in these places were as unprepared for the arrival of these outsiders as the newcomers themselves were unprepared for life in a new country. Alongside the well-documented hostility of some, there was also a story of support and generosity and, probably for the majority, grudging acceptance.

The period of the 'Great Arrival' in the 1950s and 1960s was in many ways a golden age for working-class Britain. Incomes were rising rapidly, there was full employment, the expanded welfare state was providing health care, pensions and new housing. There was still a sense of a working-class culture and politics, often built around great industrial villages.

Nearly one third of the population lived in public housing and many of them on big public housing estates, which accommodated a surprising range of incomes and occupations and at their best produced tightly-knit communities, of a kind that is rare today – except perhaps among minority communities.

The culture was also introverted, conservative and illiberal, at least by today's standards. But the understandable nostalgia for this 'golden age' among older working-class people has created a strong association between mass immigration and loss, the loss of that world.

It is a sense of loss sometimes tinged with bitterness and a sense of unfairness. The sociologist Geoff Dench writes about a belief in the East End of London that no sooner had the working class there come into its inheritance after the sacrifice of the war years than it was snatched away by the arrival of people who had had little to do with that story.[1]

There was a variation on that theme in the North, especially in those places where industrial decline had already begun in the 1960s. Graham Mahony, former head of race relations in Bradford, describes the sentiment: 'White people knew that the immigrants were not to blame for the decline of their towns, indeed that they may have helped to slow it down. Yet decline is inevitably associated with their arrival in the 1950s and 1960s, so the whole thing got off on the wrong psychological footing in a place like Bradford.'

Social and economic change would have swept away the old working-class ways even if there had been zero immigration. Nevertheless, looking over their shoulder it is easy to imagine how an unprejudiced man or woman from what was a thriving working-class community in the 1960s might reasonably feel that the next fifty years have been kinder to the rising immigrant population than to the declining white working-class one.

The British working class no longer exists in the way it did fifty years ago when, notwithstanding big regional differences, it had a sense of itself as a distinct group with its own interests and institutions, a central part of the

1. *The New East End*: 'The post-war compact was understood by working-class East Enders as admitting them to full membership of British society. To some extent this itself recognised historical debts by the nation to its lowest orders. A further compact made soon afterwards with colonial citizens, especially one not properly discussed within the nation in the way that the creation of the welfare state had been, was felt as a serious diminution, even a snatching back, of their own recent "reward".'

country but at an angle to it as well. I remember when I was at university in the late 1970s listening to some of my fellow students from working-class backgrounds talking about the generational tensions associated with 'leaving' the working class and going to university; I am reminded of those conversations when listening to young second- or third-generation people of immigrant background talking about trying to combine their British and ancestral identities.

Of course it has not all been bad news for white working-class people over the past fifty years. Most have moved on and up in those years: they are mainly richer and better educated than their parents and if only some have moved, via higher education, directly into the professional elite, many more have moved into safer, less strenuous non-manual jobs and into private housing in suburbs or new towns.

Over the course of the twentieth century the proportion of people classified as manual workers in Britain fell from about three-quarters to about one third. So even if you do the same sort of job as your father your status is likely to have declined quite sharply. And in the last few decades quite a sizeable group have got more visibly left behind in this process – people who struggled at school and are now too old to retrain for anything – and they have experienced multiple losses. The old industrial communities have mainly gone and with them the decently paid low-skilled or semi-skilled manual jobs too (those jobs that remain have to be competed for with immigrants). Status and esteem is now associated with education, not with skilled or hard manual labour. The white working classes no longer enjoy privileged access to public housing. And they have also lost a place in the national culture – they were once that section of society that the liberal middle classes worried about, perhaps feared slightly, and wanted to improve. That role is now taken by minority Britain.

As the number of industrial jobs fell sharply in the 1980s and 1990s, the attention that had once been focused on striking miners or unemployed workers shifted to issues of race and racial discrimination.[1] And in the 1980s,

1. I remember being struck by how dominant questions of racial justice had become in modern Britain when I opened a copy of the *Evening Standard* – it was the issue of 17 November 2011 – and the three biggest stories on the front and the back pages, and about seven pages

just as multiculturalism began to stress the value of minority cultures, the industrial working-class culture that had given many people their connection to and place in British society began to fade away. No wonder the white child, famously quoted in Keith Ajegbo's commission on diversity and citizenship in education, said that unlike her Indian, Somalian and Caribbean classmates she came 'from nowhere'.[1]

Minority Britain in places like Merton is, for all its struggles, on a journey of discovery and in most cases improvement. Even the 'stuck' groups are slowly improving their educational and employment outcomes; for the bottom end of the white working class that is not the case and most families, as we have seen, are less educationally aspirational than their ethnic minority equivalents.

There has always been a 'rough' end of society somewhat apart from the mainstream working class. It's now called the underclass, and deindustrialisation has swelled its numbers in certain parts of the country, though welfare payments have kept it better looked after than in previous generations. In the mid-2000s it became commonly described as the 'Shameless' underclass, after the Channel 4 television series which painted a fond picture of a hedonistic, post-work-ethic Salford family.

This group and its usually more respectable real-life equivalents are over-represented in former industrial areas and in the coastal towns of the South – places which have had the energy and purpose sucked out of them. The children of this group (and especially boys), white children who qualify for free school meals, came bottom of the whole educational pyramid, with the exception of Somalis: only just over 25 per cent get five decent GCSEs, lower than Caribbean children on free school meals, of whom one third clear that hurdle. In the early 2000s, as the rest of Britain woke up to its existence, it came to be thought of almost as a separate ethnic group, and one which attracted less sympathy from liberal Britain than the real ethnic minorities.

---

inside, were about racism: the new trial of the Stephen Lawrence murder defendants, John Terry's alleged racial abuse of Anton Ferdinand and, on the back page, the lead story, Tiger Woods's white caddy using a racial insult.

1. Sir Keith Ajegbo, 'Diversity and Citizenship Curriculum Review', Department for Education 2007.

But this white 'ethnic minority' did begin to attract the sympathy and interest of the British National Party, which after the collapse of the National Front in the 1980s was the new and less fascistic face of far right Britain.

The 1990s had been a meagre time for the far right. Opposition to large-scale immigration, although a more or less permanent feature of public opinion in almost all countries at all times, had receded in importance in Britain after new immigration fell to low levels in the early 1990s. And the worst of the majority-minority conflict seemed to be over in areas of high minority settlement, with a process of integration, or at least peaceful co-existence, well under way in most places.

This rather placid period came to an end in the late 1990s/early 2000s thanks to the convergence of several factors: a big increase in the number of asylum-seekers and a noisy newspaper campaign against them; a more assertive Muslim presence leading to riots in the northern mill towns and then political conflict over the Iraq war and the 'war on terror'; and the start of the biggest single wave of immigration in British history, in part due to the opening up to workers from Eastern Europe.

When Britons were asked between 1990 and 2007 to rate the most important issues facing the country, the percentage choosing immigration rocketed from under two per cent to a record peak of 46 per cent (and in 2005 20 per cent thought it was the *most* important issue). At various points in 2006 and 2007 immigration was considered more important than education, crime, the NHS and foreign affairs. The west Midlands is generally the most hostile region to immigration and London and Scotland the least.

Overall, the proportion favouring a reduction in immigration rose from two-thirds to three-quarters in this period; six out of ten agreed that 'some parts of the country don't look like Britain any more because of immigration'. Also polls taken after the 7/7 terrorist attacks found that more than half of Britons thought Muslims should do more to integrate and 60 per cent thought they were more loyal to other Muslims around the world than to their fellow Britons.

Newspapers and the electronic media are sometimes held responsible for these negative views. And it is true that views on everything from public services to immigration are usually far more favourable at local level, based on more direct experience, than at national level mediated through newspapers and television. But there is little evidence to suggest that if newspapers reported immigration stories in a more neutral way that opinion would be significantly more favourable.

Electoral support for the BNP, another measure of discontent, also rose sharply in the early and mid-2000s. Neither the British Union of Fascists nor the National Front had ever won a single council seat, but starting in the early 2000s the BNP started to win several and reached a total of fifty-seven in 2009 (out of 22,000), mainly in the northern mill towns, the East End of London (it won eleven seats on Barking and Dagenham Council, making it the second largest party) and places like Stoke and Sandwell in the Midlands – places with a disproportionate number of that left-behind white 'ethnic minority'.

In the 2005 general election the BNP saved its deposit in several seats and won 10 per cent of the vote in Burnley and 16 per cent in Barking. In national opinion polls its support reached a peak of 5 per cent around 2007, when the party claimed about 10,000 members. It won more than 5 per cent of the vote in the London Assembly elections of 2008, and in 2009 it scored its greatest electoral triumph with almost 1 million votes (6.2 per cent of the total) in the European elections, winning two seats in the European Parliament for Yorkshire and Humberside and the North-West regions.

The BNP is comfortably the most successful far right party in modern British history.[1] And its burst of electoral success focused the attention of the political class. Margaret Hodge, the Labour MP for Barking, said that in the late 2000s for the first time in her life mainstream voters on the doorstep were expressing no shame or embarrassment about their preference for a far right party; in some corners of run-down Britain it had become socially acceptable. (Many in Barking and Dagenham just voted with their feet: the white British proportion of the population fell by 40,000 or almost one third between 2001 and 2011.) Other senior Labour figures like John Denham and Jon Cruddas worried publicly about the left-behind white working class, and the Labour government's Connecting Communities initiative in 2009 was

---

1. It grew out of the overtly fascist National Front but has moderated some of its policies. It wants for example to halt all immigration but is now in favour of only voluntary repatriation.

expressly designed to shovel some money and attention in the direction of high-BNP-voting areas.

Even liberal Britain started to take note: BBC 2 had a 'white season' in March 2008; Channel 4 commissioned Rageh Omaar to make an extended television essay on the failures of mass immigration and multiculturalism called *Immigration: the inconvenient truth*. And the Joseph Rowntree research organisation started commissioning studies of the white working class – it was very much as if a new minority with its own traditions and grievances had, indeed, been discovered. The refrain that 'no one is listening to us, only to the immigrants' became harder to maintain after this period.

The academics Matthew Goodwin and Robert Ford have established that the BNP voter is older and more northern than the NF support base in the 1970s, though both have generally been drawn from poorly educated working-class males. BNP supporters are pessimistic about the future but not generally the most economically marginalised of the underclass. Many are in steady skilled or semi-skilled jobs; they are protesting for larger cultural and political reasons centred on immigration.

And sometimes hostility to immigration itself seems to be emblematic of a wider disillusionment with the way that the terms of trade of the modern world have turned against them. In places like Stoke and Burnley the ethnic minority population is still relatively small, and talking to local people there a more diffuse sense of being ignored and left behind is what motivates many people to vote for the BNP, rather than issues relating to race or competing with minorities.

Since 2009 the BNP has seen its electoral fortunes slump, winning less than 2 per cent of the national vote in the 2010 general election (though still nearly 600,000) and holding on to only three council seats after the 2012 local election. Internal squabbles, the attraction of more moderate right-wing populist parties like UKIP (and the rise of the English Defence League on the streets), and perhaps also the return of the Conservative Party to power and its concerted attempt to bring down immigration numbers, may all have contributed.

But disaffection with large-scale immigration, with the ideology of multi-culturalism and with politics itself, remains a powerful current in Britain, and not just in the problem places like the northern mill towns. The important large-scale opinion survey by the anti-fascist Searchlight Educational Trust, *Fear and Hope*, published at the end of 2010, revealed just how few people embrace the liberalism of the metropolitan political class on immigration and multiculturalism. It divided respondents into six identity tribes, only the first two of which seem happy with multiculturalism: Confident Multiculturalists (8 per cent of the population); Mainstream Liberals (16 per cent); Identity Ambivalents (28 per cent); Cultural Integrationists (24 per cent); Latent Hostiles (10 per cent); and Active Emnity (13 per cent).

On my travels around the country I have talked to many dozens of white people who would probably be categorised as Active Enmity, the sort of people who might hang the English flag in a window of their house all year round as an act of defiance. Some admit to being racists, such as the middle-aged men in a pub in Newham: 'None of us were racists to start with … the first wave were good people who wanted to integrate, but then it got worse … we've been taken over by other cultures, it's been a one-way street.'

Almost all people, even in the Active Emnity group, will strenuously deny racism and will say that they would prefer a decent Asian family as neighbours than a noisy white one. They often talk like thwarted idealists rather than haters; people who, as many of them say, are tired of seeing this country's traditions and beliefs pushed aside while others seem to get favoured treatment, like the young man in Leeds who pointed to the Pakistani community centre on one roundabout and the Bangladeshi centre at the next roundabout and asked, 'Where is *our* community centre?'

The belief in institutionalised favouritism towards minorities is particularly acute in housing. 'The people in the council never listen to us, it's one law for us and another law for the people who have just arrived,' is a common refrain. According to the 2009–10 Citizenship Survey which looked at perceptions of racial disadvantage, the group which had the largest proportion of aggrieved people on any subject were whites, with 26 per cent saying that they felt at a disadvantage to other groups on housing.

Is there any truth behind this feeling of injustice? Ever since the abolition of local preference and the shift to 'need' as the main criterion for public housing in the late 1970s, many white working-class people have felt pushed out from a part of their historic welfare inheritance. The rules now favour those with large families, those with health problems and with low or no incomes, and that tends to favour poorer minority families and even some relative newcomers. About 27 per cent of minority Britain is in social housing compared with 16 per cent of the white British.

Of those who have arrived in recent years the numbers are less clear. An Institute for Public Policy Research report in 2009 found that only 11 per cent of non-British citizens who had arrived in the last five years were in social housing. But an EU citizen with a job can qualify straight away for such housing and some believe the proportion of new lets going to newcomers is much higher: an inquiry by Migration Watch into London social housing found that in the boroughs of Ealing and Haringey half of all new social housing lets went to foreign nationals.

There seems to be a group of about 15 per cent of the population, mainly among the well off and well educated, who are comfortable with large-scale immigration and contemporary multiculturalism; and another 15 per cent, mainly in the bottom half of the income spectrum, who are unremittingly hostile. The *Fear and Hope* report and a host of other opinion survey reports in recent years have reflected the large majorities in between those two groups who are not in general illiberal or racist – some might be described as 'conflicted populists' – but are opposed to large-scale immigration and, more broadly, do not share the world-view of the mobile, liberal, graduate elite.

They are likely to belong to the (almost) half of the population that still lives within five miles of where they were when they were fourteen.[1] They want a narrower and more conditional welfare state, they are strong believers in the distinction between the deserving and the undeserving (both among the poor and the bankers), and worry that some minorities are not integrating.[2] They are not opposed to, say, gay marriage but think that metropolitan

1. Ludi Simpson and Nissa Finney, 'How mobile are immigrants after arriving in the UK?', Understanding Society: Findings 2012.
2. According to Ipsos MORI, 87 per cent of people think immigrants should be made to learn English and 77 per cent think immigrants should have citizenship lessons to learn about the British way of life. And, as mentioned in a footnote in the previous chapter, Ipsos MORI has also found that only 16 per cent of the native born (of native parents) strongly agree that ethnic minorities should maintain their traditions, rising to about one third for

liberals give such issues too high a priority. They are post-liberal rather than anti-liberal. They think that Britain is a better place for the advances in sex and race equality of recent decades, but also think that somewhere along the way we have lost a sense of moral community and common sense. This group includes many Labour voters – perhaps including Gillian Duffy, famously described as 'that bigoted woman' by Gordon Brown during the 2010 election campaign.

The 2000s clearly did see an adjustment of focus in politics and public opinion: not an abandonment of the idea that newcomers should be allowed to be different but a feeling that it needed to be balanced with more concern with what people share in common; plus a greater awareness of the legitimate grievances of some in the white working-class, especially in the declining industrial regions.

The far right has a larger base of support in some depressed corners of urban Britain than in the past but this does not mean that a new racism has been sweeping the country since the mid-2000s, as is sometimes claimed. Indeed, taking the longer view, the remarkable thing is how weak organised racism, or even populism, has remained. Powellism in the 1960s and 1970s never developed into a British equivalent of the French Front National; that was partly because the 'first past the post' electoral system made it harder but also because British common sense is generally hostile to anything associated with extremism. The tabloid press is often blamed for fanning prejudice but its bluntness may also have acted as a psychological safety valve for those who feel unrepresented by the mainly liberal political class.[1] And though there is disillusionment with the way in which Britain has managed large-scale immigration, generally speaking hostility to immigration does not extend to hostility to the immigrant. Even half of BNP voters accept that you can be non-white and British.

Throughout most of the post-war period British views on race and immigration have been in the middle of the range of European views. Opposition

---

non-European immigrants who have lived in Britain for more than seven years.

1. It could be argued that the uninhibited popular press in Britain has given voice to ideas and feelings that in continental Europe, with its more establishment newspaper culture, has only found expression in right-wing populist parties.

to immigration did rise more sharply than elsewhere in the mid-2000s but that was itself in response to a sharper actual increase in immigration, and it did not coincide with a significant increase in racist attitudes or evidence of racism. Britain generally comes out well on international attitude surveys. The European Values Survey of 2008 found only 6 per cent of Britons saying they would not like to have someone of a different race as a neighbour, one of the very lowest.[1]

Despite the general decline of racist beliefs, a small minority of people continue to believe that you cannot be 'fully British' if you are not white – 9 per cent in a 2008 Ipsos MORI poll.[2] But a much larger group continues to have some discomfort with the idea of living among people who are not like themselves. Another Ipsos MORI poll in 2003 found that 39 per cent of people preferred to live in an area 'where most people are from the same ethnic background as you' – 41 per cent white British people and 26 per cent ethnic minority British people. A continuing low-level groupishness, perhaps no more than preferring familiarity, is neither surprising nor necessarily regrettable.

The immigration-related changes of the past few decades have, of course, been overwhelmingly accepted by white Britain and in some cases even celebrated. The Caribbean men and Caribbean and Chinese women who 'marry out' in large numbers are generally forming relationships with white British people. And there are many places where a cross-ethnic common life and an uncomplicated hybridisation is the norm, especially among younger people.

One of the challenges to our immigration story is how to allow older and poorer white people a safe space in which to express a sense of loss, and homesickness for the past, without this mood becoming destructively pessimistic or spilling over into racism.

1. The 2010 European Social Survey found a relatively small difference between British people saying few or no immigrants of a different race should be allowed in (50 per cent) and those saying the same about people from the same race (40 per cent). And Britain comes third from the top of the Gallup Diversity Index, a measure of European countries' acceptance of people from different ethnic backgrounds.
2. In another Ipsos MORI poll, 7 per cent agreed strongly and 11 per cent tended to agree that 'to be truly British you have to be white'.

For some white people large-scale immigration has, indeed, been experienced as loss, either directly because they lived in a neighbourhood that was rapidly changed by it or indirectly because their working-class culture and institutions seemed to be pushed aside by the same market forces that then ushered in the newcomers. As the Oldham-based community worker Maxine Moar puts it: 'What you so often hear is, "Why did no one ask us, they just changed our communities."'

Part Three

Why It Matters and What We Do About It

CHAPTER 6

Progressive Dilemmas

The Heart of the Matter

So why should we worry about the 'little Pakistans' or 'little Somalias' and the white working-class ghettoes that dot many of our big cities? Why should we worry about modern liberalism's indifference to a sense of belonging or multiculturalism's inability to speak to majorities? What is at stake here? I do not believe that a Mad Max dystopia is around the corner, although ultimately what is at stake is the smooth running of a liberal democracy and even social peace. What is far more imminent is the slow disappearance in Britain, and probably the rest of Europe too, of the rather miraculous, and historically unique, institution of the modern welfare state.

This brings the argument back to the progressive dilemma. The conflict between solidarity and diversity. The fact that as we become more different from one another in lifestyle, values, ethnic and national origins, we become less willing to sacrifice, trust and share. Is it a fact? Common sense says it is, but common sense is often wrong, and many social scientists are working away at this moment trying to prove it wrong. And they make some good points that I will consider later. But there is enough evidence from observation, from history, from natural science and from opinion surveys to suggest that we are dealing with one of the big social facts of modern life. It is not immutable; like most social facts it can be mitigated in many ways. Nor is it only about *ethnic* diversity, although that is certainly part of the dilemma.

Moreover, the increase in diversity is evidently not the only cause of pressure on the welfare state – indeed at any particular moment it is unlikely to be the most important – but it is a powerful underlying current that policy-makers need to think about and address.

The progressive dilemma was my starting point – it is where I came into this rolling argument about immigration, multiculturalism, integration and national identity. And, as I mentioned in the introduction, it was thanks to the leading Conservative politician and thinker David Willetts. Here is a fuller extract from the *Prospect* round table debate that Willetts was taking part in back in 1998:

> The basis on which you can extract large sums of money in tax and pay it out in benefits is that most people think the recipients are people like themselves, facing difficulties which they themselves could face. If values become more diverse, if lifestyles become more differentiated, then it becomes more difficult to sustain the legitimacy of a universal risk-pooling welfare state. People ask 'Why should I pay for them when they are doing things I wouldn't do?' This is America versus Sweden. You can have a Swedish welfare state provided that you are a homogenous society with intensely shared values. In the US you have a very diverse individualistic society where people feel fewer obligations to fellow citizens. Progressives want diversity but they thereby undermine part of the moral consensus on which a large welfare state rests.[1]

I remember at the time being impressed by this insight and I began to see evidence for the dilemma all around me. (The progressive dilemma was also a conveniently controversial idea for the editor of a small political magazine.)

The dilemma draws attention to the messy intertwining of generous and mean human impulses: how solidarity with and fellow-feeling towards one's own group can become, if it is too intense, indifference towards or even

---

1. Sweden is now rather less homogeneous than when David Willetts spoke in 1998, with a minority population of around 15 per cent rising to 40 per cent in Malmö. Some academics see an erosion of traditional Swedish support for a strong welfare state; see Maureen Eger, 'Even in Sweden: the effect of immigration on support for welfare state spending', *European Sociological Review*, 2009, vol. 26, issue 2.

hatred of outsiders.[1] Equally, too much diversity with its challenge to familiarity, moral consensus and trust makes co-operative living harder.

The 'progressive dilemma' is a permanent balancing act and part of an even bigger tension, at the heart of the individual human condition itself, between commitment and freedom. We want the freedom to be geographically and socially mobile, to break free of commitments if we find them too burdensome – to get divorced if our marriages are not happy, to park our elderly relatives in care homes if they become too burdensome – yet these choices can be disruptive to strong, stable communities. We value the liberal idea of self-realisation, autonomy and the free authorship of our own lives, yet we also acknowledge our dependence on others to realise those goals and seek to embed ourselves in human groups both small and big.

In politics the progressive dilemma takes many forms. Today it is often found in arguments between a communitarian notion of reciprocity/club membership and the more universal cross-border rights championed by modern liberalism – this was the conflict in places like Tower Hamlets in the 1980s, between the locals-first 'sons and daughters' housing policy and the more pressing housing needs of the recent immigrant with a big family.

Natural science stands on both sides of the argument. Evolutionary psychology stresses both the universality of most human traits and – through the notion of kin selection and reciprocal altruism – the instinct to favour one's own group. Most social psychologists also argue that the tendency to perceive in-groups and out-groups is innate.[2]

It is now widely agreed that many features of the modern human personality were shaped during the late Pleistocene era (126,000–11,700 years ago) when people lived in bands of around seventy-five individuals united by bonds of kinship. These bands were organised into tribes of a few hundred to a few thousand people. This form of organisation can still be seen amongst modern hunter-gatherers.

---

1. Too much of what the American political scientist Robert Putnam called 'bonding capital', which intensifies group solidarity, can make it harder to establish 'bridging capital' across different groups.

2. See Donald R. Kinder and Cindy D. Kam, *Us Against Them: Ethnological Foundations of American Opinion*, University of Chicago Press, 2009.

Competition between tribes for resources was often fierce and warfare endemic. Tribes that could not hold their own in this competition would either be eliminated or absorbed into another tribe. Extensive evidence on the prevalence and nature of warfare in this period has recently been popularised by Steven Pinker in *The Better Angels of our Nature*. Pitched battles were infrequent and the favourite method of warfare was to ambush an outnumbered opponent or to raid an unsuspecting settlement. Cumulatively, however, the loss of life was often very large as a proportion of the total population. It is estimated that average human mortality rates from inter-group violence in hunter-gatherer societies was around 15 per cent for adults (25 per cent for men). This is many times greater than in most modern wars.

Such intense inter-group rivalry created a strong evolutionary pressure in favour of behaviour for promoting group cohesion, such as loyalty and self-sacrifice. It also favoured the selection of genes that predispose individuals towards the suspicion of outsiders and preference for insiders. This was not simply xenophobia, which is an irrational fear of outsiders, but a well-founded fear given the real danger that strangers posed. Of course, excessive suspicion of strangers today – or even in ancient times – is harmful and limiting, and excessive conformism is an obstacle to inventiveness and flexibility. But in-group preference has a solid base in human evolution.

That does not mean that hostility to outsiders is inevitable. Humans have many other instincts that promote other kinds of behaviour. And when people are feeling secure and have time to become familiar with other kinds of people, the idea of the 'in-group' expands to include people who are initially regarded as outsiders. Moreover, as traditional, collectivist societies with high levels of social obligation and conformity have given way to freer, more individualistic, urban societies, 'groupishness' has weakened.

This has also made altruism more complex. In pre-industrial societies, David Miller has argued (in the paper 'Are they my poor?'[1]), there was no such thing as altruism as 'obligation was localised: people had responsibility for those who stood close by, according to rules that everybody understood'.

1. David Miller, 'Are they my poor? The problem of altruism in a world of strangers', *The Ethics of Altruism*, Jonathan Seglow (ed.), Cass, 2004.

In today's more individualistic society, obligation and solidarity beyond the family is more abstract – mediated through bureaucracy and the tax system – but also more discretionary: who to support, and by how much? Miller's conclusion was that people take into account a variety of factors, including the attributes of the potential recipient (whether ethnic, sexual, political or moral), and finds that would-be altruists are far more likely to help someone they see as similar to themselves.

David Willetts's idea has both commonsense appeal and, as we have seen, considerable support from social psychologists and other scientists of human behaviour. And it does help to explain some of the historic social and political differences between a 'communalist' and racially divided America and a historically more homogeneous Europe, the difference between an immigrant, settler country and a collection of historic nations.

Why do European governments spend something like 48 per cent of GDP compared with just 35 per cent in the US? And why is America's income tax system less progressive? It is partly a matter of simple hostility to big government, and rich Americans do give more to charity than their European equivalents. Yet it is also true that attempts to create a more universal welfare state in the US have been thwarted by the fears of voters that they would be taxed to subsidise other Americans who were unlike them in race or culture. The original social security act in the 1930s was passed only after domestic workers and farm workers – mainly black Americans at that time – were left out of its coverage at the insistence of white Southern politicians. And, more recently, Aid to Families with Dependent Children, a New Deal anti-poverty programme that was identified with non-white 'welfare queens', became a target of popular resentment until it was abolished by Bill Clinton.

Since the 1964 Civil Rights Act destroyed white supremacy in the US, every attempt to expand traditional social insurance has failed, but there has been a big increase in government welfare going disproportionately to the white and affluent, such as tax-favoured employer health insurance and childcare tax credits. Moreover, social security and Medicare, the two main examples of universal social insurance in the US, were enacted in the half-century between 1920 and 1970, when immigration was sharply reduced and America, not coincidentally, was at its most social democratic.[1] President Obama's success in implementing a more universal health system may suggest that even today's much more diverse America is still capable of solidarity, but it is a relatively weak reform and America remains deeply divided about it.

More diverse and individualistic societies simply have a weaker impulse to share, unless there are strong countervailing forces like war. The increase in diversity of many kinds – in lifestyles, morals, ethnicities, religions – has made fellow citizens less predictable, less easy to read, and therefore to trust. And this has gone hand in hand with greater urbanisation and anonymity. The consensus among researchers is that generalised trust in Britain (the proportion of people who say they generally trust other people) has fallen from 60 per cent plus in the 1950s to around 40 per cent now and sometimes lower. Meeting a stranger in a London street 100 years ago one would have been able to read from his dress his place in a clear social hierarchy, and one could also have taken for granted a Christian-inspired world-view and, probably, a shared allegiance to crown and country.

The greater unpredictability of today's stranger is a great advance in many respects – it signifies a freer and less oppressive social order in which many more people are able to focus their lives on the difficult task of being happy. As Richard Florida points out in his book *The Rise of the Creative Class*, there has been less technical change in the last fifty years than there was in the preceding fifty, but there has been a much bigger revolution in the way that people think about themselves. People in the developed world are much richer, more individualistic and egalitarian; they also have smaller families and are less dominated by obligation and conformity. When you cohabit in a single room with several people you need strict rules of behaviour; when you have your own room you can do what you want and the requirement to share is less onerous.

1. They were also, of course, a response to the Great Depression.

The Flight from State Welfare

Solidarity is a clunky, rather old-fashioned word that at its best conjures up images of people pulling together in the Second World War or the 1950s. But when many people hear it today they will think only of faceless bureaucrats trying to tax them on behalf of people they no longer feel any connection with.

The 2012 British Social Attitudes survey spells out in agonising detail the collapse in support over the last decade or so for social security spending and what might be called 'poor people's welfare'. There remains strong support for the NHS and other public services and there has even been a recent upward blip in the number of people wanting an increase in tax and spend and more redistribution.[1] But whereas in previous recessions sympathy for the poor and jobless has also risen, this time it has continued its inexorable slide downwards.

In 1991, 58 per cent of people agreed that government should spend more on welfare benefits even if it leads to higher taxes; that is now down to just 28 per cent. And more than half believe that people would 'stand on their own two feet' if benefits were less generous, with only 20 per cent disagreeing. In 1993 the responses were almost exactly the reverse.

According to a YouGov poll in *Prospect* magazine (March 2012 issue), 74 per cent agreed that welfare levels should be reduced. Less well-off voters were almost as hostile as richer voters – with even a small majority of those living on less than £10,000 agreeing – and Labour voters supported reduction by a large majority.

This is an astonishing decline. Even more striking, it is now younger people who are more hostile to redistribution and generous welfare than their elders, the reversal of a long-term trend of younger people being to the left of older people. Only about sixty years after the founding of Europe's version of the good society based on free health care and education, subsidised pensions

---

1. The number of people who agreed that government should redistribute income from the better-off to those who are less well off hovered around 50 per cent during the recession of the early 1990s. It then dropped as low as 32 per cent in 2004 before rising to 37 per cent in 2011.

and housing and a safety net for those who fall on hard times – all based on a mix of mutual insurance and redistribution – it may already be passing.

There are many possible causes for this decline. One short-term one is that the mid-2000s, when some of these surveys were taken, was both the peak of a long boom which made people less likely to imagine that they might need welfare support and also the middle of a long period of significant Labour investment in welfare and public services, which may have made people think there had been sufficient social investment.

A longer-term cause of decline is growing affluence (albeit stalled for many in recent years) – if people don't need or use most aspects of the welfare state themselves they may become less willing to pay for it. And related to affluence is the decline of collectivism in everything from the large industrial workplace (which has also meant the decline of private-sector trade unionism) to media consumption. Another longer-term trend, supported by the opinion data, is growing public scepticism about government in general and, in particular, the ability of big states to spend money effectively.

Growing inequality may be a further factor. One might expect that to produce more popular support for a strong safety net. Why has it done the opposite? One hypothesis is that the recent rise in inequality has been mainly caused by movement at the very top away from the middle. So instead of producing more sympathy for the less well off it has produced, for those on 'squeezed middle' incomes at least, a sense of living in a highly competitive and unfair society in which economic rewards have become more of a lottery.

But there also seems to be a very strong belief, which has grown in recent years, that the social security system is being asked to do too many conflicting things: to provide a decent standard of life for the genuinely needy without damaging incentives to work or save, or costing too much, or offending people's sense of fairness.

To put it more bluntly, most people seem to think that the welfare state is spending too much on the wrong things and the wrong people. Who are the 'wrong' people? People with whom we have little connection or sympathy and/or people who do not behave as we would – members of the white underclass who are content to remain welfare-dependent, or recent immigrants who have not yet earned support, or members of an introverted ethnic minority who generally do not work or make much effort to fit in. What unites hostility to 'scroungers' and migrants is the sense that neither has earned their entitlements through a record of contribution.

Many people on middling and lower incomes in welfare states have an acute sensitivity to losing their place in the queue to people they regard as 'free riders'. Actual welfare fraud has in fact been declining in recent years. Moreover, most people are net beneficiaries from state spending, they draw out more than they pay in, but it is also true that the poorest 20 per cent of the population pay slightly more as a proportion of their income in tax than the richest 20 per cent, so feel entitled to complain about freeloaders.

The senior Labour politician John Denham explained these welfare anxieties in an essay in the July 2004 issue of *Prospect* magazine, based on a focus group in his Southampton constituency:

> It's not a selfish 'I should get more' reaction, but something broader and more complex. Is good behaviour rewarded? Do I get a fair return for what I put in? Are some people getting something for nothing? There's a sense of fairness here – the belief that there is a set of obligations and opportunities that should underpin British society. When people say 'it's not fair', it is usually because they believe that the balance of duties and rewards, 'the fairness code', has been upset ... The fairness code cuts across the values of left and right. Few people express the left's traditional concern about income equality ... and there is little interest in the right's individualistic, self-reliant model of social and economic policy ... Public services should be for people who are entitled to them, need them, and use them responsibly.

Politicians of all main parties have responded to this anxiety about the 'fairness code' by talking about a 'something for something' welfare state. But in recent years the welfare system has actually been drifting in the other direction, away from a contribution-based system, with its link between what you put in and what you get out, to a 'common pool' general taxation-based system. We have come a long way from William Beveridge's contribution-based social insurance system of the 1940s – covering unemployment benefit, pensions and sickness benefit – supplemented by a non-contributory safety net. We now have a social security system that is mainly non-contributory and has relatively few conditions and short qualifying periods, and is also supposed to provide the conditions for a decent life, not just 'safety net' survival.

To preserve popular support for such a common-pool welfare system you need to have some confidence in your fellow citizens to play by the rules and not take advantage – which might include not damaging themselves through drug or alcohol abuse. But, as we have seen, we have been making this shift to more common pool welfare at a time when general trust levels have been declining and also, in an era of high immigration, when people believe that Britain no longer fully controls who becomes a fellow citizen.

Too many welfare recipients have become hard for ordinary citizens to identify with. A recent survey by the Fabian Society asked people about their attitude to people living on large council estates.[1] Around one third said they felt that they had nothing in common with tenants on such estates, and this group took a much more punitive approach to state support for tenants.

And spending seems to rise inexorably. The cost of social security and pensions, now around £200 billion a year, has increased by 40 per cent since 1999 – benefits that barely existed thirty years ago have mushroomed, housing benefit and disability benefit are each around £20 billion a year, and income support is close to £10 billion. The Coalition government's attempt to bear down on this social security bill has been one of its most popular policies.

There are good reasons why Britain has drifted away from a contribution-based system in recent decades: it reflects the end of full employment, the fact that many women work only intermittently and less caring is done within extended families. But it is no longer a majoritarian system and about 40 per cent of social security is now means-tested – disability benefit, housing benefit, income support, tax credits – creating in many cases poverty traps and disincentives to work and save, despite the best efforts of policy makers.

And when people from the social mainstream do get a contributory benefit like the Job Seekers Allowance, after paying National Insurance for, say, twenty years, they are often shocked at how little it is (£67.50 a week, and it

1. The Fabian Society report is cited in the Runnymede Trust report *Diversity and Solidarity: Crisis, What Crisis?* by James Gregory, June 2011.

stops after six months if your partner has a job or you have savings of more than £16,000). This seems to many people like nothing for something.[1]

So, the welfare state, at least the social security aspect of it, has increasingly become associated with poor others. The same is true of public housing, which after the war was occupied by a large cross-section of the population but since the late 1970s has come to be dominated by the neediest and most vulnerable.

How important is ethnic diversity to this story of declining support for welfare? Race seems to be part of the story but is probably just one aspect of that more general issue of social distance, and the decline in support for welfare has coincided with a sharp fall in racial prejudice (see a fuller consideration of this in the final section of this chapter). The 'otherness' of welfare is probably exacerbated by the relatively easy access of recent immigrants to at least some benefits. Citizens of other EU countries have essentially the same welfare rights as British citizens – including to tax credits – they merely have to prove they are 'habitually resident'.[2] Social housing, too, is available immediately to EU citizens. This offends against the common-sense idea that the welfare state is a cross-generational national club and you should not be able to just turn up and expect full rights (see 'What about the White Workers?', in Chapter 5). As I have already noted, there are huge variations in the use of welfare among both new immigrants and settled minorities. Most East Europeans, although in low-paid jobs, almost certainly pay in more than they take out; Somalis, Bangladeshis and Turks do the opposite.

Historically, immigrants to Britain received no public assistance. But for the past sixty years outsiders have been joining a society with a higher level of mutuality than in the past. In their book, *The New East End*, Geoff Dench, Kate Gavron and the late Michael Young discovered deep unease among the white working class of east London about the shift from mutual forms of welfare to

---

1. Moreover, National Insurance rights are unfairly structured as they depend on how many weeks you have worked in the past two years, regardless of whether you have paid in for thirty years or three.
2. There are more restrictions on those from outside the EU who are supposed to have no recourse to public funds for five years, but that does not exclude them from public services such as the NHS and state education.

the modern state's needs-based system, which was thought to favour outsiders, particularly the Bangladeshi newcomers, who, it was felt, had not paid their way or been part of the history behind the welfare system.

Thanks in part to a relatively open labour market, Britain has less of a problem with minority welfare dependence than some European countries like Belgium and the Netherlands. Nevertheless, because minority Britons tend to be poorer than the average, they are over-represented among welfare recipients and in social housing. As already noted, about 40 per cent of ethnic minority Britons are classified as poor, twice the rate of white Britons, and 27 per cent are in social housing compared with 16 per cent of white Britons – this, again, reinforces the idea that certain kinds of welfare are simply not for mainstream citizens. An American-style racialisation of some kinds of welfare is a dangerous possibility.[1]

People get exasperated when the teacher in their child's primary school class is having to spend extra time on the children of new arrivals, or when they see newcomers with large families jumping ahead of them in the housing queue. This exasperation is not necessarily racial; it is also a sense that John Denham's 'fairness code' has been broken, that someone who has not paid into the system for very long is subtracting from your own entitlement. This is likely to apply just as much to white, Christian East Europeans as it is to an immigrant of Asian or African descent. Even Australians resented New Zealanders' access to their labour market and social security system after a visa-free agreement was introduced in 1973, and in 2001 a caveat was introduced which insisted that New Zealanders must be resident for two years before claiming benefits.

The greater prominence given to a public philosophy of multiculturalism in recent decades may have further exacerbated social distance, though there is no clear evidence for this. But when 'hard' multiculturalism encourages minorities to give primacy to their separate identity and to lobby the state for improvements to their own welfare rather than the general welfare it can hardly reinforce solidarity with the majority.[2]

---

1. See Martin Gilens, *Why Americans Hate Welfare: Race, Media and the Politics of Antipoverty Policy*, University of Chicago Press, 2000.

2. In his paper 'Social Justice in Multicultural Societies', David Miller argues that relatively

Leading Canadian multiculturalists Keith Banting and Will Kymlicka also speculate that multiculturalism may have a political 'crowding out' effect. If political activists of the left who would once have focused on issues of social justice and redistribution are now focused on issues of racial justice and minority recognition, the politics of redistribution is bound to be weaker. And underprivileged people from the white majority will see their own claims and grievances taking second place to those of minorities on the political priority list.

Is it Poverty or Ethnicity that Reduces Trust?

In 2007 the American political scientist Robert Putnam published a famous paper, E Pluribus Unum: Diversity and Community in the 21st Century, in which he described the 'hunkering down' of residents in ethnically diverse areas in the US. He surveyed 26,200 people in forty communities and found that, after adjusting for class and income and other factors, the more racially diverse a community is, the lower the level of trust. Putnam himself is a committed liberal and was rather embarrassed by his findings, but he argues, 'the effect of diversity is worse than had been imagined. And it's not just that we don't trust people who are not like us. In diverse communities, we don't trust people who do look like us.'

Most British and European researchers put this down to American exceptionalism, in particular the legacy of slavery and black-white racial conflict, and attribute low trust in Europe to deprivation more than ethnic difference.

Putnam's work has not gone unchallenged in the US, but his broad findings are supported by the work of economist Alberto Alesina. In a series of papers with various colleagues such as Public Goods and Ethnic Divisions,[1] Alesina

---

closed and homogeneous societies create a 'social union' where 'other members' success is regarded as complementary to one's own'. Multiculturalism, however, challenges this by suggesting that for many, 'group identity has the greatest significance'. The paper is published in Cultural Diversity Versus Economic Solidarity, P. Van Parijs (ed.), Deboeck University Press, Brussels, 2004.

1. Public Goods and Ethnic Divisions, US National Bureau of Economic Research, working paper 6009, 1997.

provides detailed evidence of the progressive dilemma trade-off and argues that racial diversity accounts for about half of the difference in public spending between Europe and the US. He also shows that spending on education and benefits invariably goes down as an area becomes more mixed.

Americans are generally less sympathetic to the poor than Europeans. While 71 per cent of Americans believe that the poor have a chance to escape from poverty, only 41 per cent of Europeans do. As Alesina and colleagues put it in *Why doesn't the US have a European-style welfare state?*,[1] Americans tend to 'think of the poor as members of some different group, while Europeans think of the poor as members of their own group' – though as we have seen, Britain may be becoming more American in this respect. They show that disproportionately high poverty rates among African Americans have led to a majority 'believing that redistribution favours racial minorities'. And this belief translates into policy: more ethnically fragmented states in the US redistribute a markedly lower percentage of income.

What about the British research? Patrick Sturgis and colleagues, in 'Does Ethnic Diversity Erode Trust? Putnam's "hunkering-down" thesis reconsidered', find that diversity has some negative impact on local levels of trust but economic deprivation – and factors such as crime and housing stock – is several times more important. Natalia Letki, in 'Does Diversity Erode Social Cohesion? Social capital and race in British neighbourhoods', comes to a similar conclusion.[2]

But the confidence of the British research seems misplaced. What the researchers do is take national surveys like the Citizenship Survey or the Taking Part Survey and look at measures of trust and socialising with neighbours and volunteering, then compare the replies in four different areas (derived from the census): deprived ethnically diverse areas, deprived homogeneously white areas, affluent diverse areas and affluent homogeneous areas. The researchers then find that after adjusting for the effect of affluence there is no significant

1. *Why doesn't the US have a European-style welfare state?*, US National Bureau of Economic Research, working paper 8524, 2001.
2. The Sturgis (et al.) paper 'Does Ethnic Diversity Erode Trust?' was published in the *British Journal of Political Science*, November 2010. Natalia Letki's 'Does Diversity Erode Social Cohesion?' was published in *Political Studies*, 2008, vol. 56, 99–126.

difference between diverse and homogeneous areas – in some cases the more diverse areas have higher social trust, partly because of higher co-ethnic bonding.

But there are so many variables in play here that it is surely hard to come to such firm conclusions. Also, the researchers look at diversity in an abstract way, yet diverse areas are diverse in very different ways depending, for example, on how recently the immigrants have arrived and, in an area of long-established minority settlement, whether the minority is a relatively successful, well-integrated one or a less successful, segregated one. There is also the question of the speed of change and the size of the minority population.[1] There is strong international evidence that suggests that once an area reaches a certain minority share – around 30 or 40 per cent – it will quickly tip into becoming a minority-dominated area. An area in this transition is likely to have less trust and mixing than a more settled area.[2]

It is surely a combination of relative poverty, high minority population and lack of integration that creates the greatest social distance and lowest trust. In a poor diverse area the process of integration and mixing may not yet have taken place, or is not going to take place, so there is likely to be more wariness and ethnic boundary maintenance and feelings of competition and even conflict.

James Laurence and Anthony Heath argue (in *Predictors of Community Cohesion*, a paper for the Department of Communities and Local Government, 2008) that the worst outcomes can be found in areas of sudden immigrant inflow or in already polarised communities like the northern mill towns with

1. More circumspect findings can be found in papers by Edward Fieldhouse/David Cutts and James Laurence. Fieldhouse and Cutts in 'Does Diversity Damage Social Capital?' (*Canadian Journal of Political Science*, June 2010) find that diversity does have a negative effect on neighbourhood norms for white people but that for minorities it fosters more co-ethnic solidarity. James Laurence, in 'Wider community segregation, neighbourhood ethnic diversity and social capital: the importance of considering "nestedness" in contextual analysis' (*Social Forces*, unpublished) finds that whites distrust their neighbours in diverse neighbourhoods that are part of wider communities that are segregated but are more likely to trust them if the surrounding area is well integrated. This is another way of saying that inter-ethnic contact, 'bridging capital' in Robert Putnam's language, is crucial to trust outcomes.
2. See the work of Eric Kaufmann at Birkbeck College, University of London.

mainly Pakistani minorities. By contrast, the British Indian medical professionals and accountants in parts of Ealing or Leicester or Reading who often live in comfortably mixed, middle-class streets have passed from belonging to an 'out-group' to an 'in-group' for many of their white neighbours – they have joined the club just as Catholics did after many generations of sectarian division in many British cities.[1]

The progressive dilemma is mitigated by integration and contact and the creation of a common life across ethnic boundaries – and with some exceptions that is easier to establish in high-trust affluent areas, more likely in Wimbledon than in Mitcham. If Robert Putnam had said that it is ethnic difference *combined with segregation* that leads to lower trust, rather than ethnic difference itself, he might have got a fairer hearing from British academics.[2]

Until recently the scepticism of British and European researchers about diversity's damaging effect on solidarity may have been justified by current events – in several European countries, including Britain, diversity and social spending had been rising together quite sharply in the mid-2000s. No longer. The opinion survey evidence described earlier in this chapter suggests that the legitimacy of at least parts of the social state is in quite sharp decline.

Countries with more residual welfare states like America and Canada have been more successful than European countries, including Britain, in incorporating immigrants into work – there is often no alternative to getting a job, however poorly paid. And continental Europe, too, may be partly insulated from the progressive dilemma by the fact that more of the welfare state is

1. There is also one piece of British research – an analysis of satisfaction with local GP services by Ipsos MORI in 2004 – that finds the most important driver of dissatisfaction is living in an ethnically diverse area even after controlling for other factors like deprivation.
2. This is a highly political field of inquiry and some academic research is barely disguised advocacy. One example is the Oxford Diversity Project, funded with more than £1 million from the Leverhulme Trust, which overtly sets out to disprove the Putnam thesis, as this extract from the project's website shows. 'Our programme aims to evaluate critically [Putnam's] pessimistic prediction. Given the mixed nature of the population in England, which is set to get more diverse over time, predictions such as Putnam's offer no guidance or hope for a more cohesive society.'

insurance-based. Britain may be in a uniquely unfavourable situation with its current combination of high immigration, a relatively laissez-faire approach to integration and a common pool welfare state.

Holding on to Nurse

It is very unlikely that people in Britain today would establish from scratch anything like today's welfare state. But fortunately that is not the task, it is merely to hold on to something like the present system. Or, rather to redesign it so that instead of exacerbating social distance it minimises it.

It is often assumed that as we get richer we become less socially generous, and this tends to reinforce some of the pessimism about the future of welfare. But there is an equally powerful social stereotype that suggests that we get more benign in our attitudes as we get richer – someone from an affluent home who has had a good education is more likely to be trusting and generous than someone from a rough council estate who tends to assume the worst of people.

And there are some grounds for qualifying the pessimism I described earlier about the flight from welfare. A paper by the researcher Tom Sefton which looks at the sharp decline in those supporting redistribution to the 'less well off' concludes that support for redistribution is actually far higher than the current figure of 37 per cent suggests. He points out that other polls asking slightly different questions give much more favourable responses: when asked, for example, whether government does too much or too little to redistribute income, only 13 per cent of people say it does too much.[1]

Pessimism about long-term social generosity, thanks in part to racial and ethnic diversity, must also be qualified by the strong trends towards greater acceptance of racial equality (see 'How Racist is Britain Still?', in Chapter 2). Greater relaxation about racial and ethnic difference, and more contact with minorities, makes it easier for people to include them in the club of people they are willing to share with. The problem is that just as people have become

1. Tom Sefton, *Give and Take: Attitudes to Redistribution*, British Social Attitudes Survey 2005.

more willing to share with minority citizens, the willingness to share with *anyone* seems to be in sharp decline.

The fact that sensitivity to racial justice is increasing while social egalitarianism is decreasing is not as odd as it sounds. It is a mark of the dominance of a more individualistic-meritocratic world-view which reflects a reduced sense of collective obligation but objects to individuals being unfairly held back by racial or gender prejudice. People can still feel a growing unwillingness to share because of social distance, partly caused by large-scale immigration, while supporting the particular case of an ethnic minority acquaintance at work who is not getting the promotion they deserve. It is, of course, possible to be entirely unmarked by racism and yet feel uneasy about, or positively hostile to, the rapid demographic change in your neighbourhood or, indeed, the country as a whole.

If it is possible to combine openness to diversity and a generous welfare state one requirement is clear: those outside the in-group must be seen to be making an effort to join. A 2004 MORI survey asked people to choose between three different statements: first, immigrants should get the same level of support as existing British citizens; second, immigrants should get less welfare support than British citizens; and, third, immigrants should only get the same level of welfare support as British citizens if they demonstrate commitment to the country (for example, learning the language and history). A big majority, 58 per cent, chose the third option, compared with just 18 per cent choosing the first option and 19 per cent the second.

Another MORI poll, also from 2004, asked whether people felt that 'other people' were taking unfair advantage in their use of public services and benefits, and 45 per cent of respondents said yes. The groups most commonly blamed for taking unfair advantage were asylum-seekers and recent immigrants, but, more optimistically, the long-established minorities featured hardly at all, suggesting that given time people do extend their idea of the 'we' when it comes to sharing resources.

And people do not think outsiders have to contribute for very long before they become members of the welfare club. According to the British Social Attitudes Survey, a majority of people feel that someone who has recently come to Britain to find work should not be entitled to unemployment benefit immediately and 41 per cent feel that their access to free NHS treatment should also be restricted. On the other hand, less than 30 per cent of respondents think it is right to limit access to any benefits to immigrants who have been settled in Britain more than two years.

Another mitigating factor that can help to counter the 'social withdrawal' effect produced by social distance and ethnic fragmentation is the disproportionate number of people from settled minorities, and more recent immigrants, who actually work in the public and welfare services, from the bottom to the very top – from British Hindu Indian consultants to British black African hospital cleaners. Their very visible contribution helps to create a sense of commonality between all of us as taxpayers and users of public services and the workers – black, white and brown – who work in them. The first jobs that unskilled immigrants take are often at the lower end of the welfare economy (public or private). And for many people in middle Britain, seeing hard-working immigrant staff in the care home looking after their elderly mother or father is probably the most persuasive case for moderate immigration they will encounter.

Tom Sefton divides people's attitudes to welfare into three camps: the 'Samaritans', who are liberal and generous, the 'Club members', who support welfare but want strict conditions, are highly sensitive to free riding and want to distinguish between the deserving and undeserving poor, and the 'Robinson Crusoes', who are largely hostile to welfare. Club members are by far the largest group, representing nearly half the population. But most people from all three groups, and particularly the latter two, are allergic to people who use the system when they don't really need it.

All the surveys and focus groups conclude that if the system is to remain broadly in step with popular intuitions in an era of greater diversity and social distance 'welfare reciprocity' is the key: the contributory principle should be reintroduced as far as practical and as many 'safety net' benefits as possible should be conditional on appropriate behaviour.[1] It must be recognised,

1. The case for a more contributory welfare state is brilliantly put from the left by Kjartan Sveinsson, in *Who cares about the white working class?*, a paper for the Runnymede Trust, 2009: 'For if what one gets out of the state is determined solely by need, rather than what one has put into it, then a little dignity has been taken out of citizenship. Dependency is

however, that a shift to a more reciprocal 'Club membership' welfare state will also mean a less generous one for the worst-off groups with reduced access to housing subsidies, income supplements or support for the able-bodied long-term unemployed. It is also likely to mean a less egalitarian welfare system.

And what about new immigrants' membership of the welfare club? The same principle applies. A simpler and more transparent system of 'earned citizenship' is required. Of course anyone who is legally in the country ought to be able to use the health and education systems at once, but all social security benefits – not just contributory ones – should have a minimum two-year qualification period, including for EU citizens. And certain public goods, such as social housing, should have a longer qualification period of five years. (In the long run, if we are to remain a relatively open society with quite large flows of people in and out, to work and study, we will probably need to return to the idea of citizenship identity cards that connect entitlement to one's citizenship status and reassure people that the system is not being abused.)

Social housing, public services and even benefits should also be managed, as far as possible, to engineer mix and interaction and to prevent ethnic minority and white underclass ghettoisation.[1] There are some interesting experiments with housing associations committed to ethnic mixing in the north of England.[2]

The decline of solidarity is a slow, long-term process and with sensible policy decisions it can be slowed further. The welfare state has an institutional inertia and has created all sorts of interests that will ensure its medium-term survival. The intellectual challenge in the future may be to disentangle the

---

encouraged, the principle of reciprocity has gone, and welfare has simply become a new form of charity ... Preoccupation with the most vulnerable means that parts of all incoming groups, along with the downgraded members of the national majority, will feel that their length of residence in the country does not seem to give them a durable stake in it.'

1. See the work of Miles Hewstone and contact theory in Chapter 2, 'Thinking about Integration and Segregation'.
2. See the work of Home Group in Queensbury and Allerton, two small towns between Bradford and Halifax, cited by James Gregory in *Diversity and Solidarity: Crisis, What Crisis?*, Runnymede Trust, 2011.

causes of the welfare squeeze: is it driven more by fiscal conservatism or social distance, and how much of the social distance is related to ethnic diversity and how much to people of all races at the bottom of the pile becoming more separated from the mainstream?

As Peter Kellner has pointed out, if trust and cohesion and solidarity was all that mattered we would all live in hamlets. Families are more trusting than neighbourhoods, neighbourhoods more than villages, villages more than towns and towns more than cities. Yet the inexorable drift down the ages has been into cities, where more than half the world's population are now said to live, and into immersion among strangers. It is completely rational to be less trusting and less willing to share with people with whom we do not have repeated encounters, and indeed with whom we are often in competition economically and socially. That is the measure of the achievement of the welfare state – it has managed to project some of the sense of the 'us' of smaller communities on to the bigger, city-dominated, impersonal state of today.

As societies get richer and more diverse, accepting the inevitability of some reduction in solidarity, and a more complex mix of private and state provision, may be the best way of holding on to quite big welfare states. Even politicians of the centre left like James Purnell, the former Labour secretary of state for work and pensions, seem to accept this. Purnell favours a thicker but narrower 'protection state', with moderate taxes paying for a smaller set of stronger protections. He proposes a system of national salary insurance that would reinvigorate the contributory principle and provide satisfactory income protection for people when they lose their jobs. He points out that what binds people to the welfare state is services that they cannot buy for themselves, and believes the system should focus, in addition to salary insurance, on four things: free childcare, properly paid parental leave, reliable long-term care and a pension that is higher for those who have paid in than for those who haven't. That would mean cutting other things such as winter fuel allowances, child benefit and pension tax relief for top earners.[1]

If we are looking for a cause for declining welfare support, it seems clear

1. 'How we could come to love the welfare state', James Purnell, *The Times*, 27 July 2011.

that declining levels of interpersonal trust and rapid demographic change are making the project harder to sustain in Europe, just as they always have done in the US. And there is another related factor. Part of the liberalisation of modern societies, and the decline in discrimination, has gone hand in hand with a more general relaxation of moral boundaries. Along with the welcome decline in 'bad' discrimination (racial, gender, class and so on) there has been a decline in 'good' discrimination that has had more mixed outcomes, especially for poorer people. This creates a particular problem for some immigrant families who lose control of their children to a society that, as they see it, has no boundaries. This has probably also contributed to the size of the white underclass. Some sense of the welfare state re-establishing clearer moral boundaries, most obviously the distinction between the deserving and the undeserving, is not popular on the left but may be part of what is required to sustain welfare.

So there seems to be a fair degree of consensus on things which help to mitigate the negative effect of social distance and diversity: more conditional and insurance-based welfare and graduated access for newcomers, increased interaction with fellow citizens, across both the class and ethnic divide, and less separateness for the poor – all could help us to sustain a welfare state that softens the edges of the market economy and enables us to retain that distinct, European, combination of individual liberty and social solidarity.

CHAPTER 7

The National Question

Put Out More Flags

Almost everyone has views about national identity, about Britishness and more recently about Englishness too. These are big abstract questions but they also touch on personal feelings and sometimes evoke strong emotions. A country like Britain exists in so many different dimensions it can be hard to talk about it precisely or even coherently.

I want to find ways of thinking about the national interest and national identity that still make sense in a post-modern age. I want to try to convince a twenty-year-old who is happy enough to identify as a Londoner or a Glaswegian, and who lives most of the time in a global youth culture, that a national identity and allegiance still matters too; not that Britain is the greatest country in the world (as Tony Blair claimed in one of his final speeches as prime minister), but that it is our country and that a national idiom is still the best way to think about large-scale co-operation on everything from health care to national security.

Living in a more diverse and less collectivist country, with what seems like fewer opportunities to see fellow citizens as collaborators in a common project, moderate national feeling has become a positively progressive force. Social interaction and collective action are easier when people share at least elements of a common culture and ascribe to common norms. Citizens of course have different and sometimes conflicting interests, but without some notion of a common interest we will have too weak a collective democratic pulse to achieve even things on which there is a settled consensus. The decline of politics and the weakening of national feeling have gone hand in hand, because they are in a sense the same thing. Moderate national feeling can be the means to focus our attention on a generous idea of the public interest and the public space. It is a kind of public good – the real 'big society' – the oil that makes the giant wheels of a decent society turn; as many people discovered again to their surprise during the Olympic summer of 2012.

But for historical reasons British, and especially English, elites have had a rather oblique relationship to the idea of the nation. That has sometimes made the country seem oddly inarticulate about itself. The most striking recent example of this was the Millennium Dome, which had nothing to say about national achievement.

There is also a bigger, more international story here about liberal and left-wing intellectual scepticism towards the national that I touched on in discussing the 'universalist shift' (see 'Nations and People' in Chapter 1). Emerging from the trauma of the Second World War, a significant section of Europe's educated classes fell out of love with the national idea, holding it responsible for much of the violence of the twentieth century, for racism, for colonialism and for protectionist barriers to trade and economic progress. In continental Europe it was usually replaced with a commitment to the idea of further European integration; in Britain it was more often global and third world causes that attracted idealists. In recent decades many of the smartest people in finance, business, the universities, the arts and the liberal professions have became de-territorialised – they have come to think of themselves as belonging to a global, borderless world.

Intellectual sophistication has increasingly become associated with moving beyond the local, the everyday, the parochial, and, increasingly, the national. Transcending or replacing the nation with other allegiances has seemed an attractive, even morally superior alternative – chiming both with market freedoms and with progressive, universalist assumptions. To many people, in the era of globalisation, the nation has become just a legal entity worthy of little loyalty. We have multiple identities, commitments and networks, both sub-national and global, and our rights are protected by trans-national human rights treaties – the nation state, as the political cliché has it, is too big for most of the local things that matter, too small for most of the big international things that matter like climate change.

This scepticism was already a central part of middle-class liberal common sense when I was growing up in the 1970s and 1980s, especially if you came from a (still) powerful country like Britain, in particular its English part. I certainly believed it. As a public schoolboy leftist, briefly attracted to the intellectual certainties of Marxism while a university student, I would have considered any expression of attachment to my country – with the exception of the England cricket and football teams – as stupid. We laughed along with the Monty Python mockery of Edwardian stoicism and at the embattled campus Tories who still believed in the flag. Boundaries and borders were for the small-minded and the provincial. They were just so uncool.

I now believe this disdain for the national was immature and premature as well as loftily dismissive of majority opinion. Through reading Michael Lind, David Miller, Michael Ignatieff, Yael Tamir and others, I came to see how moderate nationalism could not only co-exist with both liberalism and internationalism but was in some ways a necessary condition of both of them. And also how liberal sceptics about national feeling lean too much on an anachronistic caricature of a violent and chauvinistic nation state and do not acknowledge how dramatically it has liberalised both internally and externally in recent decades. In any case, despite the growing importance of regional institutions like the European Union, most politics in the developed world still takes place within a liberal nationalist frame.

Of course the national interest is an idea that can be, and has been, abused by governments and elites to suppress legitimate grievances. It is obviously true that not everyone in Britain has the same economic interests or life chances and that the country is divided by class and region, and much else besides. But it has been through the claims of national citizenship, and the mutual sacrifices and commitments that it sometimes entails, that the great democratic and welfare advances of the late nineteenth and twentieth centuries were made. The equal rights of minorities, too, have been secured through an appeal to British justice.[1] As the French socialist leader Jean Jaurès put it, 'The point is not to destroy patriotism but to enlarge it.'

The extension of our sympathies beyond friends and family to the strangers (including those from minority ethnicities) who are our fellow citizens, and the recognition of at least some shared interests, is a great human achievement. It does not require one to like all one's compatriots (or indeed any of them), or dislike foreigners, or cultivate a romantic view of the nation or refrain from criticising or feeling shame for one's country's actions now or in the past.

In a liberal society the national idea is always contested, and having a strong attachment to one's country and its traditions can comfortably co-exist with criticising almost everything about it. As the first German-born US senator put it in 1872 when his patriotism was questioned: 'My country, right or wrong: if right to be kept right; and if wrong to be set right.'[2]

National attachments have become an important issue in the past few years for two reasons. The first is the political challenge to national sovereignty and the British state from European integration but now, too, from Scottish independence. The second, which affects all rich liberal democracies, and is central to the broader themes of this book, is whether a meaningful sense of national solidarity can act as a counter-weight to the pull of individualism and the call of competing group allegiances and loyalties – once class, now more likely to be religion and minority ethnic traditions.

Britain did not in the 1960s and 1970s develop a post-imperial language of national citizenship and identity. Many conservatives felt ambivalent about fully extending citizenship to non-natives (who were just starting to arrive in significant numbers), and too many on the left thought that embracing the newcomers meant discarding the nation. A more coherent 'middle way' between universalism and a tribal nationalism is what we have been reaching for ever since.

Gordon Brown tried and failed with his Britishness debate. But it was an

---

1. Consider the special passion with which civil liberty activists defended the Guantanamo prisoners who were British citizens.
2. Quoted in Tim Soutphommasane, *The Virtuous Citizen: Patriotism in a Multicultural Society*, Cambridge University Press, 2012.

interesting failure from which we can learn. He was right to ask: 'What is our equivalent of that [American] national symbolism of a flag in every garden?' But his answer was a lecture on British history and political values which misunderstood the ordinariness of national feeling.

A national identity has both a very particular aspect rooted in the customs, language, texture and reference points of everyday life, and a more universal 'citizenship' aspect derived from the political rules and procedures of liberal democracy. The two are normally mixed up together in most people's ideas of national identity, though it is the first that carries most of the emotional charge.

Even the procedural aspects of citizenship have a particular national story (and struggle) behind them, but the underlying principles – liberty, tolerance, equal treatment, fairness and so on – are common throughout the liberal democracies. These are not *national* political values, even if Britain did pioneer some of them. And while 'constitutional patriotism' and the democratic rules of the road can help us live together despite growing diversity they are not enough to create a sense of mutual attachment or shared destiny.

A story that begins with a list of attractive political values, as in Brown's Britishness debate, gets the psychology of national identity the wrong way round. National feeling and patriotic pride are rooted in the attachments of everyday life, they are not deduced from a list of historic achievements.

Indeed, Brown's stress on *values* is inappropriate on two counts. On the one hand the attachment to liberal political values is not distinctly British enough. On the other hand the values of everyday life in modern Britain are too diverse to bind us together. It is precisely because of the enormous differences in world-views contained within modern liberal societies – contrast the pious Muslim family up the road with the hedonistic, secular students next door – that values cannot be the main basis of post-racial national identities.

Values, meaning different and sometimes conflicting notions of how to live a good life, are in a way the problem, not the solution. It is shared experience and mutual interests, and the way these can be fostered by public institutions and public rituals, that are a better means for overcoming difference and creating a more transcendent in-group loyalty, a sense of fellow citizen solidarity, in a diverse era.

National identities ebb and flow in mysterious ways. Countries and the way their citizens think about them cannot be changed by political fiat, and no two individuals' national identities are exactly alike. But governments make decisions on lots of matters that have a bearing on identity – from public holidays to what is taught in schools – and telling stories about the country and where it is going is one of the main jobs of political leaders.

Big events, such as the 2012 Olympics, offer a chance to question old habits of thought and rearrange the mental furniture. Danny Boyle's opening ceremony for the Olympics did just that: rediscovering the country's ability to tell an appealing story about itself to young and old, left and right, black and white – this was not a multicultural story about a 'community of communities', it was a national story about what is special about this country but with lots of black and brown Britons playing a prominent role.

There have been other changes in the last decade or so which have helped to nudge the story in a new direction: the unselfconscious use of the language of citizenship rather than 'subjecthood', and, in the early 2000s, partly in response to Islamic extremism and the fear that multiculturalism had gone too far, the introduction by Labour ministers of those citizenship rituals for newcomers drawing attention to this national space and its value to the people who live here. This signified a belated recognition on the centre left that it makes no sense for the political right to 'own' the nation – as it has done for much of the post-war period – and that the left's universalism must make its peace with the moral particularism of the national club.

But belonging to that club no longer entails a sense of superiority. One of the reasons that the English in particular have felt awkward about their national identity is that the country's historical dominance – both within Britain and globally – fits uncomfortably in a more egalitarian age. But there is a distinction between superiority and specialness – sometimes expressed in the distinction between nationalism and patriotism.

And there are many different ways in which national specialness can manifest itself. Some people might struggle to feel a more 'special' relationship to a fellow British citizen whom they do not know than to a French or German person whom they do not know. Yet at its most basic, membership of the political community of a modern nation state places duties on us to obey laws and pay taxes, while granting us many rights and freedoms – and in doing so it places us in a special relationship to our fellow citizens, whatever their religion or skin colour.

We do not have to wave the flag or support Team GB but we do have to acknowledge that being a British citizen places us in a special network of reciprocal obligations towards our fellow citizens that we are not in with people in Stuttgart or Toulouse. And this is not just about taxes and welfare payments, though these are important. We share a physical and cultural and political space with our fellow citizens and the quality of life in Britain is the sum of our behaviour towards one another.

As well as attachment through the idea of citizenship as described above, there are, of course, 'thicker' attachments too, and most people do still feel a certain emotional attachment to their country even if it has become weaker in recent generations. An ethnic attachment to the nation through shared ancestry, and myths of ancestry, is in itself neither sinister nor threatening – and there is no reason why it should not be *chosen* by ethnic minority Britons too.

Through music or film or sport or parts of the countryside or thinking of the sacrifices and struggles of past generations I can sometimes feel an emotional link to England or Britain – and pride in much of the country's history and achievements. Minority Britons will not always feel that and can connect in other ways; my argument for the nation state is a rational and pragmatic one that includes, and is comfortable with, ethnic connections but does not depend on them.

When David Cameron said in response to Gordon Brown's Britishness debate that 'we don't do flags on the lawn', he seemed to strike a chord with the public, who are rightly sceptical of politicians presuming to tell them how to feel about their country. But he was also falling back on an Anglo-British exceptionalism, assuming that a semi-private ethnic understanding of national identity, that has no need for vulgar patriotic rituals or spelling out the citizenship contract, was still sufficient. It is not sufficient any longer. Britain may not do flags on the lawn but we do need to create a more publicly friendly environment for moderate national feeling. And as it happens those citizenship ceremonies introduced in the early 2000s have turned out to be a creative and popular innovation, despite the scepticism of much of liberal Britain when they were proposed. So, it turns out that we do indeed do flags on the lawn, or at least flags and oaths of allegiance in the town hall for newcomers.

Ahead of us in the next few years are the outlines of big national arguments about our position in Europe; about the future of Scotland in the United Kingdom and the possible re-emergence of England as a political entity; and about the nature of the monarchy when the Queen dies or abdicates. There is also the continuing background story of an ever bigger and more confident (though also in some places quite separate) ethnic minority Britain and where minorities fit into the conversation. Out of all this one would expect a somewhat different psychological and institutional texture to emerge. I hope it is one that leads to a further post-imperial 'normalisation' of national feeling and identity, especially for the English and their elites. And also a blurring of the sometimes rather artificial distinction between civic/political identities and ethnic/historic ones to produce a 'common life' identity; a national identity that feels meaningful, that is open to settled minorities and to newcomers, and is completely ordinary – the British dream in practice.

What is a National Identity, and is Britain's Declining or Evolving?

A classical definition of a nation goes something like this: a human group conscious of forming a community, sharing a common culture, language and history, attached to a demarcated territory and capable of self-government.

A nation also requires continuity in time and differentiation from others. Differentiation – the borders and boundaries that demarcate a small tribe or a modern nation state from others – is intrinsic to human life. And borders and boundaries are still necessary in a modern 'sharing' state. Most people feel a hierarchy of obligation and do not want to, nor can they, share resources equally with everyone. In Britain we spend twenty-five times more every year on the NHS than on development aid. To most people in Britain, even people who think of themselves as internationalists, that fact represents a perfectly natural reflection of our layered obligations, but to a true universalist it must seem like a crime.

Not all nations have their own states. There are 192 states in the United Nations but dozens more nations that would claim their own state if they could. And not all nation states have a single nation corresponding to the state, in the manner of, say, Denmark or France. Enormous states like China or India are in reality more like empires with different nations and quasi-nations jostling for expression within them.

There is a scholarly argument, going back several decades, about whether nations are 'real' things or modern inventions – Perennialists versus Modernists. Modernists like Ernest Gellner see a common national identity as the creation of modern industrial societies with transport and educational infrastructures able to impose common national norms in a single language. (Eugen Weber's book *Peasants into Frenchmen* illustrates this thesis by arguing that a large proportion of people living in rural areas and small towns did not conceive of themselves as Frenchmen until 1870, while many still failed to do so until 1914.)

Perennialists, by contrast, argue that common identity across large territories originates from a primordial need for connection and that national identities are modern projections of tribal and clan type relationships. Strong modern states are built around a core 'ethnos' which connects the present to the pre-modern past through myths, symbols, holy places and traditions. Of course, some of these traditions are of quite recent invention, like some aspects of Highland culture in the Scottish case, but that doesn't mean that the ethnic history itself is invented.

The leading academic in this field, Anthony D. Smith, proposes a compromise between the two schools. He acknowledges the 'invention of tradition' and the modern form of most nationalisms but also the importance of their deep ethnic roots. England itself is quite a good example of that, with a strong sense of a distinct history and shared ancestry by the eighth or ninth century which fed into the formation of the modern English nation state from the sixteenth century onwards.

Whether a nation state is a recent creation or with roots in deep history is, literally, an academic debate compared to the more pressing issue of how conscious people are of their national identity and what they make of it today.

Of course most people think only rarely about their national identity. It is, like the Queen herself (with whom for some people it is closely bound up), just a persistent backdrop to their lives, though one that occasionally moves to the foreground during big public rituals or when they go abroad or meet a foreigner at home. As the writer Michael Billig put it in his book *Banal Nationalism*, most of us are so drenched in our everyday national culture that it is a subliminal part of our identity: the symbols on money or stamps, the turns of phrase from national history ('turning a blind eye'), the pervasive assumption in the media that a national audience is being addressed.

But if a national identity is, like an iceberg, mainly beneath the surface, it is not much use in helping to create a sense of common interest or belonging. For that to happen a critical mass of the population still have to consciously think of themselves as part of a national story and to see their national identity as something meaningful and active. Is this still true in Britain?

A (multinational) nation state like Britain can be divided into two big intertwined elements. It is a state: a legal and political entity occupying a bounded territory, which people belong to usually through birth without making any conscious choice. It grants countless legal, political and social rights and in return demands obedience to its laws, and requires various minor duties (such as jury service) and payment to it of taxes. It is also a kind of emotional and moral space: a place and a group of people you (in theory) feel a special attachment to, as well as a contract between generations, between the dead, the living and the unborn. An 'ethos' and an 'ethnos'. A space for authority and the rule of law, for armies and police forces, for democratic institutions, for rights and duties, for buildings and bureaucracies and passports; and a related but more subjective space for symbols, traditions, obligations, attachments, for feelings about language, music, people and places.

It is in the second space that most of the change has taken place in the past 100 years and where most of today's arguments about national identity happen. Some people, let us call them 'declinists', sense that the overwhelming direction here has been one of loosening and weakening.

The argument of the declinists is that the background noise of national identity is becoming quieter as other calls become louder. That the British people don't really exist any longer in the sense of a large group of people who despite all their differences feel a vague allegiance to one another. How many people make important choices in their lives, about their future career, for example, based on national considerations? It would surely be rather unusual now. But I recently met a senior civil servant who remembers being at grammar school in the 1950s and deciding to become a scientist, inspired by the early developments in civilian nuclear power; he saw this explicitly as an exciting national project that he wanted to be part of.

Andrew Gamble and Tony Wright, writing for *Political Quarterly*, remind us that my civil servant was growing up in a world in which people were used to the nation state reaching deep into their daily lives: 'The establishment of democracy in the 20th century increased rather than diminished ideas of Britishness both through the creation of many new British institutions, such as the BBC and the welfare state, and through the experience of war and the enormous sacrifices made in defence of the British state and the British empire. Universal welfare and universal military service gave Britishness a solid basis in everyone's experience.'[1]

Britain was at its most national when it was also at its most equal during the Second World War and the couple of decades after. The absence of a popular revolution, as in France, does not, as is sometimes claimed, mean that the common people and the political left stood outside the national story. As Edward Thompson and others have shown, it was through myths of the rights of the freeborn Englishman, pitted against the aristocratic 'Norman Yoke', that English working-class consciousness was expressed in the eighteenth and nineteenth centuries. And as Gamble and Wright imply, in the first decades after 1945 there were few things more British than the trade-union movement and the Labour Party, and its greatest creation, the NHS.

Clearly not all of this has gone; most of us pay about a third of our income to the state and take its powerful presence in our lives for granted. But over

---

1. *Britishness: Perspectives on the British Question*, a *Political Quarterly* special, Andrew Gamble and Tony Wright (eds), Wiley-Blackwell, 2009; see introduction, p. 2.

the past twenty years many declinist historians and commentators have identified the disappearance of many of the factors that provided the 'glue' of the specifically British story from 1800 to 1950. Linda Colley's book *Britons: Forging the Nation 1707 to 1837* most famously made the case that modern British identity was built on the celebration of empire, popular Protestantism and the country's role as the first industrial nation. British liberty, expressed in part through Parliament and the common law, was contrasted with the continental European 'other' and with despotisms of various kinds. Now all these things are gone, or others do them as well or better.

The apparent weakening of Britishness in the last few decades is partly generational. The generation that fought in the Second World War and remembers the empire is dying out. Britain has been, by and large, an actively benign force in their lives. Not only that, but for perhaps 200 years being born British was to join the most successful club in the world. For most people the attachment to a country, like to a family, is unconditional – it just is. But an unconditional attachment is made even stronger by a sense of benefiting from being on the winning side, from belonging to the 'top nation' that is victorious in war, that leads the world in science and literature, and that speaks the global language.

A friend of mine told me of a conversation about the national 'contract' he had with his father just before he died a couple of years ago. His father was a manual worker from the North-East, born in the 1930s, and his life had been a pretty good one, the old man concluded: rising standard of living throughout most of his life, the NHS and an expanding welfare state if he ever needed it, two sons who went to university (one became a professor). He gave his loyalty to Britain and he got a good deal in return.

The baby boomers who came after him were even luckier in material terms but perhaps more spoiled too and less inclined to feel that they were getting a good deal from their country. Many of today's 20–30-year-olds seem to see national identity as something from an earlier age, especially if they have been to university, and tend not to connect their own good fortune to living in this particular rich and secure and liberal country. In a recent YouGov poll about how people conceive Britishness, people were asked about twelve attributes – six positive and six negative – and among the under-35s the highest scoring attribute (at 38 per cent) was a negative one, 'drunken'.[1] And as we have seen in the preceding chapter, younger people also now express less generous attitudes to welfare than older people – signifying a weakening of emotional citizenship.

The historian Robert Colls argues that national identity has an 'emergent' quality, 'it is the process of inviting people to become more equal and alike over time'. The first couple of decades after the Second World War represented a high point of that social democratic version of national identity. Since then, and especially in the last thirty years, thanks to mass immigration, rising inequality and greater freedom to be different, we have been on a gradual journey to become less like one another.[2]

That was partly about the disappearance of things that once bound people together – Protestantism, war – and partly about new forms of life emerging based more around markets and individual choice and less around collective mutual dependence; think of the decline of industrial working-class communities, the disappearance of national economic institutions and industries and the transformation of television viewing. There is also the fact of relative British decline. As international superiority faded it meant that attachment to the British national club came with fewer psychological rewards; recent immigrants who came with a belief in the mother country often felt this particularly acutely.

There are other aspects of more recent history that have also helped to unpick the 'alikeness' of the 1950s and 1960s – EU integration, cheap travel, the great moral and cultural liberalisation of the 'sixties', the promotion of ethnic difference. As David Miller and Sundas Ali have written: 'In multicultural democracies the historical trend may be towards weaker but more inclusive identities.' An inclusive and *strong* national identity is not an easy thing to achieve.[3]

Why did Britain not try to develop back in the 1970s the language of national

1. See Peter Kellner, 'What Britishness means to the British', Political Quarterly, July–September 2007.
2. Robert Colls, 'The Lion and the Eunuch: National Identity and the British Genius', Political Quarterly, October–December 2011.
3. David Miller and Sundas Ali, 'Testing the National Identity Argument', European Political Science Review.

citizenship, and pathways to citizenship for new arrivals – those practices of 'civic religions' found in settler/immigrant countries like Canada and the US – that we eventually began to establish in the early 2000s? One simple answer is that Britain is not, and was even less so then, a settler/immigrant nation or a modern political invention like America or Australia. In the 1970s it was a historic nation, just emerging from empire, with an ethnic majority that saw no need for a 'civic religion'.

But there are other reasons, arising from the political history of the 1970s, for why Britain failed to produce a new story that accommodated both the ethnic minorities and the national attachments of the majority. As I have already argued, Enoch Powell was partly to blame for this failure by polarising the debate over immigration and causing most liberal politicians to steer clear of a 'racialised' national question. But the young left, too, largely abandoned the national story in favour of an embryonic multiculturalism – for them the national flag was associated with right-wing extremism or Northern Irish unionists or an empire that made them feel ashamed.

Perhaps above all Britain did not reinvent itself as a nation because it wasn't a normal one in the first place, it was an empire. Many people, especially among the politically liberal and the highly educated, seemed to slide from an imperial idea of the country to a post-national one without passing through a 'normal' national phase. (See 'What is Multiculturalism and Where Did it Come From?' in Chapter 4.)

This story of the decline of British national identity must, however, be kept in context. Identity has been not so much fading as evolving, and often in a welcome manner. Britain in the 1950s was in many ways a miserable and small-minded place. As David Kynaston's social history of the 1950s shows, it was hierarchical and class-ridden and characterised by extraordinarily chauvinistic views about the superiority of the British people. Kynaston quotes Tom Harrison of the survey organisation Mass Observation to show how deeply conservative and individualistic, rather than community-minded, people were even in those supposedly solidarity-rich times – seven out of ten people said they were happy with the NHS but mainly because they saw it as something for nothing.[1]

1. David Kynaston, Family Britain 1951–57, Bloomsbury, 2009.

Diaries from the 1950s also show how small most people's circles were. For one middle-aged woman, the only event outside her immediate life that she records for the whole of 1955 is Princess Margaret not marrying Group Captain Townsend. It was also often a cold and repressed country. Kynaston himself remembers watching the television news every night with his father in absolute silence, with no discussion about what they had just watched.

Alongside the insularity and very local attachments there was also a deep attachment to the country, often expressed through royal events. The Queen's return from abroad in 1954 was a huge national event, let alone the Coronation a year before. Kynaston says there was indeed a strong sense of national solidarity and specialness but this did not necessarily extend to actually existing neighbours. He has some sympathy for the arguments of Joanna Bourke, who coined the phrase 'retrospective communities' – she argues that people were actually no more likely to look out for each other than they are today, though other social historians disagree.

In any case, many of the changes that I have described as the weakening of shared norms were experienced by a lot of people in the 1950s and 1960s as liberations, the freedom to escape a loveless marriage or a dreary small town. And freedom also often meant more market choice and less state uniformity; the apparent weakening of national identity was often just a straightforward de-collectivisation.

And just because some of the things that once animated Britishness have faded does not mean that national feeling itself has gone. Not so long ago Parliament and the law might have seemed central to a sense of Britishness, now sport and popular culture are probably just as important. A national identity does not stand or fall on having a 'project'. We may no longer be forced together in the collective adversity of two world wars, but the citizens of Britain (and England) still occupy the same territory, share a public culture and experience a degree of political, economic and social interdependence. And throughout Britain there is still a strong emotional attachment to the country's history. Consider the huge audiences for British history series on BBC television or the fact that every year Poppy Day seems to become more, not less, important as the great conflicts and those who fought in them fade from living memories.[1]

So, what do the polls and surveys actually show about today's national identity? All seem to agree that there has been some decline in intensity of feeling, especially among younger people. According to Anthony Heath and James Tilley, the number of people who were very proud to be British fell from 57 per cent in 1981 to 45 per cent in 2003. But the number who felt 'somewhat' proud or very proud in 2003 was still a healthy enough 86 per cent.[2] In a 2007 paper to test Ulrich Beck's 'individualisation' thesis about the decline of collective identities such as religion and class, national identity was found to have declined relatively little. A recent report by my own think tank, Demos, found that 80 per cent of people said they were proud to be British. We also discovered that most people think other people are less patriotic than they used to be.[3] And there is plenty of evidence for declining trust levels, which may be another way of measuring a decline in national feeling.

But this does not look like a crisis of national identity. Perhaps what is happening is something perfectly healthy, more like the shedding of a skin. National identity has adapted to a more individualistic society, one with fewer big collective projects. As we move further away from the purposes and symbols of one national period – the British imperial and then post-imperial period – we gradually put on the clothes of another. What does this next period look like? Britishness itself is less intensely felt than in the first half of the twentieth century, which leads naturally to a looser relationship between the constituent nations, possibly including independence for Scotland. It is also perhaps less focused on the formal symbols of Britishness – the royal family and so on – and more on the common life of citizens; more bottom up like Wootton Bassett than top down like Trooping the Colour.

There are many different ways of belonging to and identifying with a

1. Recall the unexpected outburst of public pride and mourning, and perhaps protest too, over Britain's Afghan war dead in Wootton Bassett.
2. James Tilley and Anthony Heath, 'The Decline of British National Pride', British Journal of Sociology, 2007, vol. 58, issue 4.
3. A Place for Pride, Demos, November 2011.

country. It can be weak and instrumental: I live here because it is where I come from (or where I have arrived) and so long as I pay my taxes and obey the law I want to be left alone. At the other end of the spectrum are the 'over-identifiers', people who identify ferociously, and often resentfully, with the formal symbols of the country, and may be among the relatively small minority (less than 10 per cent) who persist with a semi-racial view of what it is to be British or English. There is an oppositional anti-English edge to some of the Celtic nationalisms. There is also an oppositional ethnic edge to some white working-class expressions of English national identity.

But in the middle are the great mass of people of many different backgrounds who identify with their country through the 'little platoons' – the common life of neighbourhood, town and so on. This is usually more of a 'horizontal' identification with familiar places and fellow citizens than a 'vertical' identification with the pomp and circumstance of national symbolism, though according to Demos research the stronger people identify locally the more likely they are to feel strongly attached to the nation too. The journey of the Olympic flame through Britain in 2012, carried by local heroes surrounded by huge crowds waving the Union Jack, was evidence of that.

These Demos findings on the ordinariness of national feeling are reinforced by some large-scale focus groups conducted by the UK Borders Agency, at the prompting of Liam Byrne then a Home Office minister, on the subject of citizenship, integration of newcomers and national identity back in 2007. When asked what they would miss most if they went to live abroad, the national things (apart from friends and family and so on) that people mentioned were the NHS, pubs, the countryside and sense of humour. The royal family and the formal trappings of national identity were seldom mentioned or regarded in what the Demos researcher Max Wind-Cowie has described as a 'good-naturedly ambivalent' way.

Britain, England and All That

What is Britain? It is a physical place and all the people in it and the history that has brought us to this moment. But talking of Britishness, and indeed

Englishness, promises something more: it promises a kind of 'essence', it lends itself to lists.

There is, of course, no essence or list, that can capture the variety of ways of life across the land; there are 63 million different ways of being British. But behind the abstract language of values there is a lived experience, a common life and a public culture that is surely where we should be mainly seeking Britishness. It is perhaps less recognisable than it was, and marked by even greater variety than in the past – what do Tower Hamlets or the Thamesmead estate have in common with Hampstead; what do Ancoats and Manningham have in common with Knutsford?

This is a familiar rich-versus-poor objection to any simple account of Britishness. But this has always been the case and there can still be something called Britishness that people hold in common even if they live very separate lives and think of the country in different ways.

So perhaps Britishness is just the collective lived experience of British people? A real thing, to be sure, but impossible to describe. As Siôn Simon wrote in the November 2007 issue of *Prospect* magazine:

> The lack of a definition of Britishness is not a proof that we need one. A British person knows what it is to be British. We feel it inside us like we know the colour of our eyes. We carry it around with our kidneys, our blood and everything else about which we don't need to think but which defines who we are. We don't need to define Britishness because it defines us.
>
> The task for incomers is more than to memorise a non-existent credo. It is to imbibe, to absorb, in some ways to reshape, the spirit of the tribe … and in the medium of English – the great national glue which we underestimate both as such and as a soft power advantage.

The English language is, indeed, a useful metaphor for a British national identity that is confident in itself, but flexible, inventive and open to outside influence. And linguistic identity – the experience of shared idiom and metaphor – can be a powerful psychological bond in its own right.[1]

---

1. This point is made by the literary critic George Steiner.

But although there is something mysterious about the character of a country, especially old ones like England, Wales and Scotland, it is surely possible to generalise plausibly about common characteristics and customs – the sort of things that you recognise and feel when you return to the country from abroad, the things that create the temper and tempo of a place.

George Orwell wrote about the characteristics (rather than values) of the English in a way that didn't seem absurd at the time. But Orwell is also a reminder of how transient some customs and characteristics can be – few people would write today that 'the gentleness of England is perhaps its most marked characteristic', as Orwell did about eighty years ago (though it probably wasn't true then either).

As many people remarked at the time, the reaction to the death of Princess Diana seemed to mark the final disappearance of a quiet, stoical, stiff-upper-lip sort of Englishness/Britishness which had been fading for a generation or two. And as the writer Ian Jack has noted: 'Anyone who has witnessed the collapse of the London bus queue – they existed twenty years ago – would be puzzled by the notion that "fair play" ... is a distinctly British value.' (Though the queuing reflex seems to live on in other parts of the country.)[1]

In most respects British people today behave and respond much like people who live in similar rich, liberal, post-industrial societies. But there are customs and habits of mind and underlying assumptions that do still contribute to a sort of national style. So here is one possible list: pragmatism, empiricism, moderation and readiness to compromise; indirectness, obliqueness, a desire not to cause offence (perhaps an echo of Orwell's gentleness); sense of humour and ability to make and take a joke; love of sport and competition and gambling; sceptical verging on cynical about political power but law-abiding and relatively uncorrupt; dislike of swagger and pomposity and support for the underdog; independent, individualistic and suspicious of bureaucracy but also ready to help those in need.

There is nothing very remarkable or original about these things – many of them are commonplace in other countries too and there are lots of British citizens, and even large groups of them, who do not exemplify these attitudes

---

1. 'In search of British values', *Prospect*, November 2007.

or preferences very strongly. Some of the attitudes conflict with others. Much of the list is bequeathed by our long evolutionary history and, as we have seen, the characteristics are not set in stone. It is not even clear that they are all British, as opposed to English, characteristics. Moderation and fair play, for example, might be seen as the self-interested values of big countries. As the Scottish historian Michael Fry puts it: 'A level playing field always favours the big battalions. The wee fellow gets his way by stealth and guile ... Just ask the Celts, it is the only way to beat the plodding English.'[1]

And yet there is something there that many readers will recognise; a sort of national temperament where ethos and ethnos meet, 'the spirit of the tribe' as Siôn Simon puts it, that is more than just the sum of its individual parts and is a sort of bridge across other spirits of class, region and ethnicity. The political commentator Matthew d'Ancona once described Britishness as 'individualism plus the NHS', a neat symbol perhaps of the historic compromise between the propertied middle class and the working class, one of the main stories of modern British history. And what about creativity? It is surely not a coincidence that Britain has produced so many musical and cultural movements wth global resonance – consider how many heads of today's international fashion houses are British.

This is not something that can be easily spelt out, and individuals and groups will play different variations on the theme – but the point is there is a theme, and it helps to make more tangible the idea of the 'common life of the British people', which is what Britishness is.

This common life cannot by definition be ethnically exclusive, though the historic majority will, also by definition, have contributed more to it than recent arrivals. It is both less and more important than the formal, political form of Britishness. The latter is of course institutionalised in citizenship, in rights and duties, in the procedures of democracy – these are the basic rules that underwrite our relatively civil society. But they are not what make people feel at home or give people a sense of belonging.

This is the difference between formal and 'felt' citizenship. It is perhaps what distinguishes a second – or third – generation person of immigrant

---

1. ibid.

background from the pioneer grandparent who, having grown up somewhere else, never felt fully at home in Britain, never cracked the unwritten codes of British life.[1]

How should these reflections on Britishness make us think about the future of the United Kingdom and above all about the emergence of England? The opinion poll data tells us that the majority of English people have now joined the Scots and Welsh in identifying first with their 'home' nation rather than with Britain. In the case of the English that may have been a distinction imposed on them by a one-sided devolution settlement and a higher-profile Scottish identity creating more sensitivity to the fact that England and Britain are, indeed, different things.

It has taken the English longer to find their way to a new language of Englishness because it was submerged into Britishness in a way that Scottishness never was. As the historian David Starkey has put it, the Celtic nations have typical modern European nationalisms, positively encouraged by England in the eighteenth and nineteenth centuries. English nationalism, by contrast, expressed itself in a rather vaguer 'top nation' consciousness through the years of British supremacy. With the end of empire and then the loosening of the United Kingdom, the English were left with an absence.[2]

People are often puzzled by the claim that Britain/England has a weak or fuzzy sense of national identity compared with many equivalent countries. Surely politics in England remains as raucously national, and even at times chauvinistic, as anywhere else? And what about the accusation of arrogance – a sort of global sense of entitlement and superiority – that has often been levelled at the English?[3] And this is the paradox of English nationalism – it is *indistinctly expressed precisely because it has been so historically dominant.*

1. I came across a good example of the 'codes' of national life at a seminar on the educational under-achievement of Turkish children. In Turkey, apparently, school reports are very blunt whereas in Britain a more oblique and euphemistic style is used – satisfactory often means unsatisfactory. Turkish-born parents with children in north London schools had believed, judging from their reports, that their children were doing reasonably well and were then surprised and frustrated when they did very poorly at GCSE stage.
2. David Starkey speaking at the *Sunday Times* Education Conference at Wellington College, 2012.
3. The idea that the English thought of themselves as a new chosen people, with a special

The English have been overwhelmingly dominant within the British Isles and Britain was similarly dominant within the empire. But the point about dominance is that it is more efficiently achieved if it is less visible. This makes it sound like a plot. It is not that, rather it is about historic patterns of thought and behaviour which are handed down through institutions, cultural habits and character traits – consider Boris Johnson's disarmingly bumbling manner as an effective mask for a highly intelligent and ambitious man, and think how typically English it feels. Or think of the smooth, even-handed manner of the assured public-school-educated English civil servant over the unruly passion or romanticism of the Celtic underdog.

Some people have wondered whether this effort of suppression ended up removing all meaning from the English core of Britain. England, as Rudyard Kipling once observed, seemed to dissolve itself into the empire. Robert Young argues that apart from a brief flirtation with a racial, Anglo-Saxon idea of Englishness in the nineteenth century, it came increasingly to be defined from afar: 'Englishness paradoxically became most itself when it was far off … it was transformed into a mode of masquerade that was best performed far from home into which others could always translate themselves.'[1] As Krishan Kumar has pointed out, Rupert Brooke's 'corner of a foreign field/ That is forever England' captures this displaced, deterritorialised character of English ethnicity – though there are, of course, other more rooted industrial and working-class accounts of Englishness.[2]

The logic of an indistinct national identity has been neatly explained by the historian Linda Colley:

> Almost by definition, monarchical empires do not favour written con-
> stitutions. Nor do they normally favour precise statements as to who
> their component populations are, and of the quality of these peoples'
> rights and allegiance. Those in charge of empires are concerned to exer-
> cise often widely different levels of authority over different peoples in

---

contract with God, at least until around the First World War, was well argued by the historian Diarmaid MacCulloch in a BBC 2 television essay in March 2012.

1. Robert J.C. Young in *Locating the English Diaspora 1500–2010*, Liverpool University Press, 2012.
2. Krishan Kumar, *The Making of English National Identity*, Cambridge University Press, 2002.

geographically dispersed territories, and accordingly tend to make use of baggy and capacious political language that is focused on the person of the ruler. It is in large part because it was for so long a monarchical empire, that the language of a discrete national citizenship – of individual citizens in a bounded terrain with well defined rights – has never taken deep and unproblematic root here, only the more elastic language of subjecthood.[1]

Tentativeness in the expression of a national identity is an invitation for others to join in. That is how a confident, expanding empire works: it is the 'baggy and capacious' political language that allows others to see themselves reflected in it.

A related reason for a baggy and capacious national language is the long unbroken continuity of Anglo-Britain. So many other more 'classical' nation states have been made or reborn in the modern age – the United States bound together by a constitution and a war of independence, modern France created by a revolution, Italy and Germany both latecomers to nationhood and then recreated by defeat in war. Britain, and England before it, has no recent myths of origin, no founding document or event, no national catastrophe, hence perhaps no national day and no 'flags on the lawn'.

There is something to be said for this lack of definition, even as the underlying reasons for it shifted after 1945 from imperial 'raison d'état' to a looseness well suited to absorbing the new ethnic minority populations from the old empire. Andrew Gamble and Tony Wright again: 'The very capaciousness of "Britishness", a mansion of many rooms, enables multiple identities and loyalties to flourish within it, which is a strong argument for not trying to pin it down in a way that excludes ... There is a great merit in something so slippery and elusive, perhaps even something very British.'[2]

Being slippery and elusive is, however, perfectly compatible with being chauvinistic and arrogant, and Britain in the 1950s was often both of those things. But in the liberalisation wave of the 1960s and 1970s there was a

---

1. Linda Colley, 'Does Britishness still matter in the 21st century?', in *Britishness: Perspectives on the British Question*, Andrew Gamble and Tony Wright (eds).

2. See *Britishness: Perspectives on the British Question*, Andrew Gamble and Tony Wright (eds), introduction.

shift – from a tentativeness of English national expression born out of a need to *hide* dominance to one based on an impulse to *repudiate* dominance.

This repudiation appealed mainly to the well educated and to the political left. It was not a repudiation of nationalism as such – other people's nationalism was to be admired, in the Celtic nations or the emerging post-colonial nations of Asia and Africa – it was a repudiation of the nationalism of dominant nations like Anglo-Britain. It drew on an imperial disdain for the vulgarity of national particularism overlapped with a leftist hostility to national as opposed to class-consciousness.

This echoes the argument about the roots of multiculturalism in Chapter 4 and an imperial elite that has no national home; its allegiance is to the abstraction of the state or the monarch, not to any particular group of people – as *The Times* had claimed in 1852, the Englishman was a 'born cosmopolite' free of the 'follies of nationality'. And in the 1960s this translated easily into the cosmopolitan manners of a new liberal elite too – allegiance was now to tolerance and openness instead of the monarch, to England's 'genius' for multiculturalism.

The core members of this new elite, according to Geoff Dench, were 'policy-makers and the public servants responsible for carrying out social policy but it extends widely into the educational establishment and liberal professions ... and their role is to stand impartially above and integrate different elements of the population.' This is what both imperial and multicultural elites do.[1]

As Britain shed the empire, partially turned to Europe and acquired a new minority population in the early post-war period, the country was often said to be suffering an 'identity crisis' – as well as more straightforward decline symbolised by the Suez disaster, economic and industrial relations problems and the long, dispiriting war in Northern Ireland. And it was exacerbated by the reluctance or inability of the English post-imperial elite to think clearly about what a modern, liberal nation state looks like and feels like.

The Thatcher–Blair years helped to restore British prestige but not in ways that were always popular in Scotland. And the 1998 Scottish devolution, which was

---

1. See Geoff Dench, 'Britain's Internal Empire', unpublished paper.

meant to stop any further move towards independence, has instead fanned it. A more Scotland-focused political culture seems to have helped create a mini-national renaissance – the country's relative economic success has, for example, caused a sharp drop in the number of graduates leaving the country. This renaissance has evidently happened within the union, and it is hard to see how political connection to England is an obstacle to Scotland's freedom or success or wealth – with the possible exception of North Sea oil.

Yet the SNP has not only claimed credit for all the recent successes but has also turned them into an argument for full national independence. The economic argument is that in order to pursue an active 'developmental' economic programme Scotland needs full control of all relevant levers, including tax and investment incentives, yet it is not clear that such a policy would differ radically from current policies and there are also strict EU-related limits to such tax and subsidy competition.

So, what is going on? What Tom Nairn has called the 'revenge of the periphery' is partly a product of lower external threats and the disappearance of that 'glue' that gave Britishness its point, especially for the Scots. But it is also about changing economic structures. In the early stage of industrialisation successful countries needed large internal markets, working classes and urban centres to succeed; it made sense for smaller nations like Scotland to fuse with a larger one like England. But now those economies of scale are no longer required, and when membership of Nato and the European Union mean that you have no security worries and you can share an internal market with a different national entity, why not enjoy the warmth and excitement of a solo national journey? Even the banking crisis and the Euro crisis, which should have weakened the case for independence by reminding Scots that there is still a dangerous world out there, just provided another opportunity for SNP leader Alex Salmond to reassure people that nothing very much would change after independence. By stressing the continuities that would accompany independence – monarch, British army and now sterling – Scottish nationalism thus becomes a sort of game of identity politics at the end of history. So little was apparently at stake for most Scots that when, in a focus group exercise, Scots were told independence would make them £500 a year richer the proportion supporting it rose to over 60 per cent, and when told it would make them poorer by the same amount support dwindled to almost a single-figure percentage.

Most Scots, like most of the English, seem to feel that though the union has lost definition and meaning it is still probably worth preserving. And Alex Salmond has failed to make a convincing case that it is 'broke'. Yet this feeling that nothing serious is really at stake means that the race will go to the political group with the most momentum and vested interest behind it. At the end of 2012 independence seemed less likely than a further stage of devolution, but neither option seemed impossible.

Would a vote for Scottish independence in the 2014 referendum be a cause of regret? Britain is a multinational democratic state inevitably dominated by the sheer weight of the English – much as the Swiss-Germans dominate the Swiss federation or the Anglo-Canadians the Canadian federation. And it has been a pretty successful multinational enterprise. It is one of the world's best connected and richest countries, which, partly thanks to an illustrious past, still counts more than most countries of similar size. Uniquely it is a permanent member of the UN security council, the OECD, the G8, the EU, Nato, the Commonwealth and the Council of Europe.

And the British dimension has existed for long enough for it to have created its own loyalties and institutions – the armed forces, the monarchy and the BBC among other things – as well as an extensive mixing of families and people. Contrary to the myth of Scotland as a more Scandinavian/social democratic country, the political values of the two countries appear to be remarkably similar, especially if you compare Scotland with northern England.[1]

If Britain were to divide into at least two nation states on one island it would represent a significant diminishment, particularly for the English. For a decade or more it would probably focus English and Scottish politics on the terms of divorce and how to manage the subsequent cohabitation, and might encourage Wales to follow suit.[2] It is not clear what would be achieved

1. In 2003, in response to one rather social democratic polling question – 'ordinary people do not get a fair share of the nation's wealth' – 60 per cent of English respondents agreed compared with just 54 per cent of Scots.
2. There is also the issue of the nearly 10 per cent of Scotland's population of 5 million who are English.

by separation, except for those members of the Scottish political class who would benefit in prestige and power.

The peculiar thing about Britain is that although it was substantially made by the English they did not define their own role in it. England dissolved itself into Britain and to this day has only minimal political/institutional identity. And it does not have the option of a 'reactive' nationalism in opposition to the imperial power, for the simple reason that it is (or was) that power.

An English interviewee for the 2007 British Social Attitudes Report caught a widespread sense of regret about this: 'The Scottish, the Welsh and the Irish to an extent, seem to cling on to their identities much better than the English do. Well, I suppose some people would say that that's because the English were always seen as a little bit arrogant and not needing to have that identity, but I think the result of all that is, that the English have sort of lost ... a little bit of that, and I think we need to get a bit back. We have the Scottish Parliament and the Welsh Assembly, we don't have anything for England *per se*, so I think, I think there is a void.'

Filling that void could release creative political energies as new institutions and identities are swiftly formed. Indeed, perhaps the most desirable outcome from the current political dance over the United Kingdom would be a further stage of devolution for Scotland within a looser union that would still allow the emergence of England as a political community.

England released from Britain, at least partially, could find a new post-post-imperial resting place and finally end the residual sense of being a great power that is compelled by history to play a world role – one reason for our involvement in Iraq and Afghanistan. It might also force England to focus more on its North–South divide and its long tail of 'underclass' social failure.

The adoption of more English forms could provide a frame to the attempts to renew our jaded democracy – such as localism and city mayors and, more contentiously, English votes for English laws in Parliament. Talking about the English NHS, the English welfare or legal systems is already common.

And England needs a new song, literally. As Sunder Katwala of British Future has been pointing out for years, it is inappropriate that English sports teams still sing the British national anthem at international events, and it is particularly absurd that they do so when playing Wales or Scotland. There is a beautiful hymn perfectly designed for this task, a hymn that celebrates the specialness but not the superiority of the English people and appeals to our better selves to build together the good society – Blake's 'Jerusalem'.

The English have been semi-literate in the language of modern national identity but the Scots, by rearranging the union, present an opportunity for the English to learn to speak it normally and robustly, like the Scots do themselves. And the English appear to be warming to the idea. Some people on the left fear that a more confident English national identity would be uncomfortable for England's minorities. The opposite is more likely to be the case, as the Scottish example shows. As a small nation living in the shadow of a larger one, Scottish identity is more sharply defined and expressed than Englishness. But that seems to have made it easier for Scotland's (admittedly small) South Asian minority to adopt the symbols of Scottish nationalism.

Britishness could in future become a more formal identity for state occasions and facing the outside world, with the four nations coming together more consciously – in the monarchy, the BBC, the armed forces, foreign affairs and, of course, Team GB – where it is in their interests to do so. Englishness might then become rather more like Scottishness is now to most Scots – their 'real' national identity combining both political and ethnic aspects and grounded in a common lived experience.

Nudging the Nation

So, to summarise the argument of this chapter. Many factors in developed countries tend to weaken national identities – individualism, the decline of external threats, greater cultural and economic porousness. Britishness has been particularly vulnerable to decline because it is a political and institutional identity based on traditions which have disappeared or faded. Moreover the English language has made the British particularly open to Americanisation and cultural globalisation. And then, further complicating the story, the British elite, particularly its English part, has long had a semi-detached relationship to national identity thanks to both the imperial inheritance and the post-war 'universalist shift'.

On the other hand, the story of the decline of national identity is often exaggerated. The nation state remains central to the modern world. And people's attachment to it remains strong too, even if the current form of it – Britishness – is evolving.

Some political activists on the centre left talk about the task of nation building in today's Britain. That seems inappropriate language for an old country; nudging is more suitable. And given that a national identity is both a highly subjective individual sentiment and an objective, collective one – expressed in mass ritual and measurable, observable attitudes – it is inevitably a slippery idea. Moreover, national identity is a subject that can open a gap between intellect and emotion; while writing this chapter I had a long conversation with a friend who concluded that he loved Britain and could not imagine living anywhere else, yet did not identify with it.

So, I have no long list of policy proposals but I want to reflect, briefly, on how we think and speak about national identity under four headings: blurring the civic and the ethnic; expressing specialness without superiority (especially in England); inventing new public rites and rituals; and, finally, telling more compelling stories about ourselves – 'the British dream'.

First, blurring the distinction between civic and ethnic national identities. Too often it is just assumed that most long-standing citizens identify ethnically and more recent ones civically – it almost pits new citizens against old ones. But long-standing citizens usually identify through a mix of civic and ethnic factors, and why shouldn't new citizens identify in the same mixed way too? A post-racial ethnicity is emerging, which is another way of describing a common life and mutual identification across ethnic boundaries.

Most minority Britons, especially those born here, do join the 'we', know something about and connect to the history of this country, speak the language as a native, and so on; why should they be left to identify only through the civic realm of Parliament and equality legislation? They may retain an attachment to other traditions and memories but there are many different ways to be English or British, and hybrid ethnicities and cultures have been sprouting for several decades.

Moreover, more than almost any other nation on earth, English/British culture has been shaped from the outside and by outsiders. Krishan Kumar points out that it is impossible to analyse the meaning of Englishness in the last century or so 'without recourse to writers such as Henry James, Joseph Conrad and T. S. Eliot'. He adds a list of Jewish émigrés – Ludwig Wittgenstein, Lewis Namier, Karl Popper, Ernst Gombrich, Nikolaus Pevsner, Nicholas Kaldor, George Steiner – who have left a mark on British high culture. And a more recent list of Asian and Caribbean writers and intellectuals – V. S. Naipaul, Salman Rushdie, Kazuo Ishiguro, Stuart Hall, Bhikhu Parekh and others.

The old prejudice that minorities cannot be English is starting to fade, from both sides. Two leading minority journalists – Gary Younge and George Alagiah – have both recently written about their new comfort with the idea of being English.

It is true that some of the reflex, quasi-tribal identification with a country's history may be harder for those newcomers whose ancestors did not play a part in it, or were on the other side of the colonisation story.[1] But people can pick and mix; if you look hard enough there's something there for pretty much everyone. And is it really so much harder for a young British South Asian Muslim schoolboy to identify with Henry VIII or Gladstone than a young white British schoolboy? Both boys are living in a country that has been shaped by them and both boys needs to know something about them to understand how their country has got to where it is.

There is strong support for the belated political initiative to teach more British history in schools. This does not have to be a sanitised 'official' history or lists of the kings and queens of England but rather a sense of the narrative thread of the extraordinary English, and then British, story that pupils from all backgrounds can pick over and dispute. This desire for a connection to the past should not be dismissed as the reactionary nostalgia of middle Britain.

1. The idea of 'reclaiming' the flag became a cliché of the 2012 Olympics for people on the left. For most white people the flag never went away, but for many minority Britons it was associated with the far right, at least from the 1970s to the 1990s. And some minority Britons have also had ambivalent feelings about the flag arising from its colonial associations.

Here is historian Linda Colley:

> We need a healthier, more comprehensive, less apologetic view of our past ... We have a perfectly useable, collective past, if we only look for it and select it. Scotland, Wales, Northern Ireland and England have in some respects different visions of the past, but not entirely so. We could surely all agree to commemorate the abolition of the slave trade in 1806, something which all these islands, and black Britons as well as white, took part in. We could all commemorate the Reform Act of 1832, the first step towards achieving universal suffrage here. We could all now commemorate the Catholic Emancipation Act of 1829 or the Jewish Disabilities in the 1850s or votes for women in 1918. And why shouldn't we commemorate independence for India in 1947, since it's part of our history too? If I were in charge of currency design or in the business of inventing new national holidays, I'd be thinking hard about ways of commemorating events such as these as a means of connecting our reforming past with the extension of citizen rights today.[1]

Second, the once globally dominant English seem to be discovering that moderate national feeling can be a benign and *normal* sentiment – as it is for example in Sweden, Ireland or Scotland. Is it possible to shed a national sense of superiority without losing a national sense of specialness? Looking around England today and listening to people talk about their country I would guess – and opinion polls largely support my hunch – that this is being achieved. In an essay called 'Love, Idolatry and Patriotism', Eamonn Callan wrote about how being special is not the same as being best: 'We unashamedly love unremarkable cats and dogs, mediocre books, trivial jobs, ugly houses with unmemorable yards, in addition to our perfectly ordinary friends, kin and lovers ... The lover may be perfectly aware of the modest value that the beloved has in the larger scheme of things without that thought diminishing love.'[2]

In the long journey from superior national or racial conceptions of the

1. Linda Colley, 'Britishness in the 21st Century', lecture at No. 10 Downing Street, 28 March 2000.
2. Eamonn Callan in *Social Theory and Practice*, 2006, 32 (4), pp. 525–46.

community to an idea of equal citizenship, accommodating people of different ethnicities and religions, we do not need to abandon a sense of national history or of popular democratic 'ownership' of the country. As the 2012 Olympics suggested, an inclusive *and* strong national identity is possible.

Third, I want to speculate about how we might create more meaningful public rituals. For historical reasons that I have discussed, the public rituals in Britain, and especially England, are rather underdeveloped and recently most innovation in this area has been at the border between new citizens and existing ones – in citizenship tests and ceremonies and so on.

Politicians should step cautiously in this area – people are rightly suspicious when they wrap themselves in the flag – but there certainly appears to be a public appetite for a national bank holiday (judging by the Borders Agency focus groups and other polling). That begs the question of whether it should be a British one or separate English, Scottish, Welsh and Northern Irish holidays. We already have a kind of Britain day in Remembrance Sunday, recalling the very British (and colonial) struggles of the two world wars and subsequent smaller conflicts, and there may be a case for giving it a more explicit frame as a 'Britain day'. But given the shift towards stronger national identifications within Britain it must make sense to focus more national ritual at that level.

A St George's day national holiday in England (and the national saints' days in the other nations) should be a day for celebrating the common life of everyone who lives in England, a 'bottom up' celebration of neighbourhood, town, region and country. It should be a day for partying, for volunteering, for giving blood, for the young to pay their respects to the old and for extra large and public citizenship ceremonies in the local town hall – welcoming new citizens into English life as well as the more formal Britishness on their new passports.

Leaving the Englishness story to one side, there are also plenty of other opportunities for giving a more civic-national cast to the everyday interactions we have with the state. As the writer Ben Rogers has put it: 'State citizen encounters ... can send important messages about the standing of citizens, what is expected of them, and what they have a right to expect from the state and their fellow citizens in return. Yet as things are now, these encounters are often nothing more than dispiriting bureaucratic exchanges.'[1]

Rogers suggests various encounters which could be more heavily ritual-ised: the registration of a newborn child could become a public rite in which parents, their friends and family, and the state agree to work in partnership to support and raise the child (and perhaps a short book spelling out a citizen's rights and duties could be handed out); in the transition of a young person from childhood to adulthood, many schools have leaving ceremonies that could be made more formal; even the paying of taxes and receiving of benefits could be accompanied with much more information about, say, the alloca-tion of public spending and an invitation to contact the relevant local and national politicians.

A model here is the citizenship ceremonies and civil partnerships for same-sex couples, the two national rites successfully introduced by the last Labour government. In both cases they have a built-in local flavour. In the case of the citizenship ceremonies, Parliament merely requires the taking of the oath of citizenship and the displaying of the Union Jack – the result is that they vary enormously in content and character.

A nation state cannot just be a machine for providing individuals with rights and wealth, it needs some emotional ballast too. And the point of all these initiatives is to reinforce the idea of a 'citizen nation' – crossing class and ethnic boundaries – in which as many people as possible move beyond being 'mere' citizens who obey the law and pay their taxes to 'virtuous' citizens (in Jonathan Chaplin's distinction)[2] who join in the social and political life of the country, in however small a way. It also helps to transcend difference, in Jonathan Haidt's words, 'in a sea of similarities, shared goals and mutual interdependencies'.

One very big nudge in this direction would be compulsory citizenship service for young people. A six-month mixing together of young people from different classes and regions and ethnicities, all working on common

1. Ben Rogers, *Enhancing Citizenship through State–Citizen Encounters and Civic Rites*, IPPR, February 2007.
2. See *Multiculturalism: A Christian Retrieval*, published by the Christian think tank Theos.

projects, would be expensive and against the grain of 'choice', but it is popular and it should be done.

One of the commonest ways of joining in and being an active and virtuous citizen is through volunteering, and it also remains at the core of the two ancient institutions – the monarchy and the Church of England – which continue to play a significant, if declining, role in the story of national identity.

Arguments about whether we should have an established church, with bishops in the House of Lords, do not engage many people, especially when the minority faiths clearly have their space too in the public realm. But some modernisation of this heritage is in order, as with the monarchy itself when the Queen dies or abdicates.

The monarchy is a symbol of continuity that puts a human face on the state and there is no appetite to replace it with a republic. And a more human and less pompous monarchy is emerging – remember the Queen's 'parachute jump'. Indeed, we may be acquiring a kind of republican monarchy which is less a symbol of historic deference ('subjecthood') and more a symbol of the national collective. Linda Colley suggests that this should be formalised, with the next monarch swearing an oath of service to the 'majesty of the people'.

And finally I want us to tell better stories about Britain at its best, stories that we can live by – a 'British dream'. This starts with a mature view of the past, a view that is neither nostalgic for an imagined past nor embarrassed about the real one. There is no large country in the world which does not have bloody and oppressive episodes in its past, and Britain has more than most because of the empire. But having a connection with the past and even a certain sense of responsibility for its triumphs and disasters does not mean that we should fall into the familiar trap of judging the pre-liberal past by the standards of the liberal present.[1]

Moreover, being British no longer means so obviously belonging to a club of winners. So what does the national contract mean now? What do we get

1. Jonathan Sacks, the Chief Rabbi, describes one strand of this that emerged in the 1970s. 'The British started to see their own history as an irredeemable narrative of class, snobbery, imperialism, racism and social exclusion. It was in this atmosphere that, in the 1970s, multiculturalism was born.' *The Times*, 7 February 2011.

in return for our loyalty and our taxes? The British are still rich and free, and interesting. We no longer have the swagger and self-confidence of an imperial people but we are neither boring nor insular.

We have acclimatised ourselves to a somewhat reduced status in the world but do we still have a national project, something that gives us a larger frame and mission? Once upon a time the empire was the project, then world wars, building a welfare state; perhaps Margaret Thatcher's liberalisation period was the last time we had anything resembling a project. What might a national project look like today? Leading an outer ring of the European Union? Successfully managing the impact of globalisation on our citizens, especially the poorer ones? The former Labour minister James Purnell has suggested that we need to decide whether we want to be a larger Sweden with excellent public services but no military aspirations, or a smaller Brazil, creative, unequal, but flexible and prosperous.

But in a liberal society government is not about imposing a national blueprint. Most people would, I suspect, think an appropriate national project is simply to be a decent country that people admire and that its citizens can feel proud of belonging to, at least most of the time, a country that strives to offer a decent life and opportunity to all of its citizens and lives up to the best of its own traditions.

We do that more than we think, and we should get better at shaping a national narrative out of it. I want to end this chapter with three 'British dream' stories that I came across during the past eighteen months. Two involve immigration, opportunity and openness and all three happen to be English stories, but the idea could apply to all British citizens.

The first took place in Wolverhampton, where I had been talking to a group of British Asians, mainly of Sikh and Hindu backgrounds, about their experiences over three generations. Towards the end we touched on questions of national identity and feelings of Britishness. Afterwards a young woman came up to me and started chatting. She came from a successful Sikh family and was practising law in London. She told me how the story in her family was that they owed their success to a grandfather who had arrived here in the 1950s with £10 in his pocket. But, she said, she had come to realise over the years that was only part of the story; Britain, and the opportunities it had offered him and the subsequent generations of her family, was central to the success story too.

The second was a story told to me by the Labour MP Siobhain McDonagh. She recalled her elderly Irish father sitting in the gallery of the House of Lords in 2004 shaking his head in pride and disbelief as he watched his other daughter, Margaret, being elevated to the peerage. The Irishman had come to England in the late 1940s to work as a labourer. He met and married an Irish nurse and they had two daughters. Both did well at school, both went to good universities; one became General Secretary of the Labour Party and the other a Labour MP. And as he watched one of his girls becoming a baroness he muttered under his breath, 'Only in England, only in England.'

The old Irishman was not technically correct – these things happen in other places too, but they happen here far more than we admit and it's time that our national story reflected them. Both the two anecdotes above are about a sense of gratitude, which is not a popular idea in a democratic age, but they are not about deference nor about gratitude to a group of people but rather gratitude for the best features of an open society.

The final word goes to the political journalist Andrew Sullivan, who has lived in America for more than half his life, but returned to England for an extended stay in 2011. Reflecting on his journey home he wrote this: 'The central crisis of my youth – that of English identity – seems to me to have resolved itself. No one ... is nostalgic for global power any more, let alone empire. The whole question of Europe has palpably calmed – lulled by the very English compromise of being in the EU but not truly of it ... And what's left feels like someone emerging from a midlife crisis into a rather comfortable second wind, one in which illusions of grandeur have morphed into the modest pride of simply being who you are ... After losing an empire, England has finally found a role: just being England.'[1]

1. *Sunday Times*, 24 July 2011.

CHAPTER 8

Where Next?

The Readjustment

I have been arguing in this book for a readjustment in the way that Britain thinks about immigration, integration and national identity. The argument has been partly directed at liberal and centre-left Britain, which I still regard as my own political family. But for thirty years the left has blinded itself with sentiment about diversity, which has made it harder to understand what is actually happening in many parts of the country.

The liberal description of the world says that large-scale immigration either changes nothing or is a self-evident good; minorities are helpless victims but multiculturalism has created a Britain of happily interconnected new and old communities. The distance between this account and the lived experience of many citizens has become so wide that it has reduced overall trust in politics and our willingness to offer up our taxes to the Leviathan.

In this final chapter I want to reprise some of the arguments of the book and then, instead of a list of policy prescriptions, sketch a possible future.

Like Margaret Thatcher, most people are opposed to large-scale immigration but are happy enough with individual immigrants so long as they make some effort to join the club. As racism has declined I believe that most people in Britain today would be largely indifferent to immigration so long as they were confident that it was not undermining their economic interests or changing the country too fast.

That means numbers and speed matter, as does the way the majority think about new citizens, what is expected of them and how British society can create the right kind of space for them to flourish. Immigration and integration are intimately linked; get the second right and there is more room for the first.

The economics of immigration in Britain involves complicated trade-offs. Some people benefit as employers and consumers from certain types of immigration and, arguably, everyone benefits from some downward pressure on wage inflation and costs. But then everyone might be said to suffer from the fact that over a period of ten years' steady economic growth, from 1997 to 2007, the welfare ghettoes and the hard-to-employ were not sufficiently reconnected to economic life: thanks to mass immigration neither employers nor the government had sufficient incentive. The number on out-of-work benefits did come down from a high of 6 million in the early 1990s but remained stubbornly stuck on 4.5 million through the years of growth. The complaint that (at least from about 2002) the main beneficiaries from the boom years were bankers and immigrants has some truth.

Indeed, we have now had fifteen years of sustained large-scale immigration to test the claim of its economic benefit, and all the main macro-economic studies show that, as a result of immigration, there has been no marked improvement in growth or incomes or employment for the vast majority of the resident population. The economics of mass immigration remains broadly neutral, though negative for those at the bottom, but the social and cultural case has turned negative thanks to the scale of the inflows since 1997. Gross inflows of around 600,000 a year since 2004 and a net immigration of around 4 million foreign-born citizens from 1997 to 2012 has produced easily the most dramatic demographic change in British and English history.

We are deep into a huge social experiment, and to give it a chance of working – and of avoiding the sort of opinion swing we have seen in the Netherlands – we need to heed the 'slow down' signs that the electorate is waving, especially in a probable low-growth era when peoples' grievances cannot be too easily bought off with rising wages and public spending.

Writers of the immigrationist school, such as Philippe Legrain, Ian Goldin and Ian Birrell, reject the slow-down argument. In doing so they appeal to a spirit of openness and generosity that is one of the best things about liberal societies. But they also perpetuate an unhistorical and romantic account of the immigration story, eliding the nineteenth-century and early twentieth-century experience with today's.

Welfare states, the idea of equal citizenship, democracy – these have completely changed the context of immigration yet they are barely mentioned in the immigrationist writings. There is no sense of dilemmas or trade-offs in their work. On the contrary, it is often characterised by a self-righteous moralism. And in countless debates I have had in recent years people seem to think that the simple fact of their own immigrant ancestry is a clinching argument for high levels of immigration today. This is a kind of therapy, not rational thought.

Or consider this from Philippe Legrain, writing in the *Economist*: 'Are people who happen to be born abroad, often in circumstances less fortunate than our own, with whom you might sympathise and get on with if you met, whose motivation in moving is to better their lives and their children, are such people – human beings like us – really such a terrible threat? Are they bad people?'

Of course they are not. But neither are they morally superior people, whose interests should be placed before those of existing citizens. Indeed, given how much easier it is to be an immigrant these days they are probably far less courageous and 'exceptional' than their predecessors in earlier generations. And the one group of people in this argument who are unequivocal winners are voluntary immigrants.

The same cannot always be said for people in the receiving society, and yet immigrationist writers, though often on the political left, seem to have little interest in or sympathy for how their lives are changed.

In any case, arguing from each individual human story may seem compassionate but is a kind of moral sleight of hand; of course you can always make a case for an individual or family to enjoy the better life that most of us live in the west. But you have to look at the aggregate effects both on western societies and the societies that the individual is leaving.

In Britain, many dynamic immigrants have helped to transform companies or premier league football teams or have contributed to the country's research effort, and filled skill gaps and unpopular jobs. But supporters of large-scale immigration are here guilty of the 'fallacy of composition', the argument that something that is true for a few people is also true for a lot of people (or vice versa). Net immigration of 300,000 a year has very different short- and long-term effects to net immigration of 50,000.

And the economists who favour large-scale immigration often seem to forget how markets work. If people had not been so easily importable in the past fifteen years, price signals would have changed – in other words the pay for certain jobs would have gone up – and existing citizens would have responded.[1] In a few cases companies would have had to improve their training programmes, instead of just buying already trained foreigners off the shelf. Or if a company had not had the whole world to choose from, it might just have had to put up with a slightly less good specialist lawyer or electrical engineer. But it is my guess that there are probably only a very few thousand jobs in this country for which outsiders have unique skills that cannot already be found here.

Without large-scale immigration, governments as well as companies would have had to think a bit harder about trying to match the skilled people that we produce to the needs of business and households. Manpower planning is an unfashionable concept, but when it is known that we have shortages of, say, skilled construction workers, it ought to be possible to make sure the courses are there, and then make sure they are filled by encouraging and motivating young people to take up these potentially attractive careers. Many young people don't know what they want to do and usually follow peer group pressure or what seems the easiest or most fashionable option – the idea that their country needs them to fill certain shortage jobs, so long as pay and conditions are decent enough, could be a surprisingly attractive idea.

This argument is also about divergent attitudes to national citizenship and what special protections and entitlements it should imply. Immigrationists and libertarians argue for minimal protections while liberal nationalists, social democrats and most ordinary voters – who regard labour, like capital,

1. The experience of the introduction of minimum wage legislation in Britain suggests that employers can sometimes pay employees more without it having a negative effect on employment.

as a special kind of good – generally want some citizen favouritism in labour markets. The sweeping away of that historic protection in 2004 with the arrival of a large number of East Europeans was a political shock. An implicit part of the social contract had been removed by an elite that had no personal need for it.

The common-sense communitarianism of most ordinary voters clashed with the more universalist and free market preference of the political class, and Labour paid a heavy price for it. The latest research on the 2010 election by Geoff Evans at Nuffield College, Oxford, suggests it was immigration more than the economy that was the decisive factor in the fall in Labour's vote.[1]

But how much protection is necessary? The former Whitehall economist Jonathan Portes, one of the most influential supporters of mass immigration in the late 1990s and early 2000s, argues that it is possible in theory to spend billions on improving training and work incentives for the hard-to-employ locals, as Labour in power did, and at the same time benefit from reasonably open immigration. But the failure to make a bigger dent in the workless numbers in the 2000s suggest that, in practice, there is a trade-off – employers, given an option, will almost always opt for the cheaper and better motivated foreigner. And he or she is better motivated partly because an unemployed East European will normally improve his or her situation considerably working in a coffee shop in Croydon; an unemployed British citizen is quite likely to be worse off, or barely better off, once loss of housing and other benefits have been factored in.

This is not an argument for a closed door but for relatively low and highly selective immigration, especially at the lower and middling skill levels. Net immigration of 50,000 to 80,000 a year – which would mean a gross annual inflow of about 200,000 – still allows an immigration policy that is economically self-interested about recruiting small numbers of talented people from around the world and also generous towards those in serious need.

It is also an argument for extra protection and help for hard-to-employ

1. Geoffrey Evans and Yekaterina Chzhen, 'Explaining voters' defection from Labour over the 2005–2010 electoral cycle: leadership, economics and the rising importance of immigration', *Political Studies*, April 2013.

citizens and for further welfare reform to give people a hand back into jobs rather than being trapped in dependency – the government's new Universal Credit aims to further reduce the poverty traps associated with leaving benefit for the labour market. But extra incentives will only work if some employers change their attitude too. It has now become a cultural reflex, a sort of middle-class prejudice, to assume that British workers are always less good than foreigners.

Certain jobs, indeed whole sectors, with low pay and status often become thought of as 'migrant work' by both employers and potential employees. There are 1 million young people who are not in employment, education or training, and 300,000 unemployed graduates. And yet in the south-east of England more than 80 per cent of staff in the hospitality sector are not British citizens; it is a similar picture among London underground cleaning staff, more than half of those in the care sector, and on many big building sites, where up to 70 per cent of the skilled jobs are taken by non-citizens.

But the status of a job is a surprisingly elastic and subjective thing, and with a little bit of imagination – some training or career development – it can be made to seem more attractive to a British worker who has more options than someone from a Nigerian village.[1]

And even labour market drop-outs can re-learn the work ethic. But as anyone who has worked with the long-term unemployed will tell you, they need extra time to get back into the swing. Businesses sometimes agree to take on a certain percentage of staff from the local long-term unemployed, perhaps as part of a deal with a local authority over planning permission for a supermarket.[2] When that happens, such people invariably need weeks or even months to get used to normal work patterns but once they do they can become the best performing and most loyal staff. This sort of time and help will seldom be available if the immigration door is widely ajar.

1. This is exactly what has been happening in the social care sector. The government has quietly removed most social care jobs from the shortage occupation list which makes it much harder to import workers. This has not led to an acute labour shortage but rather to more British citizens taking up the jobs – despite the fact that they are very demanding and poorly paid. This is partly because of a lack of other work but also because the social care skills body has been able to present the jobs as the first rungs on a healthcare skills ladder.
2. See the work of some Tesco stores in Scotland.

And what about the EU? Currently the EU principle of free movement makes it illegal for British governments to provide incentives to employers to give preference to hard-to-employ locals. It was never envisaged in the late 1950s that free movement would encompass European economies with hugely different wage rates. But the principle cannot now be undone, it is part of the EU religion. It can, however, surely co-exist with special protections, opt-outs and regional or occupational exemptions. In Germany, for example, non-nationals are not allowed to work as *Beamte*, a special kind of official public sector job.[1]

Britain now requires an immigration slowdown to absorb the large inflows of recent decades – perhaps comparable to America's immigration 'pause' from 1920 to 1970 (only 4.7 per cent of the US population was foreign-born in the latter year). Denmark's switch to a more restrictive policy in the late-1990s shows it is possible even in the modern world.[2]

It is true that the recent scale of immigration has had something to do with global trends, but few of them have been completely uncontrollable. Britain *chose* after 1997 to liberalise immigration flows in the belief that it was in the interests of all citizens.

It does not, however, follow that it is simple to reverse that choice, even when both main political parties are committed to downward pressure on the numbers. One reason is what academics call 'embedded liberalism' – in open societies where everyone has plenty of rights, immigrants get them too, and one right is to bring in relatives and spouses. Nearly 70 per cent of annual immigration into the US is family reunion, and it is a similar level in Britain when you unpack the figures of those granted settlement. Another reason is conventional pressure group theory: when some people benefit significantly

1. Another option might be to levy a small tax on employers who hire non-citizens, at least outside more specialist sectors, with the proceeds going directly into appropriate training funds.
2. By its own standards, Denmark had moderately high immigration – some guest workers but mainly refugees – until the passage of two laws – an integration law in 1999 and an immigration law in 2001. Between 1995 and 2005 about 54,000 people were granted settlement but the numbers started to come down sharply in the later part of that period – around 13,000 family reunification permits were granted in 2001 but this had fallen to fewer than 5,000 in 2003.

from something – such as the businessmen who benefit from cheap immigrant labour or the minority group leaders who become more powerful the more co-ethnics they have to represent – their interests and lobbying power are likely to trump a much larger number of citizens who feel just a vague discomfort about mass immigration. For that reason, among others, it will be extremely difficult to push net immigration below 100,000 a year at least on the current counting method, which rolls up short- and longer-term movements.

Britain must, in any case, bear down carefully; even if the last fifteen years have brought few net economic gains for the resident population, untangling too fast from an immigration dependence could have damaging conse-quences. And there will be some economic costs even if the reduction is well managed. If the supply of cheap labour from abroad is reduced, people will have to pay a bit more for many services, from restaurant meals to nursing care for their ageing parents, in order to attract staff. The extra time, cost and bureaucracy required to get people into the country for long- or short-term stays means that some individuals and economic and cultural activities that we could have benefited from will be lost. And our sons or daughters may find it harder to bring in the Asian or American friend they met on their gap year. This is a price that people seem happy to pay for a return to moderate levels of immigration.

That is partly because people understand intuitively that the scale of immi-gration and integration interact. If immigration is persistently high and only semi-selective, then integration becomes harder and takes longer. Supporters of large-scale immigration ignore this time factor: they have no sense of the absorptive capacity of a society.

This is especially important in a country like Britain that, as we have seen, has never really had a political culture of integration. A more integrationist strategy was flirted with in the 1960s but it cut too sharply against the grain of laissez-faire attitudes. Instead the form of multiculturalism that evolved in the 1980s positively promoted fixed group identities and separate institu-tions, helping to extend first generation traits into subsequent generations.

The story is not very different today. Britain does not have a strategy either for new arrivals or for settled but 'stuck' communities, who often live in distinct enclaves. That is not quite true. It does have an integration plan for refugees – a year-long service that is supposed to offer help with housing, jobs, learning English, adapting qualifications and so on. There is also some help with subsidised language lessons for a broader category of newcomer, though it is estimated that two-thirds of those who arrive speaking poor English never take lessons. And for all newcomers, since the mid-2000s, there have been the rituals of citizenship: the citizenship and language tests and for those who pass them the ceremonies in which allegiance to the country is pledged.

For established minority and majority citizens there is a small 'community cohesion' budget, mainly for promoting cross-community contact – school twinning and festivals and so on – in areas of high minority settlement, but this is not significant.

What is more significant is the integration and minority support mechanisms hidden within many mainstream social welfare programmes.[1] One example is improving the English of schoolchildren who have English as a second language. There are about 500,000 children at primary school who do not speak English at home and around the same again at secondary school. According to the Institute for Fiscal Studies, the government in 2010 spent nearly £500 per head teaching the primary school pupils English and rather less for secondary school pupils, mainly late arrivals into the system. The total annual spend is hard to calculate but is probably around £300 million; an extremely good investment.

Official integration policy, then, with the exception of welfare programmes, is a slight business. Britain relies, as it always has done, on immigrants and their children integrating themselves. And, quietly, unobserved or unnoticed, that is what is happening in millions of homes around the country. Second-generation minorities report higher rates of attachment to Britain, higher rates of cross-ethnic friendship and very high rates of English speaking.

Moreover, a hands-off approach to integration, along with a laissez-faire multiculturalism, has worked well enough for some groups – better an army

---

1. See Shamit Saggar and Will Somerville, *Building a British Model of Integration in an Era of Immigration: Policy Lessons for Government*, Migration Policy Institute/Transatlantic Council on Migration, May 2012.

of volunteers than of conscripts. But for some of the groups that have been less successful, the absence of either practical support with integration or an ideology that encourages it has pushed them further back on their own networks and institutions. Absorption into some kind of common life is barely happening in some places.

The pattern most associated with failure is arriving poor and then living within a culture which does not help you to flourish in a society like this one. Indeed, in some cases it may impose patterns of behaviour that make it harder still to progress. The best example of this, and one which I have cited many times in the course of this book, is the British Kashmiri Pakistani minority: the continuing practice of transcontinental marriage which means that English is unlikely to be spoken at home; the practice of sending children to madrasas for two hours after school adds a further layer of educational disadvantage; and first cousin marriage, which is still common among some Pakistanis, appears to be responsible for a disproportionate number of minor or severe genetic defects. (Bradford has just opened two more schools for children with Special Educational Needs, and on some measures nearly half of all children in the area qualify for special help.)

We would not, surely, have started from here if we had known back in the 1950s and 1960s that our carelessness about the integration of newcomers would lead to today's Bradford or Tower Hamlets or central Birmingham. But this is where we are. And the difficult judgement that policy-makers now have to make is which minorities are going to make it into the comfortable mainstream, perhaps just rather more slowly than others, and which minorities are not and need some sort of policy intervention to tip the balance – such as placing further obstacles in the way of importing spouses, as the government is currently attempting.

Integration policy is a long-term affair, with a horizon of two or even three generations. Government policy can be a blunt instrument and can sometimes make matters worse. If government was, for example, to intervene to stop the East London Mosque in Tower Hamlets from delivering some publicly funded welfare programmes it would play into a story of Islamophobia and victimhood and might do more harm than good.

And indeed the hands-off approach in places like Tower Hamlets might work in the longer run. As we have seen, there has been a sharp improvement in results in the mainly Bangladeshi schools in the borough in the past decade, and more young people are going to college and getting decent qualifications. Though the number of young women doing so is still lower than might be expected. Nationally in 2006 about 50 per cent of Pakistani and Bangladeshi girls got A levels, compared with less than 30 per cent of the boys. Yet participation of Muslim women at university is only around 20 per cent, way below the national average for women of 50 per cent.

And even when young Bangladeshis from places like Tower Hamlets are going to university it is not clear that it is translating into successful careers. Tower Hamlets claims it has the highest graduate unemployment in the country, though the figure is disputed and there is some evidence of rising rates of employment up the road in Canary Wharf. But if it is true it suggests that qualifications on their own are not enough; if you are raised in an enclave outside mainstream society you are likely to end up with neither the social networks nor the 'soft skills' that are often a prerequisite for good careers.

Tower Hamlets may be a testing ground for the optimistic view that Britain's two biggest stuck minorities – Kashmiri Pakistanis and Bangladeshis – are gradually moving forward thanks to their young women reaching out for the opportunities that this liberal society offers them. Though that might leave some young men even more stuck, and the young women struggling to find suitable marriage partners from within their community.[1]

So what can governments do, in liberal societies, to nudge into the mainstream such groups that are both locked away and doing relatively badly and to prevent newer arrivals, such as the Somalis, from repeating the segregation story? Like most successful social policies, a more vigorous integration policy

1. This is the view of a twenty-year-old British Pakistani female university student: 'I've seen a lot of girls that have done masters and stuff, they're thirty-five and not married, and they really regret it. When they should have got married they were just so into education and they looked for someone of the same match. And Pakistani men aren't really as educated as the women, then it's so difficult, and they'll just stay spinsters for the rest of their life ...' Quoted in the chapter 'Educational Achievement and Career Aspirations for Young British Pakistanis', from *Global Migration, Ethnicity and Britishness*, Tariq Modood and John Salt (eds), Palgrave Macmillan, 2011.

would intervene early. It would provide for all people granted permanent right of residence the sort of help now provided only to refugees. This need not be prohibitively expensive – individual mentoring, for example, is something that is well suited to volunteering. (The Catalan government in Spain has an official system of 'buddies' to help immigrants fit in and learn Catalan.)

English language teaching should be more easily available to newcomers (including those who have passed English tests), and also to people who have been here for years but still speak poorly – nearly 3 million people live in homes where no one speaks English as a first language. Too many people who need lessons are not taking them.

This must be reversed. Indeed, English language lessons should be free 'at the point of use' for all who need them. This *would* be expensive but it is an extremely important investment. Every time someone's wait at an A & E department is held up by an immigrant who doesn't speak good enough English, or when a minority family move in up the road but the young mother cannot join in the social life of the street, a small setback to the establishment of a successful multiracial society is registered.

In order to reduce the cost there should be a deferred repayment system, similar to that for university fees, with payments starting only when someone has started earning above a certain threshold. Most language teaching for non-elite immigrants is currently delivered through further education colleges, though there is also a large private sector which could be integrated into such a deferred payment system, perhaps with richer students or those who need to 'fast-track' their English skills paying a top-up fee to private schools.

The central and local state should stop subsidising separation and adopt an explicit policy preference for mixed communities – on top of the current requirements of public bodies to promote both race equality and cohesion.[1] That does not necessarily mean quotas in schools or public housing, though they might be tried in some areas where it could be achieved without too much

1. This ought to rule out the extraordinary DVD about life in Britain produced by the community relations department of Slough Borough Council which starts with a South Asian man saying – with the apparent approval of the DVD producers – that 'when I arrived I did not feel I was in England... I felt I was somewhere in my own country'.

overriding of people's preferences. There have been some successful housing association experiments with the mixed communities that most people say they want but often negate through their own choices.

Actively promoting the desegregation of schools is key. Some Church of England schools have a 25 per cent quota of those from another faith, and that model might be pursued in non-faith schools too. It does not matter that schools in Cumbria and Cornwall are overwhelmingly white; it does matter in towns and cities with large minority populations that many schools are monocultural; schools should as far as possible reflect the town. Where relevant, schools should have explicit targets for becoming more mixed and catchment areas should be adapted to help in this task.

Educational white flight is not inevitable, but it requires some courage and imagination to stop it. The community cohesion expert Ted Cantle tells the story of the Minerva Primary Academy in the Fishponds area of Bristol where a major exodus of white children was prevented following the arrival of a significant cohort of Somali children. A meeting was arranged with the worried white parents and it was explained that Somali children with language difficulties would get extra support and that their own children's progress would not suffer. The result was that most of the white parents decided to stay and the school has become a local success story.

The direction of public service reform in recent years has been towards greater individual choice, which has often been a blessing, but avoiding a society scarred by segregation may require limits to be placed on individual choice – especially in pursuit of goals that people claim they want. There are plenty of examples from abroad of effective use of quotas – the city of Stuttgart, for example, has a rule that no public housing estate should be more than 20 per cent minority.

Perhaps most important, public authorities should not create and perpetuate segregation through their own policies or 'single identity' funding regimes. Clearly not all spending on a particular minority is wrong, especially when it is promoting educational or other causes that will in the longer run increase the chances of successful integration. But such spending should in all but the most exceptional cases be time limited and always include some activities that involve mixing across ethnic boundaries.

So public policy should prod where possible towards more mixing, should think long-term when it comes to integration, and have some confidence in the seductive power of a liberal society. Culture matters, of course, and is usually far stronger in its impact on people's choices than public policy, but a liberal integration policy can help to ensure that people in stuck groups are not imprisoned by their cultural inheritance. All of that becomes easier if the number of incomers, in a neighbourhood or a whole country, is relatively moderate.

And public policy should more openly publicise and welcome integration-ist trends: a decline in residential and school segregation and in the number of spouses brought over from ancestral lands, an increase in the numbers speaking English at home, an increase in minority representation in the police and armed forces. And because in a liberal society certain separatist practices are *allowed* does not mean they have to be approved of or even encouraged.

Some of the above trends are hard to measure, but I fear that thanks to the legacy of several decades of strong multiculturalism some of them at least are still moving in the wrong direction in some towns and parts of cities – in Bradford, Oldham, Dewsbury, Blackburn, Luton, Tower Hamlets and others. My hunch may be wrong, but it would be useful for citizens and policy-makers to have more reliable knowledge. Currently too much of the measurement of such things is based on perceptions such as the answers to the Citizenship Survey question, 'Do people from different backgrounds in your area get on well together?', or looks only at host society discrimination. Government, in consultation with the relevant experts, should draw up an integration measurement table, and perhaps publish an updated 'integration index' every few years, which could tell us more reliably and scientifically what is happening.

Are there lessons to be learnt from other countries? There are successful, small-scale initiatives, such as the language mentoring scheme in Catalonia, which any sensible government should look at if it is devising a more active approach to integration. Looking at the bigger picture, every country has its own history and institutions, and just as Britain cannot borrow Germany's economic model, nor can it import Canada's approach to immigration and integration. The one big thing that is worth thinking about is the way in which countries like America and Australia have created rhetorical traditions of strong but open patriotism, absorbing newcomers into a national story.

In the next twenty to thirty years Britain will start to draw closer to America's current levels of diversity – almost 25 per cent of all British primary school pupils come from ethnic minorities. Is it inevitable that we also follow America towards a more divided, less trusting society with a less supportive welfare state? Not necessarily. Britain and other European countries have a very different starting point to the US; the old societies of Europe are less 'communalist' and far more statist. Britain does not have an equivalent of the mutual fear and mistrust left by the scar of slavery in the US, nor does it have a group as large as Hispanic-Americans with a partly separate linguistic and cultural identity. And the institutionalised solidarity of Britain's welfare state has a large element of enlightened self-interest which may be able to co-exist with a higher degree of diversity than in the past. Moreover, public policy, if it is sensitive to the strain on solidarity from rising diversity, can seek to minimise that damage by increasing the insurance and conditional elements of welfare and making the access of outsiders more visibly earned (see Chapter 6).

Yet it may be that, paradoxically, in order to avoid American outcomes we need to borrow some more of America's language and practice of patriotism – a road-map for newcomers, a British dream. When people have less daily experience or shared history in common, they cannot rely on the old majority ethnic understandings and need those symbols and rituals of membership. Mass-immigration societies require a stronger and more overt national story, encompassing the old citizens and the new. A sense of national belonging and a special attachment to fellow citizens is not a prejudice but a priceless asset in an increasingly diverse and individualistic society.

About 85 per cent of Americans say they are very proud of their country compared with 55 per cent of Britons, and the latter is a high number for Europe. There is still a strong accent on joining the American way of life, normally through hard work, and there are 'symbolic pathways' for those who want to belong. (The fact that it is a religious society, too, seems to be a helpful integrating factor.) Of course to liberal European ears there is a shrillness to American patriotism that may derive in part from the very lack of real solidarity in everyday life and the sharply different lives led by some big minorities, particularly African Americans and Hispanics.

To express this schematically, America is a land of high diversity/low solidarity/high patriotism; Britain (and most of Europe too) has lower but rapidly rising diversity/high but declining solidarity/low-ish patriotism. In Britain we have made a start in recent years with more overt patriotic rituals. To go further in this direction will go against the grain of how things have been done in the past. But the times are changing and successful nations change with them, adapting their traditions and inventing new ones.

And as a guiding philosophy, colour-blind liberalism combined with an open but meaningful national identity is not a bad place to return to after the long detour of semi-separatist multiculturalism. Our starting point, at least when we are thinking politically, should be that we are first and foremost individual citizens of a liberal state, and not first of all members of an ethnic or religious minority. Colour-blind liberalism does not want to abolish ethnic cultures or expect people to live in the same way or believe the same things, and nor should it be blind to the special needs of minorities; it is colour-blind only in the sense that justice is blind. It is a liberalism that can absorb within it all the reasonable claims of multiculturalism, but does not want to abolish British history, the British majority or the idea of one law for everyone – and indeed of a core culture – because these things are thought to be unfair to minorities. It is also a liberalism that is aware of the importance of, and fragility of, a common life. Jonathan Sacks, the Chief Rabbi, talks about three different kinds of society: the country house, the equivalent of the old ethnically homogeneous society where the newcomer is only ever a guest; the hotel, the product of a cold multiculturalism where everyone has equal status but remain strangers to each other; and the home we build together, where majority and minorities come together to create a common life.

As Jews, Greek Cypriots, Sikhs, among others, have shown, it is possible both to completely belong and contribute *and* to hold on to much of your culture. Individuals from successful minorities often lead a kind of dual or bicultural life, moving comfortably between the ethnic life at home and the majority culture at work and in dealings with friends and neighbours.

We have not yet found a better way of organising human affairs than in nation states, but such nation states still need some degree of emotional commitment that isn't purely instrumental or contractual to make them work well. Patriotism, liberal nationalism, citizenship, call it what you like, it is the last form of meaningful, large-scale collectivism. The trick is to grow our own version of that American patriotism and give it a form and a language that can help our increasingly diverse old European nation state sail on into the twenty-first century.

The title of this book sounds hopeful, optimistic, sentimental even, yet throughout it I have made a virtue of talking in an unsentimental way about immigration, race and minority success and failure; indeed, I have argued that thinking and talking about these matters in a more robust way is a condition of improving our current situation.

But there is a British dream. And I want to give almost the final word to someone who exemplifies it. He is someone I have known for a few years, ever since commissioning him to write a piece for *Prospect* magazine about growing up in Luton, the son of parents from rural Pakistan. Sarfraz Manzoor has gone on to become a successful writer and broadcaster and recently married Bridget, a white British woman, with whom he has one child. This is an extract of what he had to say about Britain when I talked to him informally about the themes of this book at the end of 2011.

> Racism has not gone completely, I have come up against some barriers. But all I have I owe to this country. Multiculturalism has been too one-sided, too much about people's rights, and also we've ended up allowing private things like religion too much into the public domain ... I am concerned about some of those kids in the northern mill towns, they seem to enjoy the benefits without buying into the idea of this country ... though their disaffection is also in some ways a healthy sign of minority confidence, my parents' generation would never have dared, they did not feel secure enough here. There are so many more opportunities now than in the 1960s and 1970s, and I am basically optimistic ... look at my marriage to Bridget, it has helped to create new understandings in my own family, there are ripples of connection, we are reaching out and creating a new

England between us ... our kid will be exposed to vastly more influences than I was ... there is so much more inter-marriage now, we are creating a new national identity by just living it.

The Next Twenty Years: Ripples of Connection

It is possible to imagine Britain experiencing a Dutch-style backlash. It would require a number of perfectly plausible events: a failure to bring immigration down to more moderate levels; a new, respectable populist party emerging (perhaps some version of UKIP) with a capable leader; large parts of urban Britain, especially in the North, becoming even more ethnically segregated; Islamic extremists letting off more bombs; inner-city riots becoming a regular part of the calendar.

But a more benign future is also possible. Here is a short history of it.

Immigration and related issues did not play a significant role in the run-up to the 2015 election, though Europe did. The coalition did not quite reach its target of 'tens of thousands' of net immigrants a year but it came close enough, and anxiety about the issue was starting to decline quite sharply when Labour came to power (in coalition with the much reduced Liberal Democrats) thanks to a strong performance from UKIP.

Declining concern was also the result of Labour's conversion to a policy of being 'pro-immigrant, anti-mass immigration', as Home Secretary Jon Cruddas put it. This included its own Labour version of a 'cap', the creation of a new immigration and integration department (headed by Lord Trevor Phillips), and the renegotation of EU rules on free movement to allow for stronger local worker preferences (something that Chancellor Ed Balls had agreed in outline with his centre-left opposite numbers in France, Germany and Italy in the run-up to the election).

The new immigration and integration department became first choice for 'fast stream' graduates attracted by the challenge of how to keep Britain 'open for business', as Tory leader Boris Johnson put it, while also keeping immigration numbers as low as possible in response to voter anxiety about economic competition and rapid change. One of the first initiatives of the department was to overhaul the way in which immigration is counted, giving more accurate figures and also separating out short-term from long-term movements. Combined with counting people in and out at the border, and ID cards for those coming on a visa for more than one year, this made it possible to remove students from the headline net immigration number (unless staying on after courses), secure in the knowledge that those who had come for three-year courses left when they finished. It allowed Britain's higher education sector to continue to expand, attracting hundreds of thousands of foreign students a year.

Two further initiatives from the new department (paid for by scrapping Trident modernisation) set part of the tone for Labour in power. First, in conjunction with the Home Office and the Ministry of Defence, came the creation of a six-month compulsory citizenship service programme for all young people, to be completed between the ages of seventeen and twenty-five. As well as voluntary work in social care homes and on environmental projects, citizenship service also included a remedial teaching programme (for those unable to pass some simple tests), an arduous military-run physical fitness programme and a careers fortnight with visits to different kinds of workplaces. It became an expensive but popular national rite of passage (and the idea was exported to several other countries just as privatisation had once been), with extra resources focused on poorer participants and an explicit goal of mixing both social classes and ethnicities in the fifty-strong 'units' that were the building blocks of the programme. (It didn't always work; two units based in Pendle in Lancashire, one mainly Asian, the other mainly white, became involved in a mass brawl while supposedly co-operating to build a bicycle path.)

The other project that the new immigration and integration department drove forward was a big expansion of English language lessons both for new arrivals and for people who have been here for many years but still needed them. The lessons were paid for on a deferred repayment system similar to university student fees. Delivered alongside the English lessons was a national mentoring system of volunteers to help people not only practise their English but also navigate through their new society (or not so new in many cases).

The language and mentoring service was also directly linked to a revised system of citizenship tests and citizenship ceremonies. The citizenship oath now included not only a pledge of allegiance to Britain and its citizens but also an acceptance of the principle of equal treatment of all people regardless of gender, ethnicity or religion. (As part of the citizenship ceremony people were given as a gift a DVD of Danny Boyle's opening ceremony for the 2012 Olympic Games, with a short essay from Boyle explaining what it meant.)

In 2016 David Lammy was elected mayor of London with a pledge to, among many other things, invest in sorting out the condition of unemployed young men, black and white, in the capital, with a programme of rigorous apprenticeships focusing on the construction industry and social care. (It was paid for partly by a levy on employers who employed non-UK citizens.)

Lammy's election was the first of a series of minority Britons breaking through to the very top level of British institutions over the next few years. Lord Waheed Alli became chairman of the BBC. Victor Olisa became the first black head of the Metropolitan Police (and was stopped and searched driving his black Jaguar home on his second day in office).

A major Al-Qaeda-type bomb plot on the tenth anniversary of 7/7 was uncovered mainly thanks to the undercover work of a young British Muslim working for MI5. Islamic radicalism began to die away as a significant force in Muslim Britain, partly as a result of the greater success of young Muslims in British society – there was a particular breakthrough at the elite level in the big accountancy and law firms in the City, but also more mundane success in the teaching and medical professions as people from Pakistani and Bangladeshi backgrounds began to emulate the success of British Indians with a lag of a couple of generations. A well-known pop star, Ed Sheeran, announced his conversion to Islam, which helped its normalisation among young people.

The government's more explicit focus on encouraging integration had a slow, incremental effect. Its 'integration index' showed a more optimistic national picture than some had expected but also focused attention on the problem northern towns, some of which were put in the integration equivalent of 'special measures'. Beneath the surface various things were moving in the right direction: more English began to be spoken in minority homes, partly thanks to the government's big investment in language teaching, and there was also a sharp fall in the importing of spouses from Pakistan and Bangladesh, partly because policy had made it harder but also because actual Muslim South Asians had become less interested in marrying their rather conservative British cousins and the Biraderi clan system was taken less seriously by the younger Pakistani generations. There was even some increase in marrying 'out' among South Asians, including Muslims, though the proportion continued to lag well behind Caribbeans and the Chinese. The mixed-race part of the population (easily the largest minority group) hit 2 million in 2020, just a few years before the visible minority population as a whole hit 20 per cent.

Perhaps the biggest success of deliberate policy came in education, where there was a gradual reversal of the tendency for schools to be more segregated than the areas they serve. The success of the Oldham integration of an Asian and a white secondary school in 2012 (though not without its problems) set a model for similar mergers, and some education authorities began to apply a 50 per cent minority quota in secondary schools (though they had to do so informally after it was found to be illegal). Another policy success was increased minority recruitment to the police force and armed forces – both of which now began to look more like the Britain they recruit from – and the first wave of minority generals came through, with the first Slough-born, British Sikh chief of the general staff appointed in 2020, just in time for the Nato intervention in Moldova.

Building on the benign patriotic spirit of the 2012 Olympics, national identity among the English began to take on a new tone. Englishness was reinforced in various symbolic ways, including a national holiday on St George's day, and more importantly – after the Scots voted against independence but ended up with more devolution – an English political community was given form in Parliament. The nations of Britain 'Team GB' now came together more formally in British institutions – the armed forces, the BBC, the monarchy (the latter became more of a bicycle monarchy after William replaced Charles, whose dementia prevented him from carrying on, in 2018).

Strong economic growth after 2015, partly on the back of rising exports to a reorganised (and smaller) Eurozone, ensured that Britain voted narrowly to stay in the EU but became the explicit leader of a small 'outer ring' of semi-detached European countries. With the single exception of the controversial intervention in the Pakistani civil war, Labour's political focus was relentlessly domestic. Britain remained an open and internationally connected country but, finally, lost its sense of having the obligations of a world power. The intervention in Pakistan, originally humanitarian, came only because of intense lobbying from the British Pakistani minority. Some Pakistani refugees were accepted in Britain but most of those made homeless by the war were housed in decent temporary towns in safe zones, funded substantially by British aid.

Meanwhile, net immigration (using the revised counting system) fell to around 50,000 a year, and thanks to the introduction of a living wage, and the effect of the citizenship service programme, it became more common to find British workers on building sites, in care homes, bars and even cleaning jobs – youth and graduate unemployment were both low. The inflow from Eastern Europe fell sharply after 2015, less because governments and employers were now allowed to give preference to locally born workers than because of the take-off of the Eastern European economies following the reorganisation of the Eurozone.

When net immigration numbers did briefly rise back over 100,000 in 2022, because of acute drought in the Sahel region of Africa, there was a largely generous welcome for the refugees partly because there was an explicit commitment to help them resettle back in Africa when conditions had improved. The year was remembered more for the England football team, captained by Alex Oxlade-Chamberlain, reaching the final of the World Cup before being beaten on penalties by Belgium.

The 2025 election found Britain feeling pretty good about itself – Ireland even applied to rejoin the Commonwealth – the only remarkable thing about it being that both main parties were represented by black ex-public schoolboys, Chuka Ummuna (the black Blair) and Kwasi Kwarteng (the black Boris). Kwarteng won partly as a result of Labour's exhaustion after ten years in office but also because he represented more authentically than his opponent the socially conservative instincts of the key ethnic minority section of the inner-city electorate, which for the first time voted in larger numbers for the Conservatives than for the more liberal, suburban-based Labour Party. Even more remarkable, perhaps, no one seemed particularly bothered about the fact that Britain had its first black prime minister.

Bibliography

Keith Ajegbo, *Diversity and Citizenship Curriculum Review*, Department for Education, 2007

Navid Akhtar, *The Biraderi*, BBC radio documentary, first broadcast, 26 August 2003

George Alagiah, *A Home from Home: From Immigrant Boy to English Man* (London: Abacus, 2006)

M. Y. Alam (ed.), *The Invisible Village* (Pontefract: Route, 2011)

Alberto Alesina, *Why doesn't the US have a European-style welfare state?*, US National Bureau of Economic Research, working paper 8524, 2001

Claire E. Alexander, *The Asian Gang: Ethnicity, Identity, Masculinity* (Oxford, New York: Berghahn Books, 2000)

Monica Ali, *Brick Lane* (London: Doubleday, 2003)

N. Ali, V. S. Kalra and S. Sayyid (eds), *A Post-Colonial People: South Asians in Britain* (London: Hurst & Co., 2006)

Sundas Ali, *Muslims in Britain: National Identities and Sense of Belonging*, Compas migration workshop, June 2011

Gordon Willard Allport, *The Nature of Prejudice* (Boston, Massachusetts: Addison-Wesley, 1954)

Kurt Almqvist and Erik Wallrup (eds), *Cosmopolitanism* (Stockholm: Axel and Margaret Ax:son Johnson Foundation, 2003)

Elizabeth Anderson, *The Imperative of Integration* (Princeton: Princeton University Press, 2010)

Kwame Anthony Appiah, *Cosmopolitanism: Ethics in a World of Strangers* (London: Penguin, 2006)

Kwame Anthony Appiah, *The Ethics of Identity*, chapter 4, 'The Trouble with Culture' (Princeton: Princeton University Press, 2007)

Raymond Aron, *The Dawn of Universal History*, lecture delivered in London, 1961

Arthur Aughey, *The Politics of Englishness* (Manchester: Manchester University Press, 2007)

Brian Barry, *Culture and Equality* (Cambridge: Polity Press, 2001)

Harris Beider, *Race, Housing and Community* (New Jersey: Wiley-Blackwell, 2012)

Roger Ballard, *South Asians Overseas: Migration and Ethnicity* (Cambridge: Cambridge University Press, 1990)

Keith Banting and Will Kymlicka (eds), *Multiculturalism and the Welfare State* (Oxford: Oxford University Press, 2006)

Jamie Bartlett, Jonathan Birdwell, Mark Littler, *The New Face of Digital Populism* (London: Demos, 2011)

Michael Billig, *Banal Nationalism* (London: Sage, 1995)

Alan Billings, *God and Community Cohesion* (London: SPCK, 2009)

Nick Boles, *Which Way's Up? The future for coalition Britain and how to get there* (London: Biteback, 2010)

George Borjas, 'The Economics of Immigration', *Journal of Economic Literature*, 1994

Born in Bradford Cohort Study, Bradford Royal Infirmary, www.borninbradford.nhs.uk

Ben Bowling, Alpa Parmar and Coretta Phillips, 'Policing ethnic minority communities', *Handbook of Policing*, Tim Newburn (ed.) (London: Willan Publishing, 2003)

Roger Boyes and Dorte Huneke, *Is it easier to be a Turk in Berlin or a Pakistani in Bradford?*, Anglo-German Foundation, June 2004

British Future, *State of the Nation Report*, 2012

British Future, *Team GB: How 2012 should boost Britain*, 2012

Gordon Brown et al., 'Britain Rediscovered', *Prospect* (London: April 2005)

Rogers Brubaker, 'The Return of Assimilation?', *Towards Assimilation and Citizenship* (Basingstoke: Palgrave Macmillan, 2003)

Simon Burgess, *School Segregation in Multi-ethnic England*, Department of Economics, University of Bristol, 2003

Business in the Community, *Race into Higher Education*, 2010

Simon Burgess and David Wilson, *Ethnic Segregation in England's Schools*, Transactions of the Institute of British Geographers, 2005

Liam Byrne, *A More United Kingdom* (London: Demos, September 2008)

Christopher Caldwell, *Reflections on the Revolution in Europe: Can Europe be the same with different people in it?* (London: Allen Lane, 2009)

David Cannadine, *Ornamentalism: How the British Saw Their Empire* (Oxford: Oxford University Press, 2001)

Ted Cantle, *Community Cohesion: A report of the independent review team chaired by Ted Cantle*, Home Office, December 2001

Ted Cantle, *Community Cohesion* (Basingstoke: Palgrave Macmillan, 2005)

Ted Cantle, *Interculturalism: The new era of of cohesion and diversity* (Basingstoke: Palgrave Macmillan, 2012)

Alan Carling, *The Curious Case of the Mis-claimed Myth Claims: Ethnic segregation, polarisation and the future of Bradford*, Urban Studies, March 2008

Matt Cavanagh and Alex Glennie, *International students and net migration*, Institute for Public Policy Research, May 2012

Matt Cavanagh, *Guest Workers: Settlement, temporary economic migration and a critique of the government's plans*, Institute for Public Policy Research, October 2011

Jonathan Chaplin, *Multiculturalism: A Christian Retrieval* (London: Theos, 2012)

Citizenship Surveys, Department of Communities and Local Government, 2001–2010

Jack Citrin, *Are we all now Multiculturalists, Assimilationists, neither or both?*, paper presented at 'The political incorporation of immigrants in north America and Europe' conference, University of California, Berkeley, March 2011

Tom Clark, Robert D. Putnam, Edward Fieldhouse, *The Age of Obama: The Changing Place of Minorities in British and American Society* (Manchester: Manchester University Press, 2010)

Charles Clarke, *The EU and Migration: A call for action*, Centre for European Reform, December 2011

David Coleman, 'When Britain becomes "majority minority"', *Prospect* (London: December 2010)

David Coleman and Robert Rowthorn, *The Economic Effects of Immigration into the UK*, Population and Development Review, December 2004

Linda Colley, *Britons: Forging the Nation 1707 to 1837* (London: Vintage, 1996)

Linda Colley, 'Does Britishness still matter in the 21st century?', *Britishness: Perspectives on the British Question*, Andrew Gamble and Tony Wright (eds) (New Jersey: Wiley-Blackwell, 2009)

Linda Colley, *Britishness in the 21st Century*, lecture at No. 10 Downing Street, 28 March 2000

Michael Collins, *The Likes of Us: A biography of the white working class* (London: Granta, 2004)

Robert Colls, *Identity of England* (Oxford: Oxford University Press, 2004)

Robert Colls, 'The Lion and the Eunuch: National Identity and the British Genius', *Political Quarterly*, October–December 2011

Gary Craig et al., *Understanding 'Race' and Ethnicity* (Bristol: Policy Press, 2012)

George Crowder, *Bhikhu Parkeh's Multiculturalist Critique of Liberalism*, paper for the Australasian Political Studies Conference, 2009

Matthew D'Ancona (ed.), *Being British: The Search for the Values that Bind the Nation* (Edinburgh: Mainstream Publishing, 2009)

Geoff Dench, *Minorities in the Open Society*, (Rutgers – The State University of New Jersey: Transaction, 2003)

Geoff Dench, Kate Gavron and Michael Young, *The New East End: Kinship, Race and Conflict* (London: Profile Books, 2006)

Department for Communities and Local Government, *Creating the Conditions for Integration*, 2012

Bobby Duffy, *What do people think about integration?* Ipsos MORI Social Research, 2012

John Dunn, *Democracy: A History* (New York: Grove Atlantic, 2006)

Christian Dustmann and Francesca Fabbri, *Immigrants in the British Labour market*, Fiscal Studies, December 2005

Christian Dustmann, Stephen Machin and Uta Schönberg, 'Ethnicity and educational achievement in compulsory schooling', *The Economic Journal*, vol. 120, issue 546, 2010

Maureen Eger, 'Even in Sweden: The effect of immigration on support for welfare state spending', *European Sociological Review*, vol. 26, issue 2, 2009

Ismail Einashe, 'Mo and Me', *Prospect* (London: September 2012)

Gabriella Elgenius, *Symbols of Nations and Nationalism* (Basingstoke: Palgrave Macmillan, 2011)

Equality and Human Rights Commission, *Triennial Review*, 2010

Equality and Human Rights Commission, *Inquiry into Recruitment and Employment in the Meat and Poultry Processing Sector*, March 2010

Geoffrey Evans and Yekaterina Chzhen, 'Explaining voters' defection from Labour over the 2005–2010 electoral cycle: leadership, economics and the rising importance of immigration', *Political Studies*, April 2013

James Fergusson, *Kandahar Cockney: A tale of two worlds* (London: HarperCollins, 2004)

Edward Fieldhouse and David Cutts, 'Does Diversity Damage Social Capital?', *Canadian Journal of Political Science*, June 2010

Tim Finch and David Goodhart (eds), *Immigration under Labour*, IPPR/*Prospect* (London)

Richard Florida, *The Rise of the Creative Class* (New York: Perseus Book Group, 2002)

Robert Ford, 'Is Racial Prejudice Declining in Britain?', *The British Journal of Sociology*, vol. 59, issue 4, 2008

Patrick French, *India: A Portrait* (London: Allen Lane, 2011)

Andrew Gamble and Tony Wright (eds), *Britishness: Perspectives on the British Question*, *Political Quarterly* (New Jersey: Wiley-Blackwell, 2009)

Ernest Gellner, *Nationalism* (London: Weidenfeld & Nicolson, 1997)

Justin Gest, *Apart: Alienated and Engaged Muslims in the West* (London: Hurst & Co., 2010)

Len Gibbs and David Goodhart, 'Immigration and social housing: The story since Octavia Hill', *The Enduring Relevance of Octavia Hill* (London: Demos, 2012)

Martin Gilens, *Why Americans Hate Welfare: Race, Media and the Politics of Antipoverty Policy* (Chicago: University of Chicago Press, 2000)

GLA Economics, *Economic impact on the London and UK economy of an earned regularisation of irregular migrants to the UK*, May 2009

Ian Goldin, Geoffrey Cameron and Meera Balarajan, *Exceptional People: How Migration Shaped Our World and Will Define our Future* (Princeton: Princeton University Press, 2011)

Peter Goldsmith (Lord), *Citizenship: Our Common Bond*, a report for Prime Minister Gordon Brown, 2008

David Goodhart, 'Too Diverse?', *Prospect* (London: February 2004)

David Goodhart, *Progressive Nationalism: Citizenship and the Left* (London: Demos, 2006)

David Goodhart, *Citizens and Immigrants: Britain and the US since 1945*, Sulgrave Manor lecture, 2009

David Goodhart, 'Welcome to the new world of the post-liberal majority', *Financial Times*, 12 May 2012

David Goodhart, BBC Radio 4 Analysis, *Foreigner Policy: Labour's Immigration Policy*, broadcast 8 February 2010

David Goodhart, BBC Radio 4 Analysis, *Blue Labour: What does it mean?*, broadcast 21 March 2011

David Goodhart, BBC Radio 4 Analysis, *A New Black Politics?*, broadcast 31 October 2011

Matthew Goodwin, *New British Fascism: Rise of the British National Party* (Oxford: Routledge, 2011)

Matthew Goodwin, *The Angry White Men and their Motives*, Policy Network paper, June 2011

Ceri Gott and Karl Johnston, *The Migrant Population in the UK: Fiscal effects*, Home Office, 2002

James Gregory, *Diversity and Solidarity: Crisis, What Crisis?*, Runnymede Trust report, June 2011

James Gregory (ed.), *Homes for Citizens* (London: Fabian Society, 2011)

Montserrat Guibernau, *The Identity of Nations* (Cambridge: Polity Press, 2007)

Jonathan Haidt, *The Righteous Mind: Why good people are divided by politics and religion*, Allen Lane (London, 2012)

James Hampshire, *Citizenship and Belonging* (Basingstoke: Palgrave Macmillan, 2005)

Randall Hansen, *Citizenship and Immigration in Post-War Britain* (Oxford: Oxford University Press, 2000)

Randall Hansen, *The Poverty of Postnationalism: Citizenship, immigration and the new Europe* (Heidelberg: Springer Science and Business Media, 2008)

Randall Hansen, *Paradigm and Policy Shifts: British Immigration Policy, 1997–2011*, paper prepared for the conference: Controlling Immigration: A Global Perspective, Dallas, May 2011

Rumy Hasan, *Multiculturalism: Some Inconvenient Truths* (London: Politicos, 2010)

Anthony Heath, Jean Martin and Gabriella Elgenius, *Who do we think we are? The decline of traditional social identities*, British Social Attitudes report, Sage, 2007

Anthony Heath et al., *The Ethnic Minority British Election Survey* (EMBES), Economic and Social Research Council, 2011

Simon Heffer, *Like the Roman: The life of Enoch Powell* (London: Weidenfeld & Nicolson, 1998)

Miles Hewstone, *Intergroup Contact: A strategy for challenging segregation and prejudice*, paper for a Department for Communities and Local Government seminar, September 2012

Higher Education Commission, *An inquiry into postgraduate education*, October 2012

Ellie Hill, *Ethnicity and Democracy: A Study into Biraderi*, unpublished undergraduate dissertation, Newcastle University, 2011

Nicholas Hillman, 'A "chorus of execration"? Enoch Powell's "rivers of blood" 40 years on', *Patterns of Prejudice*, issue 42, 2008

John Hills et al., *An Anatomy of Economic Inequality in the UK*, January 2010, the report of the LSE National Equality Panel, January 2010

Home Affairs Committee of House of Commons, *Young Black People and the Criminal Justice System*, 2006–7, vol. 1

Home Office, *Secure Borders, Safe Haven: Integration with Diversity in Modern Britain*, 2002

Home Office Research, *The Migrant Journey*, September 2010

House of Lords, *Report on the Economic impact of immigration*, April 2008

Samuel P. Huntington, *Who Are We?: America's Great Debate* (New York: The Free Press, 2004)

Ed Husain, *The Islamist* (London: Penguin Books, 2007)

Asifa Hussain and William Miller, *Multicultural Nationalism* (Oxford: Oxford University Press, 2006)

Dilwar Hussain et al., *Muslims in Leicester* (New York: Open Society Institute, 2010)

Michael Ignatieff, *Identity Parades*, Prospect (London: May 1998)

S. M. Imtiaz, *Wandering Lonely in a Crowd: Reflections on the Muslim Condition in the West* (Leicestershire: Kube, 2011)

Nick Johnson, *Separate and unequal: How integration can deliver the good society* (London: Fabian Society, 2010)

Nick Johnson, *Living Through Change: The effects of global, national and local change on people and places in Bradford* (York: Joseph Rowntree Foundation, 2011)

Christian Joppke, *Citizenship and Immigration* (Cambridge: Polity Press, 2010)

Christian Joppke, *The role of the state in cultural integration* (Washington D.C.: Migration Policy Institute, February 2012

Joseph Rowntree Foundation, *Poverty and Ethnicity: A review of the evidence*, May 2011

Eric Kaufmann, *Liberal Ethnicity: Beyond Liberal Nationalism and Minority Rights*, Ethnic and Racial Studies, 2000

Eric Kaufmann, *The Rise and Fall of Anglo-America: The Decline of Dominant Ethnicity in the United States* (Cambridge, Massachusetts: Harvard University Press, 2004)

Eric Kaufmann, *Shall the Religious Inherit the Earth? Demography and Politics in the Twenty-First Century* (London: Profile, 2010)

Peter Kenway and Guy Palmer, *Poverty Among Ethnic Groups: How and why does it differ?*, New Policy Institute/Joseph Rowntree Foundation

Donald R. Kinder and Cindy D. Kam, *Us Against Them: Ethnocentric Foundations of American Opinion* (Chicago: University of Chicago Press, 2009)

Jytte Klausen, *The Islamic Challenge: Politics and Religion in Western Europe* (Oxford: Oxford University Press, 2007)

Marek Kohn, *Trust: Self Interest and the Common Good* (Oxford: Oxford University Press, 2008)

Mark Krikorian, *The New Case Against Immigration* (New York: Sentinel, 2008)

Krishan Kumar, *The Making of English National Identity* (Cambridge: Cambridge University Press, 2002)

Will Kymlicka, *Multicultural Odysseys: Navigating the New International Politics of Diversity* (Oxford: Oxford University Press, 2007)

David Kynaston, *Family Britain 1951–57* (London: Bloomsbury, 2009)

David Lammy, *Out of the Ashes* (London: Guardian Books, 2011)

James Laurence, Wider community segregation, neighbourhood ethnic diversity and social capital: the importance of considering "nestedness" in contextual analysis, *Social Forces* (unpublished)

James Laurence and Anthony Heath, *Predictors of Community Cohesion*, Department of Communities and Local Government, 2008

James Laurence, *The Effect of Ethnic Diversity and Community Disadvantage on Social Cohesion: A multilevel analysis of social capital and interethnic relations in UK communities*, European Sociological Review, December 2009

Philippe Legrain, *Immigrants: Your Country Needs Them* (London: Little Brown, 2006)

Elizabeth Legum, *Holding Us Together? Community Cohesion, superdiversity and primary schools: A case study of St Barnabas Primary School, Bristol*, a dissertation for Northumbria University, 2011

Alana Lentin and Gavin Titley, *The Crisis of Multiculturalism: Racism in a Neo-Liberal Age* (London: Zed Books, 2011)

Anthony Lester, 'Multiculturalism and Free Speech', *The Political Quarterly*, vol. 81, issue 1, March 2010

Natalia Letki, 'Does Diversity Erode Social Cohesion? Social capital and race in British neighbourhoods', *Political Studies*, vol. 56, 2008

Andrea Levy, *Small Island* (London: Headline Review, 2004)

Philip Lewis, *Young, British and Muslim* (New York: Continuum, 2007)

Philip Lewis, 'The Civic and Religious Incorporation of British Muslims: Whose Incorporation, Which Islam?', *Western Muslims and the refiguring of Liberal citizenship*, Robert Heffner (ed.) (Bloomington: Indiana University Press, forthcoming)

Simonetta Longhi, Peter Nijkamp and Jacques Poot, 'Meta-analysis of empirical evidence on the labour market impacts of immigration', *Région et Développement*, no. 27, 2008

Hassan Mahamdallie (ed.) , *Defending Multiculturalism* (London: Bookmarks Publications, 2010)

Shiraz Maher and Martyn Frampton, *Choosing our Friends Wisely* (London: Policy Exchange, 2009)

Graham Mahony, *Race Relations in Bradford: Submission to the Ouseley Report*, January 2001

Kenan Malik, *From Fatwa to Jihad: The Rushdie Affair and its Legacy* (London: Atlantic Books, 2009)

Kenan Malik, *Strange Fruit: Why Both Sides are Wrong in the Race Debate* (London: One World, 2008)

Zaiba Malik, *We Are a Muslim, Please* (London: Heinemann, 2010)

Peter Mandler, *The English National Character: The History of an idea from Edmund Burke to Tony Blair* (New Haven: Yale University Press, 2006)

Sarfraz Manzoor, *Greetings from Bury Park* (London: Bloomsbury, 2007)

Andrew Marr, *A History of Modern Britain* (London: Pan Macmillan, 2007)

Andrew Mason, 'Integration, Cohesion and National Identity: Theoretical Reflections on Recent British Policy', *British Journal of Political Science*, June 2010

Lauren McLaren, *Cause for Concern? The impact of immigration on political trust*, Policy Network/Barrow Cadbury Trust, September 2010

Lauren McLaren, David J. Cutts, Matthew Goodwin, *What Drives Anti-Muslim Sentiment?*, APSA 2011 annual meeting paper

David Metcalf, 'Work migration from outside the European Union, fifteen years of turnabout', *CentrePiece*, LSE, October 2012

Merton Community Cohesion Strategy, 2012–2015

Merton Story (The), Institute of Community Cohesion

Migration Advisory Committee, *Analysis of the impacts of migration*, January 2012

Migration Observatory (Oxford University), *Briefing: The fiscal impact of immigration to the UK*, March 2011

Migration Observatory (Oxford University), *Briefing: Immigration, diversity and social cohesion*, August 2012

Migration Observatory (Oxford University), *Briefing: Migration to the UK, Asylum*, December 2011

Migration Observatory (Oxford University), *Briefing: Settlement in the UK*, September 2012

Migration Watch, *Asylum: The Outcome*, August 2011

Migration Watch, *Who is being allocated social housing in London?*, 2012

David Miller, *Citizenship and National Identity* (Cambridge: Polity Press, 2000)

David Miller, 'Are they my poor? The problem of altruism in a world of strangers', *The Ethics of Altruism*, Jonathan Seglow (ed.) (London: Cass, 2004)

David Miller, 'Multiculturalism and the Welfare State: Theoretical Reflections', *Multiculturalism and the Welfare State*, Keith Banting and Will Kymlicka (eds) (Oxford: Oxford University Press, 2006)

David Miller, *On Nationality* (Oxford: Clarendon Press, 1975)

David Miller and Sundas Ali, 'Testing the National Identity Argument', *European Political Science Review*

Munira Mirza et al., *Living Apart Together: British Muslims and the paradox of multiculturalism* (London: Policy Exchange, 2007)

Munira Mirza, 'Rethinking Race', *Prospect* (London: October 2010)

Tariq Modood, *Multiculturalism: A Civic Idea* (Cambridge: Polity Press, 2007)

Tariq Modood and John Salt (eds), *Global Migration, Ethnicity and Britishness* (Basingstoke: Palgrave Macmillan, 2011)

Tariq Modood, *Post-immigration 'difference' and integration* (London: British Academy, 2012)

National Insitute of Economic and Social Research, *Immigration and its effects*, National Insitute Economic Review, 2006

Maajid Nawaz, *Radical* (London: W. H. Allen, 2012)

Stephen Nickell and Jumana Saleheen, *The Impact of Immigration on Occupational Wages: Evidence from Britain*, Spatial Economics Research Centre Discussion Paper, October 2009

Office for National Statistics, *Population Estimates by Ethnic Group 2002–2009*, May 2011

Office for National Statistics, *Migration Statistics Quarterly Report*, August 2012

Office for National Statistics, *Population by Country of Birth and Nationality Report*, August 2012

Office of the Deputy Prime Minister, *State of the English Cities*, vol. 1, 2006

Herman Ouseley, *Community Pride not Prejudice, making diversity work in Bradford* (Bradford: Bradford Vision, 2001)

Demetrios Papademetriou, Will Somerville and Madeleine Sumption, *The social mobility of immigrants and their children* (Washington D.C.: Migration Policy Institute, 2009)

Bhikhu Parekh (et al.), *Commission on the Future of Multi-ethnic Britain* (London: Profile Books, 2000)

Bhikhu Parekh, 'British Commitments', *Prospect* (London: September 2005)

Bhikhu Parekh, *Rethinking Multiculturalism* (Basingstoke: Palgrave Macmillan, 2000)

Philippe Van Parijs (ed.), *Cultural Diversity versus Economic Solidarity* (Brussels: Deboeck University Press, 2004)

Ceri Peach, 'Good segregation, bad segregation', *Planning Perspectives*, issue 11, 1996

Ceri Peach, *Muslims in the 2001 Census of England and Wales: Gender and economic disadvantage*, Ethnic and Racial Studies, July 2006

Ceri Peach, 'Slippery Segregation: Discovering or Manufacturing Ghettos?', *Journal of Ethnic and Migration Studies*, November 2009

Mike and Trevor Phillips, *Windrush: The Irresistible Rise of Multiracial Britain* (London: HarperCollins, 1998)

Philosophy Bites, *Multiculturalism Bites*, podcast series for the Open University, July 2011, https://itunes.apple.com/itunes-u/multiculturalism-bites-audio/

Steven Pinker, *The Better Angels of our Nature* (London: Viking Books, 2011)

Jennifer Pitts, *A Turn to Empire: The rise of imperial liberalism in Britain and France* (New Jersey: Princeton University Press, 2005)

Lucinda Platt, *Ethnicity and Family. Relationships within and between ethnic groups*, Equality and Human Rights Commission, 2011

Lucinda Platt, *Poverty and Ethnicity in the UK* (York: Joseph Rowntree Foundation, 2007)

Michael Poulsen and Ron Johnston, 'The "New Geography" of Ethnicity in England and Wales?', *New Geographies of Race and Racism*, Claire Dwyer and Caroline Bressey (eds) (London: Ashgate Publishing, 2008)

Prime Minister's Strategy Unit, *Ethnic Minorities and the Labour Market*, 2003

Prospect, 'In Search of British Values' (London: November 2007)

Robert Putnam, E Pluribus Unum: Diversity and Community in the 21st Century, Scandinavian Political Studies, June 2007

Tariq Ramadan, To be a European Muslim (Leicestershire: Leicester Islamic Foundation, 2002)

Ali Rattansi, Racism: A Very Short Introduction (Oxford: Oxford University Press, 2007)

Ali Rattansi, Multiculturalism: A Very Short Introduction (Oxford: Oxford University Press, 2011)

David Ritchie, Oldham Independent Review 'One Oldham, One Future', December 2011

Dani Rodrik, Who Needs the Nation State?, Centre for Economic Policy Research discussion paper to be published in Economic Geography

Ben Rogers and Rick Muir, The Power of Belonging (London: IPPR, 2007)

Ben Rogers, Enhancing Citizenship through State-Citizen Encounters and Civic Rites (London: IPPR, 2007)

Andrey Rosowsky, 'Decoding as a cultural practice and its effects on the reading process of bilingual pupils', Language and Education, vol. 15, no. 1, 2001

Robert Rowthorn, 'Cherry Picking: A Dubious Practice', Around the Globe, vol. 3, no. 2, Spring 2006

Robert Rowthorn, 'The fiscal impact of immigration on the advanced economies', Oxford Review of Economic Policy, vol. 24, no. 3, 2008

Robert Rowthorn, The Economic Impact of Immigration, evidence to the House of Lords Select Committee on Economic Affairs

Martin Ruhs and Bridget Anderson (eds), Who Needs Migrant Workers? (Oxford: Oxford University Press, 2010)

Jonathan Sacks, The Home We Build Together (London: Continuum, 2007)

Shamit Saggar, Pariah Politics (Oxford: Oxford University Press, 2009)

Shamit Saggar, Will Somerville, Robert Ford and Maria Sobolewska, The impacts of migration on social cohesion and integration, report to the Migration Advisory Committee, January 2012

Shamit Saggar and Will Somerville, Building a British Model of Integration in an Era of Immigration (Washington D.C.: Migration Policy Institute, May 2012)

John Salt, International Migration and the United Kingdom, OECD report 2010

John Salt, The United Kingdom experience of post-enlargement worker inflows from new EU member countries, published in Free Movement of Workers and Labour Market Adjustment, OECD 2012

Michael Sandel, 'The Procedural Republic and the Unencumbered Self',
    Political Theory, vol. 12, no. 1, February 1984
Jasvinder Sanghera, *Shame* (London: Hodder & Stoughton, 2007)
Sathnam Sanghera, *If You Don't Know Me By Now* (London: Penguin/Viking,
    2008)
Paul Scheffer, *Immigrant Nations* (Cambridge: Polity Press, 2011) (originally
    published in the Netherlands, 2007)
Samuel Scheffler, *Boundaries and Allegiances* (Oxford: Oxford University Press,
    2001)
Thomas Schelling, 'Models of segregation', *American Economic Review*, 1969
Roger Scruton, *England: An Elegy* (London: Continuum, 2001)
Searchlight Educational Trust, *Fear and Hope: The new politics of identity*, 2010
Tom Sefton, *Give and Take: Attitudes to Redistribution*, British Social Attitudes
    Survey, 2005
Amartya Sen, *Identity and Violence* (London: Penguin, 2006)
Alison Shaw, *Kinship and Continuity: Pakistani Families in Britain* (Oxford: Taylor
    and Francis, 2000)
Naoko Shimazu, *Japan, Race and Equality* (Oxford: Routledge, 1998)
Ludi Simpson, 'Statistics of racial segregation: measures evidence and policy',
    Urban Studies, vol. 41, 2004
Ludi Simpson and Nissa Finney, *Sleepwalking into Segregation? Challenging Myths
    about Race and Migration* (Bristol: Policy Press, 2009)
Darra Singh, *Our Shared Future*, final report of the Commission on Integration
    and Cohesion, June 2007
Gurharpal Singh and Darshan Singh Tatla, *Sikhs in Britain: The Making of a
    Community* (London: Zed Books, 2006)
Ramindar Singh, *The Struggle for Racial Justice: The Story of Bradford 1950–2002*
    (Bradford: Bradford Arts, Museums and Libraries Service, 2002)
Michael Skey, *National Belonging and Everyday Life* (Basingstoke: Palgrave
    Macmillan, 2011)
Anthony D. Smith, *National Identity* (London: Penguin, 1991)
Will Somerville, *Immigration Under New Labour* (Bristol: Policy Press, 2007)
Tim Soutphommasane, *The Virtuous Citizen: Patriotism in a Multicultural Society*
    (Cambridge: Cambridge University Press, 2012)
Sarah Spencer (ed.), 'The Politics of Migration', *Political Quarterly* (Oxford:
    Blackwell Publishing, 2003)
Sarah Spencer, *The Migration Debate* (Bristol: Policy Press, 2011)

Danny Sriskandarajah (et al.), *Paying their way: fiscal contribution of immigrants in the* UK (London: IPPR, 2005)

Burton Stein, *A History of India* (Oxford: Blackwell, 1998)

Patrick Sturgis (et al.), 'Does Ethnic Diversity Erode Trust? Putnam's "hunkering-down" thesis reconsidered', *British Journal of Political Science*, November 2010

Madeleine Sumption and Will Somerville, *The UK's New Europeans*, Equality and Human Rights Commission/Migration Policy Institute, January 2010

Kjartan Sveinsson, *Who cares about the white working class?*, Runnymede Trust, 2009

Yael Tamir, *Liberal Nationalism* (New Jersey: Princeton University Press, 1993)

Charles Taylor et al., *Multiculturalism: Examining the Politics of Recognition* (New Jersey: Princeton University Press, 1994)

Margaret Thatcher, *The Path to Power* (London: HarperCollins, 1995)

Paul Thomas, *Youth, Multiculturalism and Community Cohesion*, (Basingstoke: Palgrave Macmillan, 2011)

James Tilley and Anthony Heath, 'The Decline of British National Pride', *British Journal of Sociology*, vol. 58, issue 4, 2007

Adair Turner, *Do We Need More Immigrants and Babies?*, LSE lecture, 28 November 2007

Varun Uberoi, 'Do Policies of Multiculturalism Change National Identities?', *The Political Quarterly*, vol. 79, no. 3, July–September 2008

Varun Uberoi and Tariq Modood, 'Inclusive Britishness: A Multicultural Advance', *Political Studies*, vol. 60, issue 4, 2012

Michael Walzer, *Spheres of Justice* (New York: Basic Books, 1983)

Vron Ware, *Who Cares About Britishness?* (London: Arcadia Books, 2007)

Eugen Weber, *Peasants into Frenchmen: The Modernisation of Rural France 1870–1914* (Palo Alto: Stanford University Press, 1976)

Unni Wikan, *Generous Betrayal* (Chicago: The University of Chicago Press, 2002)

David Willetts, *Prospect* round table on welfare reform, March 1998

Max Wind-Cowie and Thomas Gregory, *A Place for Pride* (London: Demos, 2011)

Max Wind-Cowie (ed.), *Are We There Yet?: A Collection on Race and Conservatism* (London: Demos, 2011)

Robert Winder, *Bloody Foreigners: The Story of Immigration to Britain* (London: Little, Brown, 2004)

Alan Wolfe and Jytte Klausen, 'Other People: A critique of the Parekh report', *Prospect* (London: December 2000)

Robert J.C. Young, 'The Disappearance of the English: Why is there no English Diaspora?', *Locating the English Diaspora 1500–2010* (Liverpool: Liverpool University Press, 2012)

NOTE ON THE AUTHOR

David Goodhart is the director of the think tank DEMOS, and the editor-at-large of *Prospect* magazine, which he founded in 1995. He was previously a senior correspondent for the *Financial Times*.

Index